MENTAL CAPACITY, DIGNITY AND THE POWER OF INTERNATIONAL HUMAN RIGHTS

Personhood, in liberal philosophical and legal traditions, has long been grounded in the idea of autonomy and the right to legal capacity. However, in this book, Julia Duffy questions these assumptions and shows how such beliefs exclude and undermine the rights of adults with cognitive disability. Instead, she reinterprets the right to legal capacity through the principle of the interdependence and indivisibility of human rights. In doing so, she compellingly argues that dignity and not autonomy ought to be the basis of personhood. Using illustrative case studies, Duffy demonstrates that the key human rights values of autonomy, dignity and equality can only be achieved by fulfilling a range of interdependent human rights. With this innovative book challenging common assumptions about human rights and personhood, Duffy leads the way in ensuring civil, economic, political, social and cultural inclusion for adults with cognitive disabilities.

JULIA DUFFY is Research Fellow at the Australian Centre for Health Law Research at the Queensland University of Technology. She writes and publishes in the areas of cognitive disability, decision-making and human rights law and theory and provides research and consultancy services to government and non-government agencies on supported decision-making and related areas. She has been a member of two health practitioner regulatory boards, a legal member of Queensland's Mental Health Review Tribunal and was for many years a member of the board of Family Planning Queensland. Julia has also had a substantial career as a government policy advisor, lawyer and senior executive, including roles as Chief Executive of a major Commission of Inquiry into Child Protection and as Deputy Public Guardian.

CAMBRIDGE BIOETHICS AND LAW

This series of books – formerly called Cambridge Law, Medicine and Ethics – was founded by Cambridge University Press with Alexander McCall Smith as its first editor in 2003. It focuses on the law's complex and troubled relationship with medicine across both the developed and the developing world. In the past twenty years, we have seen in many countries increasing resort to the courts by dissatisfied patients and a growing use of the courts to attempt to resolve intractable ethical dilemmas. At the same time, legislatures across the world have struggled to address the questions posed by both the successes and the failures of modern medicine, while international organisations such as the WHO and UNESCO now regularly address issues of medical law. It follows that we would expect ethical and policy questions to be integral to the analysis of the legal issues discussed in this series. The series responds to the high profile of medical law in universities, in legal and medical practice, as well as in public and political affairs. We seek to reflect the evidence that many major health-related policy and bioethics debates in the UK, Europe and the international community over the past two decades have involved a strong medical law dimension. With that in mind, we seek to address how legal analysis might have a trans-jurisdictional and international relevance. Organ retention, embryonic stem cell research, physician-assisted suicide and the allocation of resources to fund health care are but a few examples among many. The emphasis of this series is thus on matters of public concern and/or practical significance. We look for books that could make a difference to the development of medical law and enhance the role of medico-legal debate in policy circles. That is not to say that we lack interest in the important theoretical dimensions of the subject, but we aim to ensure that theoretical debate is grounded in the realities of how the law does and should interact with medicine and health care.

Series Editors

Professor Graeme Laurie, *University of Edinburgh*
Professor Richard Ashcroft, *City, University of London*

Mental Capacity, Dignity and the Power of International Human Rights

JULIA DUFFY
Queensland University of Technology

CAMBRIDGE
UNIVERSITY PRESS

CAMBRIDGE
UNIVERSITY PRESS

Shaftesbury Road, Cambridge CB2 8EA, United Kingdom

One Liberty Plaza, 20th Floor, New York, NY 10006, USA

477 Williamstown Road, Port Melbourne, VIC 3207, Australia

314–321, 3rd Floor, Plot 3, Splendor Forum, Jasola District Centre, New Delhi – 110025, India

103 Penang Road, #05–06/07, Visioncrest Commercial, Singapore 238467

Cambridge University Press is part of Cambridge University Press & Assessment, a department of the University of Cambridge.

We share the University's mission to contribute to society through the pursuit of education, learning and research at the highest international levels of excellence.

www.cambridge.org
Information on this title: www.cambridge.org/9781009304498

DOI: 10.1017/9781009304481

First published 2023
First paperback edition 2026

A catalogue record for this publication is available from the British Library

ISBN 978-1-009-30452-8 Hardback
ISBN 978-1-009-30449-8 Paperback

In memory of
Lloyd Davis

Contents

Acknowledgements

There are many people without whose support this book would never have been written. My PhD supervisors Professors Ben White and Lindy Willmott and Associate Professor Andy McGee shared with me their extensive knowledge in health law and bioethics and pushed me in new and challenging directions, while providing a safety net of kindness and encouragement. They also provided a wonderfully collegial environment for what may otherwise have been a solitary pursuit, introducing me to their team of brilliant and dedicated researchers and other colleagues. I'd especially like to thank Professor Shih-Ning Then and members of her writing group, as well as Dr Katrine Del Villar and Dr Sam Boyle for reading and critiquing drafts of various chapters. Monica Chaplain and Kristina Chelberg provided invaluable support with copy-editing and indexing and Annabelle Duffy with proofreading.

Many friends and family members encouraged me, supported me and showed interest along the way (as they still do). Thanks to Annabelle, and especially to Charlotte and Joey Davis who inspire me every day.

Table of Cases

Table of Treaties

Abbreviations

1971 Declaration	*Declaration on the Rights of Mentally Retarded Persons*
1975 Declaration	*Declaration on the Rights of Disabled Persons*
Ad Hoc Committee	Ad Hoc Committee on a Comprehensive and Integral International Convention on the Protection and Promotion of the Rights and Dignity of Persons with Disabilities
ALRC	Australian Law Reform Commission
ALRC Report	*Equality, Capacity and Disability in Commonwealth Laws: A Final Report*
Article 12	Article 12 of the United Nations *Convention on the Rights of Persons with Disabilities* – the 'right to enjoy legal capacity on an equal basis with others'
CEDAW	*Convention on the Elimination of All Forms of Discrimination against Women*
CERD	*International Convention on the Elimination of All Forms of Racial Discrimination*
civil-political rights	civil and political rights
CRC	*Convention on the Rights of the Child*
CRPD	*Convention on the Rights of Persons with Disabilities*
Disability Royal Commission	Royal Commission into Violence, Abuse, Neglect and Exploitation of People with Disability [Australia]
ECHR	*European Convention on Human Rights*

ESCR Committee	Committee on Economic, Social and Cultural Rights
ESCR *General Comment No 3*	Committee on Economic, Social and Cultural Rights, *General Comment No 3: The Nature of State Parties' Obligations*
ESCR *General Comment No 5*	Committee on Economic, Social and Cultural Rights, *General Comment No 5: Persons with Disabilities*
GAOR	General Assembly Official Records [United Nations]
General Comment No 1	Committee on the Rights of Persons with Disabilities *General Comment No 1 (2014) – Article 12: Equal Recognition before the Law*
General Comment No 4	Committee on the Rights of Persons with Disabilities, *General Comment No 4 (2016) – Article 24: Right to Inclusive Education*
General Comment No 5	Committee on the Rights of Persons with Disabilities, *General Comment No 5 (2017) on Living Independently and Being Included in the Community*
General Comment No 6	Committee on the Rights of Persons with Disabilities, *General Comment No 6 (2018) on Equality and Non-Discrimination*
General Comment No 7	Committee on the Rights of Persons with Disabilities, *General Comment No 7 (2018) on the Participation of Persons with Disabilities, Including Children with Disabilities, through Their Representative Organizations, in the Implementation and Monitoring of the Convention*
ICCPR	*International Covenant on Civil and Political Rights*
ICESCR	*International Covenant on Economic Social Cultural Rights*
IDC	International Disability and Caucus
MCA	*Mental Capacity Act* 2005 (England and Wales)
NDIS	National Disability Insurance Scheme [Australia]
Optional Protocol to the ICESCR	*Optional Protocol to the International Covenant on Economic, Social and Cultural Rights (2013)*

principle of indivisibility	the principle of the indivisibility, interdependence and interrelatedness of human rights
Proclamation of Teheran	*Proclamation of Teheran* in the *Final Act of the International Conference on Human Rights*
PVS	persistent vegetative state
QLRC	Queensland Law Reform Commission
socio-economic rights	economic, social and cultural rights
Standard Rules	*Standard Rules on the Equalisation of Opportunities for Persons with Disabilities*
UN	United Nations
UN Charter	*Charter of the United Nations*
UN Declaration	*Universal Declaration of Human Rights*
UN Disability Committee	United Nations Committee on the Rights of Persons with Disabilities
VCLT	*Vienna Convention on the Law of Treaties*
Vienna Declaration	*Vienna Declaration and Programme of Action* (1993)

1

Introduction and Background

In our daily lives as adults, we make many decisions that we consider determinative of our futures – where to live, what education to undertake and what health treatment to accept. Many of us may consider that we have a human right to make personal decisions and that such a right is key to our individual autonomy, essential to our dignity, and should be claimed equally by all. Article 12 of the United Nations *Convention on the Rights of Persons with Disabilities* ('CRPD')[1] is said to enshrine such a human right for people with disability when it provides for the right to 'enjoy legal capacity on an equal basis with others'. However, historically and currently, challenges arise in recognising legal capacity or decision-making ability in the case of adults with cognitive disability – that is, disability associated with intellectual disability, acquired brain injury, aged dementia or mental illness.[2] Adults with cognitive disability have historically been denied (and for the most part, still are denied) the opportunity to make decisions that are recognised at law as their own and acted upon as such. They may have decisions made for them by substitutes, including guardians, attorneys or even clinicians,[3] and such decisions may directly conflict with their own expressed desires or wishes.

This book interprets Article 12 of the CRPD – the 'right to enjoy legal capacity on an equal basis with others' – through the principle of the indivisibility, interdependence and interrelatedness of all human rights (the 'principle of indivisibility'). It concludes that the principle of indivisibility underpins an interpretation of Article 12 that requires adults with cognitive disability to be supported in making decisions but that also may require decision-making by substitutes in cases of last resort. Contrary to the view of the Committee on the Rights of Persons with Disabilities ('UN

[1] *Convention on the Rights of Persons with Disabilities*, opened for signature 30 March 2007, 2515 UNTS 15 (entered into force 3 May 2008) ('CRPD').

[2] See Section 2 – 'A Note on Terminology and Concepts'.

[3] Ben White, Lindy Willmott and Shih-Ning Then, 'Chapter 7: Adults Who Lack Capacity: Substitute Decision Making' in Ben White, Fiona McDonald and Lindy Willmott (eds), *Health Law in Australia* (Lawbook Co, 3rd ed., 2018) 207.

Disability Committee')[4] and others,[5] it argues that in 'hard cases', decision-making by substitutes may be required to uphold an adult's indivisible human rights. In interpreting Article 12, the book examines the role of the three human rights values of autonomy, dignity and equality and explains how these can be rearticulated in the language of indivisible human rights to support the above interpretation. It applies a concept of indivisibility that recognises the interdependencies between rights and the equal importance of economic, social and cultural ('socio-economic') rights with civil and political ('civil–political') rights.

This chapter provides context and background by explaining the ongoing contention around Article 12, the book's aims and scope, and why I have chosen to use certain key terms. It also introduces the CRPD, explains the book's structure and how it contributes in an original and significant way to the existing research and literature in this area.

1 ARTICLE 12 AND THE PROBLEM OF INTERPRETATION

The first three paragraphs of Article 12 provide that:

> (1) States Parties reaffirm that persons with disabilities have the right to recognition everywhere as persons before the law.

[4] Committee on the Rights of Persons with Disabilities, *General Comment No 1 Article 12: Equal Recognition before the Law*, UN Doc CRPD/C/GC/1 (19 May 2014) ('*General Comment No 1*').

[5] Tina Minkowitz, 'Legal Capacity: Fundamental to the Rights of Persons with Disabilities' (2007) 56(1) *International Rehabilitation Review* 25; International Disability Alliance, *Legal Opinion on Article 12 of the CRPD* https://disability-studies.leeds.ac.uk/wp-content/uploads/sites/40/library/legal-opinion-LegalOpinion-Art12-FINAL.pdf ('*Legal Opinion*'); Fiona Morrissey, 'The United Nations Convention on the Rights of Persons with Disabilities: A New Approach to Decision-Making in Mental Health Law' (2012) 19 *European Journal of Health Law* 423; Amita Dhanda, 'Legal Capacity in the Disability Rights Convention: Stranglehold of the Past or Lodestar of the Future' (2007) 34 *Syracuse Journal of International Law and Commerce* 429; Gerard Quinn and Anna Arstein-Kerslake, 'Restoring the "Human" in "Human Rights": Personhood and Doctrinal Innovation in the UN Disability Convention' in Costas Douzinas and CA Gearty (eds), *Cambridge Companion to Human Rights Law* (Cambridge University Press, 2012) 36; Theresia Degener, 'Editor's Foreword' (2017) 13(1) *International Journal of Law in Context* 1; Gerard Quinn and Abigail Rekas-Rosalbo, 'Civil Death: Rethinking the Foundations of Legal Personhood for Persons with a Disability' (2016) 56 *Irish Jurist* 286; Eilionóir Flynn and Anna Arstein-Kerslake, 'The Support Model of Legal Capacity: Fact, Fiction, or Fantasy?' (2014) 32(1) *Berkeley Journal of International Law* 124; Michael Bach and Lana Kerzner, *A New Paradigm for Protecting Autonomy and the Right to Legal Capacity: Advancing Substantive Equality for Persons with Disabilities through Law, Policy and Practice* (Law Commission of Ontario, October 2010); Nandini Devi, 'Supported Decision-Making and Personal Autonomy for Persons with Intellectual Disabilities: Article 12 of the UN Convention on the Rights of Persons with Disabilities' (2013) 41(4) *The Journal of Law, Medicine & Ethics* 792; Clíona de Bhailís and Eilionóir Flynn, 'Recognising Legal Capacity: Commentary and Analysis of Article 12 CRPD' (2017) 13(1) *International Journal of Law in Context* 6; Anna Arstein-Kerslake, *Restoring Voice to People with Cognitive Disabilities: Realizing the Right to Equal Recognition before the Law* (Cambridge University Press, 2017); Kristin Booth Glen, 'Changing Paradigms: Mental Capacity, Legal Capacity, Guardianship and Beyond' (2012) 44 *Columbia Human Rights Law Review* 93.

(2) States Parties shall recognize that persons with disabilities enjoy legal capacity on an equal basis with others in all aspects of life.
(3) States Parties shall take appropriate measures to provide access by persons with disabilities to the support they may require in exercising their legal capacity.

There is wide if not universal agreement that paragraph 3 of Article 12 requires States to provide decision-making supports for adults with cognitive disability so that they can endeavour to exercise legal capacity in fulfilment of their human rights.[6] These supports may be in the form of, for example, mentoring, communication assistance or advocacy, according to what have become known as systems of 'supported decision-making'.[7] However, while promotion of supported decision-making is widely endorsed, there remains significant and entrenched disagreement about whether Article 12 allows for decision-making by substitutes in cases of last resort. These cases of last resort include those described in the literature as 'hard cases' (as discussed in the following section) but also potentially when a supporter chosen by the adult is exercising undue influence or abuse.[8]

1.1 *Case Studies*

The term 'hard cases' is used in the Article 12 literature to describe those situations where traditionally an adult would have a decision made for them by a guardian and where there are particular challenges for supported decision-making. This may be in cases of severe and profound cognitive disability;[9] in situations where an adult

[6] Rosemary Kayess and Therese Sands, *Convention on the Rights of Persons with Disabilities: Shining a Light on Social Transformation* (UNSW Social Policy Research Centre, 2020); Ron McCallum, *The United Nations Convention on the Rights of Persons with Disabilities: An Assessment of Australia's Level of Compliance* (Royal Commission into Violence, Abuse, Neglect and Exploitation of People with Disability, 2020) 46–55.

[7] See Section 2 of this chapter. Piers Gooding, 'Supported Decision-Making: A Rights-Based Disability Concept and Its Implications for Mental Health Law' (2013) 20(3) *Psychiatry, Psychology and Law* 431, 432–39.

[8] Also, note the challenges of supported decision-making in these cases, in particular in ascertaining an adult's autonomous will and preferences: see Section 5 of this chapter.

[9] Anna Arstein-Kerslake and Eilionóir Flynn, 'The General Comment on Article 12 of the Convention on the Rights of Persons with Disabilities: A Roadmap for Equality before the Law' (2016) 20(4) *The International Journal of Human Rights* 471, 482; Anna Arstein-Kerslake, 'An Empowering Dependency: Exploring Support for the Exercise of Legal Capacity' (2016) 18 *Scandinavian Journal of Disability Research* 77, 84; for the example of an adult in a persistent vegetative state, see Mary Donnelly, *Healthcare Decision-Making and the Law: Autonomy, Capacity and the Limits of Liberalism* (Cambridge University Press, 2010); Jillian Craigie et al, 'Legal Capacity, Mental Capacity and Supported Decision-Making: Report from a Panel Event' (2019) 62 *International Journal of Law and Psychiatry* 160, 162; Wayne Martin et al, *Three Jurisdictions Report: Towards Compliance with CRPD Article 12 in Capacity/Incapacity Legislation across the UK* (Essex Autonomy Project, 2016) 34; Australian Law Reform

wants to make a decision that will result in harm or serious harm to themselves or others;[10] or where an adult is supported by someone who exercises undue influence over their decision-making.[11] The three case studies below are discussed in Chapters 4, 5 and 6, respectively, to illustrate the arguments made in this book. They have been chosen and shaped to illustrate where decision-making with support is challenging or complex and where decision-making by a substitute may be considered necessary as a last resort to uphold human rights.

ALEX

Alex is a 30-year-old man with an intellectual disability who refuses dental treatment because he is scared of, and doesn't trust, the dentist. Collateral information is that his fear is linked to post-traumatic stress disorder from childhood abuse. Counsellors have been unable to assuage his fears or convince him to have the treatment. They have warned him that he will lose all of his teeth if he does not have the treatment. His support workers and family all know that one of his real joys in life is to partake of gourmet food, and it is a significant social interest that he can share with others. If Alex loses all of his teeth, he will need to live chiefly on pureed food. It is not clear whether he understands this longer-term adverse impact (as opposed to the shorter-term impact of undergoing the treatment). It appears to Alex's supporters that he thinks that his teeth will get better on their own, and he will be able to eat steak again soon.

The case of Alex is a version of various hypothetical scenarios discussed in the Article 12 literature.[12] It illustrates challenges with supported decision-making when the

Commission, *Equality, Capacity and Disability in Commonwealth Laws: A Final Report* (2014) 33; Kristin Booth Glen, 'Introducing a New Human Right: Learning from Others, Bringing Legal Capacity Home' (2018) 49(3) *Columbia Human Rights Law Review* 1, 7, 15.

10 Arstein-Kerslake and Flynn (n 9); Lucy Series, 'Relationships, Autonomy and Legal Capacity: Mental Capacity and Support Paradigms' (2015) 40 *International Journal of Law and Psychiatry* 80, 87; Martin et al, *Three Jurisdictions Report* (n 9) 34.

11 'There is a risk that people in positions of power, such as medical professionals and supporters, may profess to be acting on the will and preference of the individual when they are really carrying out their own desires': Arstein-Kerslake and Flynn (n 9) 482; Arstein-Kerslake, 'An Empowering Dependency' (n 9) 88; 'Risk-taking behaviour presents a particular challenge in implementing the principle of support, as do the accompanying moral dilemmas, where the person rejects support and/or intimates a wish to place themselves in a situation of danger, exploitation, abuse or undue influence': Martin et al, *Three Jurisdictions Report* (n 9) 36.

12 Arstein-Kerslake and Flynn (n 9) 483–84; de Bhailís and Flynn (n 5), 16; Rosemary Kayess and Ben Fogarty, 'The Rights and Dignity of Persons with Disabilities' (2007) 32(1) *Alternative Law Journal* 22, 26; also for where dental treatment was ordered in the face of an adult's refusal: *In the matter of: Deon Wessels and Hayden William Kelly* [2012] NZFC 9487.

adult expresses desires or intentions that conflict; or when one or other of those desires or intentions might harm the adult.

SESHA

Philosopher Eva Feder Kittay describes her daughter Sesha as a girl and now woman, who 'was diagnosed as having severe to profound retardation'. Kittay describes Sesha as 'enormously responsive, forming deep personal relationships with her family and long-standing caregivers and friendly relations with her therapists and teachers'.[13] Kittay has written quite a bit about her daughter's love of music, especially but not exclusively classical symphonic music, Beethoven being on the top of her list. Sesha cannot read, and Kittay says she cannot 'engage in moral practical reasoning'[14] or participate in political life but that her life is full. It is hard to know what cognitive capacities Sesha possesses because she cannot speak. She also has physical functional limitations, with unsteady legs and no dexterity with a spoon or knife. Kittay is fortunate enough to have the material resources to provide her daughter with carers, therapists and teachers. As an adult, Sesha lives in supported accommodation – a group home with five other young people who are also described as having cognitive and multiple disabilities.

The case of Sesha is referred to by Kittay[15] and others[16] in the philosophical literature on personhood, autonomy and dignity. Sesha's life and circumstances, and her

[13] Eva Feder Kittay, 'The Personal Is Philosophical Is Political: A Philosopher and Mother of a Cognitively Disabled Person Sends Notes from the Battlefield' (2009) 40(3–4) *Metaphilosophy* 606, 616.

[14] Eva Feder Kittay, 'Equality, Dignity and Disability' in Mary Ann Lyons and Fionnuala Waldron (eds), *Perspectives on Equality: The Second Seamus Heaney Lectures* (Liffey Press, 2005) 100.

[15] Kittay, 'Equality, Dignity and Disability' (n 14); Eva Feder Kittay, 'At the Margins of Moral Personhood' (2005) 116(1) *Ethics* 100; Kittay, 'The Personal Is Philosophical Is Political' (n 13) 624.

[16] Susan Dodds, 'Depending on Care: Recognition of Vulnerability and the Social Contribution of Care Provision' (2017) 21(9) *Bioethics* 500, 508; Alice Crary, 'Cognitive Disability and Moral Status' in David T Wasserman and Adam Cureton (eds), *The Oxford Handbook of Philosophy and Disability* (Oxford University Press, 2018) 2; Camillia Kong, *Mental Capacity in Relationship: Decision-Making, Dialogue and Autonomy* (Cambridge University Press, 2017) 205–7; Christie Hartley, 'An Inclusive Contractualism: Obligations to the Mentally Disabled' in Kimberley Brownlee and Adam Cureton (eds), *Disability and Disadvantage* (Oxford University Press, 2009) 138, 151; Lorraine Krall McCrary, 'Hannah Arendt and Disability: Natality and the Right to Inhabit the World' in Barbara Arneil and Nancy J Hirschmann (eds), *Disability and Political Theory* (Cambridge University Press, 2016) 198, 201, 215; Bach and Kerzner (n 5) 70; Martha C Nussbaum, *Frontiers of Justice Disability, Nationality, Species Membership* (Harvard University Press, 2009) 96.

inability to 'engage in moral reasoning', means that she presents as a hard case of severe and profound cognitive disability.

> JESS
>
> Jess, aged 76, has advanced dementia and lives on a rural property with her adult son. The property has been in the family for generations and Jess has always wanted it to stay in the family. She has also been very house-proud in the past.
>
> To 'manage' her dementia, her son has placed Jess in the laundry under the house and locked the door to prevent her from wandering. Jess does not object to her living situation and appears acquiescent or compliant, always favouring her son over her other children.
>
> Neighbours report the situation to the police, who find Jess under the house, malnourished and soiled.

The case of Jess illustrates the complexities surrounding severe cognitive disability in the case of aged dementia and where the adult has chosen a supporter whose neglectful and abusive actions result in harm to the adult.[17]

1.2 *The Problem the Book Is Addressing*

On the one hand, there is a prevailing view held by the UN Disability Committee and others that decision-making by a substitute will breach Article 12 legal capacity rights because it constitutes a denial of autonomy for adults with cognitive disability and constitutes unlawful discrimination.[18] Under the tenets of liberal philosophy, autonomy is the foundation of personhood.[19] According to this logic, denial of legal capacity and autonomy constitutes a violation of all human rights by situating adults with cognitive disability as 'non-persons'. Their position as ostensible non-persons,

17 This is similar to a hypothetical scenario described in Elizabeth Anderson, 'Animal Rights and the Values of Non-human Life' in Cass R Sunstein and Martha C Nussbaum (eds), *Animal Rights: Current Debates and New Directions* (Oxford University Press, 2004) 277, 282.

18 *General Comment No 1*; Lucy Series and Anna Nilsson, 'Article 12 CRPD: Equal Recognition before the Law' in Ilias Bantekas, Michael Ashley Stein and Anastasiou Dimitris (eds), *The UN Convention on the Rights of Persons with Disabilities: A Commentary* (Oxford University Press, 2018) 339, 340.

19 John Christman, 'Autonomy in Moral and Political Philosophy', *The Stanford Encyclopedia of Philosophy* (Fall 2020 Edition), Edward N Zalta (ed) [1.2] https://plato.stanford.edu/archives/fall2020/entries/autonomy-moral/. See also Chapter 4.

in turn, amounts to unlawful discrimination because they are treated unequally in all aspects of their lives.[20]

On the other hand, there is also a widely held view that decision-making by substitutes may be reasonable, necessary and inevitable in some cases, and that Article 12 allows for substitute decision-making 'as a last resort'.[21] I argue for this second interpretation – that in some cases where an adult has impaired capacity, Article 12 allows for and may even require a decision to be made by a substitute. There is no widely held agreement as to the basis for this interpretation. Some writers refer to the inevitability of substitute decision-making;[22] some seek alternative bases for personhood to replace autonomy;[23] some view prevention of harm as a permissible exception to legal capacity rights;[24] and others consider how equality may be

[20] *General Comment No 1*; Arstein-Kerslake, *Restoring Voice to People with Cognitive Disabilities* (n 5) 38.

[21] See Chapter 2, Section 4.2.

[22] Scott Kim: 'The debate should not be over whether we sometimes should decide for others. The fact is that we inevitably do, whether we acknowledge this or not': Craigie et al (n 9) 165; 'Our own approach incorporates the frank admission that the exercise of legal capacity may not always be possible, even when all possible supports are provided.' Martin et al, *Three Jurisdictions Report* (n 9) 37; 'A more common interpretation, supported by most States Parties, is that certain or all situations necessitate substitute rather than supportive decision-making.' Kjersti Skarstad, 'Ensuring Human Rights for Persons with Intellectual Disabilities?' (2018) 22(6) *International Journal of Human Rights* 774, 777; 'The position taken by the Committee on the issue of legal capacity is a challenge for common sense' in Silvana Galderisi, 'The UN Convention on the Rights of Persons with Disabilities: Great Opportunities and Dangerous Interpretations' (2019) 18(1) *World Psychiatry* 47, 47.

[23] Skarstad suggests that autonomy in a descriptive sense is not necessary for personhood or for claiming human rights because 'By focusing on the process or act of just treatment, human rights can include all persons on equal terms' in Kjersti Skarstad, 'Human Rights through the Lens of Disability' (2018) 36(1) *Netherlands Quarterly of Human Rights* 24, 40; Nussbaum proposed dignity as the foundation for moral personhood in various writings including Martha Nussbaum, *Creating Capabilities: The Human Development Approach* (Harvard University Press, 2011); Kittay proposes an ethics of care as an inclusive foundation for moral personhood in, for example, Licia Carlson and Eva Feder Kittay, 'Introduction: Rethinking Philosophical Presumptions in the Light of Cognitive Disability' (2009) 40(3–4) *Metaphilosophy* 307; Bilchitz proposes dignity as either 'the capacity of individuals to have a conscious experience of the world …' or 'the ability of individuals to develop purposes and to seek to achieve them': in David Bilchitz, 'Dignity, Fundamental Rights and Legal Capacity: Moving beyond the Paradigm Set by the General Comment on Article 12 of the Convention on the Rights of Persons with Disabilities' (2016) 32(3) *South African Journal on Human Rights* 410, 430–31; Hall proposes vulnerability as the foundation for moral personhood in Margaret Isabel Hall, 'Mental Capacity in the (Civil) Law: Capacity, Autonomy, and Vulnerability' (2012) 58(1) *McGill Law Journal – Revue de Droit de McGill* 61.

[24] 'A representative may override the person's will and preferences only where necessary to prevent harm': ALRC (n 9) 13; Martin et al endorse a functional capacity test and decision-making by substitutes when the aim of fostering autonomy conflicts with protecting life or ensuring protection and safety, in Wayne Martin et al, *Achieving CRPD Compliance: Is the Mental Capacity Act of England and Wales Compatible with the UN Convention on the*

considered differently for adults with cognitive disability.[25] All of these arguments are considered at various points in the book.

I argue that autonomy is one very valuable good amongst others for those who are capable of autonomy. However, for adults who are not capable of decision-making autonomy (even with support), we can still respect their personhood through respecting their human dignity. If we respond to them through the lens of substantive 'inclusive equality', then decision-making by a substitute as a last resort will not violate human rights but may actually be required in order to uphold them.

1.3 *An Overview of the Argument*

The book makes the argument that Article 12 requires both supported decision-making *and* decision-making by substitutes as a last resort. It does this by using a human rights framework that recognises the principle of indivisibility to interpret Article 12 as:

(1) refashioning liberal autonomy from non-interference to a process of achieving autonomy or developing autonomy competencies, and incorporating a demand for the provision of real options;
(2) underpinned by a concept of personhood based on dignity as inclusive of people with a cognitive disability, rather than on autonomy as rationality, which is inevitably exclusive; and
(3) acknowledging that the difference of cognitive disability allows for differential treatment in the form of supported decision-making and also decision-making by substitutes to achieve non-discrimination and what the UN Disability Committee has itself described as 'inclusive equality'.[26]

Rights of Persons with Disabilities? If Not, What Next? (Essex Autonomy Project, 2014) 19; Jeanne Snelling and Alison Douglass, 'Legal Capacity and Supported Decision-Making' in Iris Reuvecamp and John Dawson (eds), *Mental Capacity Law in New Zealand* (Thomson Reuters, 2019) 163, 172.

[25] Martin et al, *Achieving CRPD Compliance* (n 24) 14–26; 'Moreover, these errors reveal the Committee's flawed conception of discrimination.' In John Dawson, 'A Realistic Approach to Assessing Mental Health Laws' Compliance with the UNCRPD' (2015) 40 *International Journal of Law and Psychiatry* 70, 73; Katrine Del Villar, 'Should Supported Decision-Making Replace Substituted Decision-Making? The Convention on the Rights of Persons with Disabilities and Coercive Treatment under Queensland's Mental Health Act 2000' (2015) 4(2) *Laws* 173, 183; Anita Smith, 'Are Guardianship Laws and Practices Consistent with Human Rights Instruments?' in A Kimberly Dayton (ed), *Comparative Perspectives on Adult Guardianship* (Carolina Academic Press, 2014) 247, 264.

[26] Committee on the Rights of Persons with Disabilities, *General Comment No 6: On Equality and Non-Discrimination*, UN Doc CRPD/C/GC/6 (26 April 2018) ('*General Comment No 6*').

1.3.1 The Principle of Indivisibility

The principle of indivisibility is investigated and described in Chapter 3 as requiring recognition of:

(1) the interdependency of human rights, both between the two categories of civil-political rights and socio-economic human rights, and between individual rights within or across those categories; and
(2) the equal importance of socio-economic with civil–political human rights.

Civil rights are traditionally associated with negative state action (or restraint), protecting personal life from state interference. They are presumed to be cost-free, capable of being implemented immediately and are justiciable. Socio-economic rights are, on the other hand, traditionally framed as requiring positive state actions, intervention in the personal sphere, intensive resources, progressive realisation and as non-justiciable.[27] The principle of indivisibility recognises that these ostensible differences between the two categories of rights are far from clear-cut and are frequently overstated.[28]

The principle of indivisibility has been chosen as the central and coherent organising concept for the book's argument. This is because, as referenced in the literature, the CRPD, more than any other convention, embodies the indivisibility, interdependence and interrelatedness of human rights.[29] It is the only convention to have a statement of indivisibility in its Preamble,[30] and it includes civil–political and socio-economic rights not just within the one convention but within the same articles.[31] It demands that Article 12 be interpreted in the context of the whole of the CRPD in a way that is consistent with the convention in its entirety.

1.3.2 Autonomy, Dignity and Equality

Both the right to legal capacity and the right to equality expressed in Article 12 (i.e. the right 'to enjoy legal capacity on an equal basis with others') are traditionally

[27] Kristin Henrard, 'Introduction: The Justiciabiity of ESC Rights and the Interdependence of all Fundamental Rights' (2009) 2(4) *Erasmus Law Review* 373, 373.

[28] Ibid 373–34.

[29] Janet E Lord, 'Preamble' in Ilias Bantekas, Michael Ashley Stein and Dēmētrēs Anastasiou (eds), *The UN Convention on the Rights of Persons with Disabilities: A Commentary* (Oxford University Press, 2018) 1, 11; Arstein-Kerslake, *Restoring Voice to People with Cognitive Disabilities* (n 5) 19; Arlene S Kanter, *The Development of Disability Rights under International Law from Charity to Human Rights* (Routledge, 2015) 9; Ida Elizabeth Koch, 'From Invisibility to Indivisibility: The International Convention on the Rights of Persons with Disabilities' in Oddný Mjöll Arnadóttir and Gerard Quinn (eds), *The UN Convention on the Rights of Persons with Disabilities: European and Scandinavian Perspectives* (Nijhoff, 2009) 67, 77; Gauthier DeBeco, 'The Indivisibility of Human Rights and the Convention on the Rights of Persons with Disabilities' (2019) 68 (January) *International and Comparative Law Quarterly* 141; Michael Ashley Stein, 'Disability Human Rights' (2007) 95(1) *California Law Review* 75, 77–79.

[30] 'Reaffirming the universality, indivisibility, interdependence and interrelatedness of all human rights and fundamental freedoms …' *CRPD* Preamble para 3; DeBeco (n 29) 149.

[31] Koch, 'From Invisibility to Indivisibility' (n 29) 77; DeBeco (n 29) 149–51.

categorised as civil–political rights.[32] The principle of indivisibility demands both recognition of the interdependence of rights and acknowledgement that socio-economic rights are as important as civil–political rights. I argue, therefore, that indivisibility (as applied to Article 12) leads to the disruption of the hegemony of the right to legal capacity over other rights, autonomy (as the basis for personhood) over other values (including dignity), and formal over substantive equality.

First, this disruption allows for recognition that achievement of the civil–political rights of legal capacity (or autonomy) and equality may depend on fulfilling socio-economic rights. It further recognises that autonomy for adults with cognitive disability is more than the right to non-interference. Second, it recognises that equality is achieved not just by restraint from the state but sometimes by positive, differential treatment in the form of supported decision-making *or* decision-making by substitutes. Third, it recognises that personhood is not just located in the abstraction of rationality but is inter-relational and embodied. I draw on philosophical and legal literature and jurisprudence to argue for a concept of dignity (instead of autonomy) to underpin Article 12 personhood. I argue that this 'five-dimensional' concept of human dignity, infused as it is with the principle of indivisibility, underpins the CRPD and Article 12.

This book focuses on the values of, or rights to, autonomy, dignity and equality for reasons explained in Chapters 4, 5 and 6, respectively. Overarching these explanations is the fact that the text of the CRPD itself places particular emphasis on these three values as being fundamental to disability human rights. Specifically, Article 12 is explained widely in the literature as upholding autonomy and often as asserting a right to *equal* autonomy. Further, the right to legal capacity is frequently described as respecting human dignity as the 'dignity of risk'.[33] This book examines how the case of cognitive disability denies a simplistic understanding of these central concepts as they have developed and been applied in the liberal tradition.

2 A NOTE ON TERMINOLOGY AND CONCEPTS

Morris observes how writing and speaking in disability studies is fraught with complexity 'because non-disabled people have had … "absolute power" over narrative when it comes to the representation of impairment …'.[34] In this context, I have settled on using the following terms.

[32] *General Comment No 1* [30].

[33] ALRC (n 9) 75; Suzanne Doyle and Eilionóir Flynn, 'Ireland's Ratification of the UN Convention on the Rights of Persons with Disabilities: Challenges and Opportunities' (2013) 41(3) *British Journal of Learning Disabilities* 171, 174. For further discussion on the 'dignity of risk', see Chapter 2, Sections 3.2.2 and 3.3.2, and Chapter 5, Sections 3.2.1 and 4.1.

[34] Jenny Morris, 'Impairment and Disability: Constructing an Ethics of Care that Promotes Human Rights' (2001) 16(4) *Hypatia* 1, 6; note also that 'disabled people' is the language favoured by British theorists because according to the social model of disability 'Disabled people are those people with impairments who are disabled by society': Ibid 2.

2.1 'Cognitive Disability'

I use the umbrella term 'cognitive disability'[35] to describe impairments in adults associated with intellectual disability, acquired brain injury, age-related dementia[36] and mental illness. For the term 'intellectual disability', I rely on the definition provided by the American Association of Intellectual and Developmental Disabilities as: 'a disability characterised by significant limitations in both intellectual functioning and in adaptive behaviour, which covers many everyday social and practical skills [and which] originates before the age of 18'.[37] The term 'mental illness' is chosen because it reflects the language used predominantly in legislation relating to involuntary treatment.[38]

Many adults will have cognitive disability associated with more than one of these conditions, but these categorisations are still used widely. While to an extent these labels or 'diagnoses' reflect a much-criticised 'medical' model of disability, of which I write further in Chapter 2,[39] they also indicate broadly different individual, social and legal circumstances embodied in and around the person.

2.2 'Impairment' and 'Disability'

The terms 'impairment' and 'disability' have attracted particular and distinct meanings in the commentary. As explained in Chapter 2, the social model of disability

35 The terminology used takes account of the approach of the Royal Commission into Violence, Abuse, Neglect and Exploitation of People with Disability ('Disability Royal Commission'): 'This report uses the singular term "disability" rather than the plural "disabilities" to adhere to the human rights model of disability … and uses the more common term "people" instead of the specific legal use of "persons" used in the CRPD' in Kayess and Sands (n 6) 49.

36 Cahill notes that although the CRPD uses the terms 'mental' and 'intellectual' impairment in Article 1, she recommends a change of wording to include 'cognitive' to recognise dementia more squarely: Suzanne Cahill, *Dementia and Human Rights* (Policy Press at the University of Bristol, 2018) 49; Article 1 [2] provides that 'Persons with disabilities include those who have long-term physical, mental, intellectual or sensory impairments which in interaction with various barriers may hinder their full and effective participation in society on an equal basis with others'.

37 Website of the American Association on Intellectual and Developmental Disabilities https://aaidd.org/intellectual-disability/definition, retrieved 17 September 2018. Used in Devi (n 5) 794. An alternative definition is used by Bach and Kerzner, that is, 'generally means having greater difficulty than most people with intellectual and adaptive functioning due to a long term condition that is present at birth or before the age of eighteen': Bach and Kerzner (n 5) 14.

38 See, for example, *Mental Health Act 2016* (Qld) s 10(1), *Mental Health Act* (Vic) s 4(1). Note that the CRPD refers to 'mental impairment': Article 1; the World Network of the Users and Survivors of Psychiatry uses 'psychosocial disability': World Network of Users and Survivors of Psychiatry, 'Implementation Manual for the United Nations Convention on the Rights of Persons with Disabilities' (February 2008) www.wnusp.net/documents/WNUSP_CRPD_Manual.pdf; but that this terminology is not universally adopted: Anne Plumb, 'UN Convention on the Rights of Persons with Disabilities: Out of the Frying Pan into the Fire? Mental Health Service Users and Survivors Aligning with the Disability Movement' in Helen Spandler et al (eds), *Madness, Distress and the Politics of Disablement* (Bristol University Press, 2015) 183, 184.

39 See Chapter 2, Section 2.2.

makes a distinction between them. In short, the social model frames disability as being caused by the failure of society to accommodate an individual's impairment.[40] However, in Chapter 2, I also explain how the interpretation of Article 12 presented in this book is premised on acceptance of a critique of the social model of disability that questions the basis of the distinction between these two concepts.[41] For these reasons, I use the words 'impairment' and 'disability' largely interchangeably, except where the context requires or implies otherwise – for example, when describing or critiquing the social model of disability and related commentary.

2.3 *'Legal Capacity'*

'Legal capacity' is not defined in the CRPD, thereby contributing to the interpretive contention around Article 12. But in *Equality, Capacity and Disability in Commonwealth Laws: A Final Report* ('the ALRC Report'), the Australian Law Reform Commission ('ALRC') provides usefully that:

> Capacity in a general sense refers to decision-making ability ...; Legal capacity sets the threshold for individuals to take certain actions that have legal consequences ... [and] ... Legal capacity goes to the validity, in law, of choices and being accountable for the choices made.[42]

The significance of the concept of legal capacity for adults with cognitive disability is that where an adult lacks capacity to make legally enforceable decisions (or has impaired capacity), a substitute may in some cases make a decision or decisions on the adult's behalf.[43]

2.4 *'Decision-Making by a Substitute'*

Much of the debate around Article 12 has been complicated and confused by different understandings of the terminology used to describe decision-making by substitutes for an adult with impaired capacity.[44] In 2014, the UN Disability Committee published its General Comment No 1 Article 12: Equal Recognition before the Law ('General Comment No 1'), explaining its interpretation of Article 12. However, the definition it contained of 'substitute decision-making', was later made subject to a corrigendum, the status of which is unclear, adding yet more confusion.[45] The

[40] See Chapter 2, Section 2.3. See also Kayess and Sands (n 6) 33.
[41] See Chapter 2, Section 2.4.
[42] ALRC (n 9) 44.
[43] See Chapter 2, Section 3.2, for a description of the different capacity tests.
[44] Ibid 52; Series and Nilsson (n 18) 347.
[45] Committee on the Rights of Persons with Disabilities, *General Comment No 1 (2014) Article 12: Equal Recognition before the Law, Corrigendum*, 11th sess, UN Doc CRPD/C/GC/1.Corr.1 (26 January 2018). See further Chapter 2, Section 4.1 including footnotes.

UN Disability Committee generally uses the terms 'guardianship' and 'substitute decision-making'.[46] In other contexts, the terms 'surrogates'[47] or 'representatives'[48] may be used to include: guardians who make decisions for personal matters;[49] administrators[50] and managers[51] who make financial decisions; and clinicians who may make decisions for adults relating to mental health treatment.[52] The *Mental Capacity Act 2005* (England and Wales) ('MCA') uses the term 'deputy' to describe a substitute appointed to make decisions on financial or personal matters.[53]

In an attempt to find some clarity, this book uses the term 'decision-making by a substitute' to refer to decisions made by a second person for an adult with impaired capacity, where the decision is legally recognised as having been made by the second person rather than the adult.[54] Unless the context demands otherwise, this would include decisions by all those types of decision-makers referred to above. The more specific terms are used in the context of particular situations, legislation or commentary.

2.5 *'Supported Decision-Making'*

Article 12(3) provides that States shall provide for people with disabilities, 'the support they may require in exercising their legal capacity'. Chapter 2 surveys the historical and ongoing development of various practices of providing support for an adult to exercise legal capacity to make their own decisions.[55] It shows that there is no universal consensus on what the practice entails, or where the line should be drawn between supported decision-making and substitute decision-making. Different terms including 'assisted decision-making', 'support for decision-making'

46 *General Comment No 1*.

47 Allen Buchanan and Dan W Brock, *Deciding for Others: The Ethics of Surrogate Decision Making* (Cambridge University Press, 1989).

48 ALRC (n 9).

49 Legislation in Australian jurisdictions tends to make a distinction between a 'guardian' and 'administrator' as indicated; for example, *Guardianship and Administration Act 2000* (Qld) ('*GAA Qld*') sch 4, Dictionary.

50 For example, *Guardianship and Administration Act 2019* (Vic) ('*GAA Vic*') pt 3 provides for guardianship orders for personal matters and administration orders for financial matters.

51 For example, *Guardianship Act 1987* (NSW) ('*GA NSW*') pt 3A provides for managers to be appointed under 'Financial management orders'.

52 For involuntary mental health treatment, see White, McDonald and Willmott (n 3) 735, 743–50.

53 Section 16.

54 Note that although legislation recognises that the decision is made by the guardian, it also provides that the decision has an effect against third parties as if it were made by the adult. For example, s 38(3) *GAA Vic* (n 50) provides that: '(3) A decision made, action taken, consent given or thing done by a guardian under a guardianship order has effect as if it were made, taken, given or done by the represented person and the represented person had decision-making capacity for the matter in relation to which the order was made.'

55 See Chapter 2, Sections 3.4, 4.1.3 and 4.1.4.

and 'supported decision-making' all have some currency.[56] The Law Commission of England and Wales usefully provides that 'Supported decision-making refers to the process of providing support to a person whose decision-making ability is impaired, to enable them to make their own decisions wherever possible'.[57] The term 'supported decision-making' is used in this book to refer to this collection of informal and formal practices.

3 THE CONVENTION ON THE RIGHTS OF PERSONS WITH DISABILITIES

In using the principle of indivisibility to understand and interpret Article 12, this book examines the right to legal capacity in the context of the whole of the CRPD. The CRPD and the Article 12 literature are in turn situated in the broader context of the development of disability policy and human rights – a history that has shaped the text of the convention as well as the interpretations surrounding it. This section briefly describes this history of the CRPD's development, which is further elaborated on in later chapters, especially Chapter 3, in its explanation of the principle of indivisibility.

3.1 *Development of Human Rights Instruments for People with Disability*

Historically, disability was not referred to as a human rights issue, reflecting the social, political and legal exclusion of people with disability.[58] Gradually, non-binding human rights instruments began to recognise people with disability as attracting specific claims to human rights, culminating in the 2006 adoption of the CRPD, which signalled formal inclusion of people with disability on the human rights agenda.

The two foundational UN human rights conventions – the International Covenant on Civil and Political Rights ('ICCPR')[59] and the International Covenant on Economic Social and Cultural Rights ('ICESCR')[60] – both expressly apply to 'all

[56] Then refers to terminology including 'assisted decision-making also known as supported, interdependent or co-decision-making'. In Shih-Ning Then, 'Evolution and Innovation in Guardianship Laws: Assisted Decision-Making' (2013) 35(1) *Sydney Law Review* 133, 134.

[57] Law Commission, *Mental Capacity and Deprivation of Liberty* (Report No 372, 2017) 167.

[58] Theresia Degener and Andrew Begg, 'From Invisible Citizens to Agents of Change: A Short History of the Struggle for the Recognition of the Rights of Persons with Disabilities at the United Nations' in Valentina Della Fina, Rachele Cera and Giuseppe Palmisano (eds), *The United Nations Convention on the Rights of Persons with Disabilities: A Commentary* (Springer International Publishing, 2017) 1, 2–15.

[59] *ICCPR*, opened for signature 16 December 1966, 999 UNTS 171 (entered into force 23 March 1976).

[60] *ICESCR*, opened for signature 16 December 1966, 993 UNTS 3 (entered into force 3 January 1976).

members of the human family',[61] thereby including people with disability. However, the prohibited grounds of discrimination list (inclusively) '...race, colour, sex, language, religion, political or other opinion, national or social origin, property, birth or other status'.[62] The omission of disability from this list meant that disability was implicitly or arguably included in the catch-all of 'other status'.[63]

Beginning in the 1970s, the UN began to develop non-binding instruments that acknowledged the human rights of people with disability. In 1971, the UN adopted the 'Declaration on the Rights of Retarded Persons' ('1971 Declaration')[64] and in 1975 the 'Declaration on the Rights of Disabled Persons' ('1975 Declaration').[65] The 1971 Declaration specifically provides that it may be 'necessary to restrict or deny'[66] some human rights of persons with cognitive disability provided that legal safeguards are put in place to prevent abuse. Rather than view guardianship as a potential tool of human rights abuse, the 1971 Declaration included a 'right to a qualified guardian'.[67] The 1975 Declaration uses the language of paternalism rather than human rights when it defines a 'disabled person' as 'any person unable to ensure by himself or herself, wholly or partly, the necessities of a normal individual and/or social life, as a result of deficiency, either congenital or not, in his or her physical or mental capabilities'.[68]

Increasing recognition of the human rights of people with disability led in 1981 to the UN declaring the International Year of Disabled Persons, which also launched the United Nations World Programme of Action Concerning Disabled Persons.[69] These were followed by the adoption in 1993 of the 'Standard Rules

[61] *ICCPR* (n 59) Preamble para 2; *ICESCR* (n 60) Preamble para 2.

[62] *ICCPR* (n 59) Article 2(1); *ICESCR* (n 60) Article 2(1).

[63] Moreover, the requirement contained in Article 2 (2) of the Covenant that the rights 'enunciated ... will be exercised without discrimination of any kind' based on certain specified grounds 'or other status' clearly applies to discrimination on the grounds of disability'. Committee on Economic Social and Cultural Rights, *General Comment 5: Persons with Disabilities*, 11th sess (9 December 1994) ('*ESCR General Comment No 5*'). It was not until the adoption of the UN Convention on the Rights of the Child in 1989 that discrimination based on disability was expressly articulated in a UN treaty as a violation of human rights. *Convention on the Rights of the Child*, opened for signature 29 November 1989, 1577 UNTS 11 (entered into force 2 September 1990) ('*CRC*'). Article 2(1).

[64] 1971 Declaration, proclaimed by General Assembly resolution 2856 (XXVI) (20 December 1971).

[65] 1975 Declaration, UN Doc GA, Res, 3447 (XXX), at 88, UN GAOR, Supp, No 34, UN Doc, A/10034 (9 December 1975).

[66] 1971 Declaration (n 64) [7].

[67] Ibid [5].

[68] 1975 Declaration (n 65) [1]; 'the 1971 Declaration on the Rights of Mentally Retarded Persons and the 1975 Declaration on the Rights of Disabled Persons – did state that persons with disability are subjects of international human rights law, but did this largely within the context of the medical model of disability': Kayess and Sands (n 6) 8. The language of 'deficiency' also embodies the much criticised 'medical model' of disability: see Chapter 2, Section 2.2.

[69] United Nations, General Assembly, *World Programme of Action Concerning Disabled Persons*, GA Res 37/52, UN Doc A/RES/37/52 (3 December 1982)

on the Equalisation of Opportunities for Persons with Disabilities' ('the Standard Rules'),[70] which are referred to in the CRPD's Preamble[71] and which have been described as having a 'significant impact on the emergence of disability-based anti-discrimination legislation in many countries around the globe'.[72]

3.2 *Inclusion of People with Disability in the Development of the CRPD*

On 12 March 2000, the 'World NGO Summit on Disability' meeting in Beijing made a declaration ('the Beijing Declaration'), urging that:

> people with diverse disabilities and their organizations, and other civic organizations, local and national governments, members of the United Nations system and other inter-governmental bodies, as well as the private sector, … collaborate closely in an inclusive and wide consultative process aimed at the development and adoption of an international convention to promote and protect the rights of people with disabilities, and enhance equal opportunities for participation in mainstream society.[73]

By resolution on 19 December 2001 the United Nations ('UN') General Assembly established an 'Ad Hoc Committee on a Comprehensive and Integral International Convention on the Protection and Promotion of the Rights and Dignity of Persons with Disabilities' ('the Ad Hoc Committee').[74] As urged by the Beijing Declaration, collaboration and consultation were considered key to the development of what became the CRPD, and it has indeed been lauded as the first UN treaty to be negotiated directly with civil society organisations.[75] In the past, such organisations had made known their views through States parties. However, in the case of the CRPD, given the historical social and political exclusion of those with disability, it

[70] *Standard Rules*, 48th sess, UN Doc A/RES/48/96 (4 March 1994).

[71] Preamble para 6.

[72] Degener and Begg (n 58) 9.

[73] *Beijing Declaration on Disabled Persons in the New Millennium*, World NGO Summit on Disability (12 March 2000); Anna Lawson, 'The United Nations Convention on the Rights of Persons with Disabilities: New Era or False Dawn?' (2007) 34(2) *Syracuse International Journal of Law and Commerce* 563, 586.

[74] Comprehensive and integral international convention to promote and protect the rights and dignity of persons with disabilities, UN Doc A/Res/56/168 (19 December 2001).

[75] See, for example, Barbara Carter, 'Seeking the Essence of Guardianship: Beyond the United Nations Convention on the Rights of Persons with Disabilities' (Conference Paper, World Guardianship Congress, 15–16 October 2012) 1 https://agac.org.au/conference-papers/72-2012-oct-2nd-world-congress-melbourne; Kayess and Fogarty (n 12) 22; World Network of Users and Survivors of Psychiatry (n 38) 4–5; Sarah Arduin, 'Article 3: General Principles' in Ilias Bantekas, Michael Ashley Stein and Anastasiou Dimitris (eds), *The UN Convention on the Rights of Persons with Disabilities: A Commentary* (Oxford University Press, 2018) 85, 97; Rosemary Kayess and Philip French, 'Out of Darkness into Light? Introducing the Convention on the Rights of Persons with Disabilities' (2008) 8(1) *Human Rights Law Review* 1, 3–4.

was considered of paramount importance that their voices be heard directly in negotiations, reflecting what had become the slogan of the disability movement: 'nothing about us, without us'.[76] The CRPD was to become a convention developed by people with disability *for* people with disability as subjects and claimants of human rights.[77] Their autonomy, personhood and equality were recognised in the drafting process itself.

3.3 *A Disability-Specific Convention*

In 2002, the year following the formation of the Ad Hoc Committee, the UN High Commissioner on Human Rights released a report titled *Human Rights and Disability: The Current Use and Future Potential of United Nations Human Rights Instrument in the Context of Disability* ('the 2002 Report').[78] The 2002 Report conceives the then-proposed disability-specific treaty as underpinning the existing conventions by particularising human rights norms in the context of disability in a binding instrument.[79] Reflecting these beginnings, the UN Disability Committee has affirmed that the CRPD does not create new rights but is to be articulated as interpreting pre-existing rights. Nevertheless, several commentators have queried whether this is, in fact, the case, or whether the CRPD has actually created new rights, including those expressed in Article 12.[80]

During the drafting of the CRPD, there had been some discussion as to whether a narrow, non-discrimination approach, such as that in the *International Convention on the Elimination of All Forms of Racial Discrimination* ('CERD')[81] and the *Convention on the Elimination of All Forms of Discrimination against Women* ('CEDAW'),[82] should be adopted. The alternative proposal was for a broader,

[76] McCallum (n 6) 156.

[77] The ongoing participation of those with disability in the review and monitoring of the CRPD is also ensured by Articles 33 and 34. Article 33 provides that 'Civil society, in particular persons with disabilities and their representative organisations, shall be involved and participate fully in the monitoring process'. Article 34 provides that when nominating members of the UN Disability Committee to oversee and monitor the CRPD, States Parties shall give consideration to 'the participation of experts with disabilities'.

[78] Gerard Quinn and Theresia Degener, *Human Rights and Disability: The Current Use and Future Potential of United Nations Human Rights Instruments in the Context of Disability* (United Nations, 2002).

[79] Ibid 294–95.

[80] Kayess and French (n 75) 32; María Soledad Cisternas Reyes, 'Foreword' in Valentina Della Fina (ed), *The United Nations Convention on the Rights of Persons with Disabilities: A Commentary* (Springer, 2017) v; Elif Celik, 'The Role of CRPD in Rethinking the Subject of Human Rights' (2017) 21(7) *The International Journal of Human Rights* 933, 935.

[81] *CERD*, opened for signature 21 December 1965, 660 UNTS 195 (entered into force 4 January 1969).

[82] *CEDAW*, opened for signature 1 March 1980, 1249 UNTS 8 (entered into force 3 September 1981).

comprehensive rights approach modelled on the United Nations *Convention on the Rights of the Child* ('CRC').[83] The travaux préparatoires indicate that the Ad Hoc Committee ultimately decided on the CRC model and drafted a comprehensive convention expressing the full range of human rights. They further indicate that paragraph 3 of the CRPD's Preamble, which recognises the 'universality, indivisibility, interdependence and interrelatedness of all human rights and fundamental freedoms', was inserted in recognition of this approach.[84] This broader, comprehensive approach means that the principle of indivisibility is particularly prominent in the text of the convention,[85] and also (as explained in Chapter 6) that it embraces a broad concept of substantive equality.

In summary, the CRPD was the first stand-alone, binding human rights instrument that dealt wholly with disability rights. From their invisibility in the category of 'other status' in the ICCPR and ICESCR, people with disability came to be included as subjects of rights, and their autonomous personhood was respected in the drafting process itself. The CRPD was intended to achieve not just non-discrimination for people with disability but inclusion as people with substantive equality.

3.4 *The Drafting of Article 12: A 'Flashpoint'*

The CRPD – and Article 12, in particular – has been referred to as representing and effecting a 'paradigm shift' in disability human rights.[86] During the drafting process, Australia was one of many States acknowledging this paradigm shift to supported decision-making away from substitute decision-making. The Australian delegate described Article 12 as providing: '…the seeds for an important paradigm shift by giving primacy to supported decision making … [and] continues that shift by providing for personal representation only as a last resort'.[87] However, many of the civil society organisations involved in drafting considered that the 'paradigm shift' of supported decision-making needed to be more radical. As drafting progressed, these organisations had formed a coalition – the International Disability Caucus ('IDC') – whose representative said that:

> Substituted decision making is based on the premise of incompetence and must not be legitimized. Supported decision making is based on the premise of

[83] *CRC* (n 63).

[84] Degener and Begg (n 58) 13.

[85] See Chapter 3, Section 5.

[86] Quinn (n 20) 12; Quinn and Arstein-Kerslake (n 5) 44; ALRC (n 9) 24; 23; Amita Dhanda, 'Constructing a New Human Rights Lexicon: Convention on the Rights of Persons with Disabilities' (2008) 8 *Sur – Revista Internacional de Direitos Humanos* 43, 45; Bach and Kerzner (n 5).

[87] Ad Hoc Committee, *Daily Summary of the Seventh Session: Discussions Related to Article 12 Equal Recognition as a Person before the Law (continued)* (18 January 2006) www.un.org/esa/socdev/enable/rights/ahc7sum18jan.htmAd Hoc Committee ('*Daily Summary 18 January 2006*').

> competence. The two cannot exist together and successfully achieve the paradigm shift desired.... Addressing states' concerns for safeguards for guardianships and worrying about implementation does not promote the paradigm shift but reinforces the traditional abusive systems.[88]

As stated above following ratification of the CRPD, the UN Disability Committee's *General Comment No 1* was published in 2014. It adopted an interpretation effectively supporting the IDC's view that adults with cognitive disability have their legal capacity recognised, their will and preferences given effect to, and their autonomy preserved.[89] Many commentators, both before and after *General Comment No 1*'s publication, have expressed strong endorsement of the interpretation it prescribes.[90] Others have continued to pursue some of the counter arguments raised during drafting. These include that decision-making by substitutes is required as a safeguard[91] and that implementing supported decision-making for all adults with cognitive disability has unresolvable challenges in implementation.[92]

While all parties agree that *General Comment No 1* is not technically binding, it is also widely agreed that it has significant normative force.[93] In particular, under the CRPD, the UN Disability Committee has responsibility for monitoring states' compliance with the convention. It does this by considering States' reports[94] as well as through hearing and considering 'communications' or complaints of human rights violations.[95] As a result of both of these processes, the UN Disability Committee can make suggestions or recommendations for compliance, and will be guided by its own General Comments in doing so.[96] States' parties compliance (or non-compliance) with *General Comment No 1* will continue to be monitored as a critical issue.

While this book agrees that a paradigm shift is needed, it argues that recognition of universal legal capacity may actually serve to perpetuate the old paradigms. The

88 Ibid.

89 *General Comment No 1.*

90 Minkowitz, 'Legal Capacity' (n 5); International Disability Alliance (n 5); Morrissey (n 5); Dhanda, 'Legal Capacity in the Disability Rights Convention' (n 5); Quinn and Arstein-Kerslake (n 5); Flynn and Arstein-Kerslake, 'The Support Model of Legal Capacity' (n 5); Bach and Kerzner (n 5); Devi (n 5); de Bhailís and Flynn (n 5) Arstein-Kerslake, *Restoring Voice to People with Cognitive Disabilities* (n 5); Glen, 'Changing Paradigms' (n 5).

91 Nicholas Caivano, 'Conceptualizing Capacity: Interpreting Canada's Qualified Ratification of Article 12 of the UN Disability Rights Convention' (2014) 4(1) *Western Journal of Legal Studies* 1, 23. See also Chapter 2, Section 4.2.4.

92 See criticisms of the 'best interpretation' principle in Chapter 2, Section 4.2.5.

93 Martin et al, *Three Jurisdictions Report* (n 9) 56.

94 See Articles 34 and 35.

95 *Optional Protocol to the Convention on the Rights of Persons with Disabilities*, opened for signature 30 March 2007, 2518 UNTS 283 (entered into force 3 May 2008) Article 1.

96 See for example where the UN Disability Committee has referred to several of its General Comments, including General Comment No 1 in: Committee on the Rights of Persons with Disabilities, *Concluding Observations on the Combined Second and Third Period Reports of Australia*, UN Doc CRPD/C/AUS/CO/2-3.

continued privileging of autonomy as the basis for personhood may only serve to further embed existing stigmatisation of adults who lack decision-making autonomy.[97] I further argue that a conception of equality that demands all adults with severe cognitive disability be treated the same 'as others' in the area of decision-making will fail to achieve substantive, inclusive equality.[98]

4 RESEARCH METHOD AND SCOPE

4.1 *Doctrinal and Theoretical Analysis and Research*

The book uses legal doctrine and legal and philosophical theory to answer the central question of how Article 12 can be interpreted to require both supported decision-making and decision-making by substitutes as a last resort in order to uphold the human rights of adults with cognitive disability. Legal doctrine is drawn upon first to describe key legal concepts in guardianship, decision-making by substitutes and supported decision-making and to provide context for the interpretation and application of Article 12. The book refers to human rights law and doctrine, so as to describe and explain the principle of indivisibility. It further describes, analyses and applies the CRPD and Article 12 through reference to General Comments and other publications and decisions of UN committees. It also reviews cross-jurisdictional jurisprudence, which considers the role and meaning of dignity as a legal value or principle.

Some reliance is placed on the *Vienna Convention on the Law of Treaties* ('VCLT').[99] Article 31 provides a general rule that a treaty is to be interpreted 'within the ordinary meaning to be given the terms of the treaty in their context and in the light of its object and purpose'[100] including its Preamble.[101] Article 32 VCLT further provides that when the meaning of a provision is 'ambiguous or obscure', recourse can be made to the 'preparatory work of the treaty and the circumstances of its conclusion' to aid interpretation.[102]

The book also includes a substantial theoretical research component, in describing, reviewing, analysing and critiquing the literature in law and philosophy relating to the central concepts of disability, human rights, autonomy, dignity and equality.

97 See Chapter 4, Sections 4.1 and 4.6.

98 See Chapter 6.

99 Opened for signature 18 December 1979, 1155 UNTS 331 (entered into force 27 January 1980).

100 Ibid Article 31(1).

101 Ibid Article 31(2).

102 'Recourse may be had to supplementary means of interpretation, including the preparatory work of the treaty and the circumstances of its conclusion, to confirm the meaning resulting from the application of Article 31, or to determine the meaning when the interpretation according to Article 31 (a) leaves the meaning ambiguous or obscure; or (b) leads to a result which is manifestly absurd or unreasonable.'

The research is cross-disciplinary, referring to the work of lawyers, philosophers, psychologists and sociologists, many of whom have written on Article 12 directly, as well as on the human rights values and concepts on which it is founded.

4.2 *Scope*

The focus of this book is on how Article 12 can be interpreted as allowing for decision-making by substitutes, arguing that such decision-making can actually uphold human rights. Its focus is not on the latest developments in supported decision-making. Rather, it examines the principles and values underpinning supported decision-making to the extent required to explain how autonomy, dignity and equality are theorised and applied across decision-making by, with and for adults with cognitive disability.

I wish to clarify that there are several other extremely important areas of investigation that are nevertheless beyond this book's scope. Chapter 2 describes the different decision-making principles used by substitutes – that is, 'best interests'[103] or adopting the adult's 'will and preferences'.[104] The argument in this book for the retention of decision-making by substitutes as a last resort assumes that such decisions will take account of an adult's will and preferences and that there will be time and domain limits on the appointments of substitutes.[105] The book contributes to the development of those principles by anticipating that the adult's full range of indivisible human rights will be considered when a substitute makes a decision. However, it does not investigate the challenging and important question of how rights are to be balanced, whether through the principle of proportionality[106] or otherwise, in any particular case.

Also beyond scope of this book is how decisions by substitutes are implemented. The book's argument assumes that once decisions are made (whether supported or by a substitute), goods and services must be provided to adults in ways that respect their personhood, ensure their social inclusion and uphold their rights. Important considerations of modes and methods of service delivery are beyond scope.

Decision-making by a substitute may occur when an adult's capacity is impaired, whether such impairment is associated with intellectual disability, acquired brain injury, dementia or mental illness. The literature referenced in the book includes consideration of how Article 12 applies in decision-making practices in all of the

103 See Chapter 2, Section 3.3.1.

104 Also referred to as 'substituted judgement'. See Chapter 2, Section 3.3.2.

105 Chapter 2, Section 4.2.3.

106 'The principle of proportionality is the means by which a court or tribunal applying international human rights law determines whether a particular restriction on a human right is a justified restriction …': Justice Virginia Bell, 'Equality, Proportionality and Dignity: The Guiding Principles for a Just Legal System' (2017) 42(1) *Alternative Law Journal* 4, 5.

above cases. However, the case studies chosen are related to guardianship and don't include cases of involuntary treatment for mental illness. This is because of the significant amount of controversy and disagreement over which mental health treatments are effective and justified, quite apart from whether they are provided voluntarily or at the direction of a substitute decision-maker.[107] The effectiveness of any particular type of treatment is beyond the scope of this book. To avoid using case studies that deflect attention from the method of decision-making to the nature of the treatment itself, case studies in the area of mental health treatment have not been used. Case studies used in this book describe adults with physical health and support needs, where the premise is clear that the health or support service in question would be beneficial in some way to the adult.

Partly for the same reason, that it would lead to a diversion into another major field of study, the impact of Article 12 on the criminal law is beyond scope. While there has been some important commentary around how Article 12 affects the criminal defence of unsound mind and pleas of unfitness for trial,[108] consideration of the interpretation and application of Article 12 in the criminal context is not considered. Others have commented and proposed that interpreting Article 12 as recognising universal legal capacity in the criminal context would require a much-needed wholesale review of criminal law and procedure internationally.[109] Hall, on the other hand, has expressed the view that Article 12 and the right to legal capacity have no relevance to interpretation and application of the criminal law.[110]

[107] 'A growing research base has produced evidence indicating that the status quo, preoccupied with biomedical interventions, including psychotropic medications and non-consensual measures, is no longer defensible in the context of improving mental health': Pūras, Dainus, Special Rapporteur, *Report of the Special Rapporteur on the Right of Everyone to the Enjoyment of the Highest Attainable Standard of Physical And Mental Health*, UN Doc A/HRC/35/21 (28 March 2017) [5].

[108] Melvyn Colin Freeman et al, 'Reversing Hard Won Victories in the Name of Human Rights: A Critique of the General Comment on Article 12 of the UN Convention on the Rights of Persons with Disabilities' (2015) 2(9) *The Lancet Psychiatry* 844, 844; Piers Gooding et al, 'Unfitness to Stand Trial and the Indefinite Detention of Persons with Cognitive Disabilities in Australia: Human Rights Challenges and Proposals for Change' (2017) 40 *Melbourne University Law Review* 816; Peter Bartlett, 'The United Nations Convention on the Rights of Persons with Disabilities and Mental Health Law' (2012) 75(5) *The Modern Law Review* 752, 753–54; Tina Minkowitz et al, 'Advancing the Rights of Users and Survivors of Psychiatry using the UN Convention on the Rights of Persons with Disabilities: An Interview with Tina Minkowitz' in Helen Spandler, Jill Anderson and Bob Sapey (eds), *Madness, Distress and the Politics of Disablement* (Bristol University Press; Policy Press, 2015) 171, 178; Meron Wondemaghen, 'Testing Equality: Insanity, Treatment Refusal and the CRPD' (2018) 25(2) *Psychiatry, Psychology and the Law* 174.

[109] Amita Dhanda and Gabor Gombos, 'Questions of Criminal Culpability and Persons with Disabilities' in Eilionoir Flynn, Anna Arstein-Kerslake, Clíona De Bhailís and Maria Laura Serra (eds), *Global Perspectives on Legal Capacity Reform: Our Voices, Our Stories* (Routledge, 2018) 32, 40

[110] Margaret Isabel Hall, 'Putting the Pieces Together: Article 12, 'Safeguarding' and the Right to Legal Capacity' in Mary Donelly, Rosie Harding and Ezgi Tascioglu (eds), *Supporting Legal Capacity in Socio-Legal Context* (Hart Publishing 2022) 273, 278.

Finally, as described in Chapter 3, the indivisibility of human rights as doctrine or principle is contested by some scholars and theorists.[111] Chapter 3 reviews the dominant writings on this topic and draws on these to formulate the concept of indivisibility relied on by this book. Further consideration as to whether indivisibility is officially recognised as a doctrine or principle or otherwise is beyond scope. Chapter 3 refers to and reviews a body of literature that affirms the incorporation of the principle of indivisibility into the CRPD.

5 THE BOOK'S STRUCTURE AND ARGUMENT

This chapter has introduced the research problem, explained key terms, provided background to the development of the CRPD and Article 12, described the research methodology, and defined the book's scope. This section provides an overview of the book's interpretive argument, as it is developed chapter by chapter – in particular, how it relates to the principle of indivisibility and the key values of autonomy, dignity and equality.

Chapter 2 explains the historical and contemporary policy, legal and human rights contexts for decision-making by, with and for adults with cognitive disability.[112] It describes the dominant narrative in the literature as depicting a journey from paternalism to autonomy, from exclusion to inclusion, and from discrimination to equality. This journey is reflected in the development of three widely recognised models of disability: the charity, medical and social models.[113] The development of these models, in turn, parallels and charts the development of decision-making frameworks from mass institutionalisation, through guardianship to supported decision-making. Chapter 2 also reviews widespread critiques of the social model of disability and argues that a social model that recognises the residual impacts of impairment[114] serves as a more useful reference point for the development of law and policy than what some have referred to as a 'strict' social model.

Chapter 2 also summarises the major arguments grounding different interpretations of Article 12. Arguments for abolition of decision-making by substitutes are: legal capacity includes the ability to act on rights and not just hold them;[115]

[111] See Chapter 3, Section 2.4.

[112] See Chapter 2, sections 2 and 3.

[113] Theresia Degener, 'A New Human Rights Model of Disability' in Valentina Della Fina, Rachele Cera and Giuseppe Palmisano (eds), *The United Nations Convention on the Rights of Persons with Disabilities: A Commentary* (Springer, 2017) 41; Shane Clifton, *Hierarchies of Power: Disability Theories and Models and Their Implications for Violence against, and Abuse, Neglect, and Exploitation of, People with Disability* (Royal Commission into Violence, Abuse, Neglect and Exploitation of People with Disability, 2020).

[114] 'But to properly grasp the normative obligations entailed in the provision of decisional support, differences that are residual from impairment must be taken into account.' Kong, *Mental Capacity in Relationship* (n 16) 152.

[115] *General Comment No 1* [12]–[13;] International Disability Alliance (n 5).

decision-making by substitutes can never be a safeguard;[116] and (3) it is always discriminatory against people with cognitive disability.[117] Related to these arguments is the proposal that it is always possible to recognise an adult's decision-making autonomy by making a 'best interpretation' of his or her will and preferences.[118] The chapter explains the limitations of these arguments as privileging autonomy at the expense of other values; and in privileging the civil-political right to legal capacity over other civil, economic, political, social and cultural human rights.

Arguments for interpreting Article 12 as allowing for retention of decision-making by substitutes include that legal capacity means only the ability to hold rights and not the ability to act on them.[119] Alternatively, or in addition, there are arguments that substitute decision-making is allowable as 100% support[120] or as a safeguard[121] and that the hard reality is that some adults with cognitive disability are not capable of decision-making autonomy.[122] There are associated arguments that making a 'best interpretation' of an adult's will and preferences lacks transparency,[123] is vulnerable to manipulation,[124] and amounts to substitute decision-making under a different guise.[125] The chapter explains how recognition of hard reality is consistent with the interpretive argument in this book, based as it is on a social model of disability, which recognises the residual impacts of impairment.

Chapter 3 introduces and explains the principle of the indivisibility of human rights. It explains how the principle of indivisibility is embodied in and developed by the CRPD, and how the commentary around the CRPD engages with the principle of indivisibility.[126] It establishes that the principle of indivisibility relied upon in this

[116] 'The "best interests" principle is not a safeguard which complies with article 12 in relation to adults': *General Comment No 1* [21].

[117] Ibid [32]–[34].

[118] Ibid [21].

[119] Ad Hoc Committee, *Daily Summary of the Fifth Session* (25 January 2005) www.un.org/esa/socdev/enable/rights/ahc5sum25jan.htm ('*Daily Summary 25 January 2005*').

[120] Ad Hoc Committee, *Daily Summary 18 January 2006* (n 87); ALRC (n 9) 94.

[121] Caivano (n 91) 23.

[122] Martin et al, *Achieving CRPD Compliance* (n 24) 23.

[123] Matthew Burch, 'Autonomy, Respect, and the Rights of Persons with Disabilities in Crisis' (2017) 34(3) *Journal of Applied Philosophy* 389, 390, 397; Malcolm Parker, 'Getting the Balance Right: Conceptual Considerations Concerning Legal Capacity and Supported Decision-Making' (2016) 13(3) *Journal of Bioethical Inquiry* 381, 389.

[124] Anita Smith (n 25) 266–67.

[125] Terry Carney, 'Supported Decision-Making for People with Cognitive Impairments: An Australian Perspective?' (2015) 4 *Laws* 37, 45; Parker, 'Getting the Balance Right: Conceptual Considerations Concerning Legal Capacity and Supported Decision-Making' (2016) 13(3) *Journal of Bioethical Inquiry* 381, 387.

[126] Dhanda, 'Constructing a New Human Rights Lexicon' (n 86) 48–50; Marianne Schulze, 'Chapter 16: The Human Rights of Persons with Disabilities' in Anja Mihir and Mark Gibney (eds), *The SAGE Handbook of Human Rights* (SAGE Publications Ltd, 2014) 267, 277; Andrea Broderick, 'Harmonisation and Cross-fertilisation of Socio-Economic Rights in the Human Rights Treaty Bodies: Disability and the Reasonableness Review Case Study' (2016) 5 *Laws* 38, 42; DeBeco (n 29) 154; Koch, 'From Invisibility to Indivisibility' (n 29).

book recognises: (a) the interdependencies between rights within and across categories, and (b) the equal importance of socio-economic rights with civil-political rights. It further reviews and agrees with the literature that proposes the particular importance of socio-economic rights to people with disability, given their disproportionate levels of poverty and disadvantage.

Chapter 3 also describes and analyses how existing interpretations of Article 12 have accounted for the principle of indivisibility. It explains how disability issues had historically been sidelined by being included only on socio-economic rights agendas at a time when civil-political rights were regarded as the only 'true' human rights.[127] It argues that the framing of the civil-political right to legal capacity as fundamental to all other rights is an over-correction to this historical subordination of disability rights and thus fails to account for the principle of indivisibility.[128] It explains how civil-political rights are underpinned by the value of autonomy and how their privileging frames negative state actions and non-interference as always rights-affirming. Such framing, in turn, demands abolition of guardianship and involuntary treatment in pursuit of fulfilling civil-political human rights over socio-economic rights and the value of autonomy over other human rights values.

It describes how Carney[129] (and some other writers more tentatively)[130] has described Article 12 as embodying the principle of the indivisibility of human rights. While the right to legal capacity is more appropriately categorised as civil-political, Article 12(3) as a right to support is more convincingly categorised as a socio-economic right. It begins the analysis of Article 12 according to the principle of indivisibility, by explaining the interdependency of the two rights within Article 12 itself – that is, the right to legal capacity and the right to support.

Chapter 4 considers how the concept of autonomy relates to Article 12, and looks at endeavours in the literature to reconceptualise autonomy so as to include adults with cognitive disability. It explains how, in traditional liberalism, autonomy as the ability to reason has been recognised as the foundation for personhood, thereby excluding adults with cognitive disability.[131] Interpretations of Article 12 that require the abolition of decision-making by substitutes refashion autonomy from being marked by rationality and independence to being marked by shared personhood[132]

[127] Degener and Begg (n 58) 10; Gerard Quinn, 'The International Covenant on Civil and Political Rights and Disability: A Conceptual Framework' in Theresia Degener and Yolan Koster-Dreese (eds), *Human Rights and Disabled Persons* (Martinus Nijhoff, 1995) 69, 70.

[128] Chapter 3, Section 4.1.

[129] Terry Carney, 'Prioritising Supported Decision-Making: Running on Empty or a Basis for Glacial-to-Steady Progress?' (2017) 6(4) *Laws* 18, 18–23.

[130] Quinn and Rekas-Rosalbo (n 5) 303; Degener, 'A New Human Rights Model of Disability' (n 113) 45–46.

[131] Christman, 'Autonomy in Moral and Political Philosphy' (n 19) [1].

[132] Gerard Quinn, 'From Civil Death to Civil Life: The Decay and Re-Birth of Legal Capacity Law around the World' (Conference Paper, Australian Guardianship and Administration Council National Conference: Reflecting Will and Preference in Decision-Making, 17–18 October 2016) 10 www.agac.org.au/images/stories/2016nsw/quinn-decay-rebirth-legal-cap-law.pdf.

and interdependence or 'positive liberty'[133] so as to include adults with cognitive disability.

I argue that these refashionings of autonomy ultimately fail because despite avowals to the contrary, they perpetuate the privileging of rationality and of the bounded, independent individual. The only difference is that the boundary now extends to include the supporter to the extent only that they are instrumental to the personhood of the adult. I further argue that such an interpretation also ignores the indivisibility of human rights by failing to recognise the interdependency of Article 12 with other rights in the CRPD, especially socio-economic rights.

Chapter 4 does acknowledge autonomy as a fundamental human rights value that underpins the CRPD and Article 12 but argues that the type of autonomy envisaged by Article 12 embodies the indivisibility of human rights. It draws on the relevant literature to affirm a conception of autonomy as only one good amongst others but decries its privileged position as the basis for universal personhood. It argues that a concept of autonomy as achievement, as the development of autonomy competencies, as demanding the availability of a range of options, and as demanding recognition of the indivisibility of human rights is the autonomy underpinning Article 12 and the CRPD.

Chapter 5 proposes an interpretation of Article 12 that allows for the abolition of decision-making by substitutes as a last resort through relocating personhood from recognition of an adult's autonomy to recognition of their dignity. It describes and analyses the literature that considers the role that dignity plays in interpreting Article 12. It finds that the literature almost always equates dignity with autonomy, with autonomy described as respecting the 'dignity of risk'.[134] It further describes the very limited forays in the Article 12 literature into proposing dignity as a value distinct from autonomy in order to justify decision-making by substitutes.[135]

Drawing on the text of the CRPD and other human rights instruments, philosophy, legal commentary and jurisprudence, it settles on a concept of dignity as inherent in all humans,[136] as a legal principle (not a right) that underpins human rights and the

133 Bach and Kerzner (n 5) 40–42.

134 de Bhailís and Flynn (n 5) 17; Bach and Kerzner (n 5) 54, 86, 89, 134, 153, 163, 178, 184; Bruce Alston, 'Towards Supported Decision-Making: Article 12 of the Convention on the Rights of Persons with Disabilities and Guardianship Law Reform' (2017) 35(2) *Law in Context* 21, 24; ALRC (n 9) 53, 75, 85, 102, 153, 170.

135 Mary Donnelly, 'From Autonomy to Dignity: Treatment for Mental Disorders and the Focus for Patient Rights' (2008) 26(2) *Law in Context* 37, 431; Marcus Düwell, 'Setting the Agenda for Ethical Debates about the Rights of Persons with Disabilities' in Joel Andersen and Jos Philips (eds), *Disability and Universal Human Rights: Legal, Ethical, and Conceptual Implications of the Convention on the Rights of Persons with Disabilities* (Netherlands Institute of Human Rights, 2012) 185, 190–94; Bilchitz (n 23) 431.

136 CRPD Preamble para 1 'Recalling the principles proclaimed in the Charter of the United Nations which recognize the inherent dignity and worth and the equal and inalienable rights of all members of the human family as the foundation of freedom, justice and peace in the world ...'

CRPD, and as having five dimensions. The first dimension of human dignity is that it means equal worth or value of all humans and demands that they be treated as ends in themselves and not merely means. The second dimension recognises autonomy as an important component of dignity for people who have autonomy but seeks to position autonomy as only one very valuable good amongst others. The third dimension recognises that human dignity is reflexive and acknowledges the interdependent, interpersonal and social nature of being human. The fourth dimension of human dignity is that it underpins a concept of personhood that is embodied and particular, thereby recognising the residual impacts of impairment and the materiality of our lives. The fifth dimension of human dignity is that it embodies and demands an understanding of rights as interdependent and indivisible.

Chapter 6 considers the meaning of equality in Article 12, describing and explaining how equality is a fundamental human rights value foregrounded in the CRPD.[137] It describes the development of concepts of discrimination and equality in human rights law and theory, from direct to indirect discrimination, from formal to substantive equality, to transformative equality and ultimately 'inclusive equality'. Inclusive equality has been developed and described by the UN Disability Committee in its *General Comment No 6 (2018) on equality and discrimination* ('General Comment No 6') as having four dimensions and as being the type of substantive equality that underpins the CRPD.[138]

Chapter 6 goes on to describe how the phrase 'on an equal basis with others' in Article 12 has been interpreted to mean that Article 12 requires either the abolition of decision-making by substitutes[139] or its retention as a last resort.[140] It identifies unresolved contradictions in the arguments that decision-making by substitutes always or necessarily results in failure to achieve substantive equality. It describes those interpretations of Article 12 that explain how decision-making by substitutes can achieve equality,[141] but develops and builds on these by applying the four dimensions of inclusive equality to interpret Article 12.

It argues that inclusive equality recognises that difference requires differential treatment in the form of supported decision-making or decision-making by substitutes to achieve equality. The chapter draws on existing commentary explaining the 'hybrid' nature of the right to equality in bridging both socio-economic and

[137] Ibid Preamble paras 1, 5, 6, 11, 18 and 24, and Articles 1, 3 and 5.

[138] *General Comment No 6.*

[139] *General Comment No 1*; *General Comment No 6* [3], [47]–[51].

[140] Martin et al, *Three Jurisdictions Report: Towards Compliance with CRPD Article 12 in Capacity/Incapacity Legislation across the UK* (n 9); Del Villar (n 25); George Szmukler, Rowena Daw and Felicity Callard, 'Mental Health Law and the UN Convention on the Rights of Persons with Disabilities' (2014) 37(3) *International Journal of Law and Psychiatry* 245.

[141] Martin et al, *Achieving CRPD Compliance* (n 24); Del Villar (n 25) 183; Szmukler, Daw and Callard (n 140).

civil-political rights.[142] It affirms that inclusive equality, which underpins the CRPD and Article 12, is driven by the indivisibility of human rights.

The final chapter summarises the book's argument and conclusions, and explains their implications for advocacy and law reform.

6 WHY THE BOOK IS IMPORTANT

This book addresses a key and prominent area of dispute over the interpretation and application of the CRPD, a convention that marks an important step forward in recognising the human rights of people with disability. It endeavours to make a significant and original contribution to the debate in several areas.

First, it situates the development and interpretation of the civil-political right in Article 12[143] against the background of the historical marginalisation of socio-economic rights. It then goes on to argue that an interpretation of the right to legal capacity as a right foundational to all other rights over-corrects the historical marginalisation of disability as relevant to socio-economic rights only.[144] Second, it critiques existing analysis of how the principle of indivisibility of human rights infuses the CRPD by dissolving distinctions between the two categories of rights, to propose instead a concept of indivisibility that retains those distinctions (albeit porous).[145]

Third, it demonstrates through the case study of Alex how attempts to attribute autonomy to all adults with cognitive disability risk perpetuating the exclusion of adults with cognitive disability from personhood,[146] and argues that Article 12 autonomy demands fulfilment of both civil-political and socio-economic rights, according to the principle of indivisibility.[147] Fourth, with autonomy failing to include all adults with cognitive disability in personhood, the book proposes dignity as an alternative, inclusive basis for personhood in the CRPD (and in human rights law and theory more widely), and develops a novel concept of five-dimensional dignity, which incorporates the principle of indivisibility.[148] Fifth, the book reviews the

[142] Anna Lawson, 'The UN Convention on the Rights of Persons with Disabilities and European Disability Law: A Catalyst for Cohesion?' in Oddný Mjöll Arnadóttir and Gerard Quinn (eds), *The UN Convention on the Rights of Persons with Disabilities: European and Scandinavian Perspectives* (Nijhoff, 2009) 81, 104–7; Rebecca Brown and Janet Lord, 'The Role of Reasonable Accommodation in Securing Substantive Equality for Persons with Disabilities' in Marcia H Rioux, Lee Ann Basser Marks and Melinda Jones (eds), *Critical Perspectives on Human Rights and Disability Law* (Martinus Nijhoff, 2011) 273, 281; Broderick, 'Harmonisation and Cross-Fertilisation of Socio-Economic Rights in the Human Rights Treaty Bodies' (n 126) 38.

[143] See *General Comment No 1* [30].

[144] See Chapter 3, Section 4.1.

[145] See Chapter 3, Section 5.4.

[146] See Chapter 4, Sections 3 and 4.

[147] See Chapter 4, Section 6.

[148] See Chapter 5, especially Section 3.

literature on equality and *General Comment No 6* in the context of Article 12.[149] In doing so it interprets recognition of legal capacity 'on an equal basis with others', according to the principle of indivisibility, as demanding decision-making by substitutes as a last resort.[150]

In its argument for interpretating Article 12 according to the principle of indivisibility, the book weaves together a range of otherwise disparate analyses and complex ideas found in the Article 12 and CRPD literature, human rights law and theory, philosophy, legal commentary and jurisprudence. As a whole, it analyses, draws connections between, critiques and builds on existing bodies of knowledge and ideas in new ways. It presents an argument for interpreting Article 12 as requiring both supported decision-making and decision-making by substitutes in order to uphold the human rights of all adults with cognitive disability and recognise their human dignity and personhood.

7 CONCLUSION: THE SIGNIFICANCE OF THE CRPD AND ARTICLE 12

The CRPD is universally recognised as a major step forward for disability human rights, including for adults with cognitive disability. However, as a relatively recent UN convention, it is still subject to ongoing interpretation, and this book contributes to that significant project. Despite the authoritative status of the UN Disability Committee, a wide range of commentators have opposed its interpretation of Article 12 – in particular, it has not been supported by any law reform commission in the English-speaking world to date.[151] More significantly, many States parties including Australia, Canada, France, Ireland, the Netherlands, Norway and Poland have made interpretive declarations or reservations stating that Article 12 still allows for decision-making by substitutes as a last resort.[152] This exposes governments to condemnation from the UN, but even more problematically, such wide 'non-compliance' potentially undermines the moral and legal authority of Article 12, and

149 See Chapter 6, especially Sections 2 and 3.

150 See Chapter 6, Section 5.

151 Shih-Ning Then et al, 'Supporting Decision-Making of Adults with Cognitive Disabilities: The Role of Law Reform Agencies – Recommendations, Rationales and Influence' (2018) 61 *International Journal of Law and Psychiatry* 64.

152 Also, Canada, France, Ireland, the Netherlands, Norway, and Poland have lodged interpretative declarations or reservations in relation to Article 12. Interpretive declarations by Egypt, Estonia and Kuwait assert their understanding that legal capacity does not necessarily include the capacity to act or exercise rights. The implication is that decision-making by representatives is still permitted (see discussion in Chapter 2, Section 4.1.1). The declarations and reservations were made upon ratification. For a full list of reservations and declarations and their full text, see https://treaties.un.org/Pages/ViewDetails.aspx?src=TREATY&mtdsg_no=IV-15&chapter=4&clang=_en#EndDec

the CRPD more broadly,[153] a result that would be widely decried by all of those seeking equality and inclusion for people with disability.

In Australia, at the time of writing, the ongoing neglect and stigmatisation of people with disability was being investigated and exposed by the Royal Commission into Violence, Abuse, Neglect and Exploitation of People with Disability ('the Disability Royal Commission').[154] The Disability Royal Commission has emphasised the role of the CRPD as a framework for upholding the rights of people with disability, including their decision-making rights.[155] In 2013, Australia began its rollout of the National Disability Insurance Scheme ('NDIS'), which is premised on the right of people with disability to have choice and control in service provision.[156] In this project it follows other western nations including the UK, Europe, North America, Norway, Iceland, Israel and New Zealand, in introducing a system of individualised funding and budgeting for accommodation and services for people with disability. Such systems based on individualised budgets have been referred to variously as '… person-centred support, self-directed care, cash for care, personalised allocations, personal budgets, case and counselling, and individualised funding…'.[157] At their core they emphasise the value of autonomy over the old paternalisms, '…the key idea being that individuals should be empowered to have choice, control and flexibility in making their own decisions to spend money on the services that best suit their needs.'[158] In Australia, the NDIS is a significant and impressive venture that

[153] George Szmukler, '"Capacity", "Best Interests", "Will and Preferences" and the UN Convention on the Rights of Persons with Disabilities' (2019) 18(1) *World Psychiatry: Official Journal of the World Psychiatric Association (WPA)* 34, 40; 'Structurally, an interpretation by a UN body that is not feasible risks undermining the authority of the wider UN human rights machinery': Craigie et al (n 9), 165.

[154] https://disability.royalcommission.gov.au/

[155] Kayess and Sands (n 6); McCallum (n 6).

[156] www.ndis.gov.au/ *National Disability Insurance Scheme Act 2013* (Cth). s 4 'General principles guiding actions under this Act … (8) People with disability have the same right as other members of Australian society to be able to determine their own best interests, including the right to exercise choice and control, and to engage as equal partners in decisions that will affect their lives, to the full extent of their capacity. (9) People with disability should be supported in all their dealings and communications with the Agency and the Commission so that their capacity to exercise choice and control is maximised in a way that is appropriate to their circumstances and cultural needs'; s 17A '(2) People with disability will be supported in their dealings and communications with the Agency so that their capacity to exercise choice and control is maximised. (3) The National Disability Insurance Scheme is to: (a) respect the interests of people with disability in exercising choice and control about matters that affect them; and (b) enable people with disability to make decisions that will affect their lives, to the extent of their capacity; and (c) support people with disability to participate in, and contribute to, social and economic life, to the extent of their ability.'

[157] Laura Davy and Celia Green, 'The Right to Autonomy and the Conditions that Secure it: The Relationship Between the UNCRPD and Market-Based Policy Reform' in Franziska Felder, Laura Davy and Rosemary Kayess (eds), *Disability Law and Human Rights: Theory and Policy* (Palgrave, 2022) 127–45, 135–36.

[158] Ibid.

promises improved living conditions and social inclusion for many people with disability. However, it is vital – in all of these systems premised on the right to make decisions freely – that the specific challenges of cognitive disability are acknowledged, recognised and responded to in a way that upholds human rights.

Some commentators reject a human rights framework as being inadequate to ensure that adults with cognitive disability are treated in a way that social justice and ethical demands require.[159] However, the prevalence of human rights talk in our community, together with the high status that human rights are widely accorded,[160] demand that social justice solutions be articulated within a human rights framework to attract the moral and practical urgency that they deserve. This book aims to contribute to that significant project.

159 Barbara Carter, 'The Case for Dignity as the Governing Principle in Adult Guardianship' (2010) 19(1) *Res Publica* 1.

160 'Human rights traditionally have been thought of as moral right of the highest order …': Jack Donnelly, *Universal Human Rights in Theory and Practice* (Cornell University Press, 3rd ed, 2013) 11; 'But human rights are also a powerful discourse and practice in domestic and international law': Costas Douzinas, *The End of Human Rights: Critical Legal Thought at the Turn of the Century* (Hart, 2000) 4.

2

Article 12 – Context and Background

1 INTRODUCTION

This chapter introduces the main interpretive arguments surrounding Article 12. It does this by first contextualising them against key policy and legal concepts in disability and decision-making by, with and for adults with cognitive disability, as they have developed over the twentieth and twenty-first centuries. Chapter 1 described how disability human rights development culminated in the CRPD, tracking a journey from paternalism to autonomy, from invisibility to visibility and from discrimination to equality. It also introduced the idea of autonomy – demanding the ability to reason, to be independent and to be free from interference from the State – as the foundation of personhood. The development of relevant policy and legal concepts in disability is explained in this chapter in terms of how it reflects that evolutionary journey to increasing levels of autonomy, recognition of personhood, and equality. However, it also anticipates a radical disruption of that dominant narrative (to be developed in subsequent chapters) and examines the complexities around those concepts, as revealed by the case of cognitive disability.

Section 2 describes the different 'models' of disability – the charity, medical and social models – as developed and widely used by disability advocates and commentators to explain how various policy and legal responses to disability have developed and functioned. Section 3 describes how the development of the CRPD was hailed as articulating a social model of disability, whereby disability is framed as a product of a prejudiced, ableist society. It further explains how a strict social model of disability has since been subject to wide critique. It describes how the interpretive arguments made in this book are explained by referencing a social model of disability that recognises the residual impacts of impairment.

Section 3 goes on to describe the different policy and legal responses to decision-making by, with and for adults with cognitive disability that have aimed to improve adults' autonomy, increasingly recognise their value as persons and eliminate discrimination. The era of mass institutionalisation was followed by the development and implementation of personal guardianship regimes. Within those regimes, capacity tests evolved from status and outcome tests to functional tests. Decision-making principles have begun to evolve from paternalistic 'best interests' tests to acknowledging the will and preferences of adults and recognising their individual autonomy. Since the 1990s, supported decision-making practices and legislation have developed, which aim to further increase the autonomy of adults with cognitive disability and reduce or eliminate discrimination on the basis of capacity.

Section 4 provides first an overview of the major arguments made during the drafting of Article 12, and afterwards, for interpreting Article 12 as requiring the abolition of decision-making by substitutes. This is followed by an overview of those arguments that interpret Article 12 as allowing for or requiring decision-making by substitutes as a last resort. Section 4 describes how the interpretive contention over Article 12 led to the publication of *General Comment No 1* in 2014, which prescribes an interpretation of Article 12 as requiring the abolition of decision-making by substitutes and guardians in all cases, and their replacement with practices of supported decision-making.[1] There are various arguments made in support of this interpretation, all based on the premise that the right to legal capacity equates with a right to autonomy, and that denial of legal capacity therefore means denial of personhood.[2] It follows that to deny recognition of legal capacity to people on the basis of their disability will always constitute unlawful discrimination.[3] The contrary arguments are premised, to a greater or lesser extent, on an understanding that hard reality dictates decision-making by substitutes may not be a choice but an inevitability,[4] and respect for human rights demands that it be recognised as such and made transparent and accountable.[5]

[1] *Committee on the Rights of Persons with Disabilities, General Comment No 1 Article 12: Equal Recognition before the Law UN Doc CRPD/C/GC/1 (19 May 2014)* ('*General Comment No 1*') [3], [7], [26].

[2] 'The right to equal recognition before the law implies that legal capacity is a universal attribute inherent in all persons by virtue of their humanity …': *General Comment No 1* [8], [26], [29]; 'It has been found that denial of legal capacity to any individual or group has also meant negation of both the right to personhood and the capacity to act': International Disability Alliance, *Legal Opinion on Article 12 of the CRPD* (disability-studies.leeds.ac.uk/wp-content/uploads/sites/40/library/legal-opinion-LegalOpinion-Art12-FINAL.pdf008) 38–52; Nandini Devi, 'Supported Decision-Making and Personal Autonomy for Persons with Intellectual Disabilities: Article 12 of the UN Convention on the Rights of Persons with Disabilities' (2013) 41(4) *The Journal of Law, Medicine & Ethics* 792; Jillian Craigie et al, 'Legal Capacity, Mental Capacity and Supported Decision-Making: Report from a Panel Event' (2019) 62 *International Journal of Law and Psychiatry* 160, 161; Glen, Kristin Booth, 'Introducing a New Human Right: Learning from Others, Bringing Legal Capacity Home' (2018) 49(3) *Columbia Human Rights Law Review* 1, 20.

[3] *General Comment No 1* [7], [15]; Anna Arstein-Kerslake and Eilionóir Flynn, 'The General Comment on Article 12 of the Convention on the Rights of Persons with Disabilities: A Roadmap for Equality before the Law' (2016) 20(4) *The International Journal of Human Rights* 471, 478.

[4] Wayne Martin et al, *Achieving CRPD Compliance: Is the Mental Capacity Act of England and Wales Compatible with the UN Convention on the Rights of Persons with Disabilities? If Not, What Next?* (Essex Autonomy Project, 2014) 23; Craigie et al (n 2).

[5] Matthew Burch, 'Autonomy, Respect, and the Rights of Persons with Disabilities in Crisis' (2017) 34(3) *Journal of Applied Philosophy* 389, 390, 397; Malcolm Parker, 'Getting the Balance Right: Conceptual Considerations Concerning Legal Capacity and Supported Decision-Making'

2 DIFFERENT 'MODELS' OF DISABILITY

From the late twentieth century, the commentary on disability has described what are widely acknowledged as three dominant models of disability – the charity, medical and social models – which underlie, or have driven, the development of disability policy and law.[6] These models are described in the following sections as they have been widely presented in the disability literature – that is, as reflecting evolving social attitudes to people with disability along a continuum from paternalism to respect for autonomy, from exclusion to inclusion and from discrimination to equality. The section goes on to describe wide criticisms of the social model and how the arguments in this book are premised on a social model of disability that recognises the residual impacts of impairment.

2.1 *Charity Model*

Commentators relate how, before the late twentieth century, the only morally defensible attitude of the State and the wider community towards people with disability was to view them as objects of pity and charity.[7] People with disability were also encouraged to perceive themselves in this limited role, internalising community prejudices. The Article 12 literature and the commentary surrounding the CRPD continually reiterate that Article 12 and the CRPD more broadly represent a move away from the 'charity model' of disability to either a 'social model' or 'human rights model' of disability (see further sections).[8]

This perception, of people with disabilities as objects of charity, is reflected in the work of the legal philosopher John Rawls, whose broader influence on the liberal theory of autonomy is described in Chapter 4.[9] Rawls, in his book *A Theory of Justice*, drew upon Kantian theories to develop his theory of justice as fairness.[10] For Rawls, society is constituted by individuals who each agree to enter into a 'social contract' with each other so that the State operates on a foundation of common rules and understandings for the mutual advantage of individuals who pursue their own conceptions of 'the good': 'A person's good is determined by what is for him

(2016) 13(3) *Journal of Bioethical Inquiry* 381, 389; Kjersti Skarstad, 'Ensuring Human Rights for Persons with Intellectual Disabilities?' (2018) 22(6) *International Journal of Human Rights* 774, 777; Silvana Galderisi, 'The UN Convention on the Rights of Persons with Disabilities: Great Opportunities and Dangerous Interpretations' (2019) 18(1) *World Psychiatry* 47, 47.

6 Shane Clifton, *Hierarchies of Power: Disability Theories and Models and Their Implications for Violence against, and Abuse, Neglect, and Exploitation of, People with Disability* (Royal Commission into Violence, Abuse, Neglect and Exploitation of People with Disability, 2020) 4–13.

7 Australian Law Reform Commission, *Equality, Capacity and Disability in Commonwealth Laws: A Final Report* (2014) 4–5.

8 For the 'social model', see Section 2.3, and for the 'human rights model', see Section 2.4.4.

9 See Chapter 4, Section 2.

10 John Rawls, *A Theory of Justice* (Harvard University Press, 1971).

the most rational long-term plan'.[11] This 'contract' model or metaphor relies on the individual having reasoning abilities to a requisite 'level', so that citizenship is only bestowed on those who are 'beyond a certain age and possessed of the requisite intellectual capacity'.[12]

The social contract can include some rules for redistribution of resources from the more advantaged to the disadvantaged when this redistribution is for the benefit of society overall. However, it does not provide for redistribution to those who are deemed unable to contract and are therefore ineligible for the rights of citizenship.[13] For Rawls, citizens have liberties and are the subjects of rights, but those denied citizenship because of their cognitive impairment are the objects of paternalism.[14] So, any distribution of resources to those 'non-citizens' is entirely discretionary. This positions those with cognitive disability as objects of pity, not the subjects of rights, and it imposes the values of the donor on the charitable objects, who are assumed to have no ability to know what is good for them.[15]

Disability advocates and scholars clearly reject the '…old worldview (objectification of persons with disabilities)',[16] which defined any social or economic distribution to people with cognitive disability as an act of 'charity' for those outside the citizenship State.[17] The so-called 'charity model' of disability, although still lingering (or some may say pervasive) in various community responses and attitudes,[18] is widely rejected in disability commentary and advocacy.[19] A charity model denies autonomy and personhood to adults with disability and fails to position them as holders of human rights.[20]

[11] Ibid 25.
[12] Ibid 46.
[13] Ibid 87.
[14] Ibid 250.
[15] Ibid 249.
[16] Gerard Quinn, 'Resisting the "Temptation of Elegance": Can the Convention on the Rights of Persons with Disabilities Socialise States to Right Behaviour?' in Oddný Mjöll Arnadóttir and Gerard Quinn (eds), *The UN Convention on the Rights of Persons with Disabilities: European and Scandinavian Perspectives* (Nijhoff, 2009) 215, 216.
[17] Barbara Arneil and Nancy J Hirschmann, 'Introduction' in Barbara Arneil and Nancy J Hirschmann (eds), *Disability and Political Theory* (Cambridge University Press, 2016) 1, 7.
[18] Clifton (n 6) 6.
[19] Ibid 4–6; John Chesterman, 'The Future of Adult Guardianship in Australia' (2013) 66(1) *Australian Social Work* 26, 30; Gerard Quinn and Anna Arstein-Kerslake, 'Restoring the "Human" in "Human Rights": Personhood and Doctrinal Innovation in the UN Disability Convention' in Costas Douzinas and C A Gearty (eds), *Cambridge Companion to Human Rights Law* (Cambridge University Press, 2012) 36; Tom Shakespeare, *Disability: The Basics* (Routledge, 2018) 15; Rosemary Kayess and Philip French, 'Out of Darkness into Light? Introducing the Convention on the Rights of Persons with Disabilities' (2008) 8(1) *Human Rights Law Review* 1, 3.
[20] Often the commentary will equate the 'charity' model with a 'welfare' model of disability, so that the two terms are elided or used interchangeably. See Arstein-Kerslake and Flynn (n 3) 471. This elision I suggest reflects the experiences of people dealing with state welfare agencies that administer their services in ways that objectify and humiliate recipients. See Shakespeare,

2.2 Medical Model

The pre-eminence of the charity model was to some extent displaced by the emergence of the 'medical model' of disability. The medical model is described as constructing disability purely or foremostly as a condition to be remedied or rectified (or not) by intervention – whether medical or otherwise.[21] There were and are good reasons for encouraging medical and health responses to impairments, and Arneil describes how the medical model was associated with rehabilitation programmes for injured World War One veterans. However, Arneil also describes how this focus led to rehabilitation being an 'overarching paradigm governing disability in the twentieth century' to the exclusion of other paradigms. To this extent, there became a dominant societal assumption behind the medical model that those who were unable to be fully rehabilitated were somehow lesser beings.[22]

This so-called medical model has been described as constructing disability as being essentially caused by a fault or defect within the individual.[23] As such, it was the individual's responsibility to either remedy the disability by seeking intervention or, failing that, the disability was to be borne by the individual through personal adaptation or stoicism.[24] In a society where people with disability were largely socially and politically excluded, the idea that disability should, if possible, be rectified or remedied by medical science engaged the corollary implication that people with untreatable conditions or impairments were 'defective' or less than normal.[25] As Erevelles has described it, the medical model served to position disability 'as a

Disability: The Basics (n 19) 76; Clifton (n 6) 6–7; Jennifer Nedelsky, *Law's Relations: A Relational Theory of Self, Autonomy, and the Law* (Oxford University Press, 2012) 66. However, I argue that equating the words 'charity' and 'welfare' in this context risks perpetuating the stigmatisation of social welfare claimants and the services to which they are entitled as a matter of human rights (see especially Chapter 3, and Section 4.2.1 of this chapter). For this reason, I exclusively use the term 'charity model'.

21 Clifton (n 6) 7–9; Michael Ashley Stein, 'Disability Human Rights' (2007) 95(1) *California Law Review* 75, 87–8.

22 Arneil and Hirschmann (n 17) 30.

23 Stephen R Smith, 'Social Justice and Disability: Competing Interpretations of the Medical and Social Models' in Kristjana Kristiansen, Simo Vehmas and Tom Shakespeare (eds), *Arguing about Disability: Philosophical Perspectives* (Routledge, 2008) 15, 15.

24 Martha Rioux, 'On Second Thoughts: Constructing Knowledge, Law, Disability and Inequality' in Stanley S Herr and Lawrence O Gostin (eds), *The Human Rights of Persons with Intellectual Disabilities: Different but Equal* (Oxford University Press, 2003) 287, 291.

25 'The medical (or biomedical) model considers disability to be a problem with the individual that is directly caused by a disease, an injury, or some other health condition and requires medical care in the form of treatment and rehabilitation': Willene Holness, 'Equal Recognition and Legal Capacity for Persons with Disabilities: Incorporating the Principle of Proportionality' (2014) 30(2) *South African Journal on Human Rights* 313, 316; Stein (n 21); Jan Wallcraft and Kim Hopper, 'The Capabilities Approach and the Social Model of Mental Health' in Helen Spandler, Jill Anderson and Bob Sapey (eds), *Madness, Distress and the Politics of Disablement* (Policy Press at the University of Bristol, 2015) 83, 84; Shih-Ning Then, 'Evolution and Innovation in Guardianship Laws: Assisted Decision-Making' (2013) 35(1) *Sydney Law Review* 133, 136–7.

pathological abnormality [and] has been used to support the exclusionary, segregationist, and exploitative practices of an ableist society'[26] with 'ableism' defined elsewhere as 'modalities, mechanisms, and techniques of marginalisation and oppression specifically directed at disabled persons due to their disabilities'.[27] Ableism has the potential to make society view people with disability as merely 'potential beings', as not fully formed, and thus fail to deny them full personhood.[28] The dominance of the medical model, as described above, to the exclusion of alternative perspectives has been widely criticised as inconsistent with a human rights approach to disability, which demands social inclusion.

2.3 *Social Model*

With the increasing emergence of human rights movements, disability advocates began to reject the old constructs of disability in favour of what is now known widely as the 'social model' of disability.[29] The social model was initially developed by

[26] Nirmala Erevelles, *Disability and Difference in Global Contexts: Enabling a Transformative Body Politic* (Macmillan, 2011) 151. Some philosophers have argued (contentiously) that the descriptors 'abnormal', 'atypical' or 'pathological' in relation to biological functioning can be descriptive without being normative; that is, there is an argument that they can be value neutral, without implying *inferiority* of functioning. See Christopher Boorse, 'On the Distinction between Disease and Illness' (1975) 5(1) *Philosophy & Public Affairs* 49, 555; Christopher Boorse, 'Health as a Theoretical Concept' (1977) 44(4) *Philosophy of Science* 542; Christopher Boorse, 'Disability and Medical Theory' in D Christopher Ralston and Justin Ho (eds), *Philosophical Reflections on Disability* (Springer, 2010) 55. For arguments against, see Ron Amundson, 'Against Normal Function' (2000) 31(1) *Studies in the History and Philosophy of Biology and Biomedical Science* 33; Elselijn Kingma, 'What Is It To Be Healthy? (Boorse's Biostatistical Theory)' (2007) 67(2) *Analysis* 128. Of relevance here is that even if we accept that some functioning is atypical in a descriptive sense, the *dominance* of the medical model meant that certain impairments have been *socially* constructed as 'abnormal' in a way that stigmatises, marginalises and devalues the person with disability.

[27] Lucas G Pinheiro, 'The Ableist Contract: Intellectual Disability and the Limits of Justice in Kant's Political Thought' in Barbara Arneil and Nancy J Hirschmann (eds), *Disability and Political Theory* (Cambridge University Press, 2016) 43, 46.

[28] Licia Carlson defines cognitive abelism as 'a prejudice or attitude of bias in favour of the interests of individuals who possess certain cognitive abilities … against those who are believed not to actually or potentially possess them.': Licia Carlson, 'Cognitive Ableism and Disability Studies: Feminist Reflections on the History of Mental Retardation' (2001) 16(4) *Hypatia* 124, 140.

[29] Anna Arstein-Kerslake, *Restoring Voice to People with Cognitive Disabilities: Realizing the Right to Equal Recognition before the Law* (Cambridge University Press, 2017) 12; Rannveig Traustadóttir, 'Disability Studies, the Social Model and Legal Development' in Oddný Mjöll Arnadóttir and Gerard Quinn (eds), *The UN Convention on the Rights of Persons with Disabilities: European and Scandinavian Perspectives* (Nijhoff, 2009) 3, 3–4; Oddný Mjöll Arnadóttir, 'A Future of Multidimensional Disadvantage Equality' in Oddný Mjöll Arnadóttir and Gerard Quinn (eds), *The UN Convention on the Rights of Persons with Disabilities: European and Scandinavian Perspectives* (Nijhoff, 2009) 41, 59; Theresia Degener, 'A New Human Rights Model of Disability' in Valentina Della Fina, Rachele Cera and Giuseppe Palmisano (eds), *The United Nations Convention on the Rights of Persons with Disabilities: A Commentary* (Springer International Publishing, 2017) 41, 41–4.

British scholars whose Marxist leanings led them to focus on disadvantage and economic inequality in the external, social environment as defining the notion of disability.[30] This model distinguishes between 'impairment' and 'disability'. Physical or cognitive disability is not framed as defining the individual or his or her identity but is understood as a product and function of the social and physical environment in which the individual is situated.[31] This model emphasises that it is the social and physical environment that places barriers to functioning on those with disability or fails to accommodate their impairments.

Because the emphasis is on barriers to functioning, a social model does not construct disability as an immutable status imposed on the person or as something that needs to be addressed by 'fixing' the person. Instead, the social model recognises the need for the State to provide supports and 'reasonable accommodation' to promote equality of opportunity for those with disability.[32]

The wide acceptance of this social model of disability led to the call for the development of the CRPD, and the CRPD is touted by many as being the first human rights instrument that fully incorporates the social model of disability.[33] The CRPD is said to embrace the social model by rejecting both the charity model's positioning of people with disability as objects of pity and the medical model's framing of disability as personal affliction or tragedy, so as to reposition people with disability as rights bearers.[34] As many commentators have written, the social model has served as an extremely effective political and advocacy tool in providing visibility to those with disability, in giving people with disability the confidence to make claims against governments, and in holding governments and the community responsible for addressing the needs of those with impairments.[35]

[30] Shakespeare, *Disability: The Basics* (n 19) 12.

[31] Then (n 25) 137, 138.

[32] 'Reasonable accommodation means necessary and appropriate modification and adjustments not imposing a disproportionate or undue burden, where needed in a particular case, to ensure to persons with disabilities the enjoyment or exercise on an equal basis with others of all human rights and fundamental freedoms': *CRPD* Article 2.; see further in Chapter 6, Section 2.6.1.

[33] Anna Lawson and Mark Priestley, 'The Social Model of Disability: Questions for Law and Legal Scholarship?' in Peter Blanck and Eilionoir Flynn (eds), *Routledge Handbook of Disability Law and Human Rights* (Routledge, 2016) 3; 'The social model is embedded within the CRPD'. Arstein-Kerslake, *Restoring Voice to People with Cognitive Disabilities* (n 29) 72; 'The salience of support is a concrete expressoin of the social, interactive model of disability that animates the Convention …': Robert D Dinerstein, 'Implementing Legal Capacity under Article 12 of the UN Convention on the Rights of Persons with Disabilities: The Difficult Road from Guardianship to Supported Decision-Making' (2012) 19(2) *Human Rights Brief* 8, 9; Australian Law Reform Commission ('ALRC'), *Equality, Capacity and Disability in Commonwealth Laws: A Final Report* (2014) 38; Michael Perlin, 'Understanding the Intersection between International Human Rights and Mental Disability law: The Role of Dignity' in Bruce Arrigo and Heather Bersot (eds), *Routledge Handbook of International Crime and Justice Studies* (Routledge, 2013) 191, 195.

[34] ALRC (n 33) 44.

[35] Kayess and French (n 19) 7; Shakespeare, *Disability Rights and Wrongs* (Routledge, 2006) 18; William J Penson, 'Unsettling Impairment: Mental Health and the Social Model of Disability' in Helen Spandler, Jill Anderson and Bob Sapey (eds), *Madness, Distress and the Politics of*

2.4 *Beyond the Social Model of Disability*

Despite its wide influence, the social model of disability has never been universally accepted by people with disability, or their supporters and carers, and has been subject to widespread criticism.[36] Debate and confusion around how the social model is meant to operate, how many 'versions' of it there are, and what it really means[37] have fed much of the criticism. However, it has been largely defined by way of opposition to the medical model, with the social model locating disability in society and the medical model in the individual.[38] Commentators sometimes refer to a 'strict'[39] or 'strong'[40] version of the social model, and it is this strict version – which is the one that has proliferated in popular advocacy – that attracts most of the criticism. According to this version, impairment and disability are separate concepts, and disability is caused solely by the existence of ableist prejudices and barriers and their effect on impairment.[41]

2.4.1 Strict Social Model Does Not Reflect Embodied Experience of Impairment

What I will refer to as the strict version of the social model – that disability is *entirely* a product of environment – has been criticised for discounting or ignoring the reality or experience of impairment.[42] It potentially denies the real difference that people

Disablement (Bristol University Press, 2015) 57, 66; D Christopher Ralston and Justin Ho, 'Introduction: Philosophical Reflections on Disability' in D Christopher Ralston and Justin Ho (eds), *Philosophical Reflections on Disability* (Springer, 2010) 1, 4.

36 Barbara Arneil, 'Disability in Political Theory versus International Practice: Redefining Equality and Freedom' in Barbara Arneil and Nancy J Hirschmann (eds), *Disability and Political Theory* (Cambridge University Press, 2016) 10, 26.

37 Mitra suggests that there are at least nine different versions of the social model: Sophie Mitra, 'The Capability Approach to Disability' (2006) 16(4) *Journal of Disability Policy Studies* 236, 237. Commentators describe, for example, a 'minority rights' version of the social model as being prevalent in the United States: Lawson and Priestley (n 33) 3, 5.

38 Jonas-Sébastien Beaudry, 'Beyond (Models of) Disability?' (2016) 41(2) *Journal of Medicine and Philosophy* 210, 210.

39 Ralston and Ho (n 35) 2; referring to the 'strict materialist view': Simo Vehmas and Pekka Mäkelä, 'The Ontology of Disability and Impairment: A Discussion of the Natural and Social Features' in Simo Vehmas, Kristjana Kristiansen and Tom Shakespeare (eds), *Arguing about Disability: Philosophical Perspectives* (Taylor and Francis, 2008) 42, 43; refers to the 'strict constructionist argument'. Bryan S Turner, *Vulnerability and Human Rights* (Pennsylvania State University Press, 2006) 101–2; Andrea Broderick, *The Long and Winding Road to Equality and Inclusion for Persons with Disabilities: The United Nations Convention on the Rights of People with Disabilities* (Intersentia, 2015) 78.

40 Emily Julia Kakoullis and Yoshikazu Ikehara, 'Article 1: Purpose' in Ilias Bantekas et al (eds), *The UN Convention on the Rights of Persons with Disabilities: A Commentary* (Oxford University Press, 2018) 35, 38; Jackie Leach Scully, 'Disability and the Thinking Body' in Simo Vehmas, Kristjana Kristiansen and Tom Shakespeare (eds), *Arguing about Disability: Philosophical Perspectives* (Taylor and Francis, 2008) 57, 58.

41 Clifton (n 6) 10–11.

42 Degener, 'A New Human Rights Model of Disability' (n 29) 41, 47; Lawson and Priestley (n 33) 7–8; Kakoullis and Ikehara (n 40) 38; Beaudry, 'Beyond (Models of) Disability' (n 38) 212;

with disability may experience through their impairment, apart from any real or perceived failure of social or environmental accommodation or change.[43] Critics of the premise that disability is purely caused by environment consider it inadequate at explaining the lived experience of those with disability and realising their rights.[44] For some people, the experience of impairment or its manifestations (e.g. pain, discomfort and increased morbidity) is real and lived, and needs to be recognised as different.[45] As Shakespeare writes, 'in most cases, disabled people are experiencing both the intrinsic limitation of impairment, and the externally imposed social discrimination'.[46] Kong writes that these 'differences that are residual from impairment', even after supports are provided and barriers removed, 'must be taken into account'.[47] In its ostensible and outright rejection of a medical model, the social model has also been criticised for minimising or rejecting the need for prevention of disability and for rehabilitation.[48]

2.4.2 Cognitive Disability and the Challenges of the Social Model

The social model originally developed in the context of advocacy groups that consisted predominantly of people with physical disability,[49] and some commentators have criticised it for not providing a useful model when it comes to responding to cognitive disability. Daniels et al acknowledge that the social model in its strict

Katrine Del Villar, 'Should Supported Decision-Making Replace Substituted Decision-Making? The Convention on the Rights of Persons with Disabilities and Coercive Treatment under Queensland's Mental Health Act 2000' (2015) 4(2) *Laws* 173, 182.

43 Jenny Morris, 'Impairment and Disability: Constructing an Ethics of Care that Promotes Human Rights' (2001) 16(4) *Hypatia* 1, 9–11.

44 Kakoullis and Ikehara (n 40) 36.

45 Jonas-Sébastien Beaudry, 'Theoretical Strategies to Define Disability' in David T Wasserman and Adam Cureton (eds), *The Oxford Handbook of Philosophy and Disability* (Oxford University Press, 2019), 6; the social model 'overlooks aspects of pain, fatigue and sometimes illness relating to certain impairments': Lorella Terzi, 'Vagaries of the Natural Lottery? Human Diversity, Disability, and Justice: A Capability Perspective' in Kimberley Brownlee and Adam Cureton (eds), *Disability and Disadvantage* (Oxford University Press, 2009) 86, 91–92. Margaret Price explores the tension between 'desiring' disability and the reality and problem of pain in Margaret Price, 'The Bodymind Problem and the Possibilities of Pain' (2015) 30(1) *Hypatia* 268, 272.

46 Shakespeare, *Disability Rights and Wrongs* (n 35) 41.

47 Camillia Kong, *Mental Capacity in Relationship: Decision-Making, Dialogue and Autonomy* (Cambridge University Press, 2017) 152; Scully suggests similarly that disability is a set of complex interactions between the 'experience of anomalous embodiment', or 'being physically unusual', and social and cultural factors: Scully (n 40) 60.

48 Arneil (n 36) 30; Shakespeare, *Disability Rights and Wrongs* (n 35) 29; Degener, 'A New Human Rights Model of Disability' (n 29) 52; in the CRPD there is no absolute right to prevention of disabilities but only a right to prevent further disabilities: Article 25 – the Right to Health.

49 Shakespeare, *Disability Rights and Wrongs* (n 35) 2; Anne Plumb, 'UN Convention on the Rights of Persons with Disabilities: Out of the Frying Pan into the Fire? Mental Health Service Users and Survivors Aligning with the Disability Movement' in Helen Spandler et al (eds), *Madness, Distress and the Politics of Disablement* (Bristol University Press, 2015) 183, 184.

form may be useful in framing and therefore addressing (often through technology) the needs of people with a very narrowly defined, but prevalent, range of specific motor and sensory impairments.[50] However, they comment that: 'For significant mental illness and for many brain injuries, neither existing technology nor robust social inclusion can make up for the disability that results'.[51] Plumb (identifying as a survivor of psychiatry) describes how a person experiencing psychosis may be exercising will or agency, but their preferences and actions are based on assumptions that are not just unusual or eccentric but qualitatively different. The concepts of self-determination and autonomy, which Plumb describes as being central to the social model, are problematic for those experiencing these 'non-ordinary' states.[52]

2.4.3 Mixed Models: 'Interactive', 'Biopsychosocial', and 'Multifactorial'

These criticisms have led to arguments for recognising impairment or disability as 'difference', but a difference that should not lead to inequality or social exclusion. Kayess and Sands write, 'that impairment is valued as part of human diversity and human dignity, and therefore people with disability are critical to all aspects of life'.[53] Morris explains why disability activists often deny difference, but also why and how difference should be asserted. She explains that:

> our difference has been the gateway to a denial of human and civil rights: to be recognized as 'severely disabled,' for example, all too often leads to segregation in an institutional setting. We need to change this situation so that the recognition of our difference becomes the gateway to the provision of what we require in order to access our human and civil rights. We have to recognize that disabled people will not get access to full human and civil rights by being treated the same as non-disabled people.[54]

In other words, it is not the recognition of difference in itself that leads to rights-denying behaviour but the nature of the social response that ensues. She affirms, however, that difference needs to be recognised before an appropriate and effective human rights response can be designed and provided.

Many critics of the social model have been advocating for its replacement by a more complex one whereby disability is understood as an 'interaction between medical, psychological, environmental, economic and political factors', some of

[50] Norman Daniels, Susannah Rose and Ellen Daniels Zide, 'Disability, Adaptation and Inclusion' in Kimberley Brownlee and Adam Cureton (eds), *Disability and Disadvantage* (Oxford University Press, 2009) 54, 80.

[51] Ibid 81; see also Peter Bartlett, 'The United Nations Convention on the Rights of Persons with Disabilities and Mental Health Law' (2012) 75(5) *The Modern Law Review* 752, 761.

[52] Plumb (n 49) 186, 187, 194.

[53] Rosemary Kayess and Therese Sands, *Convention on the Rights of Persons with Disabilities: Shining a Light on Social Transformation* (UNSW Social Policy Research Centre. 2020) 46.

[54] Morris (n 43).

which are within the individual and some embedded in the environment.[55] In 2011, the World Health Organization redefined disability as the 'dynamic interaction between health conditions and contextual factors, both personal and environmental', explaining that this reflected a 'biopsychosocial model of disability'.[56] Shakespeare adopts what he refers to as a 'multi-factorial' concept of disability, which recognises the myriad factors that contribute to the 'complexity of disability'.[57]

2.4.4 The 'Human Rights Model' of Disability

The UN Disability Committee in its General Comments describes the CRPD as promoting a 'human rights model' or a 'human-rights-based' model of disability.[58] The human rights model has been described by Degener and endorsed by Kayess (former Chairs of the UN Disability Committee)[59] as an 'alternative to' and 'improvement on the social model of disability' to be used as 'a tool to implement the CRPD'.[60] The human rights model has six features, with two of them prescribing relevantly that 'impairment matters' and that 'identity is composed of different layers'.[61] Under this human rights model, 'impairment' is used

55 Paul Harpur and Heather Douglas, 'Disability and Domestic Violence: Protecting Survivors' Human Rights' (2014) 23(3) *Griffith Law Review* 405, 415; 'even in the disability movement there are disagreements about this strong version of the social model': Wallcraft and Hopper (n 25) 85; a 'growing number of disability scholars' understand disability as 'the interactoin between the body/mind and the social context. Disability thus exists in the interactive processes of bodies living in social space': Arneil and Hirschmann (n 17) 15.

56 Arneil (n 36) 26–7; see also reference in: Suzanne Cahill, *Dementia and Human Rights* (Policy Press at the University of Bristol, 2018) 33.

57 Shakespeare (n 19) 19–21; a more interactive model of disability has been dominant in Scandinavian countries, referred to as the Nordic 'relational' approach, 'which stresses the complex and situational interactions between individual factors and the environment': Traustadóttir (n 29) 12.

58 *General Comment No 1* [3]; Committee on the Rights of Persons with Disabilities, *General Comment No 4: On the Right to Inclusive Education*, UN Doc CRPD/C/GC/4 (25 November 2016) [4(a)], [36], [44], [62], [71]; Committee on the Rights of Persons with Disabilities, *General Comment No 5: On Living Independently and being Included in the Community*, UN Doc CRPD/C/GC/5 (27 October 2017) [60]; Committee on the Rights of Persons with Disabilities, *General Comment No 6: On Equality and Non-Discrimination*, UN Doc CRPD/C/GC/6 (26 April 2018); Committee on the Rights of Persons with Disabilities, *General Comment No 7: On the Participation of Persons with Disabilities, Including Children with Disabilities, through their Representative Organizations, in the Implementation and Monitoring of the Convention*, UN Doc CRPD/C/GC/7) [1], [60], [76].

59 As of the time of writing Rosemary Kayess has been appointed Vice Chair until 2026.

60 Degener, 'A New Human Rights Model of Disability' (n 29) 41; Kayess and Sands (n 53) 2, 9, 20, 21, 29–34, 37.

61 The six features are: 'First, the human rights model ensures that no person with a disability is denied legal capacity. Second, it goes beyond non-discrimination rights and includes first and second generation human rights. Third, it acknowledges that impairment matters in the life of persons with disabilities. Fourth, it recognizes that identity is composed of different layers. Fifth, it provides a roadmap for non-discriminatory preventative health policy. Sixth, the human rights model proves a roadmap for disability inclusive development and humanitarian aid': Degener, 'A New Human Rights Model of Disability' (n 29) 56.

descriptively, and to the extent that it has normative implications, the model is celebratory of impairment, with Degener describing how the human rights model 'values impairment as part of human diversity and human dignity'.[62]

The human rights model thus responds to the criticisms of the social model by recognising the lived experience of impairment.[63] Of note, though, is that the human rights model includes as its first feature, the recognition of universal legal capacity[64] – an inclusion I argue that fails to recognise the difference of cognitive impairment. For this reason, the human rights model contains internal contradictions and, as a reference point for interpreting and applying Article 12, fails to remedy the limitations of the social model. Although it asserts that 'impairment matters', in the specific case of decision-making ability it fails to acknowledge that decision-making impairment as a matter of fact has an adverse impact on decision-making ability or capacity.

2.4.5 Commentary and Conclusion on Models of Disability and the CRPD

The charity model of disability situated people with disability as objects of pity and discretionary beneficence rather than as subjects of rights, and the dominance of a medical model meant that if a person could not have his or her disability 'fixed' or 'cured', then they were somehow lesser persons. The social model, therefore, developed as an important advocacy tool to accommodate impairment and to include people with disability as subjects of rights. However, a strict version of the social model emphasises that people with disability – once environments have been adapted to support them – are intrinsically 'the same' as each other and the same as those without disability. I argue further in Chapter 6 that this assumption of sameness risks treating people with disability identically, even when their impairment demands differential supports and services for them to achieve equality and social inclusion.[65]

In its effort to de-stigmatise disability, the strict social model risks denying difference, both the different experience of impairment and the disadvantages associated with impairment or disability.[66] I argue that it is important and useful for impairment to be recognised descriptively as atypical or 'non-ordinary' so that it can be responded to in a way that will ensure human rights are fulfilled. There is a plethora of terms (e.g. biopsychosocial, multi-factorial, interactive) to describe disability as something created by ableist social and environmental responses and also by the concrete reality of embodied, lived impairment. There is no consensus on what any new model should be called, so I choose to refer to a social model that recognises the

62 Kayess and Sands (n 53) 9.
63 Degener, 'A New Human Rights Model of Disability' (n 29) 56.
64 Ibid.
65 See Chapter 6, especially Section 2.
66 See for example Chapter 3, Section 4.2.1, which describes the socio-economic disadvantages disproportionately associated with disability.

residual impacts of impairment.[67] In using this terminology, I seek to acknowledge both the social determinants of disability and the lived experience of impairment, even after all requisite and available social and environmental supports have been provided. This terminology is also consistent with the description of disability in the CRPD as: 'an evolving concept … that … results from the interaction between persons with impairments and attitudinal and environmental barriers that hinders their full and effective participation in society on an equal basis with others'.[68]

3 DECISION-MAKING AND PEOPLE WITH COGNITIVE DISABILITY

The three dominant models of disability – charity, medical and social – have been used to explain the development of different approaches to decision-making for, with and by adults with cognitive disability. Historically, decisions were made for adults by the institutions where they lived; but, with a move to de-institutionalisation, personal guardians began to be appointed to make decisions for adults in recognition of their individual needs and interests. Guardianship frameworks, in turn, have evolved from strictly paternalistic models to ones that increasingly recognise adults' autonomy. The dominance of guardianship is, in turn, starting to be challenged by the development of supported decision-making practices that endeavour to enable adults with cognitive disability to make their own autonomous decisions.

The next three subsections trace this development in decision-making practices in relation to people with cognitive disabilities – from the routine imposition of institutionalisation to the advent of supported decision-making.

3.1 *The Era of Mass Institutionalisation*

The dominance of the charity and medical models of disability has become associated with the historical practice of routinely 'placing' adults with cognitive disability in institutions run by the State or church, where they resided until death.[69] In these cases, the institution made all decisions for the adults, who had no choice as to where they would live, what they would eat, what (if any) health care would be

[67] See 'differences that are residual from impairment must be taken into account' and 'residual difficulties caused by bodily impairment': Kong, *Mental Capacity in Relationship* (n 47) 152.

[68] *CRPD* Preamble para 5; and this definition is reiterated with minor changes in Article 1; Broderick has written that this definition reflects what she calls a 'social-contextual model of disability', which appears to approximate what I have called a social model that acknowledges the residual impacts of impairment. See: Broderick, *The Long and Winding Road to Equality and Inclusion for Persons with Disabilities* (n 39) 77–9.

[69] Ron McCallum, *The United Nations Convention on the Rights of Persons with Disabilities: An Assessment of Australia's Level of Compliance* (Royal Commission into Violence, Abuse, Neglect and Exploitation of People with Disability, 2020) 91.

provided or the friends or family with whom they would associate. Such adults were truly denied autonomy in their lives in that they were not permitted any personal space over which they could rule nor allowed to make decisions independently, according to their own values. In 2005, an Official Visitor to one such institution in Australia wrote:

> I found an institution used mainly as a place for keeping certain people out of circulation. Remedial treatment and turnover were practically nil. Patients were eking out a 24-hour daily existence in impoverished conditions and some practically in squalor. Many requests for discharge were ignored and not worth recording. Paramedics were unknown.[70]

In the 1980s and 1990s, Australia and other Western nations began de-institutionalising people with disability by moving them into community living.[71] This move was driven by revelations of significant abuse and exploitation behind closed walls,[72] and a belief that de-institutionalisation would increase the adults' autonomy and lead to fewer human rights abuses.[73] I note that while the era of mass institutionalisation has ostensibly ended, in reality institutionalisation continues, with significant concerns prevailing about the lack of appropriate community-living options for people with disability.[74]

70 Office of the Public Advocate (Qld), Submission No 73 to Senate Standing Committee on Community Affairs, Parliament of Australia, *Inquiry into Violence, Abuse and Neglect against People with Disability in Institutional and Residential Settings, Including the Gender and Age Related Dimensions, and the Particular Situation of Aboriginal and Torres Strait Islander People with Disability, and Culturally and Linguistically Diverse People with Disability* (June 2015) 5 ('*Submission to Senate Standing Committee*'); see also description of people being 'mopped down' in an institution in the 1960s: Raimond Gaita, *A Common Humanity: Thinking about Love & Truth & Justice* (Text Pub, 2nd ed, 2000) 17–18.

71 Frances Owen and Gillian MacKinnon, 'The Right to Community Living' in Dorothy Griffiths, Frances Owen and Shelley L Watson (eds), *The Human Rights Agenda for Persons with Intellectual Disabilities* (NADD, 2012) 39.

72 Office of the Public Advocate (Qld), *Submission to Senate Standing Committee* (n 70).

73 Mary Donnelly, 'Deciding in Dementia: The Possibilities and Limits of Supported Decision-Making' (2019) 66 *International Journal of Law and Psychiatry* 101466: 1–7; given the alternative motivations of cost-reduction, de-institutionalisation in itself has not always resulted in improved living conditions or greater choices of support services. This is despite the fact that one of the aims of de-institutionalisation was to increase the autonomy of adults with disabilities: see Jonathan Herring, *Caring and the Law* (Hart Publishing, 2013) 91, 146; Allen Buchanan and Dan W Brock, *Deciding for Others: The Ethics of Surrogate Decision Making* (Cambridge University Press, 1989) 313–15. Also relevant was the development of psychotropic drugs, which could be used to treat (but some would still say 'contain') adults within community settings: Owen and MacKinnon (n 71) 41–2. For use of psychotropic drugs as a form of containment, see Office of the Public Advocate (Qld), *Upholding the Right to Life and Health: A Review of the Deaths in Care of People with Disability in Queensland* A Systemic Advocacy Report (February 2016) 47.

74 McCallum (n 69) 91–9; Disability Royal Commission, *Group Homes* (Issues Paper, 28 November 2019); Disability Royal Commission, *Overview of Responses to Group Homes* (Issues Paper, September 2020).

3.2 *Legal Capacity Tests*

Under current guardianship regimes, a decision can generally be made for an adult when the adult lacks decision-making capacity or legal capacity. As the ALRC explains, 'Legal capacity sets the threshold for individuals to take certain actions that have legal consequences' and 'Legal capacity goes to the validity, in law, of choices and being accountable for the choices made'.[75] So, if an adult is not accorded legal capacity for a decision, any decision the adult makes may not be legally enforceable. Capacity has been described as the 'gateway to autonomy'[76] so that if a person is found to lack legal capacity, another person (i.e. a substitute – whether a guardian, surrogate, representative, or clinician in health-service provision) may be empowered to make a decision for them that will be legally recognised and for which the substitute will be legally accountable. If a substitute is making a decision for an adult in this way, the substitute is ostensibly or potentially stepping into the adult's own sovereign, personal space, and compromising or denying the adult's autonomy.[77] The three commonly described tests for capacity are the status, outcome and functional tests, with the functional test generally seen as showing greater respect for autonomy than the other two.[78]

3.2.1 **Status Test**

Legal capacity in some cases is said to be determined by status – for example, a person currently lacks legal capacity if they are under eighteen years of age; historically, both women[79] and slaves lacked capacity by virtue of their status as such.[80] An example of a capacity test that is *partially* status based can be found in the Mental Capacity Act 2005 (England and Wales) ('MCA'). Under the first limb of this test, a guardian can only be appointed for a person who is unable to make a decision 'because of *an impairment of or disturbance* in the functioning of, the *mind or brain*' [emphasis added];[81] with the MCA's Code of Practice providing diagnostic examples of '…a disability, condition or trauma …'

75 ALRC (n 33) 44.

76 Mary Donnelly, *Healthcare Decision-Making and the Law: Autonomy, Capacity and the Limits of Liberalism* (Cambridge University Press, 2010) 2.

77 See Chapter 4.

78 Lucy Series and Anna Nilsson, 'Article 12 CRPD: Equal Recognition before the Law' in Ilias Bantekas, Michael Ashley Stein and Anastasiou Dimitris (eds), *The UN Convention on the Rights of Persons with Disabilities: A Commentary* (Oxford University Press, 2018) 339, 356; Suzanne Doyle and Eilionóir Flynn, 'Ireland's Ratification of the UN Convention on the Rights of Persons with Disabilities: Challenges and Opportunities' (2013) 41(3) *British Journal of Learning Disabilities* 171, 174.

79 Law Commission, *Mental Incapacity* (Report No 231, 1995) 32.

80 Anna Arstein-Kerslake et al, 'Future Directions in Supported Decision-Making' (2017) 37(1) *Disability Studies Quarterly* 5–5.

81 *Mental Capacity Act 2005* (England and Wales) ('MCA') s 2(1); see also, 'a person in need of a guardian' is defined as, 'a person who because of a disability, is totally or partially incapable of managing his or her person', *Guardianship Act 1987* (NSW) ('GA NSW') s 3; in Tasmania a guardian or administrator can be appointed 'for a person with disability', *Guardianship and*

The status-based approach to determining capacity aligns most clearly with a medical model of disability, and in some jurisdictions mere determination of medical conditions or identification of impairments can be enough to rebut the presumption of capacity and confer a status of mental and legal incapacity.[82] The status approach lay behind what was historically the default model of 'plenary' guardianship, which had and still has the effect of depriving the adult of decision-making power in all areas of life.[83] Moreover, an overturning of that determination would be extremely unlikely, particularly as the individual might be denied legal standing to challenge it. Under this model, an individual could therefore be said to have the 'status' of disability and incapacity with their autonomy being significantly undermined or denied. A status test for capacity on the basis of impairment or disability is also widely perceived to be discriminatory and in breach of Article 12.[84]

3.2.2 Outcome Test

An outcome-based approach to determining capacity considers the probable outcome of a particular decision if it were to be made by the adult, and effectively works backwards to determine if the adult has capacity to make the decision.[85] Examples of an outcome-based test can be found in legislation that allows for the appointment of a guardian if an adult is unable to make 'reasonable' decisions or judgements.[86]

Administration Act 1995 (Tas) ('GAA *Tas*') s 20 (1); in South Australia the definition of 'mental incapacity' includes a test of inability 'as a result of … damage to, or any illness, disorder, imperfect or delayed development, impairment or deterioration of the brain or mind'. *Guardianship and Administration Act 1993* (SA) ('GAA SA') s 3(1); the legislation in the Australian Capital Territory sets a condition that 'the person's decision-making ability is impaired because of a physical, mental, psychological or intellectual condition or state, whether or not the condition or state is a diagnosable illness'. *Guardianship and Management of Property Act 1991* (ACT) ('GMPA ACT') s 5. By way of contrast, the *Guardianship of Adults Act 2016* (NT) ('GAA *NT*') s 5(5) expressly rejects a status-based test when it provides that for the purposes of guardianship appointment: 'The cause of the impairment of an adult's decision-making capacity is immaterial'.

82 Ben White, Lindy Willmott and Shih-Ning Then, 'Chapter 7: Adults Who Lack Capacity: Substitute Decision Making' in Ben White, Fiona McDonald and Lindy Willmott (eds), *Health Law in Australia* (Lawbook Co, 3rd ed, 2018) 207, 230.

83 Terry Carney, 'Searching for Workable Alternatives to Guardianship for Vulnerable Populations?' (2015) 1(1) *Ethics, Medicine and Public Health* 113, 115; John Chesterman, 'The Review of Victoria's Guardianship Legislation: State Policy Development in an Age of Human Rights' (2010) 69(1) *Australian Journal of Public Administration* 61, 61. Further, a determination of incapacity could mean that an adult was stripped of civil participation in all of its facets so as to be unable to vote or run for public office: Quinn and Arstein-Kerslake (n 19) 44.

84 *General Comment No 1* [15]; Martin et al, *Achieving CRPD Compliance* (n 4) 31.

85 White, Willmott and Then (n 82) 231.

86 Ibid; e.g., the Western Australian legislation has as a precondition for a guardian that a person is 'unable to make reasonable judgements in respect of any treatment proposed to be provided'. *Guardianship and Administration Act 1990* ('GAA WA') ss 110ZD(1), 110ZG(1), 110ZJ(1); and simlarly the second limb of the test in the Tasmanian legislation is that a person 'is unable … to make reasonable judgements in respect of all or any matters relaing to his or her person or circumstances': GAA *Tas* s 20(1)(b).

The test of reasonableness tends to focus on the effect of the decision itself rather than on the person's decision-making ability in proceduralist terms.[87] When it comes to health decisions, this means that greater capacity may be required to refuse treatment than to consent to the same treatment, because refusal is seen to be riskier.

The outcome test has been criticised for holding an adult with cognitive disability to a higher standard of decision-making than those in the wider community, who are indeed free to make bad or unwise decisions.[88] For this reason, it has been widely decried as denying adults' autonomy and what is referred to as their 'dignity of risk' (i.e. the right to made 'bad' or risky decisions).[89] The outcome test infringes a proceduralist account of autonomy because it imposes on the adult an idea of the good that may be outside their own value system.[90] This test has been criticised as the one most profoundly based on lack of respect for the autonomy of the adult, because it pays no heed to their will or preferences.[91] Despite the ongoing existence of outcome tests in some legislation, Quinn wrote in 2010 that 'Nobody seriously suggests an outcomes approach now'.[92]

[87] Clíona de Bhailís and Eilionóir Flynn, 'Recognising Legal Capacity: Commentary and Analysis of Article 12 CRPD' (2017) 13(1) *International Journal of Law in Context* 6, 10; Leslie Salzman, 'Guardianship for Persons with Mental Illness – A Legal and Appropriate Alternative' (2011) 4 *St Louis University Journal of Health Law and Policy* 279, 303. It has applied in some cases to find an adult incapacitous when they've entered a mental health facility voluntarily, only to find that they are involuntarily detained when they wish to exit: Buchanan and Brock (n 73) 217; Donnelly, *Healthcare Decision-Making and the Law* (n 76) 105.

[88] de Bhailís and Flynn (n 87) 10.

[89] For further discussion of the 'dignity of risk', see Chapter 5, Sections 3.2.1 and 4.1; 'It is to recognise the "dignity of risk" so that individuals with impairments are allowed to make unwise choices without paternalistic incursions into their lives': Camillia Kong, 'The Convention on the Rights of Persons with Disabilities and Article 12: Prospective Feminist Lessons against the "Will and Preferences" Paradigm' (2015) 4(4) *Laws* 709, 725; 'The General Comment No 1 states that there must be safeguards to protect against undue influence, yet these must respect the rights, will and preferences of the person, including the right to take risks and make mistakes'; Series and Nillson (n 78) 371.

[90] 'A results-based approach is objectionable because of the inherent contradiction between allowing the majority to make bad mistakes without intervention and disallowing a minority to make the same mistakes and overplaying the protective role of the law …' Gerard Quinn, 'Concept Paper "Personhood and Legal Capacity": Perspectives on the Paradigm Shift of Article 12 of the CRPD' (Conference Paper, HPOD Conference, 20 February, 2010) 14 www.inclusiveirelandie/document/HarvardLegalcapacitygqdraft2.doc; on the dignity of risk, see also Quinn and Arstein-Kerslake (n 19) 41; reflecting the concern that an outcome test denies the dignity of risk, some legislation acknowledges that for an adult 'the right to make decisions includes the right to make decisions with which others may not agree'. See, for example, *Guardianship and Administration Act 2000* (Qld) ('GAA *Qld*') s 5(a); similarly the Victorian legislation provides that, 'it should not be assumed that a person does not have decision-making capacity in relation to a matter merely because the person makes a decision that, in the opinion of others, is unwise': *Guardianship and Administration Act 2019* (Vic) ('GAA *Vic*'); see also MCA s 1(4).

[91] Arstein-Kerslake, *Restoring Voice to People with Cognitive Disabilities* (n 29) 85.

[92] Quinn, 'Concept paper "Personhood and Legal Capacity"' (n 90) 13.

3.2.3 Functional Test

The third approach to testing capacity is the functional test, which ostensibly considers only the process by which a decision is made. The functional test differs from a status-based approach in that a person may have capacity to make decisions in some domains – for example, everyday shopping – but may not have the capacity to enter into a complex financial transaction.[93] Under this test, capacity is domain-specific but also time-specific.[94]

The functional test can be found in the MCA as well as in the guardianship legislation of Australian states. A typical version of a functional test can be found in the *Guardianship and Administration Act 2019* (Vic), which requires that the adult be able:

> (a) to understand the information relevant to the decision and the effect of the decision; and
> (b) to retain that information to the extent necessary to make the decision; and
> (c) to use or weigh that information as part of the process of making the decision; and
> (d) to communicate the decision …[95]

A functional test of capacity, which assesses whether the adult has the ability to understand the decision to be made, weigh the relevant information and communicate their decision, is consistent with a liberal view of autonomy whereby the adult's own perception of 'the good' must be respected.[96] The functional test is ostensibly a procedural, 'value neutral' test of capacity that doesn't require the adult to hold any particular view or values to be found capacitous.[97] The functional test is also, however, subject to criticism for largely following a medical model, with findings of incapacity being almost entirely determined on the basis of psychiatric evidence.[98] It has also been criticised by the UN Disability Committee and others for being

[93] White, Willmott and Then (n 82) 229–30.

[94] In cases of both mental illness and aged dementia, this temporal limitation if applied carefully can have a significant impact, as capacity can fluctuate on a daily basis.

[95] Section 5; see also definition of 'person in need of a guardian' in *GA NSW* s 3; *GAA Tas* s 6(2); in Queensland, the test for capacity is similar to that above, but includes a third limb, that the person also has to be 'capable of … (b) freely and voluntarily making decisions about the matter', *GAA Qld* sch 4 Dictionary – definition of 'capacity'; MCA s 2 retains a status approach as a threshold, with an overlay of a functional test.

[96] Rawls (n 10) 11.

[97] Lucy Series, 'Relationships, Autonomy and Legal Capacity: Mental Capacity and Support Paradigms' (2015) 40 *International Journal of Law and Psychiatry* 80, 81.

[98] Quinn and Arstein-Kerslake (n 19) 45; Sam Boyle, 'Medical Evidence of Capacity in a Legal Setting: To What Extent Do Courts and Tribunals Make Their Own Decisions?' (2018) 25(2) *Journal of Law and Medicine* 572, 580–5. Also, the time-specific aspect of the functional test can be difficult to apply in practice, with many health-care decisions related to ongoing treatment rather than one-off procedures: Donnelly, *Healthcare Decision-Making and the Law* (n 76) 120.

discriminatory, because it impacts disproportionately on adults with cognitive disability (as discussed further in Chapter 6).[99] Behind this conclusion is an assumption that a finding of incapacity and the appointment of a substitute will always be deleterious for the adult and constitute a breach of human rights and Article 12 in particular.[100]

3.3 *Decision-Making Principles*

Once a determination of incapacity is made, legal frameworks may allow for a substitute to make a decision for the adult. This section provides a description of principles that may apply in cases of decision-making by substitutes, from 'best interests' to substituted judgement' and 'will and preferences'.

3.3.1 'Best Interests' Principle

Liberal theory demands that autonomy and self-determination be respected for those with capacity, but the 'best interests' test is used to ensure that adults with impaired capacity do not make decisions that place them or others at high risk of harm.[101] In practice, a decision made by a substitute according to a pure 'best interests' test[102] may deny the adult any role or voice in decision-making. In addition, a substitute could make a decision that he or she believed to be for the well-being of the adult, whether or not the adult objected to it.[103] The best interests test has been widely criticised for its encapsulation of a paternalistic attitude towards adults with cognitive

99 *General Comment No 1* [15]. See further critique in Renato Antonio Constantino Caycho, 'The Flag of Imagination: Peru's New Reform on Legal Capacity for Persons with Intellectual and Psychosocial Disabilities and the Need for Understandings in Private Law' (2020) 14(June) *The Age of Human Rights Journal* 155, 166; Mary Keys, 'Article 12' in Valentina Della Fina, Rachele Cera and Giuseppe Palmisano (eds), *The United Nations Convention on the Rights of Persons wtih Disabilities: A Commentary* (Springer International Publishing, 2017) 263, 266. For further discussion of the functional test in the context of Article 12 see Chapter 6, Section 4.

100 The status, outcome and functional tests are described above as if they are separate and distinct, but they are sometimes mixed together and incorporated into multi-level legislative tests, as in the MCA. Commentators have also pointed out that no matter what the legislative requirements may be, in practice the tests overlap, and courts tend to rely heavily on psychiatric evidence when purportedly applying any of the three different tests: Quinn and Arstein-Kerslake (n 19) 45; Donnelly, *Healthcare Decision-Making and the Law* (n 76) 115; also Boyle's view is that under the MCA while outcome cannot be determinative of capacity, it can be considered as *one* factor amongst others: Sam Boyle, 'Is the Wisdom of a Person's Decision Relevant to Their Capacity to Make that Decision?' (2020) 46(1) *Monash University Law Review* 39, 41–7; see also Series (n 97) 82.

101 Buchanan and Brock (n 73) 21–2.

102 Section 4 *MCA* provides that in determining a person's best interests, their 'past and present wishes and feelings ...' must be considered 'so far as is reasonably ascertainable' – i.e. it softens a traditional, 'pure' best interests test by explicitly requiring consideration of the adult's will and preferences.

103 ALRC (n 33) 49–50; commentators have also suggested that achievement of self-determination and autonomy in itself may promote well-being: Buchanan and Brock (n 73) 37.

impairment, because it may diminish the freedom of the adult and threaten his or her self-determination.[104] Under the best interests test, an adult whose decisions are made by a substitute may be denied the dignity of risk (i.e. the right to make unwise decisions).[105] The best interests test is still prevalent in legislation in common law jurisdictions,[106] although considered by many to be anachronistic and contrary to a twenty-first-century human rights approach to disability. In particular, the UN Disability Committee is of the firm view that it is contrary to Article 12 CRPD.[107] In imposing external values onto the adult, best interests decision-making is perceived by many as undermining the adult's autonomy and to be discriminatory on the basis of disability.[108]

3.3.2 Substituted Judgement and 'Will and Preferences'

Given the concerns described above, the best interests test has been replaced in some cases with 'substituted judgement'. According to this practice, the substitute must consider what decision the adult would have made had he or she *not* lost capacity and then give effect to their views.[109] In refraining from imposing the substitute's own views on the adult, substituted judgement is less paternalistic than 'best interests' decision-making and places greater weight on the adult's right to self-determination.[110] Most guardianship legislation in Australian states, as well as the MCA, now acknowledge and apply the substituted judgement test, at least to a limited extent.[111]

However, there are many occasions where a person may never have had capacity, most notably in cases of intellectual disability from birth, or in cases of brain injury

104 ALRC (n 33) 49–50.

105 For further discussion of the concept of 'dignity of risk' see Chapter 5, Section 4.1.

106 For example: GA NSW s 4(a) states that 'the welfare and interests of … persons should be given paramount consideration', s 16(2A) provides that the tribunal must consider 'best interests' when reviewing an appointment, and s 21A(2) provides that whether a guardian has acted in 'best interests' is one criterion to be considered to grant the guardian immunity, and see also ss 25G, 25P(2)(b) and s 25D in relation to financial management orders; GAA NT s 4(1); GAA WA s 51; in relation to the MCA see Donnelly, *Healthcare Decision-Making and the Law* (n 76) 179–80; for the United States see: Julia Duffy, 'What if Britney Spears Lived in Australia? Disrupting the Binary Framing of Guardianship versus Supported Decision-Making', (forthcoming 2023) 30 *Transnational Law and Contemporary Problems*.

107 *General Comment No 1* [21].

108 Anna Arstein-Kerslake, 'An Empowering Dependency: Exploring Support for the Exercise of Legal Capacity' (2016) 18 *Scandinavian Journal of Disability Research* 77, 84; Arstein-Kerslake and Flynn (n 3) 479.

109 White, Willmott and Then (n 82) 210–11.

110 'the value of self-determination can still be indirectly respected by guidance principles for surrogates that require them to seek to make decisions that are most in accordance with the person's values while competent …': Buchanan and Brock (n 73) 38.

111 See: 'the principle of substituted judgement' in GAA *Qld* s 11B(3); GA NSW ss 4(d), 14(2)(a), 28(2)(a), 40(3)(a), 44(2)(a), 45(5)(a); GMPA ACT s 4(2); GAA *Vic* s 8(c); GAA *Tas* s 6(c); GAA NT s 4(3)(1); GAA SA s 5(a); GAA WA s 51.

acquired before the age of eighteen years.[112] Moreover, in cases of acquired brain injury, mental illness or age-related dementia, an adult's values post-injury or illness may change.[113] In increasing recognition of the importance of autonomy for adults with disability, legislation has begun to require that substitutes make decisions that accord with the 'will and preferences' of the adult as expressed at the time that the decision is made.[114] The UN Disability Committee, in its prescription of universal legal capacity, favours the view that Article 12 demands that the adult's will and preferences, as expressed contemporaneously with the decision, be recognised and upheld.[115] This practice recognises the adult as always autonomous, the UN Disability Committee prescribing such autonomy as a pre-condition for recognising personhood.

3.4 *Supported Decision-Making*

In the 1990s, there was a move towards supported decision-making as an adjunct to existing guardianship regimes.[116] Supported decision-making is aimed at maximising an individual's autonomy so that, ideally, an adult who would otherwise have been assessed as not having legal capacity can make decisions that are recognised as their own, and for which they are therefore legally accountable. This movement towards supported decision-making led to the adoption of Article 12(3) CRPD, which provides in full that: 'States Parties shall take appropriate measures to provide access by persons with disabilities *the support they may require* in exercising their legal capacity' [emphasis added].

112 White, Willmott and Then (n 82) 211. Donnelly opines that in cases where the substituted judgement approach was used by courts for an adult who never had capacity, it was beginning to: 'look more and more like a legal fiction whereby judges made decisions which they considered appropriate under the guise that this was what the patient would have wanted': Donnelly, *Healthcare Decision-Making and the Law* 186.

113 See Buchanan and Brock (n 73) 155; 'the issue of changing identity following lack of capacity arises' in terms of the moral authority of advance directives, in Donnelly, *Healthcare Decision-Making and the Law* (n 76) 199; note that, 'The profile of people who are the subject of guardianship applications in NSW has … changed. Initially, the largest group was people with intellectual disability. Cases involving people with dementia are now the most common. Cases involving people with a mental illness or brain injury also make up a significant number of applications': New South Wales Law Reform Commission, *Review of the Guardianship Act 1987* (Report No 145, May 2018) xxii.

114 For example, in Queensland the 'structured decision-making' process appears to provide that it is the will and preferences at the time that the substitute decision is being made that are primarily relevant. It is only when these contemporaneous wishes cannot be determined that the adult's previously expressed will and preferences should be considered: GAA *Qld* s 11B General Principle 10 'Structured decision-making' (1)(4). This potential for tension and conflict is an issue of some significance given that guardianship appointments in Australia and elsewhere are increasingly and disproportionately being made for persons over the age of 65 years.

115 The exception to this is that the UN Disability Committee *does* endorse the use of advance planning instruments, or advance directives: *General Comment No 1* [17].

116 Then (n 25) 134.

Under a strict social model, an impairment is only framed as a disability because our ableist environment fails to accommodate it.[117] So, in the case of decision-making, the provision of social and environmental supports minimises the impact of cognitive impairment on decision-making ability so that legal capacity may be achieved and recognised. Adults who would otherwise be considered to lack capacity or decision-making ability can be supported by assistants, mentors, translators, technology or education to make legally effective and recognised decisions. In this way, they can be recognised as having legal capacity on an equal basis with others. While there is contention as to whether or not supported decision-making can or should totally replace decision-making by substitutes, there is nevertheless broad common ground that Article 12(3) CRPD should apply when feasible.

Support can include enlisting a trusted support person for the adult, advocacy, or communication assistance.[118] The UN Disability Committee has indicated no one-size-fits-all model of supported decision-making but that the diversity of individuals and situations should be respected and taken into account.[119] It provides that a support person 'formally chosen' by an adult must have legal recognition; there must be legal mechanisms to 'challenge the action of a support person', and an adult has a right to refuse support.[120] While practices of supported decision-making are still evolving, provided below is a brief overview of the principles espoused, some practices developed to date, and the ongoing challenges.

3.4.1 Supported Decision-Making in Legislation

Canadian provinces were at the forefront in developing legislative models for supported decision-making even before adoption of the CRPD. For example, the

[117] See discussion of the social model at Section 2.3 of this chapter.

[118] In 2012, Dinerstein referred to Inclusion Europe's position paper on supported decision-making, which prescribes eight key elements of a supported decision-making model: promotion of self-advocacy; 'using mainstream mechanisms …' to protect an adult's best interests; replacing substitute decision-making; formal support and registered supporters only for significant decisions; selection and training of supporters; overcoming communication barriers; preventing conflicts between the adult and their supporter; and the inclusion of safeguards: Dinerstein (n 33) 10, citing Inclusion Europe, *Key Elements of a System of Supported Decision-Making* (Position Paper, 2018) http://inclusion-Europe.org/images/stories/documents/PositionPapers/Position_Supported_Decision_Making_EN.pdf.; Gooding suggests broad principles for supported decision-making as: protects autonomy by offering support appropriate to an individual when he or she is exercising choice; embraces an 'inter-dependent' concept of autonomy, i.e. interdependence between the adult making the decision and a support person; acknowledges the dignity of risk but protects the individual from abuse; respects equality and non-discrimination; and reflects the norms of international human rights law: Piers Gooding, 'Supported Decision-Making: A Rights-Based Disability Concept and Its Implications for Mental Health Law' (2013) 20(3) *Psychiatry, Psychology and Law* 431, 445; see also Chris Bigby, et al, *Diversity, Dignity, Equity and Best practice: A Framework for Supported Decision-making. Royal Commission into Violence, Abuse, Neglect and Exploitation of People with Disability* (2023) https://disability.royalcommission.gov.au/policy-and-research/research-program

[119] *General Comment No 1*.

[120] Ibid [29].

Representation Agreement Act 1996 of British Columbia allows for an adult who may otherwise lack capacity but who has enough 'capability' to appoint a supporter, to do so. The goal is that once the supporter is in place, this person can assist in raising the adult's capability or capacity to a level where the adult can make a range of other decisions.[121] Another early adopter was Sweden where legislation introduced the role of the 'god man' or mentor. The 'god man' is a support person and decision-making assistant appointed informally or by a tribunal with the consent of the adult with cognitive disability.[122] Since ratification of the CRPD, legislation formally recognising supported decision-making has been enacted in several other countries including the Republic of Ireland,[123] the United States,[124]

[121] *Representation Agreement Act* 1996 (BC) s 8. Although enacted almost 30 years ago, the Act provides a useful example of typical legislative scaffolding incorporated in the increasing number of supported decision-making statutes. The agreement with the supporter is called a representation agreement, which is a novel combination of a supported decision-making agreement and enduring power of attorney. The effect of the legislation is that supporters or representatives have the same rights to access information relating to the adult as the adult themselves (s 10); protective factors include exclusion of real property deals (s 2); representatives/supporters have obligations to keep accounts (s 16(8)); and there are requirements for an additional representative or 'monitor' in the case of financial matters, and oversight by the Public Trustee (s 12). Other examples of Canadian legislation are the *Adult Guardianship and Trusteeship Act* 2008 (Alberta), which allows for both supported decision-making and co-decision making (ss 4, 13); and the *Adult Guardianship and Co-Decision-Making Act* 2000 (Saskatchewan), which allows for appointment of a co-decision-maker if an adult's capacity is impaired so that he or she requires assistance to make 'reasonable' decisions (s 14(a)(i)). For further description and analysis of this and other Canadian legislation, see Julia Duffy and Kelly Unsworth, 'Supported Decision-Making, Legal Risk and Commercial Uncertainty' (Conference Paper, Australian Guardianship and Administration Council National Conference: Reflecting Will and Preference in Decision-Making, 17–18 October 2016) <https://agac.org.au/images/stories/2016nsw/duffy-et-al-supp-dec-mk-legrsi-comm-unc.pdf>; also, Then (n 25) 151–4.

[122] Usually, the appointment is of a friend or relative, but professionals can also be appointed and paid a small fee. The introduction of this concept of a legally recognised mentor avoids the need for a determination of incapacity and has served to greatly decrease the appointment of 'forvaltare', i.e. guardians or administrators: Office of the Public Advocate (Qld), *Decision-Making Support and Queensland's Guardianship System: A Systemic Advocacy Report* (A Systemic Advocacy Report, April 2016) 167; Arstein-Kerslake and Flynn (n 3) 478; Christine Bigby et al, 'Delivering Decision Making Support to People with Cognitive Disability – What Has Been Learned from Pilot Programs in Australia from 2010 to 2015' (2017) 52(3) *Australian Journal of Social Issues* 222, 223; Gooding (n 118) 444; Jacinta Douglas et al, 'Factors That Underpin the Delivery of Effective Decision-Making Support for People with Cognitive Disability' (2015) 2(1) *Research and Practice in Intellectual and Developmental Disabilities* 37, 39.

[123] *Assisted Decision-Making (Capacity) Act* 2015 (Republic of Ireland) s 10 provides that an adult who considers that their capacity 'is in question or may shortly be in question' can appoint a person to assist them in making decisions on personal welfare or property matters.

[124] In Texas, legislation was introduced in 2015 that provides for the recognition of supported decision-making agreements and includes some immunity for third parties acting in good faith who rely on the agreement: Eliana J Theodorou, 'Supported Decision-Making in the Lone-Star State' (2018) 93(4) *New York University Law Review* 973, 996; see also California: 'What if Britney Spears Lived in Australia? Disrupting the Binary Framing of Guardianship versus Supported Decision-Making' (forthcoming 2023) 30 *Transnational Law and Contemporary Problems*; as of

and Peru,[125] and there have been some limited endeavours to introduce legislation for supported decision-making in the Australian State of Victoria.[126] However, it is noteworthy that none of these legislative models has functioned so as to abolish decision-making by substitutes in all cases.[127] Some further analysis of the limitations of legislative regimes is revisited in later chapters.[128]

3.4.2 Informal Support Trials in Australia

Australia has been described as a leader in its development of supported decision-making trials outside of legislative frameworks, with trials led by government and academics in several Australian states and territories.[129] Results from supported decision-making trials have shown overall that the participants completing the trials had 'increased confidence, interpersonal skills, greater self-determination, success within the workplace, the ability to sustain important relationships' and sometimes the ability to transition from a guardianship order.[130] All of this would point to increased autonomy for the participants, consistent with the policy aims. However, the trials have also revealed challenges, which include conflicts between supporters and others involved in the adult's life[131] and reluctance by service providers to

October 2022 15 states and the District of Columbia had passed supported decision-making laws: sdmy Supported Decision-Making New York, *SDMA Legislation in the US and Elsewhere* web page, 11 October 2022) https://sdmny.org/supported-decision-making-legislation/supported-decision-making-agreement-legislation-in-the-u-s-and-elsewhere/

125 In 2018, Peru repealed antiquated guardianship laws and replaced them with legislation that recognises a decision-making supporter appointed by an adult, and also allows for court appointment of supporters where an adult cannot communicate their will and preferences: Antonio Martiniez-Pujalte, 'Legal Capacity and Supported Decision-Making: Lessons from Some Recent Legal Reforms' (2019) 8(3) *Laws* 1.

126 Allows for 'supportive guardianship orders': *GAA Vic*; allows for a person to appoint 'another person to support the person and represent the interests of the person in making medical treatment decisions': *Medical Treatment Planning and Decisions Act 2016* (Vic); allows for the appointment of a 'supportive attorney': *Powers of Attorney Act 2014* (Vic).

127 No law reform agency in English-speaking jurisdictions has recommended complete abolition of decision-making by substitutes: Shih-Ning Then et al, 'Supporting Decision-Making of Adults with Cognitive Disabilities: The Role of Law Reform Agencies – Recommendations, Rationales and Influence' (2018) 61 *International Journal of Law and Psychiatry* 64, 69; also, the legislation in Peru has been criticised for failing to completely abolish decision-making by substitutes: Caycho (n 99) 162–4.

128 See Chapter 4, Section 4.5 and Chapter 6, Section 5.1.

129 Kristin Booth Glen, 'Supported Decision-Making from Theory to Practice: Further Reflections on an Intentional Pilot Project' (2020) 13 *Albany Government Law Review* 94, 104; Bigby et al (n 122) 224; Terry Carney et al, 'Realising "Will, Preferences and Rights": Reconciling Differences on Best Practice Support for Decision-Making?' (2019) *Griffith Law Review* 357, 365–75; Office of the Public Advocate (Qld), *Decision-Making Support and Queensland's Guardianship System* (n 122).

130 Office of the Public Advocate (Qld), *Decision-Making Support and Queensland's Guardianship System* (n 122) 172; Bigby et al (n 122) 231–2.

131 Bigby et al (n 122) 233; a supported decision-making trial in New York City included mediation services as a component: Glen, 'Supported Decision-Making from Theory to Practice' (n 129) 97, 115–16.

recognise decisions or acknowledge supporters.[132] One trial revealed that some degree of interpretation was always required to determine an adult's will and preferences, suggesting 'a fine line between realisation of will and preference and substitution for it'.[133] Supported decision-making trials have yet to be attempted with adults with severe cognitive disability, leaving it unknown or unclear how those hard cases are to be dealt with in practical terms.[134]

3.4.3 Advance Planning

Advance planning directives are typically understood to be written directives made by an adult when they have capacity. The directives either appoint a person to make decisions for the adult at a future time when they have impaired capacity or provide specific directions for how their health or other needs should be met at that future time.[135] *General Comment No 1* endorses the use of advance planning directives as a tool for supported decision-making. There is broad agreement that they can further the autonomy and self-determination of adults with cognitive disability as required by Article 12.[136]

3.5 *Summary and Conclusions*

This section has mapped out a brief history of legal and policy frameworks for decision-making for, with and by adults with cognitive disability from the era of mass institutionalisation to current practices of decision-making by substitutes and supported decision-making. Although policy frameworks have shifted from promoting paternalism to valuing autonomy, it is important to note that implementation is still a work in progress and that neglect and abuse of many adults with cognitive disability is still a grim reality.

Nevertheless, the trajectory of development from institutionalisation to supported decision-making reflects the increasing endeavours of policymakers to recognise

[132] Office of the Public Advocate (Qld), *Decision-Making Support and Queensland's Guardianship System* (n 122) 173.

[133] Carney et al (n 129) 169; see also description below of use of the 'best interpretation' principle in supported decision-making at Section 4.1 and criticisms of it at Section 4.2.5.

[134] Bigby et al (n 122) 235.

[135] White, Willmott and Then (n 82) 217–27; Lindy Willmott, Ben White and Ben Matthews, 'Law, Autonomy and Advance Directives' (2010) 18 *Journal of Law and Medicine* 366.

[136] *General Comment No 1* [17]; Jill Stavert, 'Supported Decision-Making and Paradigm Shifts: Word Play or Real Change?' (2020) 11 *Frontiers in Psychiatry* 571005: 1–9; however, *General Comment No 1* only endorses advance directives if they are *not* triggered by a determination of incapacity but by the occurrence of some other event or condition. The UN Disability Committee's view is that a trigger not associated with disability or incapacity (i.e. a disability 'neutral' trigger) is allowable under Article 12. In such a case, an advance directive could deny legal capacity, but not discriminatorily on the basis of disability. However, I argue in Chapter 6 (Sections 4.1 and 4.2) that relying on a concept of disability 'neutrality' fails to interrogate what equality means when we are all situated differently and when we recognise the residual impacts of impairment.

the personhood and autonomy of adults with cognitive disability. This, in turn, reflects a desire to respond to adults' needs in ways that respect their rights to non-discrimination and equality. This growing focus on autonomy and equality has been explained or supported by the parallel development of different models of disability – the charity, medical and social models.

Originally, decisions by substitutes were always made according to paternalistic best interests principles; but then substituted judgement and 'will and preference' tests developed to recognise the adult's own autonomous wishes and value system. However, even under the substituted judgement and 'will and preference' models, decision-making impinges on the adult's autonomy in that a substitute can be appointed without an adult's consent and even in the face of their objection. Autonomy is compromised because such an appointment is seen as intervention by the State in the adult's personal sphere.[137] In addition, under contemporary legislative regimes, decisions can be made by a substitute that conflict with the adult's expressed wishes.

Concern that decision-making by substitutes still compromises an adult's autonomy and is also discriminatory on the basis of disability has led to the promotion and development of supported decision-making. Through supported decision-making, a friend, family member or other support person can assist an adult to make 'autonomous' decisions. It aims to promote the autonomy and equality of the adult's decision-making, so as to recognise their legal capacity 'on an equal basis with others'. Supported decision-making is said to be more respectful of autonomy when it is informal, unregulated and 'least restrictive'.[138] However, there is also a drive to legislate for supported decision-making and to regulate support relationships to promote transparency and accountability.[139]

There are ongoing challenges with supported decision-making. It fails to fully account for severe and profound cognitive disability[140] and for cases when an adult decides to harm themselves or others.[141] Challenges also arise by the fineness of the line between supporting an adult's will and preferences and substituting for them.[142]

137 See Chapter 4, Section 2.3 for an understanding of autonomy as demanding non-intrusion in the private sphere.

138 Dinerstein (n 33) 10.

139 *General Comment No 1* [29(d)].

140 Wayne Martin et al, *Three Jurisdictions Report: Towards Compliance with CRPD Article 12 in Capacity/Incapacity Legislation across the UK* (Essex Autonomy Project, 2016) 34; 'this is where the General Comment comes closest to massaging the facts and closing its eyes to the actual real-life situation that many people with severe psychosocial disabilities find themselves in': David Bilchitz, 'Dignity, Fundamental Rights and Legal Capacity: Moving beyond the Paradigm Set by the General Comment on Article 12 of the Convention on the Rights of Persons with Disabilities' (2016) 32(3) *South African Journal on Human Rights* 410, 417.

141 Arstein-Kerslake and Flynn (n 3) 482; Amita Dhanda, 'Conversations between the Proponents of the New Paradigm of Legal Capacity' (2017) 13(1) *International Journal of Law in Context* 87, 89; Craigie et al (n 2) 161; Series (n 97) 81.

142 Carney et al (n 129) 169.

Supported decision-making under Article 12(3) CRPD is said to have been driven by the social model of disability, whereby disability is located in society and not the individual; hence, all adults can achieve decision-making autonomy if they have the appropriate social and environmental supports. Under the strict version of the social model, all adults are to be considered and treated the same, once these supports have been provided. In this way, adults with cognitive disability can have their legal capacity recognised 'on an equal basis with others'.

However, there has also been widespread critiques of the strict social model, and I describe how the interpretation of Article 12 argued for in this book is best explained by a social model that recognises the residual impacts of impairment. A strict social model aligns with a trajectory of policy development from paternalism to autonomy, and from discrimination to equality (the latter aligned with a journey from difference to sameness). Recognition of the residual impacts of impairment disrupts the simplicity of this narrative. It challenges the privileging of autonomy in human rights law and theory as a basis for personhood and demands that we seek other values, such as dignity, on which to found personhood. Recognition of the residual impacts of impairment also demands interrogation of what is meant by equality and non-discrimination in a world where we are all situated differently. Investigation of these issues forms the subject matter of Chapters 4–6.

The historical overview provided above serves as important policy and legal context for understanding the CRPD and the ongoing arguments around the interpretation of Article 12. The next section provides an overview of the main interpretive arguments found in the literature.

4 THE CRPD AND ARTICLE 12 AS A 'PARADIGM SHIFT' BUT ALSO A SITE OF CONTEST

Chapter 1 described how the CRPD grew out of an increasing recognition of the historical exclusion of people with disability from human rights agendas;[143] how the drafting process included a wide range of civil society organisations;[144] how it was agreed that the CRPD should include a broad range of human rights;[145] and that Article 12 was said to represent a 'paradigm shift' in recognising people with disability as subjects of human rights.[146]

The travaux préparatoires reveal that the contention over whether or not Article 12 should require the abolition of decision-making by substitutes was left unresolved during drafting, with the IDC ultimately acknowledging that it could accept the final text because it 'has created silence on this issue by neither prohibiting nor

[143] Section 3.
[144] Section 3.2.
[145] Section 3.3.
[146] Section 3.4.

endorsing substitutive [sic] decision making'.[147] The literature survey below shows that because of this silence, many of the arguments ventilated during drafting continued after adoption and ratification, as different commentators advocated for conflicting interpretations.

Subsection 4.1 summarises the major arguments made in favour of interpreting Article 12 as requiring the abolition of decision-making by substitutes. This is followed in Subsection 4.2 by arguments interpreting Article 12 as allowing for its retention as a last resort. This survey is intended as context for the more extensive interpretive arguments relating specifically to autonomy, dignity and equality, which are elaborated further in Chapters 4, 5 and 6, respectively.

4.1 *Arguments That Recognition of Legal Capacity Demands the Abolition of Substitute Decision-Making*

Throughout drafting negotiations, the IDC argued that Article 12 must require the abolition of all forms of guardianship, substitute decision-making and involuntary treatment or the paradigm shift required by the CRPD would not be achieved.[148] Following ratification of the CRPD, *General Comment No 1*, published in 2014, adopted an interpretation effectively supporting the IDC's view, affirming that adults with cognitive disability have their legal capacity recognised, their will and preferences given effect to, and their autonomy preserved. It further provided that Article 12 should be interpreted as requiring the abolition of guardianship and other substituted decision-making practices.[149] Many commentators, both before and after *General Comment No 1*'s publication, have endorsed this interpretation.

147 Ad Hoc Committee, *Daily Summary of the Seventh Session: Discussions Related to Article 12 Equal Recognition as a Person before the Law (continued)* (18 January 2006) www.un.org/esa/socdev/enable/rights/ahc7sum18jan.htm Ad Hoc Committee ('*Daily Summary 18 January 2006*').

148 'Substituted decision making is based on the premise of incompetence and must not be legitimized. Supported decision making is based on the premise of competence. The two cannot exist together and successfully achieve the paradigm shift desired'. Ad Hoc Committee, *Daily Summary 18 January 2006* (n 147).

149 'Substitute decision making' was originally defined in *General Comment No 1* as a system where: '1) legal capacity is removed even for a single decision; 2) a substitute is appointed by someone other than the adult, potentially against their will, *and* [emphasis added] 3) a decision is made by the substitute under best interest principles'. This conjunctive definition appeared to allow for some systems of what would usually be considered substitute decision-making – i.e. in cases where *not all* of the three criteria were met. A technical reading would, e.g., allow a scenario where a substitute makes a decision based on the adult's will and preferences and not according to best interests. However, the UN Disability Committee subsequently released a corrigendum, changing the 'and' to 'or' so that if even one only of the three criteria applied, the decision-making arrangement would fall foul of Article 12. Confusingly, the status of the corrigendum is unclear: Martin et al, *Three Jurisdictions Report* (n 140) 65; Ward, Adrian, 'Abolition of Guardianship? "Best Interests" versus "Best Interpretation"' (2015) 32 *Scots Law Times* 150, 153.

4.1.1 Legal Capacity Includes the Capacity to Act and Is a Precondition to Exercising Other Rights

In arguing that Article 12 should require the abolition of all forms of decision-making by substitutes, the IDC maintained that 'legal capacity' includes both the capacity to hold rights and the capacity to act on them because 'Legal capacity is only a shell in the absence of the capacity to act'.[150] It reiterated strongly that it did not want to 'legitimise guardianship', which it described as not allowing for the provision of support.[151] Together with Inclusion International, the IDC referred to the historical abuses of guardianship, and stated that 'The time for appointment of personal representatives, even as a last resort, is over'.[152]

In 2008, a group of 32 academics, lawyers and disability advocates signed a 'Legal Opinion on Article 12 CRPD' ('the Legal Opinion') reiterating the IDC's view that legal capacity includes the capacity to act.[153] Minkowitz, as Chair of the World Network of Users and Survivors of Psychiatry and one of the signatories of the Legal Opinion, has been and continues to be a strong opponent of an interpretation of Article 12 that allows for any decision-making by substitutes, writing that: 'Without full legal capacity, a significant proportion of people with disabilities would remain outside the protection of the Convention and be unable to exercise their human rights'.[154] Her view is that the right to 'physical and mental integrity' protected by Article 17 CRPD[155] and the right to consent to (or refuse) health care protected by Article 25(d)[156] cannot be upheld unless adults have a right to active legal capacity under Article 12.[157] Morrissey similarly espouses more broadly that:

[150] Ad Hoc Committee, *Daily Summary 18 January 2006* (n 147). The term 'legal capacity' had already been used in the CEDAW Article 14 in requiring women's legal capacity to be recognised on the same basis as men's, particularly in relation to their ability to hold property.

[151] 'Substituted decision making is based on the premise of incompetence and must not be legitimized. Supported decision making is based on the premise of competence. The two cannot exist together and successfully achieve the paradigm shift desired'. Ad Hoc Committee, *Daily Summary 18 January 2006* (n 147).

[152] Ibid.

[153] International Disability Alliance (n 2) 1–3.

[154] Tina Minkowitz, 'Legal Capacity: Fundamental to the Rights of Persons with Disabilities' (2007) 56(1) *International Rehabilitation Review* 25, 26.

[155] Article 17 'Protecting the integrity of the person – Every person with disabilities has a right to respect for his or her physical and mental integrity on an equal basis with others'.

[156] Article 25(d) – 'Require health professionals to provide care of the same quality to persons with disabilities as to others, including on the basis of free and informed consent by, inter alia, raising awareness of the human rights, dignity, autonomy and needs of persons with disabilities …'

[157] Minkowitz, 'Legal Capacity' (n 154) 25–6; see also World Network of Users and Survivors of Psychiatry, 'Implementation Manual for the United Nations Convention on the Rights of Persons with Disabilities' (February 2008) 3, 5, 16.

> Article 12 is at the core of the CRPD and the restoration of other rights such as participation and accessibility can only become fully effective if they are underpinned by the autonomous decisions of the individual.[158]

The UN Disability Committee has similarly asserted the view that fulfilment of Article 12 rights to legal capacity are foundational to claiming and fulfilling all other rights under the CRPD, and this is a view that has been expressed by other proponents of universal legal capacity.[159]

4.1.2 Denying Legal Capacity Equates to 'Civil Death'

The IDC further maintained during negotiations that denial of legal capacity is automatically rights-denying and, like many others, explains guardianship as always resulting in 'civil death'.[160] The term 'civil death' was used to describe the status of women who upon marrying had in the past been prohibited from holding property in their own name.[161] 'Civil death' references externally the denial of legal personality associated with the appointment of a plenary guardian, together with denial of political participation rights. Arstein-Kerslake and Flynn express the view that recognition of legal capacity is required to recognise legal personhood and that denial of capacity even for a single decision cannot therefore be permitted.[162] Bach equates even partial denial of legal capacity with total social and political exclusion for adults with cognitive disability.[163] Research has found that a finding of incapacity or a label of incompetence can in itself be stigmatising

[158] Fiona Morrissey, 'The United Nations Convention on the Rights of Persons with Disabilities: A New Approach to Decision-Making in Mental Health Law' (2012) 19 *European Journal of Health Law* 423, 426.

[159] See, e.g., International Disability Alliance (n 2).

[160] Ad Hoc Committee, Daily Summary of the Third Session: Discussions Related to Article 9 Equal Recognition as a Person before the Law (26 May 2004) UN Enable – Daily summary at the Third Session of the Ad Hoc Committee – Article 9, EQUAL RECOGNITION AS A PERSON BEFORE THE LAW; Quinn and Arstein-Kerslake (n 19) 42; Theresia Degener, 'Editor's Foreword' (2017) 13(1) *International Journal of Law in Context* 1; Anna Lawson, 'The United Nations Convention on the Rights of Persons with Disabilities: New Era or False Dawn?' (2007) 34(2) *Syracuse International Journal of Law and Commerce* 563, 569; Gerard Quinn and Abigail Rekas-Rosalbo, 'Civil Death: Rethinking the Foundations of Legal Personhood for Persons with a Disability' (2016) 56 *Irish Jurist* 286, 286–9; George Szmukler, '"Capacity", "Best Interests", "Will and Preferences" and the UN Convention on the Rights of Persons with Disabilities' (2019) 18(1) *World Psychiatry: Official Journal of the World Psychiatric Association (WPA)* 34, 35; Morrissey (n 158) 427.

[161] Bernadette McSherry, 'Legal Capacity under the Convention on the Rights of Persons with Disabilities' (2012) 20 *Journal of Law and Medicine* 22, 23.

[162] Eilionóir Flynn and Anna Arstein-Kerslake, 'The Support Model of Legal Capacity: Fact, Fiction, or Fantasy?' (2014) 32(1) *Berkeley Journal of International Law* 124, 126.

[163] Michael Bach, 'Inclusive Citizenship: Refusing the Construction of "Cognitive Foreigners" in Neo-liberal Times' (2017) 4(1) *Research and Practice in Intellectual and Developmental Disabilities* 4, 10–14.

and lead to learned helplessness.[164] Philosophically, the concept of civil death is premised on acceptance of the liberal tradition whereby civil and moral personhood are denied to an individual who lacks a sufficient amount of reason to be autonomous – that is, children and adults with cognitive disability.

4.1.3 Bach and Kerzner's Proposal for 'Facilitated Decision-Making'

In 2010, Bach and Kerzner argued that Article 12 required the abolition of guardianship and decision-making by substitutes and prepared a report for the Law Reform Commission of Ontario proposing a three-tier system of supported decision-making. They proposed three different decision-making 'statuses' differentiated *not* by assessing legal capacity, but by determining differential decision-making capability. Under the 'legally independent status', an adult makes a decision without formal support and the decision is recognised as his or her own. Under 'supported decision-making status', an appointed or recognised person (a supporter) supports the adult to make a decision that accords with the adult's own will and preferences. The third status of 'facilitated decision-making' would be available to adults with 'significant disabilities' who also find themselves in situations of isolation and who have no advance planning documents.[165]

Facilitated decision-making status would apply in two circumstances. First, it would apply where an adult's will and preferences cannot be communicated; and second, when adults would otherwise have supported decision-making status except that they intend to make a decision with 'serious adverse effects'.[166] In the first situation, the facilitator must gather whatever information may be available about the person's history and circumstances in order to make a decision consistent with the adult's coherent life narrative.[167] In the second situation, the facilitator should consider which decision would best outweigh the risk of harm to the adult or improve their quality of life.

Despite Bach and Kerzner describing their model as supported decision-making, several commentators have pointed out that the facilitated decision-making status equates to substituted decision-making under a different guise.[168] The proposal has also been criticised for applying what amounts to a best interests test to protect the adult from harm. As such, it is considered by some advocates of universal legal capacity to be in breach of Article 12.[169]

164 Bruce Winick, 'The Side Effects of Incompetency Labelling and the Implications for Mental Health Law' (1995) 1(1) *Public Policy and the Law* 6, 6.

165 Michael Bach and Lana Kerzner, *A New Paradigm for Protecting Autonomy and the Right to Legal Capacity: Advancing Substantive Equality for Persons with Disabilities through Law, Policy and Practice* (Law Commission of Ontario, October 2010) 83–91.

166 Ibid 92; see also Chapter 6, Section 4.1.1.

167 Ibid 66; see also Chapter 4, Section 3.3 for an explanation of how the idea of a 'coherent life narrative' underpins some accounts of autonomy.

168 Devi (n 2) 803; see also: Terry Carney, 'Supported Decision-Making for People with Cognitive Impairments: An Australian Perspective?' (2015) 4 *Laws* 37, 45; Parker (n 5) 387.

169 Devi (n 2) 803; Series also describes it as a 'modified outcome' approach: Series (n 97) 87.

4.1.4 The 'Best Interpretation Principle': In Pursuit of Autonomy

General Comment No 1 provides that where it is 'not practicable to determine the will and preferences of an individual' the support person must make a 'best interpretation' of the adult's will and preferences ('the best interpretation principle'). In these cases, the adult still retains their legal capacity and the adult (not the support person) would be held legally accountable for the decision.[170]

De Bhailís and Flynn describe the best interpretation principle as reflecting:

> the presumption that it is almost always possible to come to some level of understanding of a person's values, beliefs and views, and that the person's values, beliefs and views ultimately underpin their will and preferences'.[171]

This echoes the earlier commentary of Bach and Kerzner, who also argue for universal legal capacity and refer to the importance of decisions being made that reflect the 'narrative coherence' of an adult's life so that the decision is in some cases admittedly an 'ascription by others of [the adult's] will and/or intentions'.[172] Alston describes the best interpretation principle as a legal fiction but, despite this, suggests it is 'probably' justified on the basis that it is common for legal fictions to be used 'in pursuit of important societal aims'.[173] Glen argues that there is a real value to *General Comment No 1*'s 'insistence' on will and preferences, despite its challenges, because the 'expressive' value of the law in asserting universal legal capacity can lead to cultural change in ascribing personhood to people with disability.[174] The above commentary elevates the best interpretation principle and the principle of autonomy to a privileged position, with autonomy conceived of as self-determination, the freedom to make choices and to act in accordance with one's own values.[175]

4.1.5 Substitute Decision-Making Is Discriminatory on the Basis of Disability

Despite the rhetoric of universality, *General Comment No 1* does give weight and meaning to the equality proviso – that legal capacity be recognised 'on an equal basis with others'. It explains that Article 12 allows for denials of legal capacity, provided they do not discriminate on the grounds of disability or mental incapacity.[176] *General Comment No 1* distinguishes mental capacity as 'the decision making skills of a person' from legal capacity, being 'the ability to hold rights and duties (legal standing) and to exercise those rights and duties (legal agency)'.[177] According to this

170 *General Comment No 1* [21].
171 de Bhailís and Flynn (n 87) 16.
172 Bach and Kerzner (n 165) 66; see further discussion Chapter 4, Section 4.1.
173 Bruce Alston, 'Towards Supported Decision-making: Article 12 of the Convention on the Rights of Persons with Disabilities and Guardianship Law Reform' (2017) 35(2) *Law in Context* 21, 38.
174 Glen, 'Introducing a New Human Right' (n 2) 20.
175 See further Chapter 4 for different meanings attributed to 'autonomy'.
176 *General Comment No 1* [25].
177 Ibid [13].

logic, denial of legal capacity (as the ability to hold and exercise rights) should not be denied to an adult because the adult lacks decision-making skills. It explains that on this basis, not only status and outcome tests for capacity are discriminatory but also functional tests because they test an individual's mental capacity.[178]

4.1.6 Summary and Conclusions: Article 12 Requires the Abolition of Decision-Making by Substitutes

The drafting of Article 12 was contentious from the start, with arguments centring on whether it should abolish decision-making by substitutes or allow it to be retained as a last resort. While many commentators have resorted to the travaux préparatoires to settle the interpretive position, the polarity in views expressed means that they are far from determinative. I propose that the only consensus between delegates was that the text remain silent on the issue and that there was agreement to disagree.[179]

Delegates ultimately did agree that Article 12 should include a right to legal capacity, given that the language of 'legal capacity' had been used in CEDAW. However, the IDC and Inclusion International argued that legal capacity necessarily includes not just legal standing or the capacity to hold rights, but also the right to act on and exercise those rights. For the IDC,[180] Inclusion International,[181] Minkowitz[182] and others,[183] because legal capacity means the ability to hold *and* act on rights, Article 12 prohibits any form of guardianship or decision-making by substitutes. Arguments were also made, and continue to be made, that all forms of guardianship, even the appointment of a substitute for a single decision, amounts to an adult's civil death, whereby they are denied recognition of personhood. This argument, in turn, relies on an understanding of the right to legal capacity as being a foundational right that, if unfulfilled, leaves an adult unable to claim any other rights under the CRPD.

In 2010, Bach and Kerzner developed a supported decision-making model that they proposed was compliant with Article 12 because it ostensibly abolished substitute decision-making. However, their proposal for a 'facilitated' decision-making status has been criticised as de facto substitute decision-making, with the test of 'serious adverse effects' also approximating a 'best interests' determination. The criticisms of this proposed model illustrate the challenges of recognising legal capacity and autonomy as universal. This is, as also reflected in *General Comment No 1*'s acknowledgement, that in some cases it may 'not [be] practicable to determine the

[178] Ibid [29(i)].

[179] To interpret Article 12 by referring to the travaux préparatoires to 'avoid leaving a gaping hole in the Convention ... would enforce an interpretation where the negotiators could not reach a consensus'. Bartlett (n 51) 756.

[180] Ad Hoc Committee, *Daily Summary 18 January 2006* (n 147).

[181] Ibid.

[182] Minkowitz, Legal Capacity' (n 154) 25–6; see also World Network of Users and Survivors of Psychiatry (n 157) 26.

[183] International Disability Alliance (n 2) 1–3.

will and preferences of an individual'. Despite these challenges, *General Comment No 1* provides that, a 'best interpretation' of an adult's 'will and preferences' must be made and attributed to the adult as his or her own decision.

Underlying the above interpretive arguments is the view that recognition of active legal capacity amounts to recognition of autonomy; that autonomy is a human rights value to be privileged above all other values; and that legal capacity is to be privileged as a human right above all other rights. According to the logic of these arguments, any denial or limitation on legal capacity (i.e. autonomy) on the grounds of disability constitutes unlawful discrimination. *General Comment No 1* affirms this by providing expressly that 'Freedom from discrimination in the recognition of legal capacity restores autonomy'.[184] *General Comment No 1* and the literature that endorses its position argue that denial of legal capacity on the basis of mental incapacity violates Article 12 because it constitutes prohibited discrimination based on disability.

4.2 *Arguments That Recognition of Legal Capacity Allows for Retention of Decision-Making by Substitutes as a Last Resort*

General Comment No 1 is not legally binding but as explained in Chapter 1, it has significant influence and normative force[185] so that States Parties are not simply free to ignore General Comments without at least engaging with them.[186] Arguments in the literature for an interpretation of Article 12 as allowing for decision-making by substitutes include those directly rebutting the arguments summarised above. An overarching argument is based on acknowledgement of the hard reality that some adults do not have the autonomy to make their own decisions, and that decision-making by substitutes is therefore not discriminatory; it is not a choice, but an inevitability.

4.2.1 The Right to Legal Capacity as a Presumption that Is Rebuttable

Interpretive arguments have been made that, given the prevalence of substitute decision-making as an 'instrument of legal protection' across the world, explicit wording would be required to mandate its abolition. It would follow, therefore, that in the absence of such explicit wording in the CRPD, substitute decision-making is permitted.[187] These arguments align with notes in the drafting documents that

[184] *General Comment No 1* [33].

[185] Chapter 1, Section 3.

[186] Martin et al, *Three Jurisdictions Report*' (n 140) 56. See also CPRD Articles 35 and 36 establish a system whereby States report regularly to the UN Disability Committee on their compliance with the convention.

[187] Volker Lipp and Julian O Winn, 'Guardianship and Autonomy: Foes or Friends?' (2011) 5 *Journal of International Aging, Law & Policy* 41, 48; Martin et al, *Achieving CRPD Compliance*

provided that in 'exceptional circumstances' decisions would be allowed to protect persons with disability who could not exercise their legal capacity.[188] During drafting negotiations, Australia had argued similarly that since guardianship regimes would 'remain for the foreseeable future', the 'paradigm shift' required by Article 12 from a medical to a social model of disability could be effected by having supported decision-making as the default model but allowing for substitute decision-making in outlying cases.[189]

4.2.2 Legal Capacity Means Only the Capacity to Hold Rights

An argument for a narrow definition of legal capacity as the capacity to hold rights but not to necessarily act on them was first raised during drafting. The Coordinator suggested that: 'His impression of the group's consensus is that there will be exceptions to exercising legal capacity, but not to having legal capacity', pointing out that even adults with serious disability can inherit, own, buy and sell property, but it would only be to perform the actions of buying and selling on their behalf that a guardian would be required.[190]

There had been an attempt to emphasise this distinction by the insertion of a footnote in the draft to the effect that 'In Arabic, Chinese and Russian, the term "legal capacity" refers to "legal capacity for rights", rather than "legal capacity to act"'.[191] The implication was that all language versions would attribute the same, more limited meaning to legal capacity, thereby recognising an adult's legal capacity even when a decision was made by a substitute. While the footnote was ultimately omitted, two letters were later tabled in the UN General Assembly, the signatories representing over 40 States Parties, each letter affirming that the omission of the footnote was only a technical, not substantive, change and that legal capacity therefore attracted the more limited meaning.[192] In the context of the arguments made

(n 4) 12; McSherry argues that article 12 provides for a *presumption* of legal capacity, but acknowledges uncertainty as to when such a presumption may be displaced: McSherry (n 161) 23; Kayess and Fogarty describe Article 12 as requiring supported decision-making, but as allowing for substitute decision-making 'in some rare circumstances, after all other support measures have been exhausted': Rosemary Kayess and Ben Fogarty, 'The Rights and Dignity of Persons with Disabilities' (2007) 32(1) *Alternative Law Journal* 22, 25.

188 *Report of the Working Group to the Ad Hoc Committee, Annex 1, 'Draft Articles for a Comprehensive and Integral International Convention on the Protection and Promotion of the Rights and Dignity of Persons with Disabilities, Draft Article 9: Equal Recognition as a Person before the Law'* A/AC.265/2004/WG/1 (14 January 2004).

189 Ad Hoc Committee, *Daily Summary 18 January 2006* (n 147).

190 Ad Hoc Committee, *Daily Summary of the Fifth Session* (25 January 2005) www.un.org/esa/socdev/enable/rights/ahc5sum25jan.htm ('*Daily Summary 25 January 2005*').

191 Ad Hoc Committee, *Interim Report – Article 12 Equal Recognition as a Person before the Law*, 8th sess, A/AC.265/2006/4 (14–25 August 2006). www.un.org/esa/socdev/enable/rights/ahc8intreporte.htm

192 *Letter Dated 5 December 2006 from the Permanent Representative of Iraq to the United Nations Addressed to the Chairman of the General Assembly*, resumed 8th sess, UN Doc

during drafting, the effect of these letters is that they endorse an interpretation of Article 12 that allows for decision-making by substitutes as a last resort.

4.2.3 Substitute Decision-Making Is Allowed Because It Is Equivalent to 100% Support

The Chair of the Ad Hoc Committee suggested that decision-making by substitutes could be allowed under a supported decision-making paradigm because it could be justified as '100% support'.[193] The IDC emphatically rejected this suggestion, but this approach has nevertheless been adopted in the ALRC Report referred to above. The ALRC argues that the paradigm shift proposed by Article 12 can be effected by replacing an inquiry into an adult's capacity with an investigation of the supports needed by them to make a decision. It goes on to recommend a set of decision-making principles to guide law reform so that: 'supported decision-making is encouraged'; and 'representative' (i.e. substitute) decision-makers are appointed only 'as a last resort'. The ALRC describes how different levels of support may be required, including full support in the form of decision-making by a representative.[194] It argues that even in liberal philosophy, autonomy is not always privileged if in doing so, harm would result to the adult or to others.[195] It recommends that where it is not possible to determine an adult's will and preferences, or where there may be risk of harm, a decision-maker should 'consider the person's human right relevant to the situation and… act in a manner promoting the personal, social, financial and cultural wellbeing of the person'.[196] However, it is yet to be seen how this would operate in practice, and Alston queries whether the test of well-being would be very different in practice from a best interests determination.[197]

The ALRC's recommendation follows the wording of Australia's interpretive declaration, which provides that Article 12 allows '…full supported or substituted decision-making arrangements, which provide for decisions to be made on behalf of a person, only where such arrangements are necessary, as a last resort and subject to safeguards'.[198] Commentators arguing for retention of decision-making by substitutes widely agree that Article 12 demands that appointments be time- and domain-limited, subject to review and other safeguards, and that denial of legal capacity under such regimes does not amount to civil death.[199]

A/AC.265/2006/5 (5 December 2006); *Letter Dated 5 December 2006 from the Permanent Representative of Finland to the United Nations Addressed to the Chairman General Assembly*, resumed 8th sess, UN Doc A/AC.265/2006/6 (5 December 2006).

193 Ad Hoc Committee, *Daily Summary 18 January 2006* (n 147).

194 ALRC (n 33) 94.

195 Ibid 83–4.

196 Ibid 15.

197 Alston (n 173) 38.

198 CRPD Article 4.

199 Donnelly, *Healthcare Decision-Making and the Law* (n 76) 93.

I note that the UN Disability Committee in 2019 did to an extent endorse the ALRC Report in that it recommended that Australia, 'Implement a nationally consistent supported decision-making framework, as recommended …' by the ALRC Report. However in the same document the Committee went on to express concern about Australia's '…lack of progress made to abolish the guardianship system and substituted decision-making regime, particularly in decisions concerning forced psychiatric treatment…'.[200] It would appear that the Committee's endorsement of the ALRC's recommendations is somewhat limited, and does not extend to the ALRC's position on representative decision-making, or to its recommendation to retain the concept of capacity in the context of the law of contract.[201]

4.2.4 Substitute Decision-Making as an Article 12(4) Safeguard

Paragraph (4) of Article 12 provides that:

> States Parties shall ensure that all measures that relate to the exercise of legal capacity provide for appropriate and effective safeguards to prevent abuse in accordance with international human rights law. Such safeguards shall ensure that measures relating to the exercise of legal capacity respect the rights, will and preferences of the person, are free of conflict of interest and undue influence, are proportional and tailored to the person's circumstances, apply for the shortest time possible and are subject to regular review by a competent, independent and impartial authority or judicial body. The safeguards shall be proportional to the degree to which such measures affect the person's rights and interests.

The ALRC Report recommends that when making a decision a representative should consider the adult's 'will, preferences and rights', thereby using the language found in paragraph (4) of Article 12. The travaux préparatoires reveal that some delegates intended the above paragraph (4) to authorise substitute decision-making as a protection from potential abuse from 'supporters'.[202] This is consistent with Donnelly's view that Article 12 allows for retention of guardianship where it is personally tailored, respects will and preferences, is time-limited and subject to review.[203] Alston notes the ALRC's addition of 'rights' to the usual rubric of will and preferences, and endorses this approach to the extent that it is a 'defensible interpretation of what the treaty demands'.[204]

In recommending that a representative (or substitute decision-maker) should consider the adult's *rights* when making a decision, the ALRC is advancing its view that guardianship and decision-making by substitutes is not always rights-denying. The

[200] Committee on the Rights of Persons with Disabilities, *Concluding Observations on the Combined Second and Third Period Reports of Australia*, UN Doc CRPD/C/AUS/CO/ ('*Concluding Observations on Australia*') 6.

[201] ALRC (n 33) 290–1.

[202] Ad Hoc Committee, *Daily Summary 25 January 2005* (n 190).

[203] Donnelly, *Healthcare Decision-Making and the Law* (n 76) 93.

[204] Alston (n 173) 37–8.

ALRC's clear view is that abuse does not result from the appointment of a representative in itself but depends on the nature of the powers exercisable and exercised.[205] Several other commentators make the argument that in certain circumstances a substitute decision-maker can actually make decisions that uphold the human rights of the adult,[206] an argument that is expressly made in this book through applying the principle of indivisibility of human rights to interpret Article 12.

4.2.5 Best Interpretation Principle Could Justify a Decision Illegitimately

Interpretations of Article 12 as allowing for the retention of substitute decision-making as a last resort are frequently critical of the best interpretation principle. First, there is a lack of clarity over what 'will' and 'preference' mean, with suggestions that a person's long-term will may conflict with a more fleeting preference.[207] Second, the best interpretation principle doesn't account for the interactive process of supported decision-making.[208] In some cases, a supporter may explain real options, but in other cases an adult may merely be given a binary choice, or no choice at all.[209] Also, a supporter who spends more time with the adult may actually have the effect of determining an adult's preference.[210] Third, there is a questioning of the principle's premise that the supporter may be better placed than the adult to determine the adult's own will and preferences.[211] A corollary of this is that the principle ignores the reality that there are some things that a supporter will not and cannot know.[212] Fourth, there is an overarching concern that the best interpretation principle could be used to justify a decision illegitimately.[213] Chapter 4 considers some of these criticisms through applying the 'best interpretation' test to the particular case of 'Alex'.

205 ALRC (n 33) 52.

206 Anita Smith, 'Are Guardianship Laws and Practices Consistent with Human Rights Instruments?' in A Kimberly Dayton (ed), *Comparative Perspectives on Adult Guardianship* (Carolina Academic Press, 2014) 247, 268; Martin et al, *Achieving CRPD Compliance* (n 4) 19, 27.

207 Szmukler, '"Capacity", "Best Interests", "Will and Preferences" and the UN Convention on the Rights of Persons with Disabilities' (n 160) 39; see discussion in Chapter 4, Section 3.3 on 'hierarchical' accounts of autonomy.

208 Paul Skowron, 'Giving Substance to "the Best Interpretation of Will and Preferences"' (2019) 62 *International Journal of Law and Psychiatry* 125.

209 Ibid 130.

210 Ibid 128–30.

211 Ibid 129.

212 Mary Donnelly, 'Best Interests in the Mental Capacity Act: Time to Say Goodbye?' (2016) 24 *Medical Law Review* 318, 327; Carney, 'Searching for Workable Alternatives to Guardianship for Vulnerable Populations?' (n 83) 117.

213 Series and Nilsson (n 78) 371. See also the concept of 'full support' that 'some commentators claim that, even then, the disabled individual's will and preference can dictate the decision, suggesting the facilitator can have an almost preternatural ability to 'divine' the individual's wishes. This is extremely problematic … It is implausible that a third party facilitator has such capacity, and potentially disingenuous …': Jeanne Snelling and Alison Douglass, 'Legal Capacity and Supported Decision-Making' in Iris Reuvecamp and John Dawson (eds), *Mental Capacity Law in New Zealand* (Thomson Reuters, 2019) 163, 170.

4.2.6 Decision-Making by Substitutes Recognises 'Hard Reality' and Is Not Discriminatory

Several commentators who advocate for the retention of decision-making by substitutes as a last resort expressly base their argument on recognition of the factual reality and inevitability that decisions *will* be made for adults at times, especially for adults with severe and profound cognitive disability. Such writers acknowledge the hard reality that in cases of advanced dementia,[214] severe and profound intellectual disability, acquired brain injury,[215] as well as for adults suffering certain psychotic conditions, adults will lack decision-making autonomy and decisions will inevitably be made for them by others.[216]

Once this 'hard reality' is acknowledged and accepted, it follows that decision-making by substitutes is not discriminatory because it happens as a matter of fact, whenever some adults do not have the capability to make their own decisions. Galderisi's view is that decision-making processes and capability are integrally dependent on mental capacity, and people with impaired capacity will be at a greater risk of exploitation than many others.[217] In the same vein, Kim writes:

> There is a place for mental capacity assessments in determining decisional authority because there is no choice in the matter … The debate should not be over whether we sometimes should decide for others. The fact is that we inevitably do, whether we acknowledge this or not.[218]

Martin et al similarly assert that, 'The crucial point is that autonomy is intrinsically related to decision making ability' and that a person who lacks decision-making ability 'in a domain, even when support is provided, cannot accurately be described as acting autonomously in that domain'.[219] Martin et al further argue that different treatment in the form of decision-making by substitutes can actually result in substantive equality,[220] a position consistent with that argued for in Chapter 6 of this book.

[214] Nick O'Neill and Carmel Peisah, 'Beware the New Paternalisms: Capacity As a Means of Achieving the Goals of the Convention on the Rights of Persons with Disabilities' (Conference Paper, World Guardianship Congress, 15–16 October 2012) 9; Cahill (n 56) 94; Martin et al, *Three Jurisdictions Report* (n 140) 11; Anita Smith (n 206) 257.

[215] Nick O'Neill, 'From Parens Patriae to Advance Personal Planning – Guardianship in Australia 1824–2016' (Conference Paper, Australian Guardianship and Administration Council National Conference: Reflecting Will and Preference in Decision-Making, 17–18 October, 2016); including, for example, in the case of PVS: Lipp and Winn (n 187) 51.

[216] Plumb (n 49) 187, 191.

[217] Galderisi (n 5) 47–8.

[218] Craigie et al (n 2) 164.

[219] Martin et al, *Achieving CRPD Compliance* (n 4) 19.

[220] Ibid 16–19. They therefore view substitute decision-making as inevitable as a last resort – e.g. for people in comas, with advanced dementia, severe brain injury, profound learning difficulties or situations involving self-harm or suicidal tendencies: Martin et al, *Three Jurisdictions Report* (n 140) 34. Further discussed in Chapter 6, Section 4.2.

4.2.7 Summary and Conclusions: Article 12 Allows for Decision-Making by Substitutes to be Retained as a Last Resort

The interpretation of Article 12 as requiring the abolition of decision-making by substitutes has been widely criticised. Arguments were made during drafting, and have continued to be made, that Article 12 only creates a very strong presumption of legal capacity that the right to legal capacity in Article 12 is limited to the ability to hold rights so that they can be exercised by others on an adult's behalf; and also that substitute decision-making is allowed because it is equivalent to 100% or 'full' support. The argument has also been made that, given the prevalence of substitute decision-making and guardianship in jurisdictions internationally, clear and unequivocal wording would be needed should the intention of Article 12 be to abolish it.

In asserting that decision-making by a substitute or representative is not in itself rights-denying, the ALRC's position is consistent with the argument in this book; but it is the extent and nature of the representative's authority and how they exercise their power that will determine whether or not an adult's rights are either upheld or denied. The ALRC's recommendations are also premised on an understanding of paragraph (4) of Article 12 as allowing for representative decision-making as a protection against undue influence or abuse by supporters, an interpretation supported by the comments of some delegates during negotiations and shared by others since.[221]

A more concrete and fundamental argument, which is built upon in later chapters, is that, as a matter of hard fact, some adults will not have decision-making capability, no matter what supports are provided. It follows that such adults do not have decision-making autonomy in a descriptive sense and that they do not therefore have legal capacity. Related to this conclusion is a view that denial of recognition of legal capacity based on mental capacity is not, therefore, discriminatory on the basis of disability but constitutes recognition of an empirical and material difference. These interpretations, based on recognition of hard reality, align with the premises of a social model of disability that recognises the residual impacts of impairment and challenges the assumption that denial of legal capacity is automatically rights-denying.

[221] I note that the UN Disability Committee in 2019 did to an extent endorse the ALRC Report in that it recommended that Australia, 'Implement a nationally consistent supported decision-making framework, as recommended in a 2014 report of the Australian Law Reform Commission entitled *Equality, Capacity and Disability in Commonwealth Laws*'. However the Committee also expressed concern 'about the lack of progress made to abolish the guardianship system and substituted decision-making regime, particularly in decisions concerning forced psychiatric treatment…'. *Concluding Observations on Australia* (n 200) 6. The endorsement of the ALRC Report would appear to be only in respect of the ALRC's recommendation to implement a supported decision-making regime. Contrary to the prescriptions of the UN Disability Committee, the ALRC Report does also recommend the retention of the concept of 'legal capacity': ALRC Report (n 33) 290–1. One article does query whether the 2019 comments of the UN Disability Committee (above) indicate a softening of its position: Alex Ruck Keene et al, 'Mental Capacity - Why Look for a Paradigm Shift?' Medical Law Review (2023) 00, 1–18 https: // doi-org/10/1093/medlaw/fwac052

5 SUMMARY, COMMENTARY AND CONCLUSIONS

The policy and legal responses to disability and decision-making have evolved from mass institutionalisation, through guardianship to supported decision-making. Such evolution is frequently portrayed as a progression from paternalistic, autonomy-denying and discriminatory practices to ones that increasingly recognise autonomy and equality as human rights. The charity model of disability described a system where adults with cognitive disability were situated outside the Rawlsian social contract and, therefore, had no entitlement to social goods, only receiving them as an act of discretionary beneficence. A so-called medical model of disability then developed and dominated, having the detrimental impact of framing people with disability as inferior and defective, and of quarantining disability as a responsibility of and problem for the individual and not of and for society. The social model developed as a critique of the medical model to argue that it was prejudiced attitudes and ableist environments that framed impairment as disability and that impairments should be accommodated by society. Article 12 reflects the influence of the social model in its requirement that legal capacity may be achieved by adults with cognitive disability if they have the supports around them to make decisions.

The social model has been widely hailed as an extremely effective and useful advocacy tool; but it has never been fully accepted by people with disability and their supporters and has been subject to wide critique and significant review. Criticism has focused on what I refer to as the 'strict' social model, which effectively denies the reality of impairment, or the lived experience of impairment and its associated disadvantages. 'Mixed' models, referred to variously as 'biopsychosocial', 'interactive' or 'multi-factorial' have been suggested to address the limitations of the strict social model and the UN Disability Committee itself refers to a 'human rights model' of disability that recognises the impacts of impairment (albeit also endorsing recognition of universal legal capacity). I endorse what I refer to as a social model that recognises the residual impacts of impairment, arguing in later chapters that such a model demands an interpretation of Article 12 that allows for decision-making by substitutes as a last resort.

The development of the different models of disability reflects the evolution of different legal and policy responses to disability and decision-making over time, responses that have increasingly responded to calls for recognition of autonomy and personhood and the end of discrimination. Mass institutionalisation was replaced by personal guardianship, and within guardianship, capacity tests and decision-making principles evolved from paternalistic models to ones that increasingly recognised individuality and autonomy. Discriminatory capacity tests based on status and outcome have increasingly been replaced with functional tests that consider an adult's ability to understand, retain and weigh relevant information, and communicate a decision. Decision-making according to a paternalistic best interests test has started to be replaced or complemented by the substituted judgement test, whereby a substitute makes a decision in accordance with the adult's will and preferences. Since the 1990s, supported decision-making, both informal and legislated, has begun to be practised alongside decision-making by substitutes, in increasing efforts to recognise the autonomy of adults with cognitive disability. There is wide recognition, however, that the supported decision-making model is challenged by hard cases. These hard cases include decision-making by adults with severe and profound cognitive disability, where supported decisions may result in harm and when there is a fine line as to whether the adult or the supporter has actually made the decision.

Article 12 now drives the move to supported decision-making, although with ongoing contention as to whether it allows for decision-making by substitutes as a last resort. The interpretation of Article 12 as requiring the abolition of decision-making by substitutes has been bolstered by the authoritative (although not binding) prescriptions of *General Comment No 1*. Interpretative arguments supporting the abolition of decision-making by substitutes are that legal capacity includes the capacity to act, and that denial of legal capacity amounts to civil death and loss of personhood. The privileging of the value of autonomy in these arguments is especially evident in accompanying assertions that it is always possible to elicit an adult's will and preferences or make a 'best interpretation' of them; and that denial of legal capacity on the basis of mental incapacity is always discriminatory because it amounts to a denial of autonomy.

Contrary arguments are as follows: Article 12 only creates a presumption of capacity; legal capacity means only capacity to hold rights (and not to act on them); substitute decision-making amounts to 100% support; the best interpretation principle lacks transparency and accountability; decision-making by substitutes is not always rights-denying; Article 12(4) allows for decision-making by substitutes as a safeguard. An overarching argument is based on recognition of 'hard reality', which effectively acknowledges the residual impacts of impairment. In hard cases where an adult does not, in fact, have decision-making ability, decision-making by a substitute is not in itself discriminatory. In some cases, decision-making by substitutes will be inevitable; therefore, it should be made transparent and accountable.

I argue in this book against the privileging of the right to legal capacity as a human right foundational to all others. Such a privileging is unsustainable because first, it assumes that individual rights are independent and bounded, and second, it is linked with the privileging of civil–political over socio-economic rights. The principle of indivisibility of human rights challenges these assumptions and Chapter 3 begins the investigation of why and how the principle of indivisibility drives an interpretation of Article 12 as requiring decision-making by substitutes as a last resort.

3

The Principle of Indivisibility and Article 12

1 INTRODUCTION

Chapter 2 described how different capacity tests and decision-making principles have developed from the increasing acknowledgement of the right of adults with disability to lead autonomous, self-determined lives, to be respected as persons, and to be free from discriminatory treatment. It outlined the history of the debate around the drafting of Article 12, as to whether it should abolish substitute decision-making or retain it as a last resort and how the final draft represents a compromise by remaining silent on the issue. Following ratification, this debate evolved into an interpretative one. The UN Disability Committee's *General Comment No 1* prescribes that Article 12 requires recognition of universal legal capacity and the abolition of decision-making by substitutes, while many commentators advocate for an interpretation that allows decision-making by substitutes as a last resort.

Arguments that all adults can be supported to make their own decisions privilege the liberal value of autonomy and therefore conclude that decision-making by substitutes constitutes unlawful discrimination through its denial of autonomy. Arguments for retention of decision-making by substitutes as a last resort emphasise the importance of other values or outcomes, including protection from harm. They conclude that decision-making by substitutes is not always discriminatory but may be an empirical inevitability that does not necessarily result in disadvantage. I argue that recognition of this empirical reality is premised on a social model of disability that acknowledges the residual impact of impairment on the lived experience of people with cognitive disability.

This chapter introduces the main argument of this book – that the principle of indivisibility demands an interpretation of Article 12 that allows for, and even requires, decision-making by substitutes as a last resort to promote equality and social inclusion for some adults with cognitive disability, while still recognising personhood. The principle of indivisibility demands an interpretation and application of Article 12 that recognises the material reality of adults' lives, including the residual impacts of impairment and the associated socio-economic disadvantage disproportionately associated with disability. Section 2 begins by describing the history of the principle of indivisibility of human rights in UN law and doctrine. It originated with statements by the UN General Assembly in 1950 when the UN decided to split the human rights in the Universal Declaration of Human Rights ('UN Declaration')[1] between the two binding covenants: the International Covenant on Civil and Political Rights ('ICCPR')[2] and the International Covenant on Economic, Social and Cultural Rights ('ICESCR').[3] Section 3 establishes the particular concept of indivisibility, which is used as the basis for this thesis, as incorporating (a) recognition of the interdependence of human rights, and (b) recognition of the equal importance of economic, social and cultural ('socio-economic') rights with civil and political ('civil–political') rights. It further explains how the two separate categories of rights are typically demarcated from one another, but also shows that the differences are frequently overstated if not non-existent. Section 4 explains the particular importance of the principle of indivisibility in claiming the rights of people with disability because of the disproportionate levels of socio-economic disadvantage among people with disability.

Section 5 goes on to establish both the legitimacy and urgency of applying the principle of indivisibility to an interpretation of the CRPD. It describes how the principle of indivisibility is emphasised and evidenced in the text of the CRPD, more than in any other convention, and how much of the CRPD literature recognises and emphasises the principle. While much of the literature seeks to conceptualise indivisibility in the CRPD as dissolving the categories between rights, I argue that a concept of indivisibility as dissolution risks actually perpetuating the privileging of civil–political rights under the cloak of indivisibility.

Section 6 begins the analysis of how the principle of indivisibility demands an interpretation of Article 12 as requiring both supported decision-making and decision-making by substitutes as a last resort. It does this first by considering how the rights within Article 12 itself – the right to legal capacity and the right to support – are interdependent and interrelated. It shows that, while the right to legal capacity is widely agreed to be a civil-political right, the right to support is more a socio-economic right.

2 THE HISTORY OF THE PRINCIPLE OF INDIVISIBILITY

The United Nations Bill of Rights consists of the UN Declaration, adopted in 1948, and the two foundational covenants – the ICCPR and the ICESCR – both adopted

[1] *Universal Declaration*, GA Res 217A (III), UN GAOR, 3rd sess, 183rd pen mtg mtg, UN Doc UN Doc A/810 (10 December 1948) ('*UN Declaration*').

[2] *International Covenant on Civil and Political Rights, opened for signature 19 December, 1966, 999 UNTS, (entered into force 23 March 1976) ('ICCPR').*

[3] *International Covenant on Economic, Social and Cultural Rights, opened for signature 16 December, 1966, 993 UNTS 3 (entered into force 3 January 1976) ('ICESCR').*

in 1966 and ratified in 1976.[4] The rhetoric of interdependence and indivisibility began in the context of the drafting of the two foundational UN human rights covenants and has continued to evolve and be increasingly recognised in human rights instruments since that time.

2.1 *The Universal Declaration of Human Rights*

The UN Declaration is a non-binding instrument with all rights in the one document. However, when it came to incorporating these human rights into a binding treaty, it was ultimately agreed to split the rights between the two covenants, each incorporating one category of what have become known as two separate categories of rights – civil–political on the one hand and socio-economic on the other. A popular theory for why the split occurred is that it was due to Cold War Cold politics, with the West aiming to subordinate the significance of socio-economic rights and the Soviet Union aiming to privilege them. However, some theorists argue that Cold War politics were not the original cause of the schism and that the idea that only socialist political systems endorsed socio-economic rights was a later, inaccurate and ideological superimposition.[5] These two categories of rights have come to be known as 'first generation' rights (i.e. civil–political) and 'second generation' rights (i.e. socio-economic), respectively.[6]

Whelan and Donnelly point out that the United States originally supported the development of socio-economic rights, and they trace the origins of this support to the impact of the 1930s Great Depression on US politics and society.[7] Rights to liberty and freedom are stereotypically conceived of as civil–political rights, but President Roosevelt is described as linking these to socio-economic conditions in his statement that: 'We have come to a clearer realisation of the fact … that positive individual freedom cannot exist without economic security and independence'.[8] Donnelly asserts that the recognition of the importance of socio-economic rights formed the basis of the post–World War Two liberal democratic welfare state in the West.[9] Whelan and others opine that, rather than Cold War ideologies being the

[4] Jack Donnelly, *Universal Human Rights in Theory and Practice* (Cornell University Press, 3rd ed, 2013) 26.

[5] Daniel J Whelan, *Indivisible Human Rights: A History* (University of Pennsylvania Press, 2010) 32, 54; Jack Donnelly (n 4) 235–6; Daniel J Whelan and Jack Donnelly, 'The West, Economic and Social Rights, and the Global Human Rights Regime: Setting the Record Straight' (2007) 29(4) *Human Rights Quarterly* 908, 909–10.

[6] Whelan (n 5) 209–12. I choose not to use the terminology of 'generations' of rights because of its tendency to entrench or perpetuate the hierarchy of civil–political over socio-economic rights.

[7] Whelan and Donnelly (n 5) 921; William A Schabas, 'Freedom from Want: How Can We Make Indivisibility More Than a Mere Slogan?' (1999/2000) 11 *National Journal of Constitutional Law* 189, 193; Whelan (n 5) 20–5.

[8] Whelan (n 5) 28; Schabas (n 7) 193.

[9] Jack Donnelly (n 4) 253.

cause of the split between covenants, arguments around the necessity for different enforcement mechanisms for the various categories of rights were what prevailed.[10] Further discussion of these differences is included in the following text.

2.2 *Indivisibility Invoked on Division of Human Rights into Two Binding Covenants*

It was during the discussions and negotiations around the splitting of the covenants that statements of 'interdependence' and 'indivisibility' began to appear. Neither the Universal Declaration, nor the ICCPR, nor the ICESCR include references to indivisibility, yet the rhetoric and concept have, since the 1950s, gained increasing purchase in the human rights community.[11] In a meeting of the Third Committee of the UN General Assembly in 1950, in response to suggestions that the proposed covenant be split, one delegate entreated those present 'not to divide the indivisible'.[12] Not long afterwards, the General Assembly made what is now referred to as its 'unity' resolution, resolving that: '…the enjoyment of civil and political freedoms and of economic, social and cultural rights are interconnected and interdependent'.[13] The covenants eventually provided in their Preambles, recognition of the interconnectedness of the two sets of rights, the ICCPR recognising that:

> in accordance with the Universal Declaration of Human Rights, the ideal of free human beings enjoying civil and political freedom and freedom from fear and want can only be achieved if conditions are created whereby everyone may enjoy his civil and political rights, as well as his economic, social and cultural rights.[14]

And the ICESCR provides that: 'the ideal of free human beings enjoying freedom from fear and want can only be achieved if conditions are created whereby everyone may enjoy his economic, social and cultural rights, as well as his civil and political rights'.[15]

The UN's next significant statement on indivisibility came in 1968 in the Proclamation of Teheran, *Final Act of the International Conference on Human Rights*. It provided that: 'Since human rights and fundamental freedoms are

[10] Whelan (n 5) 64; Schabas (n 7) 202; Gauthier DeBeco, 'The Indivisibility of Human Rights and the Convention on the Rights of Persons with Disabilities' (2019) 68 (January) *International and Comparative Law Quarterly* 141; Michael Ashley Stein, 'Disability Human Rights' (2007) 95(1) *California Law Review* 75, 143.

[11] Whelan (n 5) 2.

[12] Ibid 76; Dorothea Anthony, 'The Human Rights Principle of Indivisibility and Its Ideological Significance in the Contemporary Age' (Dissertation, University of New South Wales, 2018) 29 <http://unsworks.unsw.edu.au/fapi/datastream/unsworks:51572/SOURCE02?view=true>.

[13] Preamble pt E para 3; Anthony (n 12) 20.

[14] *ICCPR* Preamble para 3.

[15] *ICESCR* Preamble.

indivisible, the full realisation of civil and political rights without the enjoyment of economic, social and cultural rights is impossible'.[16] Some have interpreted the Proclamation of Teheran as asserting the importance of socio-economic rights over civil–political rights.[17] While there have been criticisms of this particular formulation of the principle of indivisibility, the principle is used by many human rights advocates to argue for the rights of marginalised and disadvantaged groups, including people with disability.[18]

2.3 *Increasing References to Indivisibility by UN Institutions from 1970s*

General Assembly resolutions proclaiming the indivisibility of human rights became more prevalent in the 1970s and 1980s, culminating in the 'Vienna Declaration and Programme of Action' ('the Vienna Declaration') at the World Conference on Human Rights in 1993. The Vienna Declaration provided that: 'All human rights are universal, indivisible, and interdependent and interrelated. The international community must treat human rights globally in a fair and equal manner, on the same footing and with the same emphasis'.[19] This declaration was made at a time when the human rights of women, children, migrants, refugees and other vulnerable populations were beginning to be emphasised. Hence, the Vienna Declaration has been described as a warning against excluding minority groups from human rights protections.[20] In this way, the principle of indivisibility is closely linked with the idea of the universality of rights.[21] Others have described the Vienna Declaration as restoring the unity of human rights as originally established in the Universal Declaration and before their splitting between the covenants.[22]

2.4 *Conclusions on Status of Indivisibility as a Human Rights Principle*

The concepts of interdependence and indivisibility had their genesis in discussions surrounding the splitting of the two covenants but have since grown organically and have been used in various ways and for different purposes ever since. Quite

[16] United Nations, *Final Act of the International Conference on Human Rights*, UN Doc A/CONF.32/41 (22 April–13 May 1968) [13].

[17] Whelan (n 5) 151, 155, 163; Anthony (n 12) 24.

[18] Philip Alston, 'Disability and the Covenant on Economic, Social and Cultural Rights' in Theresia Degener and Yolan Koster-Dreese (eds), *Human Rights and Disabled Persons: Essays and Relevant Human Rights Instruments* (Martinus Nijhoff, 1995) 94, 94; Anthony (n 12) 1, 125–6.

[19] World Conference on Human Rights, *Vienna Declaration and Programme of Action*, UN Doc A/CONF.157/24 (25 June 1993) part 1 [5].

[20] Whelan (n 5) 180.

[21] Jack Donnelly (n 4) 31–2.

[22] Whelan (n 5) 176–9.

frequently, commentators have described the notion of the interdependence and indivisibility of human rights as mere rhetoric or as aspirational.[23] However, others have described indivisibility as: 'a concept at the very root of international human rights law',[24] as 'an official doctrine of the UN, supported both by the General Assembly and by the Office of the High Commissioner for Human Rights',[25] and as 'part of the normative backbone of the UN official doctrine of human rights'.[26]

3 WHAT IS MEANT BY 'THE PRINCIPLE OF INDIVISIBILITY'?

In this book, I use the term 'the principle of indivisibility' as a convenient abbreviation for the 'principle of the indivisibility, interdependence and interrelatedness of rights'.[27] However, the terms 'indivisibility' and 'interdependence' are used differently by different theorists; the differences being sometimes only terminological but at other times substantive.[28] As indicated in Chapter 1, an investigation and critique of different concepts of indivisibility and the contentions around them is beyond the scope of this book.[29] It is identified above, however, that there is clear and growing support for recognition of the principle of indivisibility; therefore, I rely on two prevalent, if not dominant, concepts in the literature. The first concept is that indivisibility is a type of interdependence between human rights. The second is that there is no hierarchy between the two traditional categories of rights (i.e. civil–political and socio-economic). I choose this formulation of the concept because in my view, it best explains the content and structure of the CRPD as explained in Section 5.

[23] Anthony (n 12) 24, 126, 235.

[24] Victoria Hamlyn, 'The Indivisibility of Human Rights: Economic, Social and Cultural Rights and the European Convention on Human Rights' (2008) 40 *Bracton Law Journal* 13, 13.

[25] James W Nickel, 'Rethinking Indivisibility: Towards a Theory of Supporting Relations between Human Rights' (2008) 30(4) *Human Rights Quarterly* 984, 985.

[26] Ariel Zylberman, 'The Indivisibility of Human Rights' (2017) 36(4) *Law and Philosophy* 389.

[27] See Chapter 1.

[28] Whelan views 'interdependence' as different from indivisibility, with 'interdependence' referring just to the interdependent relationships: Whelan (n 5) 3; on the other hand, Scott conflates the two terms: Craig Scott, 'The Interdependence and Permeability of Human Rights Norms: Towards a Partial Fusion of the International Covenants on Human Rights' (1989) 27(4) *Osgoode Hall Law Journal* 769, 779; Nickel says indivisibility and interdependence are not the same, that 'Many more rights are interdependent than are indivisible', and that 'Indivisibility is a very strong form of interdependence': Nickel (n 25) 987; but Gilabert sees indivisibility as supporting relations between rights: Pablo Gilabert, 'The Importance of Linkage Arguments for the Theory and Practice of Human Rights: A Response to James Nickel' (2010) 32(2) *Human Rights Quarterly* 425. Anthony writes that: 'We may say, in general terms, that indivisibility refers to the undividedness of rights from one another. Further, it designates the normative importance of this undivided relationship of rights … indivisibility communicates an overall idea of an integral relationship or "firm linkages" between the human rights recognised at international law'. Anthony (n 12) 3.

[29] See Chapter 1, Section 4.2; also 'the concept of indivisibility remains much debated and its meaning is still contentious': DeBeco (n 10) 145.

3.1 *Indivisibility as Interdependence between Different Rights*

The first conception of indivisibility is what Whelan refers to as recognition of the 'interdependence' between rights – that '…enjoyment of any right or group of rights requires enjoyment of others …'.[30] Typical examples are that the right to life may depend on the right to an adequate standard of living[31] and that freedom of assembly depends on an individual's right to freedom of movement, so they may arrive at the place of assembly.[32] An interdependent or 'supporting relationship' exists between the rights because 'one of them contributes to the functioning or stability of' the other.[33] The UN Disability Committee, when it writes in *General Comment No 4* on the right to inclusive education, suggests a concept of indivisibility that incorporates this type of interdependence:

> States parties must recognise the indivisibility and interdependence of all human rights. Education is integral to the full and effective realisation of other rights. Conversely the right to inclusive education can only be realised if certain other rights are implemented.[34]

Variations on this theory of interdependence have been developed and are promulgated in the literature. Shue, for example, proposed that there are certain basic rights – security rights, liberty rights and subsistence rights – the enjoyment of which is essential to the enjoyment of all other rights.[35] There is also one theory that true indivisibility would demand a type of system-wide interdependence: 'the idea that no human right can be fully realised without fully realising all other human rights'.[36] However, arguments have also been made for a less stringent concept of indivisibility as interdependence, being where the implementation of one right is 'highly useful to the fulfilment of the other'.[37]

Some explanations of interdependence refer specifically to interdependence between the two categories of rights. This type of interdependence is driven in part by significant bodies of jurisprudence whereby socio-economic rights have been

30 Whelan (n 5) 3.
31 Scott (n 28) 780.
32 Nickel (n 25) 980.
33 Ibid 987.
34 Committee on the Rights of Persons with Disabilities '*General Comment No 4 (2016) On the Right to Inclusive Education* UN Doc CRPD/C/GC/4 (25 November 2016) [44].
35 These categories are basic in that they cannot be compromised or sacrificed if any other right is to be genuinely realised: Henry Shue, *Basic Rights: Subsistence, Affluence, and U.S. Foreign Policy* (Princeton University Press, 40th anniversary ed, 2020) 1–9; discussed in Morton Emmanuel Winston, 'Indivisibility and Interdependence of Human Rights' (Public Lecture, Nebraska Union, 3 September 1999) 7.
36 To test the validity of his thesis, Nickel divides rights into seven families, pairs them into forty-two different combinations and concludes that if a claim for indivisiibility demands system-wide interdependence, then it is too strong to be defended: Nickel (n 25) 984–6.
37 Gilabert, 'The Importance of Linkage Arguments for the Theory and Practice of Human Rights' (n 28) 430.

enforced indirectly through claims of violations of civil–political rights.[38] Indirect enforcement of socio-economic rights has been prominent both in the Council of Europe, as well as in the UN, driven historically by the absence of complaint mechanisms for violations of socio-economic rights.[39] Famously, in the case of *Airey v. Ireland*, the European Court of Human Rights found that '…the mere fact that an interpretation of the Convention may extend into the sphere of social or economic rights should not be a decisive factor against such an interpretation: there is no water-tight division separating out that sphere from the field covered by the Convention'.[40]

I note that the versions of indivisibility as interdependence discussed above recognise that, at least in some cases, fulfilment of a civil–political right (e.g. the right to life) may depend on fulfilment of a socio-economic right (e.g. the right to an adequate standard of living). This shows that the concept of indivisibility as interdependence overlaps with the concept of indivisibility as recognising the equal importance of the two separate categories of rights.[41]

3.2 *Indivisibility as No Hierarchy between the Two Sets of Rights: Civil-political and Socio-economic*

Whelan is a leading proponent of the theory that indivisibility demands no hierarchy between the two traditional categories of rights.[42] Like Whelan, Copelon harks

[38] For examples in the case law under the ECHR, see: Davíđ Þór Björgvinsson, 'The Protection of the Rights of Persons with Disabilities in the Case Law of the European Court of Human Rights' in Oddný Mjöll Arnadóttir and Gerard Quinn (eds), *The UN Convention on the Rights of Persons with Disabilities: European and Scandinavian Perspectives* (Nijhoff, 2009) 141, 145–7; for examples under the ICCPR, see: Scott (n 28).

[39] While there has always been a right of complaint or communication to the UN for breaches of the ICCPR, a corresponding right under the ICESCR was introduced only in 2014 through the adoption of the *Optional Protocol to the International Covenant on Economic, Social and Cultural Rights*, opened for signature 24 September 2009, UN Doc A/RES/63/117 (entered into force 5 May 2013) ('*Optional Protocol to the ICESCR*'). Similarly, in the Council of Europe jurisdiction, while civil-political rights are subject to formal complaint mechanisms under the *European Convention on Human Rights*, socio-economic rights are included only in the non-binding *Charter of Fundamental Rights of the European Union*, 26 October 2012, 2012/C 326/02.

[40] *Airey v Ireland* (1979) 2 EHRR 305; Hamlyn (n 24) 19; Holger Kallehauge, 'General Themes Relevant to the Implementation of the UN Disability Convention into Domestic Law: Who Is Responsible for the Implementation and How Should It Be Performed?' in Oddný Mjöll Arnadóttir and Gerard Quinn (eds), *The UN Convention on the Rights of Persons with Disabilities: European and Scandinavian Perspectives* (Nijhoff, 2009) 201, 271; Anthony (n 12) 176.

[41] Gavison argues for the interdependence of the two categories of rights on the basis that they both uphold equally 'basic interests'. He illustrates this with the example that the exercise of civil and political rights may depend on the fulfilment of the socio-economic right to accommodation – for example, the civil-political right to vote and the right to bail typically depend on having a stable residential address: Ruth Gavison, 'On the Relationships between Civil and Political Rights, and Social and Economic Rights' in Jean-Marc Coicaud, Michael W Doyle and Anne-Marie Gardner (eds), *The Globalization of Human Rights* (United Nations University Press, 2003) 23, 35, 40.

[42] Whelan (n 5) 2.

back to the Universal Declaration as affirming the interdependence of the two categories, quoting Eleanor Roosevelt as saying that: 'You can't talk human rights to people who are hungry'[43] – that is, political rights of engagement and communication depend on basic rights to subsistence and an adequate standard of living. Alston similarly describes how 'full' civil-political rights may ostensibly be granted to a person with disability, but that the person may still be disenfranchised by being denied fulfilment of social needs including effective communication or essential transport.[44] DeBeco describes how 'According to this approach, giving precedence to a particular category of rights is ineffective, as neglecting one category of rights hinders fulfilment of the other'.[45] Koch makes a further argument for indivisibility, on the basis that the human rights set out in the two foundational covenants overlap,[46] thereby undermining any argument that all of the rights in the ICCPR can be privileged over all of the rights in the ICESCR.

Some arguments have been made for a theory of indivisibility that reverses the traditional hierarchy of rights.[47] This book argues that the two categories of rights are of equal importance, but that, depending on how a person is contingently situated in the real world, their immediate need may be the fulfilment of either a civil-political *or* a socio-economic right. In some cases where an adult with cognitive disability is socio-economically disadvantaged, the fulfilment of a socio-economic right may be needed in order to exercise a civil-political right to legal capacity. As one writer has put it, needs can be hierarchised whereas rights are indivisible.[48]

In summary, the formulations of the principle of indivisibility prevalent in the human rights literature as recognising (1) the interdependence of rights in and between categories, and (2) the equal importance of socio-economic rights with civil–political rights, are applied in this book to interpret the CRPD and Article

[43] Rhonda Copelon, 'The Indivisible Framework of International Human Rights: A Source of Social Justice in the U.S'. (1998) 3(1) *New York City Law Review* 59, 59–60.

[44] Philip Alston (n 18) 95–6.

[45] DeBeco (n 10) 147.

[46] Ida Elisabeth Koch, 'Social Rights as Components in the Civil Right to Personal Liberty: Another Step Forward in the Integrated Human Rights Approach?' (2002) 20(1) *Netherlands Quarterly of Human Rights* 29, 33. Article 1 of each of the *ICCPR* and *ICESCR* establishes the right of peoples to self-determination; Articles 2 and 3 of each includes the right to non-discrimination; Article 8 *ICCPR* prohibits forced labour and Article 6 *ICESCR* recognises the right to gain a living through work; Article 23 *ICCPR* guarantees the family as the fundamental unit of society, and Article 10 *ICESCR* also recognises the right to family protection and assistance.

[47] Whelan writes how 1970s 'revisionism' held that socio-economic rights had priority over civil-political rights: Whelan (n 5) 7; Hamlyn argues that the practice of indirectly enforcing socio-economic rights through complaints mechanisms for breaches of civil-political rights, raises the status of socio-economic rights to fundamental rights: Hamlyn (n 24) 19; Anthony, on the other hand, argues that it may in fact serve to underscore the relative importance of civil-political rights: Anthony (n 12) 178.

[48] Suzanne Cahill, *Dementia and Human Rights* (Policy Press at the University of Bristol, 2018) 14.

12. Before considering how this formulation is reflected and applied in the CRPD, Section 3.3 (this chapter) explains why and how the traditional demarcation of categories has developed and Section 3.4 (this chapter) explains why the principle of indivisibility is important for disability rights.

3.3 *Traditional Demarcations Between the Two Categories of Rights and Challenges to the Hierarchy*

As described above, the principle of indivisibility began to evolve with the splitting of the human rights in the Universal Declaration into two binding covenants. While the rhetoric of interdependence and indivisibility prevailed, civil–political rights have nevertheless been widely considered of greater importance than socio-economic rights,[49] a view challenged by the principle of indivisibility as described above. This notional hierarchy has, in turn, been based on ostensible differences between the two sets of rights, the main ones being that civil–political rights are the only 'true' human rights and that, unlike socio-economic rights, they always require the State to abstain from action.[50]

This section describes the traditional markers but also how the basis of bifurcation has been challenged, such challenges lending support to the equal importance of the two categories of rights.[51] The principle of indivisibility demands recognition that rights in both categories are 'true' human rights, whether or not they require restraint or positive action by the State.

3.3.1 Socio-economic Rights Are Not 'True' Rights at All, Unlike Civil–Political Rights

One view is that socio-economic rights are not really rights at all but mere aspirations and should be treated as goals of economic and social policy[52] or as political aims rather than rights.[53] However, the Office of the High Commissioner for Human Rights has made it clear that the ICESCR 'neither requires nor precludes

49 Lisa A Crooms, 'Indivisible Rights and Intersectional Identities or, "What Do Women's Human Rights Have To Do with the Race Convention?"' (1997) 40(3) *Howard Law Journal* 619, 627; Jack Donnelly (n 4) 40.

50 Stephen P Marks, 'The Past and Future of the Separation of Human Rights into Categories' (2009) 24 *Maryland Journal of International Law* 209.

51 Kristin Henrard, 'Introduction: The Justiciabiity of ESC Rights and the Interdependence of all Fundamental Rights' (2009) 2(4) *Erasmus Law Review* 373, 373–4; Marks (n 50).

52 Philip Alston and Gerard Quinn, 'The Nature and Scope of States Parties' Obligations under the International Covenant on Economic, Social and Cultural Rights' (1987) 9(2) *Human Rights Quarterly* 156, 158. Sandra Fredman, *Human Rights Transformed: Positive Rights and Positive Duties* (Oxford University Press, 2008) 844.

53 Martha Jackman and Bruce Porter, 'Social and Economic Rights' in Peter Oliver, Patrick Macklem and Nathalie Des Rosiers (eds), *The Oxford Handbook of the Canadian Constitution* (Oxford University Press, 2017) 843, 1.

any particular form of political or economic system … provided only that it is democratic'.[54] In rebuttal to the charge that socio-economic rights are merely aspirational, Alston and Quinn argue that Article 2 ICESCR imposes a 'clear legal undertaking' on States,[55] with the words:

> 1. Each State Party to the present Covenant undertakes to take steps, individually and through international assistance and co-operation, especially economic and technical, to the maximum of its available resources, with a view to achieving progressively the full realization of the rights recognized in the present Covenant by all appropriate means, including particularly the adoption of legislative measures.

Arguments that ICESCR rights are less determinate than those in the ICCPR and much less precisely defined have been used to support the assertion that they resemble policy goals rather than rights. But once again, Alston and Quinn challenge this contention on the grounds that even if less determinate, the rights are nevertheless real and that States are obliged to give them substance and meaning.[56]

3.3.2 Negative versus Positive Obligations, Cost-Free Versus Resource-Intensive

The charge of indeterminacy of socio-economic rights, as compared with civil-political rights, is also linked to typical classifications of socio-economic rights as imposing positive obligations on states and civil-political rights as imposing negative obligations or obligations of restraint.[57] By this, it is meant, for example, that the civil-political right to freedom of speech places an obligation on the State of non-intervention (i.e. to abstain from censorship).[58] Relevantly, some would say that the civil-political right to legal capacity requires state non-interference (i.e. restraint from imposing a guardianship order). The right to health, though, is socio-economic and places a positive obligation on the State to ensure the provision of goods and services.

Aligned with the supposed negative/positive bifurcation is the distinction made between civil-political rights as being supposedly 'cost-free' and socio-economic rights as being 'resource-intensive'.[59] Acknowledgement of the resource-intensiveness

[54] Committee on Economic Social and Cultural Rights, *General Comment No 3: The Nature of States Parties' Obligations*, UN Doc E/199/23 (14 December 1990) [8] ('ESCR *General Comment No 3*').

[55] Alston and Quinn (n 52) 166.

[56] Alston and Quinn (n 52) 220, 222.

[57] Fredman asserts that positive duties in human rights are sufficiently determinative to be normative, and that precise standards for implementation are not essential as long as clear parameters can be set: Fredman (n 52) 65.

[58] Ida Elisabeth Koch, 'From Invisibility to Indivisibility: The International Convention on the Rights of Persons with Disabilities' in Oddný Mjöll Arnadóttir and Gerard Quinn (eds), *The UN Convention on the Rights of Persons with Disabilities: European and Scandinavian Perspectives* (Nijhoff, 2009) 67, 71.

[59] Henrard (n 51) 373–4; Fredman (n 52) 70; Marks (n 50) 236.

of socio-economic rights, together with the practical need to place limits on expenditure, can be found in Article 2 ICESCR. Article 2 requires states '…to take steps … to the maximum of [their] available resources' to progressively implement the rights in the ICESCR. There is no equivalent provision in the ICCPR, implying that implementation of those rights is resource-free.[60]

However, the idea that the bifurcation of rights can be justified on the basis that they are supposedly realised through either positive or negative actions is now widely challenged,[61] with assertions made that: 'All human rights require both positive action and restraint on the part of the State'.[62] A common example is the right to a fair trial,[63] a civil right that demands the active creation of an independent, accountable (and costly) courts system. Fredman gives the example of the right to adequate housing, which can require either the positive provision of goods and services or restraint by way of abstention from eviction.[64] Alston and Quinn conclude that:

> the reality is that full realisation of civil and political rights is heavily dependent both on availability of resources and the development of the necessary societal structures. The suggestion that realisation of civil and political rights requires only abstention on the part of the state and can be achieved without significant expenditure is patently at odds with reality.[65]

3.3.3 Immediate versus Progressive Implementation

The source of a further ostensible difference between the two categories is found in the exhortation in Article 2 ICESCR that the realisation of the rights it contains may be achieved 'progressively'.[66] Once again, there is no parallel provision in the ICCPR, with the result that civil–political rights have been taken to be immediately realisable.[67] Alston and Quinn point out, though, that the full realisation of civil–political rights may in practical terms also be progressive rather than immediate, given the resources required to build civil and political institutions from the ground up.[68] The Committee on Economic, Social and Cultural Rights ('the

60 *ESCR General Comment No* 3 [9].

61 Gavison (n 41) 33; Henrard (n 51) 374; Marks (n 50); Hamlyn (n 24).

62 Jack Donnelly (n 4) 443.

63 *ICCPR* Article 14.

64 Fredman (n 52) 2.

65 Alston and Quinn (n 52) 172; see also, 'The right to vote, for example, is a CP concern requiring action and positive expense …' and 'In other words, the protection of CP rights may require the imposition of positive duties and public expenditure no less than that these are required for the protection of SE rights'. Gavison (n 41) 35.

66 Article 2 requires a State 'to take steps … to the maximum of its available resources, with a view to achieving progressively the full realisation of the rights recognised in the present Covenant': *ICESCR*.

67 *ESCR General Comment No* 3 [9].

68 Alston and Quinn (n 52) 175.

ESCR Committee') points out that while there has been a widespread emphasis on the different implementation obligations under the two covenants, 'there are also significant similarities'.[69] In particular, the obligation under Article 2 is for States to 'take steps' that are '…deliberate, concrete and targeted', and that despite resource constraints, States have 'minimum core obligations', particularly in relation to vulnerable persons.[70]

3.3.4 Justiciable versus Non-Justiciable

Another argument for the lesser importance of socio-economic rights is that they are not justiciable and are therefore not enforceable like 'real' (i.e. civil–political) human rights.[71] The Optional Protocol to the ICCPR, aadopted in 1966 and entering into force in 1976, includes the right of an individual to make complaints (i.e. 'communications') to the Human Rights Committee about violations of the ICCPR.[72] One of the reasons provided at the time for splitting the covenants in two was that they required different enforcement methods for implementation,[73] with it being agreed ultimately that the appropriate enforcement method for rights under the ICESCR would be limited to States' periodic reporting.[74] The view prevailed that if socio-economic rights were made justiciable by way of communication and adjudication, this would place too much political power in the hands of the judiciary.[75] However, in 2009, the Optional Protocol to the ICESCR was adopted, and ratified in 2013, providing for a right of communication[76] and mirroring the communication mechanism in the ICCPR.

Even before formal justiciability of socio-economic rights was introduced via the Optional Protocol, challenges had been made to the premise that lack of justiciability meant that they were not 'true' rights. Arguments prevail that enforcement is not all about justiciability,[77] and also that debates about enforceability have limited value in that they take the focus away from important normative issues to consider only what happens when rights are violated.[78] Henrard points out that it is up to

69 *ESCR General Comment No 3* [1].

70 Ibid [10].

71 Ida Elisabeth Koch, 'Economic, Social and Cultural Rights as Components in Civil and Political Rights: A Hermeneutic Perspective' (2006) 10(4) *International Journal of Human Rights* 405, 405; Jack Donnelly (n 4) 242; Marks (n 50) 213; Fredman (n 52) 2.

72 *Optional Protocol to the International Covenant on Civil and Political Rights*, opened for signature 16 December 1966, 999 UNTS 171 (entered into force 23 March 1976) Article 1.

73 Whelan (n 5) 64; Schabas (n 7) 202.

74 Whelan (n 5); see *ICESCR* Articles 16, 17.

75 Alston and Quinn (n 52) 170.

76 *Optional Protocol to the ICESCR* Article 2.

77 Iain Byrne, 'The Importance of Economic, Social and Cultural Rights in Guaranteeing Civil and Political Rights within the Euro-Mediterranean Partnership' (2004) 9(3) *Mediterranean Politics* 344, 346.

78 Fredman (n 52) 175.

States and the UN system to more clearly define and circumscribe the content of socio-economic rights, so that their justiciability increases.[79] Arguments in favour of the equal justiciability of the two sets of rights are growing and, in turn, lending support to the claim for equal importance of the two sets of rights and associated claims of indivisibility.[80]

3.3.5 Protecting the Individual from the State versus State Action/Intervention/Intrusion in the Personal Sphere

A final basis for differentiating between the two sets of rights and for privileging civil-political rights is found in the widely accepted premise that human rights are 'solely designed to protect the individual from the State'.[81]

Feminists and others have criticised liberalism for constructing the family as somehow natural and apolitical, in a way that shrouds relationships of power and oppression within the family, thereby justifying the State's reluctance to interfere in family relations.[82] This privileging of the private sphere as apolitical is reflected in the traditional description of civil-political rights as requiring abstention from state interference.[83] However, as already described above, fulfilment of both civil-political and socio-economic rights can demand comprehensive government policies and programs that impact on personal lives. Civil rights require extensive legal systems, as well as health and social services, to ensure the liberty and security of the person and freedom from inhumane treatment. These services may indeed

79 Henrard (n 51) 375.

80 Li-Ann Thio, 'The Universal Declaration of Human Rights at 60: Universality, Indivisibility and the Three Generations of Human Rights' (2009) 21(1) *Singapore Academy of Law Journal* 293, 310.

81 Philip Alston, 'Disability and the Covenant on Economic, Social and Cultural Rights' in Theresia Degener and Yolan Koster-Dreese (eds), *Human Rights and Disabled Persons: Essays and Relevant Human Rights Instruments* (Martinus Nijhoff, 1995) 94, 97; 'the state is considered to be the principal source of unfreedom threatening individual rights and hence should be constrained by every available means …': Getahun A Mosissa, A *Re-examination of Economic, Social and Cultural Rights in a Political Society in the Light of the Principle of Human Dignity* (Intersentia, 2020) 36.

82 Ibid; 'The covenants, in turn, follow the traditional dichotomy between "negative" and "positive" rights. A negative right connotes freedom from interference and, as such, appears to require mere forbearance on the part of the state': Chisanga Puta-Chekwe and Nora Flood, 'From Division to Integration: Economic, Social and Cultural Rights as Basic Human Rights' in Isfahan Merali and Valerie Oosterveld (eds), *Giving Meaning to Economic, Social, and Cultural Rights* (University of Pennsylvania Press, 2001) 39, 41.

83 Camillia Kong, 'The Convention on the Rights of Persons with Disabilities and Article 12: Prospective Feminist Lessons against the "Will and Preferences" Paradigm' (2015) 4(4) *Laws* 709, 714–16; 'the traditional liberal approach that civil and political rights (sometimes referred to as negative rights, in the sense of freedom from interference': Bernadette McSherry and Penelope Weller, 'Rethinking Rights-Based Mental Health Laws' in Bernadette McSherry and Penelope Weller (eds), *Rethinking Rights-Based Mental Health Laws* (Bloomsbury Publishing, 2010) 6, 6.

affect personal lives in positive ways and redefine the boundaries between the individual and the State.[84]

3.4 Conclusion and Commentary on Definition of Indivisibility

In summary, while there may still be some theorists and practitioners who consider the concepts of interdependence and indivisibility to be mere rhetorical flourishes, there is a growing body of literature that supports these principles as fundamental human rights doctrine. It would be wrong to say that there is one, settled and universally agreed meaning attributed to the principle of indivisibility. Nevertheless, by way of overview, I have distilled the various theories into two broad concepts, and it is these two associated concepts of indivisibility on which I rely in interpreting and applying Article 12.

The first concept describes indivisibility as a system of interdependency or supporting relationships between rights, so that some rights cannot be realised without the realisation of other rights. The second broad concept of indivisibility is that the two categories of rights are of equal importance, reflecting a correction to the historical privileging of civil-political over socio-economic rights. These two concepts of indivisibility are complementary and overlap, given that interdependency of rights applies within and between categories. Extensive critique and interrogation of different theories of the principle of invisibility are beyond the scope of this book, which focuses on how the principle is particularised and applied in the CRPD.

The stereotypical differences between the two categories of rights have fed into the historical and lingering framing of civil-political rights as the only 'true' human rights. civil-political rights have been typified as requiring only negative state action or restraint, as being cost-free, as immediately realisable, as justiciable, and as protecting the individual from the State. On the other hand, socio-economic rights have been typified as policy-oriented, indeterminate and aspirational; as requiring positive state action; as resource-intensive; as progressively realisable; as non-justiciable; and as requiring state intervention or intrusion into personal lives. However, the legitimacy of these stereotyped differences has been widely challenged in the literature and is further challenged by the CRPD, as explained below.

I argue, though, that interpretations of Article 12 that require the abolition of decision-making by substitutes privilege civil–political rights, contrary to the

[84] Jennifer Nedelsky, *Law's Relations: A Relational Theory of Self, Autonomy, and the Law* (Oxford University Press, 2012) 125–9; 'The [CRPD] therefore adopts a particular conceptual view of the state's role in securing individual rights as including more than simple abstinence from the abuse of individuals' civil and political rights'. Colm O'Cinneide, 'Extracting Protection for the Rights of Persons with Disabilities from Human Rights Frameworks: Established Limits and New Possibilities' in Oddný Mjöll Arnadóttir and Gerard Quinn (eds), *The UN Convention on the Rights of Persons with Disabilities: European and Scandinavian Perspectives* (Nijhoff, 2009) 163.

principle of indivisibility. In so doing, these interpretations also privilege those characteristics of rights that are stereotyped as marking civil–political rights. In particular, interpretations of the right to legal capacity as requiring the abolition of decision-making by substitutes privilege autonomy as non-interference (i.e. 'negative' state action). They also rely on a concept of equality as restraint from certain (i.e. discriminatory) state actions.[85] I argue that more complex concepts of autonomy, personhood and equality[86] are required to recognise that the indivisibility of human rights acknowledges the interdependent relationships between rights and the equal importance of socio-economic rights with civil–political rights.

4 INDIVISIBILITY, DISABILITY AND THE CRPD: THE IMPORTANCE OF SOCIO-ECONOMIC RIGHTS

Several commentators have described the CRPD as incorporating the principle of indivisibility more than does any other human rights convention.[87] This section outlines the history that led to the inclusion of both civil–political and socio-economic rights in the CRPD and why the recognition of the indivisibility of rights is of particular importance to disability.

4.1 *From Social Policy to Human Rights*

Theresia Degener, former Chair of the UN Disability Committee, describes how the UN Yearbooks from 1946 to 1970 referred to people with disability in only three roles: as refugees, as persons in need of rehabilitation and welfare, and as recipients of social security.[88] She recounts how from 1980 to 2000, people with disability came to be positioned in a human rights context, but even then, as 'objects' rather than 'subjects' of human rights. It was only with the new millennium that people with disability have come to be recognised as subjects of human rights as enshrined

85 See further discussion in Chapter 6.

86 See Chapters 4, 5 and 6, respectively.

87 '...the CRPD aspires to manifest the mandate that human rights are 'indivisible, interrelated and interconnected': Michael Ashley Stein and Janet E Lord, 'Future Prospects for the United Nations Convention on the Rights of Persons with Disabilities' in Oddný Mjöll Arnadóttir and Gerard Quinn (eds), *The UN Convention on the Rights of Persons with Disabilities: European and Scandinavian Perspectives* (Nijhoff, 2009) 17, 24; Koch, 'From Invisibility to Indivisibility' (n 58) 67–72; DeBeco (n 10) 155; Amsalu Darge Mayessa, 'Overview of the Notion of Integration of Human Rights: Giving Pragmatic Value to Socio-Economic Rights Rather Than Rim Service' (2014) 83 *Nordic Journal of International Law* 168, 192.

88 Theresia Degener and Andrew Begg, 'From Invisible Citizens to Agents of Change: A Short History of the Struggle for the Recognition of the Rights of Persons with Disabilities at the United Nations' in Valentina Della Fina, Rachele Cera and Giuseppe Palmisano (eds), *The United Nations Convention on the Rights of Persons with Disabilities: A Commentary* (Springer International Publishing, 2017) 1, 1, 3.

ultimately in the CRPD.[89] While disability had been receiving attention from UN institutions since the UN's inception, it had nevertheless originally been invisible as a human rights issue and segregated as predominantly (or only) a social policy issue.[90] This segregation also occurred at a time when the dominant view of socio-economic rights was that they merely reflected social policy, were aspirational, not enforceable as 'true' rights, and were positioned below civil–political rights in the traditional hierarchy. It was only with the new millennium that an extensive literature grew up around socio-economic rights, giving shape to them both normatively and institutionally.[91]

The subordination of socio-economic rights had been evident in and driven by the different UN institutional arrangements for the two covenants. Oversight of the ICESCR had originally been the responsibility of the Economic and Social Council;[92] while oversight and monitoring of the ICCPR had always been by the Human Rights Committee, as established under the ICCPR itself.[93] It was only in 1985 that the Economic and Social Council established the Committee on Economic, Social and Cultural Rights to specifically monitor and oversee implementation of the ICESCR.[94] These different institutional arrangements reflected and drove the conception of socio-economic rights as being social policy issues outside the agenda of 'human rights' and underpinned a lexicon whereby the term 'human rights' was taken by implication to refer to civil–political rights only. Degener further describes how until the 2000s, disability was:

> segregated as a social policy question, apart from any rights-based discussion. The Special Rapporteur, for example, reported to the Commission for Social Development in New York and not to the Commission on Human Rights in Geneva. While in theory the two commissions had equal status, the Commission for Social Development was in reality a poor cousin.[95]

At a time when socio-economic rights were widely devalued and socio-economic inequalities were still conceived of in social policy terms rather than as triggering human rights claims, disability policy was lumped with socio-economic rights and accorded the same secondary status. It was in this context that disability advocates

[89] Ibid 2, 11.

[90] Ibid 4–10; Brynhildur G Flóvenz, 'The Implementation of the UN Convention and the Development of Economical and Social Rights as Human Rights' in Oddný Mjöll Arnadóttir and Gerard Quinn (eds), *The UN Convention on the Rights of Persons with Disabilities: European and Scandinavian Perspectives* (Martinus Nijhoff, 2009) 257, 258.

[91] DeBeco (n 10) 144; Rhadhika Balakrishnan, James Heintz and Diane Elson, *Rethinking Economic Policy for Social Justice: The Radical Potential of Human Rights* (Routledge, 2016) 25.

[92] Philip Alston (n 18) 99.

[93] *ICCPR* Article 28.

[94] Philip Alston (n 18) 99.

[95] Degener and Begg (n 88) 10.

began to realise that the civil-political rights of people with disability had been largely neglected, and a move began towards recognition of disability as a human rights issue.[96] I suggest that the justified urgency around claiming disability as a human rights issue, and especially as a civil-political rights issue, was shaped in part by the traditional prejudice that civil-political rights were the only true human rights.

In 1995, Quinn suggested changing the rights focus for people with disability from socio-economic rights to civil-political rights to 'mainstream' people with disability. That this was a radical approach for the time is revealed when he writes that:

> It may therefore seem somewhat paradoxical to dwell on the civil and political rights aspects of disability as instanced by the International Covenant on Civil and Political Rights (ICCPR). Indeed, we seem more accustomed to process the legitimate claims of persons with disabilities almost exclusively through the prism of the more overtly 'substantive' catalogue of economic, social and cultural rights. However, rhetoric alone indicates the close connection between the specifically civil rights framework and such socio-economic advances. After all, the quest for greater equality and inclusion is generally framed in the language of civil rights.[97]

This passage signals an ethical, legal and institutional urgency around claiming civil-political rights for people with disability. While the passage describes a 'close connection' between the two sets of rights, I suggest that it nevertheless anticipates adoption or internalisation of the traditional prejudices against socio-economic rights. This is suggested in its counter-posing of 'civil rights' with 'socio-economic *advances*' [emphasis added] and also in proposing that claims to equality and inclusion need to be reframed as demands for civil rights, not as socio-economic rights.[98] The emerging emphasis on civil-political rights in disability advocacy, which has gained significant momentum since 1995, constitutes a much-needed correction to the historical civil-political exclusion of people with disability. However, I argue that the UN Disability Committee's assertion that the fulfilment of the civil-political right to legal capacity is a pre-condition to the exercise of all other rights[99] is an over-correction of historical prejudices, which ignores the principle of indivisibility and risks devaluing socio-economic rights for people with disability.

96 Lisa Waddington, 'Evolving Disability Policies from Social Welfare to Human Rights: An International Trend from a European Perspective' (2001) 19 *Netherlands Quarterly of Human Rights* 141, 141–2.

97 Gerard Quinn, 'The International Covenant on Civil and Political Rights and Disability: A Conceptual Framework' in Theresia Degener and Yolan Koster-Dreese (eds), *Human Rights and Disabled Persons* (Martinus Nijhoff, 1995) 69, 69, 70.

98 See further discussion in Chapter 6.

99 Committee on the Rights of Persons with Disabilities, *General Comment No 1 Article 12: Equal Recognition before the Law* UN Doc CRPD/C/GC/1 (19 May 2014) [8] ('*General Comment No 1*').

4.2 *The Importance of Indivisibility for Disability*

I argue that the principle of indivisibility is of particular consequence for people with disability. This section describes how socio-economic disadvantage is experienced disproportionately by people with disability (including cognitive disability). People with disability may be situated so that, in practical terms, the fulfilment of socio-economic rights is a pre-condition to fulfilling their right to legal capacity and other civil, economic, political and social rights. The section goes on to explain how the principle of indivisibility, aligned with a social model of disability that recognises the residual impacts of impairment, allows for much-needed welfare and health services to be claimed as rights and not received as charity or as acts of rights-denying paternalism.

4.2.1 Poverty and Disability: Indivisibility Can Reframe Welfare as a Right, Not an Act of Charity

The socio-economic disadvantage suffered by people with disability is well documented both by the UN and in regional reporting,[100] and the Preamble of the CRPD itself recognises 'that the majority of persons with disabilities live in conditions of poverty'.[101] Morris, in writing about the discrimination faced by persons with disability, states that: 'Poverty is probably the most important social factor … Impairment and illness bring additional costs, yet an increased risk of poverty also means that resources are often not available to buy equipment or personal assistance'.[102] Poverty can be a cause of or contributor to social and political (not just economic) exclusion.

[100] In 2011 the World Bank and the World Health Organization published their 'World Report on Disability', which found that people with disability have lower educational and employment outcomes and are more likely to be poor than other people, both in developed and developing countries: World Health Organization and the World Bank, *World Report on Disability 2011* (World Health Organization, 2011) 39. The Australian Council of Social Service reported in 2018 that people with disability experience risk of poverty well above the average of the wider population: Australian Council of Social Service and University of New South Wales, *Poverty in Australia 2018* (Australian Council of Social Service, in partnership with the University of New South Wales, 2018) 58. In Canada, a report published in 2009 showed that approximately 75% of adults with intellectual disabilities were living in poverty: Sheila Bennett and Tiffany L Gallagher, 'Inclusion, Education, and Transition to Employment: A Work in Progress' in Dorothy Griffiths, Frances Owen and Shelley L Watson (eds), *The Human Rights Agenda for Persons with Intellectual Disabilities* (NADD, 2012) 81, 86. In 2010, United States Census Bureau statistics showed that adults with disability were more than twice as likely to fall below the poverty line as those without: Amber Knight, 'Democratizing Disability: Achieving Inclusion (without Assimilation) through "Participatory Parity"' (2015) 30(1) *Hypatia* 97, 104–5; see also Anna Lawson, 'The Human Rights Act 1998 and Disabled People: A Right To Be Human?' in Colin Harvey (ed), *Human Rights in the Community: Rights as Agents for Change* (Hart Publishing, 2005) 135, 136.

[101] Preamble para 19.

[102] Jenny Morris, 'Impairment and Disability: Constructing an Ethics of Care that Promotes Human Rights' (2001) 16(4) *Hypatia* 1, 7.

Socio-economic rights have always included rights to welfare, social protection, social security and government assistance,[103] and yet welfare has often been derided in the disability literature as always rights-denying.[104] The CRPD has been hailed as effecting a paradigm shift by reconfiguring disability away from a 'needs-based', 'welfare' issue that portrays people as 'dependent welfare recipients',[105] and 'from medical and paternalistic approaches' that saw people with disability 'as mere receivers of protection, rehabilitation or welfare'.[106] In the twenty-first century, welfare and other forms of social security are not popularly conceived of as human rights, and historical prejudices against the legitimacy of socio-economic rights linger. Denigration of social security recipients by governments and by sections of the broader community has led to a perception of people receiving government services as a burden or a drain on society,[107] leading also to internalised self-stigma by some recipients.[108]

The stigma attaching to the term 'welfare' may mean that we need to find new language, but I argue that the principle of indivisibility can help to reinvest 'welfare' (or any term that replaces it) with the language of human rights. As many commentators have identified, provision of social goods and services by the State is not in itself rights-denying, but the arbitrary and discretionary way in which services are

103 *UN Declaration*: Article 2 protects the right to social security; Article 23 provides that work must be paid with 'just remuneration … and supplemented, if necessary, by other means of social protection'; Article 24 includes the right to '…necessary social services, and the right to security in the event of unemployment, sickness, disability … [etc.]'; Article 25 provides that 'Motherhood and childhood are entitled to special care and assistance'. *ICESCR*: Article 9 provides for the right to 'social security, including social insurance'; Article 10 provides for the right to social security benefits for mothers, and 'special measures of protection and assistance' for children.

104 Shane Clifton, *Hierarchies of Power: Disability Theories and Models and Their Implications for Violence against, and Abuse, Neglect, and Exploitation of, People with Disability* (Royal Commission into Violence, Abuse, Neglect and Exploitation of People with Disability, 2020) 4–5; 'Ambassador MacKay, Chairman of the Ad Hoc Committee … characterised the CRPD as embodyding a "paradigm shift" away from a social welfare response to disability to a rights-based approach', in Rosemary Kayess and Philip French, 'Out of Darkness into Light? Introducing the Convention on the Rights of Persons with Disabilities' (2008) 8(1) *Human Rights Law Review* 1, 3.

105 Amita Dhanda, 'Constructing a New Human Rights Lexicon: Convention on the Rights of Persons with Disabilities' (2008) 8 *Sur – Revista Internacional de Direitos Humanos* 43; Theresia Degener, 'A New Human Rights Model of Disability' in Valentina Della Fina, Rachele Cera and Giuseppe Palmisano (eds), *The United Nations Convention on the Rights of Persons with Disabilities: A Commentary* (Springer International Publishing, 2017) 41, 44.

106 Catalina Devandas Aguilar, *Report of the Special Rapporteur on the Rights of Persons with Disabilities*, UN Doc A/HRC/37/56 (12 December 2017).

107 Kayess and French point out that people with disabilities are more than justified in their mistrust of government and welfare services given the history of abuse of executive power evident in mass institutionalisation and other objectionable practices: Kayess and French (n 104) 26.

108 Shakespeare writes that 'media and government discourse around welfare benefits can result in negativity towards claimants', leading the public to make a distinction between 'genuine' recipients and others: Tom Shakespeare, *Disability: The Basics* (Routledge, 2018) 76.

often delivered can be.[109] Recognition of the interdependence of rights and of the equal importance of socio-economic rights can serve as an important platform from which people can claim social security and support services as human rights rather than receive them as objects of charity. A social model that recognises the residual impacts of impairment demands that we recognise the particular socio-economic vulnerability of many people with disability.

4.2.2 Guaranteeing the Socio-economic Right to Health: But Not under a 'Medical Model'

The higher rates of poverty experienced by people with disability generally place them at greater risk of health problems while also acting as a barrier to accessing health services.[110] People with disability can be at higher risk of respiratory disease, swallowing difficulties, use of psychotropic medication, and conditions such as epilepsy, Down syndrome and cerebral palsy.[111] Disparities in access include unavailability of dentistry[112] and gynaecological services and screening services for cancers, sexually transmitted infections and osteoporosis (the latter being more prevalent due in part to medication side effects).[113] Moreover, universal health services, as they are currently provided, are not sufficient to meet the needs of persons with disability, who often suffer particular health problems not experienced to the same degree by other members of the community.[114] These conditions are exacerbated by the lack of accessible services, but at the same time, and despite the vicious cycle of disadvantage, it is the nature of the impairment that can create the need for specialist health care in the first instance.

[109] Social services have become oppressive because of the way they have been administered – with surveillance, copious paperwork, mandatory appointments and bureaucratic decisions imposed on individuals without adequate consultation or input: Nancy J Hirschmann, 'Disability Rights, Social Rights, and Freedom' (2016) 12(1) *Journal of International Political Theory* 42, 46; Nedelsky writes that welfare itself does not inhibit autonomy, but the way the law sets up administration regimes can be demeaning, and she suggests it could be remedied partly by increased access to information and natural justice: Nedelsky (n 84) 66; Morris writes of so-called welfare 'dependence': 'Independence is not about doing everything yourself but about having control over how help is provided', in Morris (n 102) 7–8.

[110] Shelley L Watson and Stephanie Hayes, 'The Right to Accessible Health Care for Persons with Intellectual Disabilities' in Dorothy Griffiths, Frances Owen and Shelley L Watson (eds), *The Human Rights Agenda for Persons with Intellectual Disabilities* (NADD, 2012) 59, 62.

[111] Ibid; Office of the Public Advocate (Qld), *Upholding the Right to Life and Health: A Review of the Deaths in Care of People with Disability in Queensland (A Systemic Advocacy Report* (February 2016) 29–47.

[112] 'Another response described a person in residential care who had no visits to the dentist for at least five years' in Royal Commission into Violence Abuse Neglect and Exploitation of People with Disability, *Overview of Responses to Health Issues Paper* (Issues Paper, October 2020) 4.

[113] Watson and Hayes (n 110) 62–8, 75; Office of the Public Advocate (Qld), *Upholding the Right to Life and Health* (n 111) 51–4.

[114] Watson and Hayes (n 110) 59, 63.

The Disability Royal Commission has described the right to health as an 'enabling right' because: 'Health is critical to support the independence and inclusion of people with disability'.[115] Similarly, Brolan et al recognise that the fulfilment of the right to health in Article 25 CRPD:

> can facilitate the advancement of other key rights, such as the right to life (CRPD, Article 10), protecting the integrity of the person (CRPD, Article 17), and the right of persons with disability to an adequate standard of living and social protection (CRPD, Article 28).[116]

A 2016 report by Queensland's Office of the Public Advocate concluded that people with disability can have complex health needs leading to increased risks of premature mortality. It made a range of recommendations for residential facilities, including greater access to specialist medical practitioners; improved training of health professionals and support staff; accreditation of 'disability medicine' as a specialisation;[117] and 'Wherever possible, the use of agency, temporary or casual staff should be avoided'.[118] The list of recommendations illustrates how the fulfilment of rights and entitlements for adults with disability, including cognitive disability, requires significant socio-economic resources and positive measures by government, not just restraint or negative action.

4.3 *Summary and Conclusions*

This section pointed out that, while disability has been an issue of concern for the UN since its inception, its institutions originally failed to position adults with disability as claimants of civil-political rights. The institutions governing the implementation of the ICESCR (but not the ICCPR) were originally focused on disability, but at a time when the dominant framing of socio-economic rights was that they were not 'true' rights but reflected mere social policy aspirations. In this way, the lack of focus for people with disability on the more highly valued civil-political rights served to exclude them from being 'true' human rights claimants.

This led in the 1990s to a move by disability advocates to correct this exclusion by emphasising the position of people with disability as claimants of civil-political

115 Royal Commission into Violence Abuse Neglect and Exploitation of People with Disability, *Health Care for People with Cognitive Disability* (Issues Paper 2019) 2.

116 Claire E Brolan et al, 'The Right to Health of Australians with Intellectual Disability' (2011) 17(2) *Australian Journal of Human Rights* 1, 13; also Harpur makes a link between the right to health and the right to life: Paul Harpur, 'The Evolving Nature of the Right to Life: The Impact of Positive Human Rights Obligations' (2007) 9 *University of Notre Dame Australia Law Review* 95, 101–2; see also: 'The recognition that all human rights are interdependent, indivisible and interrelated further reinforces the obligation to attend to the right to health'. Penelope Weller, 'The Right to Health: The Convention on the Rights of Persons with Disabilities' (2010) 35(2) *Alternative Law Journal* 66, 66–7; McSherry and Weller (n 83) 13.

117 Office of the Public Advocate (Qld), *Upholding the Right to Life and Health* (n 111) vi–xvii.

118 Ibid ix.

rights. I argue that an interpretation of Article 12 as a civil–political right, fundamental to all other rights and as requiring the abolition of decision-making by substitutes, represents an *over*-correction to past exclusion of people with disability from the civil-political human rights agenda. Applying the principle of indivisibility to Article 12 remedies this over-correction by recognising interdependencies between rights both within and between categories, together with the equal importance of socio-economic with civil-political rights.

The principle of indivisibility is important because there is an urgency in emphasising socio-economic rights for people with disability who are disproportionately impacted by socio-economic disadvantage in a way that can also result in civil–political exclusion. Critical socio-economic rights include the right to social welfare and support services and the right of access to adequate health services. The privileging of civil-political over socio-economic rights risks perpetuating derision of much-needed 'welfare' services as being equivalent to charity, instead of being recognised as goods that can be provided and claimed as rights and entitlements. It also risks perpetuating stigmatisation of much-needed medical responses to disability as being always inappropriately paternalistic and rights-denying. The realisation of human rights can only be ensured for adults with cognitive disability if socio-economic goods and services are available to support them and if decisions are made and services delivered in a rights-affirming framework. This is the very challenge that the CRPD aims to meet by including civil, economic, political, social and cultural rights in the one convention in a way that embodies the principle of indivisibility to drive civil and social inclusion.

5 INDIVISIBILITY IN THE TEXT OF THE CRPD

The CRPD is the first UN convention to include a declaration of indivisibility, in reaffirming 'the universality, indivisibility, interdependence and interrelatedness of all human rights and fundamental freedoms and the need for persons with disabilities to be guaranteed their full enjoyment without discrimination'.[119] This section shows how the text of the CRPD reveals the two concepts of indivisibility identified above – that is, as recognising the interdependence between rights and the equal importance of socio-economic with civil-political rights. Some commentators emphasise the intertwining of the categories of rights in the CRPD to the extent that the division between them has no ongoing relevance.[120] Contrary to this, I conclude that given the historical and lingering subordination of socio-economic rights, a concept of indivisibility as 'entwining' the two categories risks shrouding ongoing prejudices against socio-economic rights while actually perpetuating the old hierarchy.

[119] *CRPD* Preamble para 3.
[120] DeBeco (n 10) 154.

5.1 *Rights from Both the ICCPR and the ICESCR and the Right of Communication*

Chapter 1 has already explained that the CPRD was designed as a comprehensive human rights treaty, not one limited to anti-discrimination obligations;[121] as such, it transposed existing rights from both the ICCPR and the ICESCR.[122] Examples of civil–political rights that have been transposed from the ICCPR into the CRPD include the right to non-discrimination (Articles 2 and 26 ICCPR), incorporated in Article 5 CRPD; the right to be free from torture (Article 7 ICCPR), found in Article 15 CRPD; the right to liberty and security of the person (Article 9 ICCPR), found in Article 14 CRPD; and the right to recognition as a person before the law (Article 16 ICCPR), found in Article 12 CRPD.

Examples of economic, social and cultural rights transposed from the ICESCR to the CRPD include the right to social security and social insurance (Article 9 ICESCR), found in Article 28 CRPD; the right to an adequate standard of living (Article 11 ICESCR), found in Article 28 CRPD; the right to the 'enjoyment of the highest attainable standard' of health (Article 12 ICESCR), found in Article 25 CRPD; the right to education (Article 13 ICESCR), found in Article 24 CRPD; and the right to partake in cultural life (Article 15 ICESCR), found in Article 30 CRPD. Almost all of the rights in the two covenants are included in the CRPD, although particularised for persons with disability.[123]

This mixing of civil-political and socio-economic rights in the one instrument is one indicator of indivisibility, reflecting what Whelan calls the original 'unity' of rights in the UN Declaration, before they were split between the covenants.[124] Contributing to this indivisibility is the right of communication in the Optional Protocol, which allows individuals or groups of individuals to bring complaints to the UN Disability Committee relating to alleged violations of the convention.[125]

5.2 *Civil–Political and Socio-economic Rights Mixed in the Same Articles*

In the case of the CRPD, rights in the two different categories are not just included in the one instrument but are also mixed within the same articles in a way that appears to defy the hierarchical classification of rights and further the principle of

[121] See Chapter 1, Section 3.3.

[122] Degener and Begg (n 88) 13.

[123] An exception may be that 'All peoples have the right to self-determination', in *ICCPR* Article 1 and *ICESCR* Article 1, but not replicated in the CRPD.

[124] Whelan (n 5) 2.

[125] *Optional Protocol to the Convention on the Rights of Persons with Disabilities*, opened for signature 30 March 2007, 2518 UNTS 283 (entered into force 3 May 2008) Article 1.

indivisibility. Koch points out that the right to life is traditionally a civil right and is expressed in Article 6 ICCPR in negative terms – that 'no one shall be arbitrarily deprived of his life'. Yet Article 10 CRPD adds to the right to life, asserting that states shall 'take all necessary measures to ensure its enjoyment by persons with disabilities on an equal basis with others'.[126] Article 7 ICCPR provides that 'No one will be subjected to torture, or to cruel, inhuman or degrading treatment or punishment'; while Article 15(2) CRPD replicates that wording but adds that states must 'take all effective legislative, administrative, judicial or other measures to prevent persons with disabilities, on an equal basis with others, from being subjected to torture'. The right to freedom of expression is traditionally a civil and political right and yet Article 21 CRPD adds positive obligations for States to ensure provision of information in accessible formats, thereby requiring the expenditure of potentially significant resources.[127]

Several commentators have noted the 'hybrid' formulation of the rights in the CRPD, a formulation that defies categorisation into civil–political or socio-economic.[128] Also noted is the mix of negative and positive obligations that defy strict alignment with either civil–political or socio-economic rights, respectively. Lawson comments that in the case of disability and the CRPD the 'classical distinction between positive and negative rights is an unhelpful one'.[129] The imposition of positive obligations on states in respect of rights that have traditionally been considered as civil-political also articulates more emphatically that realisation of those rights will require expenditure of state resources. Such positive obligations undermine the prejudice that 'true' human rights must always be implemented by State restraint. Mégret describes how disability in particular requires a mix of negative obligations and positive actions by the State because of the impact of structural discrimination, which requires more than a case-by-case response. The disproportionate incidence of poverty, for example, requires a solution, not just for an individual case but at a societal level.[130]

[126] Koch, 'From Invisibility to Indivisibility' (n 58) 69.

[127] Peter Bartlett, 'The United Nations Convention on the Rights of Persons with Disabilities and Mental Health Law' (2012) 75(5) *The Modern Law Review* 752, 757.

[128] Dhanda, 'Constructing a New Human Rights Lexicon' (n 105) 49; Marianne Schulze, 'Chapter 16: The Human Rights of Persons with Disabilities' in Anja Mihir and Mark Gibney (eds), *The SAGE Handbook of Human Rights* (SAGE Publications Ltd, 2014) 267, 277; Andrea Broderick, 'Harmonisation and Cross-fertilisation of Socio-Economic Rights in the Human Rights Treaty Bodies: Disability and the Reasonableness Review Case Study' (2016) 5 *Laws* 38, 42; DeBeco (n 10) 154.

[129] Anna Lawson, 'The UN Convention on the Rights of Persons with Disabilities and European Disability Law: A Catalyst for Cohesion?' in Oddný Mjöll Arnadóttir and Gerard Quinn (eds), *The UN Convention on the Rights of Persons with Disabilities: European and Scandinavian Perspectives* (Nijhoff, 2009) 81, 102.

[130] Frédéric Mégret, 'The Disabilities Convention: Towards a Holistic Concept of Rights' (2008) 12(2) *International Journal of Human Rights* 261, 265.

5.3 A Mix of State Restraint and State Protection/Support in the Personal Sphere

As described above, liberal theorists who privilege civil–political rights over socio-economic rights view human rights as solely designed to protect the individual from the State.[131] Mégret points to the fact that human rights law is underpinned by a public/private divide and has usually overemphasised rights owed in the public sphere at the expense of rights owed in the private sphere.[132] He contends, however, that the CRPD bridges this traditional divide. For example, Article 17 'Protecting the integrity of the person' tends to imply protection of physical and mental integrity in the public sphere, whereas Article 16 'Freedom from exploitation, violence and abuse' requires protection 'both within and outside the home' (para 1). I argue that this 'transcendence' of the 'public/private sphere divide' identified by Mégret is further evidence of the indivisibility of human rights, with civil–political rights traditionally requiring state restraint from the private sphere but socio-economic rights requiring state intervention or intrusion.

Article 19 'Living independently and being in the community' deals both with the right of a person to choose where and with whom they live, requiring state restraint from interfering in this personal matter, and obliges the State to provide in-home, residential support services, 'including personal assistance'. In Article 19, the traditional civil–political component of the right is the right to choose where to live (i.e. to exercise legal capacity), with the socio-economic component evident in the state obligation to provide services.[133] The UN Disability Committee writes in its *General Comment No 5* that:

> Article 19 entails civil and political as well as economic, social and cultural rights and is an example of the interrelation, interdependence and indivisibility of all human rights. The right to live independently and be included in the community can only be realized if all economic, civil, social and cultural rights enshrined in this norm are fulfilled.[134]

5.4 *Indivisible, but Still Visible and* Not *Totally Entwined or Dissolved into One Another*

Much of the literature on indivisibility in the CRPD doesn't engage with the broader discussion around the development of the doctrine. It tends instead to assume that the audience will understand the meaning of the terms 'interdependence' and

[131] Philip Alston (n 18) 96.
[132] Mégret (n 130) 266.
[133] Degener (n 105) 46.
[134] Committee on the Rights of Persons with Disabilities, '*General Comment No 5 (2017) On Living Independently and Being Included in the Community*' UN Doc CRPD/C/GC/5 [7]; see also Degener (n 105) 46.

'indivisibility' from very brief descriptions of the mix of rights in the CRPD. It does, nevertheless, broadly imply at times that the CRPD exhibits the interdependence of rights[135] and the equal importance of socio-economic rights with civil–political rights.[136] DeBeco is, however, one writer who has contextualised his discussion within the wider debate on indivisibility.[137] Having done so, he concludes that the hybrid nature of the rights in the CRPD leads to a new understanding of the principle. He argues that the CRPD reflects a principle of indivisibility that asserts the two sets of rights are 'mutually inextricable from each other',[138] that therefore 'the very existence of the division into civil and political and economic and social rights has itself become a hindrance to the proper interpretation of the convention', and that seeking to differentiate between them is 'pointless'.[139] This is consistent with Mégret's view that the CRPD 'transcends' the 'civil and political/economic, social

[135] Lord, for example, describes the CRPD as incorporating the principle of indivisibility on the basis that it includes both categories of rights, and, through providing examples, further implies that the CRPD demonstrates indivisibility as the interdependence of rights. Examples are of the adverse impact that inaccessible transport can have on access to education for people with disability, and how the unavailability of rehabilitation for a landmine survivor can lead to unemployment and exclusion: Janet E Lord, 'Preamble' in Ilias Bantekas, Michael Ashley Stein and Dēmētrēs Anastasiou (eds), *The UN Convention on the Rights of Persons with Disabilities: A Commentary* (Oxford University Press, 2018) 1, 11; 'Within the Convention there is an important recognition of the interdependence of all rights and a co-mingling of rights, the extent to which has never been seen in a binding human rights instrument before'. Anna Arstein-Kerslake, *Restoring Voice to People with Cognitive Disabilities: Realizing the Right to Equal Recognition before the Law* (Cambridge University Press, 2017) 19; Kanter writes that: 'Indeed the CRPD stands for the fact that all of its articles are interdependent and that civil and political rights cannot be realised unless and until the related social, economic, and cultural rights are also ensured'. Kanter (n 29) 9; Kayess and Sands explain: 'This means that the interpretation and implementatoin of … the CRPD requires applicatoin of the cross-cutting articles, but also recognition of the interrelationship between substantive articles', Rosemary Kayess and Therese Sands, *Convention on the Rights of Persons with Disabilities: Shining a Light on Social Transformation* (UNSW Social Policy Research Centre, 2020); Ron McCallum, *The United Nations Convention on the Rights of Persons with Disabilities: An Assessment of Australia's Level of Compliance* (Royal Commission into Violence, Abuse, Neglect and Exploitation of People with Disability, 2020) 37.

[136] Degener writes that: 'The legal hierarchy of civil and political rights over economic, social, and cultural rights is slowly but steadily decreasing … The CRPD is a good example of the indivisibility and interdependence of both sets of human rights': Degener (n 105) 45–6; Della Fina affirms that 'all human rights are universal, indivisible, interdependent and interrelated' after describing the inclusion of both sets of rights in the CRPD, how they are 'equally important', and how 'States are therefore responsible for violations of economic social and cultural rights as they are for violations of civil and political rights'. Valentina Della Fina, 'Article 4 General Obligations' in Valentina Della Fina, Rachele Cera and Giuseppe Palmisano (eds), *The United Nations Convention on the Rights of Persons with Disabilities: A Commentary* (Springer International Publishing, 2017) 149, 149.

[137] DeBeco (n 10) 148.

[138] Ibid 155.

[139] DeBeco's reference to differentiation being 'pointless' is made particularly in the context of implementation and the ostensible differences between progressive and immediate implementation: ibid 154.

and cultural rights divide'.[140] Koch, in the same vein, describes the CRPD as incorporating 'a certain overlapping … between the two sets of rights that seems to permit or even mandate an interpretation that dissolves the boundaries between the two distinct categories'.[141] Not dissimilarly, Stein and Lord describe the CRPD as 'holistically meld[ing] civil and political rights with economic, social and cultural rights', and that in doing so it 'aspires to manifest the mandate that human rights are 'indivisible, interrelated and interconnected'.[142]

The assertions that rights have been 'melded' or that they are inextricably intertwined and that the categories are 'inextricable' from one another have definite cogency. They accurately reflect the extent to which rights are intertwined in the drafting of the text; also, as DeBeco emphasises, they reflect the total disruption of the alignment of obligations of immediate realisation with civil-political rights and progressive realisation with socio-economic rights.[143] However, I argue against an understanding of indivisibility in the CRPD as totally dissolving the boundaries between categories to the extent that they have no ongoing relevance. The CRPD undoubtedly advances the existing challenges to the traditional bifurcation already posed by the principle of indivisibility and the eventual total dissolution of demarcation between categories of rights is a worthy aspiration. However, as long as the dichotomy is still firmly entrenched in UN and regional institutional arrangements, and there is ongoing and widespread prejudice against socio-economic rights as not being 'true' rights, it is, I propose, premature to suggest that the categories be treated as dissolved.[144]

Anthony argues that the rhetoric of indivisibility has, since the Vienna Declaration in 1993, been used to shroud the ongoing subordination of socio-economic rights, so that civil-political rights continue to be privileged, albeit under the cloak of 'indivisibility'.[145] Anthony's argument could readily be applied to *General Comment No 1*'s interpretation of Article 12 as a civil-political right fundamental to all other rights (including socio-economic rights) but at the same time recognising the principle of indivisibility.[146] In this context, I argue that it is important to emphasise that

140 Mégret (n 130) 265–6.

141 Koch, 'Social Rights as Components in the Civil Right to Personal Liberty' (n 46) 33.

142 Stein and Lord (n 87) 24; see also Michael Ashley Stein, 'Disability Human Rights' (2007) 95(1) *California Law Review* 75, 77–9; Michael Ashley Stein and Penelope JS Stein, 'Beyond Disability Civil Rights' (2006) 58 *Hastings Law Journal* 1203, 1240.

143 DeBeco (n 10) 147–8, 158.

144 Anthony notes that 'economic, social and cultural rights are still commonly recognised as marginalised rights', Anthony (n 12) 126.

145 Ibid v, 165–6.

146 Indeed, affirmations of the indivisibility of human rights are often used to affirm the importance of the civil-political right to legal capacity over and above all other rights. See, for example, the Special Rapporteur's comments, which preface a reaffirmation of the prescription of universal legal capacity under Article 12: 'In the Convention the universality, indivisibility, interdependence and interrelatedness of human rights are recalled by stressing that

indivisibility does require recognition of the equal importance of the two categories of rights. If the emphasis on socio-economic rights as being 'true' human rights is not sustained, then there are significant risks that the promotion of human rights for people with disability will emphasise civil–political rights and privilege negative state action and restraint, under the cloak of the mere rhetoric of indivisibility.

5.5 *Summary, Commentary and Conclusions*

The CRPD is the first UN Convention to include a statement of indivisibility in its text. It includes both civil–political and socio-economic rights within the one convention. It mixes civil–political and socio-economic rights within the same articles, and the Optional Protocol includes a right of communication for breach of all substantive articles. This mix of traditional categories makes it apparent that human rights, whether civil–political or socio-economic, may require either restraint or positive action from the State and support or protection in the private sphere. The way that different rights are mixed within the same articles suggests that, even at a textual level, the rights are interdependent and that civil–political and socio-economic rights have equal status. However, I argue against a conception of indivisibility in the CRPD as totally dissolving the traditional categories. The rhetoric of dissolution risks cloaking the ongoing subordination of socio-economic rights and the socio-economic needs of people with disability. Given the long history of the privileging of civil–political rights, ongoing emphasis on the legitimacy of socio-economic rights as true rights requires persistent reiteration. The chapter now turns to interpreting and applying Article 12 through the principle of indivisibility.

6 INTERPRETING AND APPLYING ARTICLE 12 THROUGH THE PRINCIPLE OF INDIVISIBILITY

It is useful to set out the full text of paragraphs (1) to (4) of Article 12 – 'Equal Recognition before the law':

(1) States Parties reaffirm that persons with disabilities have the right to recognition everywhere as persons before the law.
(2) States Parties shall recognize that persons with disabilities enjoy legal capacity on an equal basis with others in all aspects of life.

persons with disabilities should fully enjoy all their rights without any kind of discrimination'. Aguilar (n 106) [20]; *General Comment No 6* reasserts the principle of indivisibility but goes on to prescribe that Article 12 is foundational to all other rights: Committee on the Rights of Persons with Disabilities, *General Comment No 6: On Equality and Non-Discrimination*, UN Doc CRPD/C/GC/6 (26 April 2018) [9], [47]–[51].

(3) States Parties shall take appropriate measures to provide access by persons with disabilities to the support they may require in exercising legal capacity.
(4) States Parties shall ensure that all measures that relate to the exercise of legal capacity provide for appropriate and effective safeguards to prevent abuse in accordance with international human rights law. Such safeguards shall ensure that measures relating to the exercise of legal capacity respect the rights, will and preferences of the person, are free of conflict of interest and undue influence, are proportional and tailored to the person's circumstances, apply for the shortest time possible and are subject to regular review by a competent, independent and impartial authority or judicial body. The safeguards shall be proportional to the degree to which such measures affect the person's rights and interests.

This section explains how Article 12 demonstrates the principle of indivisibility by demanding recognition of the interdependence of the different rights within Article 12 itself – that is, the right to legal capacity and the right to support[147] – in a way that also illustrates the equal importance of socio-economic with civil-political rights. Later chapters consider the interdependencies between Article 12 and other rights in the CRPD.

6.1 *Article 12 as a Civil-political Right*

General Comment No 1 refers to Article 12 as a 'civil right'[148] and further states that:

> The right to equality before the law has long been recognised as a civil and political right, with roots in the International Covenant on Civil and Political Rights....The state obligation provided for in article 12, paragraph 3, to provide access to support in the exercise of legal capacity is an obligation for the fulfilment of the civil and political right to equal recognition before the law.[149]

In arriving at this categorisation of the whole of Article 12 as a civil-political right, *General Comment No 1* relies on Article 12's origins in the ICCPR, Article 16 ICCPR providing that 'Everyone shall have the right to recognition everywhere as a person before the law'.[150]

This categorisation of Article 12 as a civil-political right is also consistent with *General Comment No 1*'s interpretation of Article 12 as requiring the abolition of

[147] See below for discussion of how Article 12(3) can be conceived of as a separate but related 'right to support'.
[148] *General Comment No 1* [1].
[149] Ibid [30].
[150] Article 26 *ICCPR* also provides that: 'All persons are equal before the law and are entitled without discrimination to the equal protection of the law'.

guardianship and decision-making by substitutes. Such an abolition requires 'negative' action by the State in terms of removing guardianship and restraint from intruding into an adult's private sphere. Considered in isolation, repealing guardianship legislation is 'cost-free' and can be implemented immediately. The wording in paragraph (3) of Article 12, which obliges States to take 'measures to provide *access*' [emphasis added] to support for legal capacity could also be taken to imply that providing support requires only negative action from the State. Commentators have written that the term 'access' in Article 12(3) implies that 'dense social networks already exist',[151] and that Article 12(3) may allow for the harnessing of supports that already 'occur naturally in the community'.[152] *General Comment No 1*, in providing that all adults should be able to 'choose one or more trusted support persons … or may call on other forms of support',[153] assumes that adults have wide networks of trusted supporters and other resources at their disposal.[154]

The UN Disability Committee's view is that the whole of Article 12 is a civil–political right and *General Comment No 1* thus provides that as a civil–political right:

> the rights provided for in Article 12 apply at the moment of ratification and are subject to immediate realisation … 'Progressive realisation' Article 4(2) does not apply to the provisions of Article 12.[155]

6.2 Article 12 as a Socio-economic Right

Paragraph (3) of Article 12 is framed as a state obligation to provide supports but is nevertheless often referred to as creating a separate but related 'right to support'[156]

[151] Gerard Quinn and Abigail Rekas-Rosalbo, 'Civil Death: Rethinking the Foundations of Legal Personhood for Persons with a Disability' (2016) 56 *Irish Jurist* 286.

[152] Gerard Quinn, 'From Civil Death to Civil Life: The Decay and Re-Birth of Legal Capacity Law around the World' (Conference Paper, Australian Guardianship and Administration Council National Conference: Reflecting Will and Preference in Decision-Making, 17–18 October 2016) 10 <www.agac.org.au/images/stories/2016nsw/quinn-decay-rebirth-legal-cap-law.pdf>.

[153] *General Comment No 1* [17].

[154] Note that trials of informal supported decision-making have indicated that many adults with cognitive disability do not have 'naturally occurring' supporters but may indeed be socially isolated: Terry Carney et al, 'Realising "Will, Preferences and Rights": Reconciling Differences on Best Practice Support for Decision-Making?' (2019) *Griffith Law Review* 357, 363; Office of the Public Advocate (Qld), *Decision-Making Support and Queensland's Guardianship System: A Systemic Advocacy Report* (A Systemic Advocacy Report, April 2016) 183–4.

[155] *General Comment No 1* [30].

[156] Terry Carney, 'Prioritising Supported Decision-Making: Running on Empty or a Basis for Glacial-to-Steady Progress?' (2017) 6(4) *Laws* 18 20, 23, 24, 28; Eilionoir Flynn and Anna Arstein-Kerslake, 'Legislating Personhood: Realising the Right to Support in Exercising Legal Capacity' (2014) 10(1) *International Journal of Law in Context* 81; Elif Celik, 'The Role of CRPD in Rethinking the Subject of Human Rights' (2017) 21(7) *The International Journal of Human Rights* 933, 947.

(or 'supports'[157]) or as the 'right to supported decision-making'.[158] Some commentary is beginning to emerge suggesting either that Article 12(3) is a socio-economic right or that Article 12 as a whole is best described as a mixed civil–political and socio-economic right.

6.2.1 Supports Equate to Socio-economic Resources

Carney states that 'arguably' the right in Article 12 paragraph (3) (i.e. the right to supports) is a socio-economic right because of its 'capacity building personal development' aspects and because it gives rise to discussions akin to 'traditional welfare allocation (and priority setting) debates'.[159] Carney emphasises that fulfilment of Article 12(3) necessitates a significant injection of state resources, thus contributing to its categorisation as a socio-economic right. He further expresses the view that even if there is some disagreement about this categorisation, in the 'realpolitik of government' (i.e. in practical terms) the implementation of the necessary supports will only be achieved progressively in the tradition of socio-economic rights.[160] He concludes that, for this reason, the UN Disability Committee's requirement to abolish substitute decision-making regimes immediately[161] is not feasible. If achieved, it would leave some people with cognitive disability subject to neglect and exploitation while support systems were in development.[162]

Quinn writes of the dangers of not providing enough resources for individuals to realise their personhood through supported decision-making.[163] Further, 'at first blush' Article 12(3) appears to be subject only to progressive realisation, although in some cases immediate provision of support is possible.[164] Quinn and Rekas-Rosalbo

[157] Michael Bach and Lana Kerzner, *A New Paradigm for Protecting Autonomy and the Right to Legal Capacity: Advancing Substantive Equality for Persons with Disabilities through Law, Policy and Practice* (Law Commission of Ontario, October 2010) 112, 113, 165.

[158] Joanne Watson, 'The Right to Supported Decision-Making for People Rarely Heard' (PhD Thesis, Deakin University, 2016); Arstein-Kerslake, 'An Empowering Dependency: Exploring Support for the Exercise of Legal Capacity' (2016) 18 *Scandinavian Journal of Disability Research* 77, 87.

[159] Carney, 'Prioritising Supported Decision-Making' (n 156) 18–19.

[160] Ibid 18.

[161] As to the UN Disability's requirement to *immediately* abolish substitute decision-making: 'States parties' obligation to replace substitute decision-making regimes by supported decision-making requires both the abolition of substitute decision-making regimes and the development of supported decision-making alternatives. The development of supported decision-making systems in parallel with the maintenance of substitute decision-making regimes is not sufficient to comply with article 12 of the Convention'. In *General Comment No 1* [28].

[162] See also Terry Carney, 'Supported Decision-Making for People with Cognitive Impairments: An Australian Perspective?' (2015) 4 *Laws* 37, 41.

[163] There is a 'risk that the self will be moulded to fit the level of currently available social resources. Instead of becoming the sum total of what you consume you might just become the sum total of what we can afford'. Quinn 'From Civil Death to Civil Life' (n 152) 28.

[164] Gerard Quinn, 'Concept Paper "Personhood and Legal Capacity": Perspectives on the Paradigm Shift of Article 12 of the CRPD' (Conference Paper, HPOD Conference, 20 February, 2010) 19 www.inclusiveirelandie/document/HarvardLegalcapacitygqdraft2.doc;19.

describe how 'putting support in place takes a lot of … resources'[165] and Article 12(3) has the 'look and feel of an obligation that is to be progressively "realised"'.[166] They also describe as 'debatable' *General Comment No 1's* assertion that the right to support is a civil–political right and immediately realisable. Degener was a member of the UN Disability Committee at the time that *General Comment No 1* was made, and yet she also writes of Article 12(3) that: 'These support measures are realised by social services, which fall into the economic, social and cultural rights sphere'.[167]

Not only do trusted family and friends who act as supporters require training and resources, but the State has an obligation to provide volunteer or paid supporters for adults who find themselves isolated. Supported decision-making pilots have shown that many adults are indeed isolated, so that, where adults do not 'have access to naturally occurring supports in the community',[168] the provision of access to supports becomes a 'more muscular obligation'[169] requiring state assistance or intervention. All of this analysis supports the conclusion that Article 12(3) is more convincingly categorised as a socio-economic right.

6.2.2 Fulfilling Article 12(4) Obligations

Article 12(4) obliges the State to provide safeguards for the exercise of legal capacity, and Carney categorises paragraphs (3) and (4) together as a social right.[170] While Article 12(3) requires the availability of trusted support persons, Article 12(4) requires safeguards to 'prevent abuse' and guard against 'conflict of interest and undue influence'. In providing that safeguards must be 'proportional and tailored to the person's circumstances, apply for the shortest time possible', and be subject to regular review by an independent authority, paragraph (4) anticipates an administrative and judicial oversight scheme for supported decision-making and, I would argue (with others), a system of decision-making by substitutes.[171] *General Comment No 1* is silent on the type of safeguards to be instituted, provided that they respect the adult's 'rights, will and preferences',[172] but it seems inevitable that they will require positive actions by the State, will be resource-intensive, will take time to progress, and will necessarily intervene in the relationship between the adult and the 'supporter'. In this way,

165 Quinn and Rekas-Rosalbo (n 151) 309.
166 Ibid 303.
167 Degener (n 105) 45–6.
168 Anna Arstein-Kerslake and Eilionóir Flynn, 'The General Comment on Article 12 of the Convention on the Rights of Persons with Disabilities: A Roadmap for Equality before the Law' (2016) 20(4) *The International Journal of Human Rights* 471, 478.
169 Quinn and Rekas-Rosalbo (n 151) 301.
170 Carney, 'Prioritising Supported Decision-Making' (n 156) 18.
171 Ad Hoc Committee, *Daily Summary of the Fifth Session* (25 January 2005) www.un.org/esa/socdev/enable/rights/ahc5sum25jan.htm Ad Hoc Committee, *Daily Summary of the Fifth Session* (25 January 2005).
172 *General Comment No 1* [21].

the safeguard obligation framed as part of the right to supports bears all the indicia of a socio-economic right.[173]

6.2.3 Obligations in Article 12(3) and (4) Are Resource-Intensive

Socio-economic rights are traditionally characterised as resource-intensive, and other commentators emphasise that support for decision-making will require injection of significant state resources. Alston points out that designing legislative regimes for supported decision-making is a relatively minor challenge compared with the need for the 'availability of resources to facilitate the provision of support and effective oversight arrangements'.[174] Martin et al recommend that 'statutory advocacy services should be funded at a level that ensures genuine and effective access to independent advocates' for supported decision-making,[175] and other commentators recommend a range of relationship-building supports, administrative supports and training for support persons.[176] The Queensland Office of the Public Advocate writes that 'As this is a newly evolving concept, the costs of providing such a service will depend on the resources and economic wealth of each jurisdiction',[177] and Arstein-Kerslake and Flynn acknowledge that 'Limited resources may be one problem that prevents the development of supports for every individual that are completely tailored to their needs'.[178] These commentators are warning that increased investment in community resources is a pre-condition for increasing access to supported decision-making and minimising or abolishing the use of guardianship.[179] In other words, the fulfilment of the socio-economic rights to support is a pre-condition for fulfilling the right to legal capacity.

173 I note here that there is an argument that the rights to registration and judicial oversight do also suggest the architecture used to support civil-political rights. However, the point here is that such regulatory systems do bear the stereotyped indicia of socio-economic rights in being intrusive and resource-intensive.

174 Bruce Alston (n 134) 39; the ALRC, in prescribing the duties of a representative implies that socio-economic rights are relevant when it says that they must consider the relevant human right and a person's 'social, financial and cultural well-being': Australian Law Reform Commission, *Equality, Capacity and Disability in Commonwealth Laws: A Final Report* (2014) 105.

175 Wayne Martin et al, *Three Jurisdictions Report: Towards Compliance with CRPD Article 12 in Capacity/Incapacity Legislation across the UK* (Essex Autonomy Project, 2016) 3.

176 Bach and Kerzner (n 157) 75–80; Leslie Salzman, 'Guardianship for Persons with Mental Illness – A Legal and Appropriate Alternative' (2011) 4 *St Louis University Journal of Health Law and Policy* 279, 328.

177 Office of the Public Advocate (Qld), *Decision-Making Support and Queensland's Guardianship System* (n 154) 163.

178 Arstein-Kerslake and Flynn, 'The General Comment on Article 12 of the Convention on the Rights of Persons with Disabilities' (n 168) 477.

179 Note that Harding suggests that the costs of providing support and safeguarding could be offset by some potential savings of supported decision-making plus registration, reporting and supervision fees: Rosie Harding, 'Supporting Everyday Legal Capacity: Navigating the Complexities of Putting Rights into Practice' in Mary Donnelly, Rosie Harding and Ezgi Tascioglu (eds), *Supporting Legal Capacity in Socio-Legal Context* (Hart Publishing, 2022) 291, 312.

6.3 The 'Chicken and Egg' or 'Initiation Problem'

Carney concludes that because the right to enjoy legal capacity is conditional on realisation of the right to support, Article 12 as a whole embodies a tension between civil-political and socio-economic rights, and that this tension reflects and illustrates the principle of indivisibility.[180] This practical interdependency reveals a paradox at the heart of an interpretation of Article 12 as requiring recognition of universal legal capacity, a paradox that one writer has described as the 'chicken and egg' situation.[181] One implication of this paradox is captured by Parker when he describes the 'initiation problem' associated with supported decision-making, which arises because an adult must choose a supporter to help him or her make decisions but may not be able to freely make that initial choice of supporter, if he or she doesn't yet have support.[182] Another consequence of the 'chicken and egg' problem is that if an adult has a supporter who is exercising undue influence over him or her, then if the adult agrees to this supporter and rejects all others, the decision to continue with the existing supporter may be recognised as an exercise of legal capacity.

If, on the other hand, the principle of indivisibility is invoked to recognise that the right to legal capacity depends on the right to support, and if the socio-economic right to support is recognised as being of equal importance to the civil-political right to legal capacity, then a decision can be made to provide alternative, more trustworthy support for the adult. This would effectively require that a substitute make a decision for the adult in relation to new and different supports. This recognises the interdependence of the rights within Article 12 itself and I argue more fully in subsequent chapters that this would also recognise the interdependence of Article 12 with other articles in the CRPD. This is because the substitute would be able to make claims for fulfilment of the adults' broad range of human rights in a way that may improve the adult's legal capacity but would also serve as a vehicle through which a range of socio-economic rights – from housing and health services to social inclusion – could be claimed for the adult.

6.4 Summary and Conclusions on Article 12 and Indivisibility

The UN Disability Committee has categorised the whole of Article 12 as a civil-political right, subject to immediate realisation. This is because the right to equal recognition before the law has been adapted from the ICCCPR and is associated with civil-political status. The categorisation of Article 12 as civil-political is also associated with the UN Disability Committee's prescription that it be implemented

[180] Carney, 'Prioritising Supported Decision-Making' (n 156) 19.

[181] Amita Dhanda, 'From Duality to Indivisibility: Mental Health Care and Human Rights' (2016) 32(3) *South African Journal on Human Rights* 438, 455.

[182] Malcolm Parker, 'Getting the Balance Right: Conceptual Considerations Concerning Legal Capacity and Supported Decision-Making' (2016) 13(3) *Journal of Bioethical Inquiry* 381, 388.

through the immediate abolition of substitute decision-making (i.e. an action of state restraint that is on the face of it 'cost-free'). Commentators have pointed out, however, that Article 12(3), the right to support, has the indicia of a socio-economic right in that it demands the provision of goods and services depending on action by the State at significant cost, so that realistically it can only be implemented progressively.

The wording of Article 12(3), as providing 'access' to supports, implies that supports are already in existence in the community, to be accessed once the barrier of substitute decision-making systems is dismantled. In some cases that will be true, such as when adults are enmeshed in trustworthy social relationships and have immediate access to material resources. However, in many cases 'access' will require positive steps by States and others, and significant resources to build. Repeal of substitute decision-making regimes on the face of it signals a retreat by the State from regulating private lives. However, the reality is that the State will be intervening in private lives and personal relationships by providing, or ensuring the provision of, support services for personal decision-making and through regulating support services. The traditional bifurcation between civil-political and socio-economic rights is disrupted and the historical hierarchies disappear, demonstrating and developing one aspect of the principle of the indivisibility of human rights.

An understanding of the whole of Article 12 as a civil–political right is a limited one and, I argue, disregards any possibility of indivisibility within Article 12 itself. The assertion that the whole of Article 12 is civil–political fails to acknowledge that Article 12 could be interpreted as incorporating two interdependent rights – the right to legal capacity and the right to support. As such, it disrupts the traditional hierarchy of rights. On the other hand, interpreting Article 12 through the lens of indivisibility acknowledges that (1) Article 12 includes rights from both categories and incorporates a mix of positive and negative obligations; (2) while the abolition of guardianship may be 'cost-free', support measures may be resource-intensive, and (3) realisation of legal capacity may require some intervention or intrusion into the personal sphere to uphold human rights.

7 SUMMARY AND CONCLUSIONS

The chapter has described how the UN Declaration included both civil-political and socio-economic rights in one instrument without distinction. It was only with the transposition of these rights into an enforceable covenant that a decision was made to split the rights into the two now well-recognised categories. The dominant explanation for the splitting of the rights between the ICCPR and the ICESCR has been the impact of Cold War politics, with socio-economic rights being favoured by communist states and civil-political rights favoured by the West. An alternative or supplementary explanation is that with the development of an enforceable covenant, it became unclear if socio-economic rights could be effectively subject to the same enforcement mechanisms as civil-political ones. An exploration of why the covenants were split is beyond the scope of this book. However, from the 1950s, statements on the indivisibility and interdependence of human rights increased, leading in 1968 to the Proclamation of Teheran, followed in 1993 by the Vienna Declaration.

While there is no universal agreemenf on a definition of the principle of indivisibility, this chapter settles on a concept with two key features that are prominent in the literature. First, indivisibility asserts the interdependence of human rights, and second, it recognises the equal importance of socio-economic rights with civil-political rights. In doing so, indivisibility also reveals that the historical bifurcation of rights based on the traditional indicia cannot be sustained, those indicia being, for civil-political rights, negative action, immediate realisation and 'no cost', and, for socio-economic rights, positive action, progressive realisation and resource-intensiveness. Indivisibility, thereby, also disrupts the traditional privileging of the private and personal sphere as a space where rights are always upheld through state restraint.

The chapter situates the development of the principle of indivisibility in the context of the history of disability advocacy and rights. Originally, disability was framed in UN institutions and advocacy as a social policy issue at a time when socio-economic rights were of a lesser status than civil-political ones. As such, disability policy was subordinated to human rights issues when the only 'true' human rights were civil-political human rights. As the focus of social policy, people with disability were framed as needy and burdensome, as objects of pity and as the recipients of 'good deeds'. There was, therefore, an urgency to situate people with disability as the subjects of human rights – in particular, the 'true' human rights being civil-political. The chapter argues that this has led to an over-correction in disability advocacy to the extent that *General Comment No 1* now situates the civil-political right to legal capacity as the apex of human rights, the fulfilment of which is a pre-condition to fulfilling any other human right.

The principle of indivisibility adjusts this over-correction to assert the equal importance of both sets of rights. This recognises the material reality that, depending on an adult's contingent circumstances, the fulfilment of a socio-economic right may be a pre-condition to exercising legal capacity and achieving a range of other human rights. The chapter highlights the particular importance of the principle of indivisibility to disability rights, given that people with disability are disproportionately exposed to socio-economic disadvantage compared with other members of the community. It describes how the principle of indivisibility demands that 'welfare' and other support services be claimed as the fulfilment of socio-economic rights and entitlements and not provided or received as discretionary acts of charity. It also describes the critical importance for people with disability of the socio-economic right to health services, noting that several commentators regard such a right as a foundational and enabling right.

The chapter establishes that the CRPD, more than any other convention, expresses a commitment to indivisibility. It is the first UN Convention to include a statement of indivisibility; more significantly, it mixes rights from the traditionally separate categories and includes requirements for positive and negative state actions in the same articles. The literature on the CRPD has widely hailed the convention as revolutionary in its incorporation of the principle of indivisibility. Further, this literature has expressly or impliedly acknowledged indivisibility as the interdependence of rights and the recognition of the equal importance of socio-economic with civil-political rights.

However, I argue that those interpretations of Article 12 that require the abolition of decision-making by substitutes fail to apply the principle of indivisibility as understood in this book. In those interpretations, the 'interdependent' component of indivisibility is only ever understood as operating one way, with the fulfilment of all other rights unilaterally dependent on fulfilling Article 12. Such interpretations also ignore the second concept of indivisibility as demanding recognition that socio-economic rights in the CRPD are of equal importance to the civil-political right to legal capacity. Further, they gloss over the impact of the indivisibility of human rights to the arguably two separate rights within Article 12 itself: the civil-political right to legal capacity and the socio-economic right to support. The chapter concludes with an analysis of Article 12 that demonstrates the interdependency of the right to legal capacity with the right to support for decision-making and the equal importance of the two rights. It explains that the privileging of the right to legal capacity over the right to support cannot be sustained in the real world of people with disability.

The next three chapters consider the interdependencies between Article 12 and other rights in the CRPD and examine how the human rights values of autonomy, dignity and equality can be interpreted as embodying the indivisibility of human rights.

4

Article 12 and Autonomy

1 INTRODUCTION

Chapter 2 described key concepts in disability and decision-making and how these have driven and informed the development of policy and legal frameworks from favouring paternalism to promoting autonomy. This trajectory is evidenced by the move from institutionalisation to guardianship to supported decision-making. It parallels the development of models of disability that shifted from the dominance of a charity model though to a medical, then social model. Chapter 2 also traced the development of the CRPD, with the dominant framing of Article 12 at the highpoint on a trajectory of rights development, signalling people with disability as subjects of human rights, with full autonomy achieved through the provision of supports, when required. The chapter nevertheless anticipated complexities shrouded by the simplicity of this framing. It rejected the strict social model of disability and endorsed a social model that recognises the residual impacts of impairment.

Chapter 3 introduced the *principle of the indivisibility of human rights*, settling on an understanding of indivisibility that acknowledged interdependencies between rights and recognised socio-economic as of equal importance as civil-political rights. It further demonstrated how the principle of indivisibility infuses the text of the CRPD more than any other human rights convention. It identified that the right to legal capacity in Article 12 was widely considered a civil-political right. As such, Article 12 is typically conceived of as being achieved through negative state 'action' – in particular, restraint from the imposition of guardianship. Such restraint ostensibly respects the autonomy of the individual and his or her personal realm. However, the chapter further argued that, in requiring the positive provision of socio-economic supports, Article 12 incorporates a mix of interdependent civil-political and socio-economic rights. In doing so, the article recognises and embodies the principle of indivisibility. This current chapter investigates how, in disrupting the traditional categorisation of rights, Article 12 also disrupts the traditional concept of autonomy, which has been privileged together with the privileging of civil-political rights.

Section 2 recaps but expands upon the concept of autonomy introduced previously to explain how autonomy is traditionally conceived of as Kantian rationality and Millian liberty, demanding restraint from state interference. It reiterates how autonomy as rationality and independence underpins liberal conceptions of personhood, thereby excluding adults with cognitive disability. It further describes the challenge that this equation of rationality-with-autonomy-with-personhood has posed for disability advocates and scholars who aim to recognise adults with cognitive disability as persons.

Sections 3 and 4 describe several variants of one broad strategy to address this challenge ('the first strategy'). This first strategy still operates within the liberal tradition in privileging the value of autonomy above all other values as the basis for personhood, and the associated right to legal capacity above all other rights, but reworks, or reinvents, the concept of autonomy to include adults with cognitive disability. Autonomy is refashioned as ostensibly universal by divorcing it from rationality, reconceptualising it as *inter*dependence, and framing it as a combination of negative and positive liberty. This strategy supports an interpretation of Article 12 that requires the abolition of decision-making by substitutes to ensure the recognition of universal autonomy and legal capacity. However, I conclude that these refashionings fail because of various internal contradictions in reasoning, all linked to the resistance to recognising the residual impacts of cognitive impairment.

Section 5 describes a second broad strategy to include adults with cognitive disability as persons, this time by divorcing autonomy from personhood and allowing space for alternative bases, including dignity ('the second strategy'). This second strategy endorses or allows for an interpretation of Article 12 that, without denying personhood, permits decision-making by substitutes as a last resort where a person is non-autonomous because of cognitive impairment or disability. According to this strategy, autonomy is no longer privileged above other values; however, because it is still *highly* valued, commentators rework the concept of autonomy to be more inclusive. I conclude that a concept of autonomy as *achievement* – which recognises the need for substantive autonomy competencies and also incorporates a demand for the provision of real options – best aligns with Article 12 autonomy.

Section 6 explains how a substantive concept of autonomy as the achievement of competencies and as demanding options can be rearticulated in human rights terms as recognising the indivisibility of human rights. Autonomy in the sense of achievement of competencies no longer underpins just civil-political rights and is no longer marked by those features typically associated with civil–political rights. That is, autonomy is not always realised through negative state action, is not cost-free, may be progressively realisable and may also require intervention in the personal sphere. Section 7 argues that the concept of autonomy underpinning Article 12 is one that recognises the indivisibility of human rights. Article 12 autonomy acknowledges that not just supported decision-making but decision-making by substitutes may be required to realise a broad range of civil, social, political, economic and cultural rights to respect and achieve autonomy.

The chapter uses the case study of Alex introduced in Chapter 1 and reproduced below, to illustrate the different theories of autonomy, how they affect decision-making and personhood and how they intersect with human rights.

> ALEX
>
> Alex is a 30-year-old man with an intellectual disability who refuses dental treatment because he is scared of, and doesn't trust, the dentist. Collateral information is that his fear is linked to post-traumatic stress disorder from childhood abuse. Counsellors have been unable to assuage his fears or convince him to have the treatment. They have warned him that he will lose all of his teeth if he does not have the treatment. His support workers and family all know that one of his real joys in life is to partake of gourmet food, and it is a significant social interest that he can share with others. If Alex loses all of his teeth, he will need to live chiefly on pureed food. It is not clear whether he understands this longer-term adverse impact (as opposed to the shorter-term impact of undergoing the treatment). It appears to Alex's supporters that he thinks that his teeth will get better on their own, and he will be able to eat steak again soon.

2 THE TRADITIONAL LIBERAL VIEW OF AUTONOMY: 'TO LIVE ONE'S LIFE ACCORDING TO REASONS AND MOTIVES THAT ARE TAKEN AS ONE'S OWN'[1]

Chapter 2 described how legal capacity has served as the 'gateway for autonomy'[2] and introduced the concept of autonomy in philosophy and law.[3] It referred, in particular, to the writings of Kant and Rawls, whose constructs of moral personhood and citizenship are based on the recognition of autonomy. If, as Kant proposes, autonomy is the foundation of personhood, then logically the consequence for individuals who are non-autonomous and who have decisions made for them by substitutes is that they are non-persons.[4]

Dworkin famously wrote: 'About the only features held constant from one author to another are that autonomy is a feature of persons and that it is a

[1] John Christman, 'Autonomy in Moral and Political Philosophy' in Edward N Zalta (ed), *The Stanford Encyclopedia of Philosophy* (Fall 2020 Edition), https://plato.stanford.edu/archives/fall2020/entries/autonomy-moral/

[2] Mary Donnelly, *Healthcare Decision-Making and the Law: Autonomy, Capacity and the Limits of Liberalism* (Cambridge University Press, 2010) 90.

[3] See Chapter 2, Section 2.1 'Charity Model', Section 3.2.3 'Functional Test', and Section 3.3.2 'Substituted Judgement and Will and Preferences'.

[4] See Chapter 2, Section 2.1.

desirable quality to have.'[5] Feinberg expressed his doubts that autonomy has a single, coherent meaning.[6] An extensive description and analysis of the various conceptions and critiques of autonomy are beyond the scope of this book, which instead focuses on autonomy as understood in the Article 12 literature. For this purpose, Christman's definition provides a useful starting point:

> Individual autonomy is an idea that is generally understood to refer to the capacity to be one's own person, to live one's life according to reasons and motives that are taken as one's own and not the product of manipulative or distorting external forces.[7]

Christman's definition reveals that autonomy is associated with three dominant and overlapping features: rationality or the ability to reason, living one's life independently and being free from interference by others. I elaborate on these three features below before considering their application in Article 12 decision-making.

2.1 *Autonomy as Rationality*

For Kant, rational agency and autonomy are pre-conditions for an individual to be respected by others and recognised as having moral personhood.[8] Rawls draws on the legacy of Kant in his theory of justice as fairness by prioritising the ability for rational thinking by individuals in developing a just and fair society.[9] He theorises that such a society is based on a social contract negotiated by persons who make decisions freely and voluntarily using their ability to exercise rational judgement to develop and pursue their own conception of the good life.[10] Rawls's idea of the social contract is based on the premise that:

> each person beyond a certain age and possessed of the requisite intellectual capacity develops a sense of justice … We acquire a skill in judging things to be just and unjust and in supporting these judgments by reasons.[11]

For the exercise of rational judgement and the ability to bargain, a 'requisite' level of 'intellectual capacity' is required.[12] Because adults with cognitive disability may

5 Gerald Dworkin, *The Theory and Practice of Autonomy* (Cambridge University Press, 1998) 6.
6 John Christman, 'Constructing the Inner Citadel: Recent Work on the Concept of Autonomy' (1988) 99(1) *Ethics* 109, 109.
7 Christman, 'Autonomy in Moral and Political Philosophy' (n 1) [1].
8 David T Wasserman et al, 'Cognitive Disability and Moral Status' in Edward N Zalta (ed), *The Stanford Encyclopedia of Philosophy* (Fall 2017 Edition), <https://plato.stanford.edu/archives/fall2017/entries/cognitive-disability/>; Christman, 'Autonomy in Moral and Political Phjilosphy' (n 1) [1.1].
9 John Rawls, *A Theory of Justice* (Harvard University Press, 1971) 3, 11–12.
10 Ibid 16.
11 Ibid 46.
12 See also earlier account of Rawls in Chapter 2, Section 2.1.

lack the ability to reason, they are considered non-autonomous and non-persons.[13] Functional tests of capacity typically test what we would consider an adult's rational capacities. They consider whether an adult can understand information relevant to a decision; retain, use and weigh that information to make the decision; and communicate that decision in some way through any means.[14]

2.2 *Autonomy as Independence*

The traditional liberal accounts of autonomy are of the independent, rational individual or citizen as an isolate who can negotiate and bargain his or her position in the social contract. In acting according to his or her own values, the autonomous individual acts independently, unbowed by the influence of others. In this sense, classic liberal autonomy constitutes the capacity for '*procedural independence* or *independence of mind*' in requiring certain processes of critical reflection without dictating external, substantive values.[15] Autonomy in a procedural sense demands that a person's autonomous choices or actions be free from 'coercion or manipulation by others',[16] so an autonomous individual has strong boundaries between self and others. Mill's conception of liberty has greatly influenced contemporary concepts of autonomy, privileging the value of the individual in society and the individual's freedom to make personal life choices without interference from others. While Mill also proposed limited exceptions to the privileging of liberty in cases where the exercise of individual liberty could result in harm,[17] proceduralist autonomy is considered by many to have intrinsic value quite apart from any instrumental benefits it may bring and even if it results in harm to the self or others.[18]

2.3 *Autonomy as Non-interference in the Private Sphere*

Linked with the concept of individual autonomy in the liberal philosophy of both Mill and Rawls is a clear distinction between the public and private spheres of life.

[13] People who are non-autonomous include 'not only the permanently unconscious, but also those, such as the profoundly and permanently demented, who are not persons and who have only radically truncated interests'. Buchanan, Allen E and Dan W Brock, *Deciding for Others: The Ethics of Surrogate Decision Making* (Cambridge University Press, 1989) 12.

[14] Ben White, Lindy Willmott and Shih-Ning Then, 'Chapter 7: Adults Who Lack Capacity: Substitute Decision Making' in Ben White, Fiona McDonald and Lindy Willmott (eds), *Health Law in Australia* (Lawbook Co, 3rd ed, 2018) 207, 229.

[15] Catriona Mackenzie and Natalie Stoljar, 'Introduction: Autonomy Reconfigured' in Catriona Mackenzie and Natalie Stoljar (eds), *Relational Autonomy: Feminist Perspectives on Autonomy, Agency and the Social Self* (Oxford University Press, 2000) 3, 40.

[16] Ibid.

[17] John Stuart Mill, *On Liberty* (Routledge, 1991) 30.

[18] Viv Ashley, *Philosophical Models of Personal Autonomy (version 5)* (Essex Autonomy Project, 2013) 11.

For Mill, state interference compromises individual liberty.[19] For Rawls, the public, political sphere is situated outside of the family – the social contract is negotiated between adult men as citizens and subjects,[20] leaving the private, family sphere as an apolitical space.[21] In traditional liberal philosophy, the distinction between the individual and the State is critical. As described in Chapter 3, civil–political rights to non-interference in the personal, private realm are thereby privileged while socio-economic rights that intervene in the personal realm and impose external values are devalued as not 'true' rights.[22] Given the history of state institutionalisation of people with disability and associated abuses, it is not surprising that disability advocates are suspicious of state power.[23] In this context, the privileging of the right of people with disability to be left alone, and to be allowed to have personal, private lives without state involvement, is an important one. Guardianship and mental health legislation typically require implementation in the 'least restrictive' way in deference to the concept of autonomy as lack of interference.[24]

2.4 *The Case of Alex*

In the case of Alex, let us assume that he has been assessed according to a functional test as not having the capacity to make the decision relating to the dental treatment. He does not understand the longer-term benefits of having the treatment and cannot weigh those benefits against the shorter-term pain. A substitute decision-maker could be appointed to make a decision in Alex's best interests. The substitute may well decide that the dental work should proceed, having considered both Alex's expressed wishes and the longer-term benefits of treatment.

If, on the other hand, decision-making by substitutes were no longer an option, then Alex would instead be supported to make a decision that would be attributed to him as his own. The possible different outcomes of a process of supported decision-making are investigated further in the sections below. They show that the challenge

19 Mill (n 17) 30.

20 Dodds writes of Rawls that: 'The principles of justice were only applied to activities in the public realm': Susan Dodds, 'Depending on Care: Recognition of Vulnerability and the Social Contribution of Care Provision' (2017) 21(9) *Bioethics* 500, 501.

21 See Camillia Kong, 'The Convention on the Rights of Persons with Disabilities and Article 12: Prospective Feminist Lessons against the "Will and Preferences" Paradigm' (2015) 4(4) *Laws* 709, 608–9.

22 See Chapter 3, Section 3.3.

23 Rosemary Kayess and Philip French, 'Out of Darkness into Light? Introducing the Convention on the Rights of Persons with Disabilities' (2008) 8(1) *Human Rights Law Review* 1, 12.

24 Barbara Carter, 'The Case for Dignity as the Governing Principle in Adult Guardianship' (2010) 19(1) *Res Publica* 1, 3; for explanation of the 'least restrictive way' in mental health and guardianship legislation, see: Julia Duffy, Sam Boyle and Katrine Del Villar, 'What Does "Least Restrictive" or "Less Restrictive" Mean in Mental Health Law? Contradictions and Confusion in the Case of Queensland, Australia' (forthcoming 2023, symposium issue) *American Journal of Law and Medicine*.

for supported decision-making in this and other cases is that, under a traditional liberal view, this support could also be conceptualised as compromising Alex's autonomy. It would compromise his autonomy by limiting his independence, interfering in his personal/private realm, and potentially undermining his own value system. For this reason, advocates of universal legal capacity have sought to refashion autonomy by framing it as underpinning all supported decision-making and therefore inclusive of all adults with cognitive disability.

Sections 3 and 4 describe how the literature advocating universal legal capacity refashions autonomy to include adults with cognitive disability. It is refashioned by divorcing it from rationality; reconceptualising independence as interdependence; and reframing Millian liberty (freedom from interference) to a mix of 'positive' and 'negative' liberty. Following these descriptions, I return to the case of Alex to argue why and how none of these refashionings functions convincingly to reconceptualise autonomy as an inclusive basis for personhood.

3 AUTONOMY AS PERSONHOOD: BUT REFASHIONED BY DIVORCING AUTONOMY FROM RATIONALITY

Kantian autonomy underpins a concept of legal capacity as the right to make choices in accordance with one's own values, but, according to Kant, such choices must be rational. So, in refashioning autonomy to be inclusive of all adults with cognitive disability, many commentators have sought to de-emphasise or subordinate the role of rationality in decision-making.

3.1 *A Role for Emotions in Decision-Making and Autonomy*

General Comment No 1 criticises functional tests of capacity because they rely on testing mental capacity, a concept that 'is highly controversial in and of itself. Mental capacity is not, as is commonly presented, an objective, scientific and naturally occurring phenomenon.'[25] In this statement, the UN Disability Committee suggests that decision-making does not always rely on mental capacity as rationality. In the literature more widely, there is some controversy as to what extent decision-making processes are wholly cognitive as opposed to emotional or more broadly psychological, and therefore subject to internal influences that affect otherwise purely cognitive or rational functioning.[26]

[25] *United Nations Committee on the Rights of Persons with Disabilities 'General Comment No. 1 (2014) Article 12: Equal Recognition Before the Law CRPD/C/GC/1' (2014) ('General Comment No 1')* [13]–[15].

[26] Ashley (n 18) 11–12; Marina Oshana, 'Personal Autonomy and Society' (1998) 29(1) *Journal of Social Philosophy* 81, 81; George Szmukler, Rowena Daw and Felicity Callard, 'Mental Health Law and the UN Convention on the Rights of Persons with Disabilities' (2014) 37(3)

Some theorists argue strongly that emotional and affective factors play a significant role in decision-making, even for those who have the capacity for high-level reasoning.[27] They assert that the boundary between reason and emotion is more porous than Kantian philosophy or science allows.[28] Such arguments have been raised or relied on by those seeking to include adults with cognitive disability within the conceptions of autonomy and personhood that underpin Article 12.[29] Even though such adults may lack rational decision-making abilities, they nevertheless can exercise choice and make decisions in accordance with their own emotionally derived and constituted values, with the added implication that all of us are influenced by emotional factors in our decision-making.

In the case of Alex, if we challenge the dominance of rationality as a basis for personhood, we could ascribe capacity and personhood to Alex. There is indeed a strong emotional 'logic' to his resistance to dental treatment, given his past traumatic experiences. In this case, Alex's legal capacity would be recognised, the treatment would not proceed, and Alex would lose his teeth.

3.2 *Rationality Not Needed for Exercising 'Mere Choice' or 'Preference'*

Kant's concept of the will has been described as 'distinct from the ability to choose'. This is because the exercise of our Kantian will is constrained by our obligation to act according to the moral law and to make decisions based on reason.[30] Extrapolating

International Journal of Law and Psychiatry 245, 248; in David Bilchitz, 'Dignity, Fundamental Rights and Legal Capacity: Moving beyond the Paradigm Set by the General Comment on Article 12 of the Convention on the Rights of Persons with Disabilities' (2016) 32(3) *South African Journal on Human Rights* 410, 425; Christman writes that 'an answer to the question of whether (and to what extent) an agent must be rational to be autonomous has not been settled on in the literature': Christman, 'Constructing the Inner Citadel' (n 6) 116. The amount of literature in this area is vast, but another influential and much cited text is Daniel Kahneman, *Thinking, Fast and Slow* (Farrar, Strauss and Giroux, 2011).

[27] Donnelly (n 2) 99–100; 'Autonomous decision making is therefore built upon the interaction between cognition (giving practical reason content) and emotion (giving practical reason vision)': in Jonathan Herring and Jesse Wall, 'Autonomy, Capacity and Vulnerable Adults: Filling the Gaps in the Mental Capacity Act' (2015) 35(4) *Legal Studies* 698, 705.

[28] Mackenzie and Stoljar (n 15) 38.

[29] Gerard Quinn and Abigail Rekas-Rosalbo, 'Civil Death: Rethinking the Foundations of Legal Personhood for Persons with a Disability' (2016) 56 *Irish Jurist* 286, 322; Arstein-Kerslake writes of autonomy and personhood in the CRPD: 'It goes beyond traditional liberal notions, which restrict personhood to individual actors operating on the basis of "rationally" conscripted conceptions of their own "good"' in Anna Arstein-Kerslake, 'An Empowering Dependency: Exploring Support for the Exercise of Legal Capacity' (2016) 18 *Scandinavian Journal of Disability Research* 77, 78; Gerard Quinn, 'From Civil Death to Civil Life: The Decay and Re-Birth of Legal Capacity Law around the World' (Conference Paper, Australian Guardianship and Administration Council National Conference: Reflecting Will and Preference in Decision-Making, 17–18 October 2016) 11, <www.agac.org.au/images/stories/2016nsw/quinn-decay-rebirth-legal-cap-law.pdf>.

[30] Jerome Borges Schneewind, 'Kant on the Will' in Thomas Pink and Martin William Francis Stone (eds), *The Will and Human Action: From Antiquity to the Present Day* (Routledge, 2004)

from Kant, Frankfurt argues that the ability to have a will is what constitutes us as humans and is evidenced by our ability to reflect on our 'first-order desires' to develop and act on our 'second-order volitions'.[31] For example, our first-order desire may be to have a piece of chocolate cake, but on reflection, our second-order volition may be to refuse the cake for health reasons. Frankfurt's theory of autonomy is one of several referred to as 'hierarchical accounts', which link autonomy and the notion of the will with the capacity to reflect and reason.[32]

Szmukler applies a hierarchical account of autonomy to explain the meanings of 'will' and 'preference' as they relate to Article 12 decision-making. He argues that a person's will relates to a decision that is formed through higher-order executive functioning, and thus reflects 'a person's deep beliefs, values and commitments', whereas a preference is a more fleeting desire, and not therefore reflective of a person's autonomous will. Szmukler argues that in Article 12 terms, autonomy, legal capacity and the ability to make decisions require the ability to reflect rationally on one's preferences; and when there is a conflict or divergence between an adult's will and their preferences, the former should prevail.[33]

The idea of autonomy as the right to have choices and make decisions has dominated medical ethics and can be seen in its emphasis on the right to consent to or refuse treatment.[34] This notion of autonomy has also been shaped by Mill's idea of individual liberty as the right to make choices and take actions without interference from others, to pursue a life plan that aligns with our own 'character'.[35] Emphasis on autonomy as the right to make choices is foregrounded in the CRPD's Preamble, which recognises 'the importance for persons with disabilities of their individual autonomy and independence, including the freedom to make their own choices',[36] and the General

154, quoted George Szmukler, '"Capacity", "Best Interests", "Will and Preferences" and the UN Convention on the Rights of Persons with Disabilities' (2019) 18(1) *World Psychiatry: Official Journal of the World Psychiatric Association (WPA)* 34, 38.

31 Harry Frankfurt, 'Freedom of the Will and the Concept of a Person' (1971) 68(1) *Journal of Philosophy* 5, 6–18.

32 For example, Dworkin describes how autonomy is constituted by being able to act upon our second-order desires, which are derived from our ability to critically reflect upon our 'first-order preferences, desires, wishes, and so forth and the capacity to accept or attempt to change these in the light of higher-order preferences and values'. Dworkin (n 5) 20. See, however, some criticism of hierarchical accounts in Tom L Beauchamp and James F Childress, *Principles of Biomedical Ethics* (Oxford University Press, 6th ed, 2009) 101. Also criticised in Diana Meyers, *Self, Society and Personal Choice* (Columbia University Press, 1989) 33–4.

33 George Szmukler, 'The UN Convention on the Rights of Persons with Disabilities: "Rights, Will and Preferences" in Relation to Mental Health Disabilities' (2017) 54 *International Journal of Law and Psychiatry* 90, 96. See also in relation to Article 12, a discussion on the difference between immediate preference and 'higher-order loading of more settled values', in Terry Carney et al, 'Realising "Will, Preferences and Rights": Reconciling Differences on Best Practice Support for Decision-Making?' (2019) *Griffith Law Review* 357, 360.

34 Beauchamp and Childress (n 32) 101.

35 Mill (n 17) 33.

36 *CRPD* Preamble para 14.

Principles in Article 3, which affirm 'Respect for … individual autonomy including the freedom to make one's own choices, and independence of persons.'[37]

However, some interpretations of Article 12 as the right to choose reflect a less demanding concept of choice than that envisaged by Kant, Mill, Frankfurt or Szmukler. In this way, autonomy or legal capacity has become the right to have any desires or choices recognised at law and not just decisions made according to a process of rational deliberation reflecting an adult's will.[38] Hall is critical of such a thin concept of autonomy. She draws a distinction between 'mere choices' made by an adult with advanced dementia (which in her view may be legitimately overridden by the adult's guardian) and considered decisions that should be legally recognised as the adult's own.[39]

In the case of Alex, if he were to make a decision according to his 'mere choice', then his immediate desire and preference would be to refuse treatment. Such a decision may, however, conflict with his underlying values or will, relating to the joy he finds in dining with his friends.

3.3 *Rationality Not Needed for a Person to Have an 'Authentic' Self*

The hierarchical theories of autonomy described above suggest we have an 'authentic' self.[40] In this sense, they are premised on the idea that a person's actions and decisions have a diachronic coherence, sometimes referred to in the Article 12 literature as an adult's coherent 'life narrative'.[41] The requirement that, in cases where an adult's will and preferences cannot be determined, a decision should be made according to the 'best interpretation' of their will and preferences appears to be premised on the assumption of authenticity and narrative coherence. Bach and Kerzner, for example, write:

37 See also: Article 19 (Living independently and being included in the community), which recognises the right of persons to live in the community 'with choices equal to others'; Article 20 (Personal mobility), which requires mobility to be facilitated 'in the manner and at the time of their choice'; Article 21 (Freedom of expression and opinion, and accessible information), which requires that people have 'all forms of communication of their choice'; and Article 29 (Participation in political and public life), which provides that a person may have an assistant 'of their own choice' to facilitate voting in elections.

38 World Network of Users and Survivors of Psychiatry, 'Implementation Manual for the United Nations Convention on the Rights of Persons with Disabilities' (February 2008) 16, 20.

39 Margaret Hall, 'Rethinking Adult Guardianship: Mental Capacity and Vulnerability in the Context of Dementia in Old Age' (PhD Thesis, University of British Columbia, 2018) 13; see also: Katrine Del Villar, 'Should Supported Decision-Making Replace Substituted Decision-Making? The Convention on the Rights of Persons with Disabilities and Coercive Treatment under Queensland's Mental Health Act 2000' (2015) 4(2) *Laws* 173, 186.

40 Christman, 'Autonomy in Moral and Political Philosophy' (n 19) [1]; Dworkin (n 5) 15.

41 Lucy Series, 'Relationships, Autonomy and Legal Capacity: Mental Capacity and Support Paradigms' (2015) 40 *International Journal of Law and Psychiatry* 80, 86; Kristin Booth Glen, 'Introducing a New Human Right: Learning from Others, Bringing Legal Capacity Home' (2018) 49(3) *Columbia Human Rights Law Review* 1, 41.

> If to my actions can be ascribed intentions of my will which themselves can be woven into a coherent narrative, either by myself or others, even if the intentions or wilful behaviour represent some discontinuity with the past, then this should be sufficient ground for exercising my legal capacity.[42]

Glen similarly suggests that a 'supporter', making a decision under an advance directive, could 'make the choice consistent with the person's "general life narrative"',[43] and Quinn writes that Article 12 represents a shift 'to ensure that the authentic voice of the person is allowed to come through loud and clear'.[44]

In the case of Alex, if we were to recognise his capacity under Article 12 and then apply a hierarchical account, we could say that his preference not to have the treatment is a mere choice or desire that he hasn't reflected on, and so it doesn't represent his autonomous will. His autonomous will is expressed in the longer-term desire to eat and socialise with his friends. This social activity is part of his authentic self, according to his coherent life narrative. Under this account, the supporter would interpret his autonomous will to be to have the treatment, even though this would contradict his expressed preferences.

Alternatively, it could be argued that Alex's survival of sexual abuse as a child is part of his life narrative; that he doesn't want to just dismiss this as irrelevant to the way he conducts himself, but that it is part of his authentic self. On this account, given that the anticipation of dental treatment brings back memories of this sexual assault, a supporter would interpret his will as being to refuse the treatment, such refusal also being in accordance with his expressed preference.

If a 'best interpretation' of an adult's will and preferences is one that accords most clearly with the adult's values, according to his or her authentic self and consistent with his or her life narrative, then different interpretations will lead to alternative and potentially conflicting decisions.

3.4 *Why Autonomy without Rationality Does Not Work as Universal Personhood*

Commentators who advocate for the abolition of decision-making by substitutes argue that emotions play a significant role in decision-making and that an adult's 'mere choice' or preferences should be respected as their decision and as an exercise of legal capacity under Article 12. Consistently with this, a 'best interpretation' of an adult's will and preferences is one that reflects their authentic self or their coherent life narrative, whether such self or life are constituted by thinking rationally or by feeling emotionally.

[42] Michael Bach and Lana Kerzner, *A New Paradigm for Protecting Autonomy and the Right to Legal Capacity: Advancing Substantive Equality for Persons with Disabilities through Law, Policy and Practice* (Law Commission of Ontario, October 2010) 63–6.

[43] Glen 'Introducing a New Human Right' (n 41) 41.

[44] Quinn (n 29) 4, 24.

However, the example of Alex shows the challenges of such an approach, when a supporter is presumed to know an adult's authentic self even better than the adult themselves, and in the face of unforeseen choices. Application of the concept of 'narrative coherence' to ascribe capacity to an adult under Article 12 has been criticised for falsely attributing an unconflicted unity to the claimant of rights,[45] failing to consider external factors that might influence the adult to develop a harmful narrative,[46] and overlooking that a supporter has 'considerable power to alter a person's "narrative" through their interpretation'.[47] It also assumes that an individual's will or decision is there to be 'discovered' by the supporter and not created or derived through the interactive process of supported decision-making itself.[48]

This notion of an authentic self is a strong theme in the Article 12 commentary, but it poses two critical challenges. The first is that if autonomy is divorced from rationality or self-reflection, relying on an adult's first-order desires or preferences can lead to different outcomes or 'decisions'. The second challenge relates to determining when an adult's desires are truly their own – that is, not unduly influenced by another, including the supporter.[49] Excising rationality from autonomy is one strategy for refashioning autonomy (and therefore legal capacity) as universal. However, I argue that this strategy effaces the difference that the residual impacts of cognitive impairment may have on decision-making ability. It also stretches the concept of autonomy beyond its meaningful limits.

4 AUTONOMY AS PERSONHOOD: BUT REFASHIONED AS '*INTER*DEPENDENCE' OR RELATIONAL AUTONOMY, RELATIONSHIPS OF TRUST OR AS POSITIVE AND NEGATIVE LIBERTY

As described above, traditional accounts of autonomy emphasise independence 'as self-sufficiency, individual self-determination, and freedom from the constraint and influence of others'.[50] However, Article 12(3) explicitly provides for support in exercising legal capacity. It, therefore, acknowledges that people with disability are not always independent, self-sufficient or unaffected by others in their decision-making

45 Paul Skowron, 'Giving Substance to "the Best Interpretation of Will and Preferences"' (2019) 62 *International Journal of Law and Psychiatry* 125, 133.

46 Camillia Kong, *Mental Capacity in Relationship: Decision-Making, Dialogue and Autonomy* (Cambridge University Press, 2017) 65.

47 Series (n 41) 87.

48 Carney et al (n 33) 360–1.

49 Lucy Series and Anna Nilsson, 'Article 12 CRPD: Equal Recognition before the Law' in Ilias Bantekas, Michael Ashley Stein and Anastasiou Dimitris (eds), *The UN Convention on the Rights of Persons with Disabilities: A Commentary* (Oxford University Press, 2018) 339, 370. Note: 'All people risk being subject to "undue influence", yet this may be exacerbated for those who rely on the support of others to make decisions'. In *General Comment No 1* [22].

50 Laura Davy, 'Philosophical Inclusive Design: Intellectual Disability and the Limits of Individual Autonomy in Moral and Political Theory' (2015) 30(1) *Hypatia* 132, 138.

processes and that support can enhance their autonomy and decision-making ability. To include adults with cognitive disability in conceptions of autonomy and personhood, some commentators have refashioned autonomy so that it is constituted by shared personhood or *inter*dependence; relational autonomy; cooperative relationships of trust, or as both positive and negative liberty. Sections 4.1–4.5 below provide a summary of some of these theories, while Section 4.6 argues why and how they ultimately fail to justify recognition of universal legal capacity or serve as a foundation for acknowledging inclusive personhood. Section 4.7 returns to the case study of Alex to illustrate these limitations.

4.1 *Autonomy as Shared Personhood or* Inter*dependence*

Adults with disability have been culturally marked as dependent, such dependency being a significant factor in society's protective attitude towards them and the associated denial of their autonomy and legal capacity. By contrast, Bach and Kerzner describe the autonomy envisaged by Article 12 as exhibiting 'interdependence' or as incorporating the notion of interdependence.[51] In doing so, they reconfigure liberal autonomy by ostensibly challenging the notion of the bounded and independent individual as the ideal of Kantian personhood.

Quinn and Arstein-Kerslake describe how the CRPD shifts the balance from protection to autonomy. They criticise the various capacity tests as failing to acknowledge that all of us 'rely on a wide variety of supports, social cues and the benefits of social capital to give context, meaning and direction to [our] choices' and that decision-making with others is the norm for all of us.[52] Quinn describes how the CRPD, with Article 12 at its epicentre, restores moral authority and personhood to adults with cognitive disability by acknowledging that 'our personhood' is 'primarily shared'[53] and that 'our autonomy is fundamentally relational'.[54] For these writers, Article 12 articulates a concept of 'shared'[55] personhood through its promotion of supported decision-making.

These writers seek to destigmatise dependence, reconceive it as 'interdependence' or 'shared personhood' and value it as essential to autonomy.[56] Dependence

[51] 'Rather autonomy is a social and inter-dependent accomplishment': Bach and Kerzner (n 42) 95.

[52] Gerard Quinn and Anna Arstein-Kerslake, 'Restoring the "Human" in "Human Rights": Personhood and Doctrinal Innovation in the UN Disability Convention' in Costas Douzinas and CA Gearty (eds), *Cambridge Companion to Human Rights Law* (Cambridge University Press, 2012) 36, 46.

[53] Quinn (n 29) 12.

[54] Ibid 10.

[55] Quinn and Arstein-Kerslake (n 52) 40.

[56] Bach and Kerzner (n 42) 96; Quinn (n 29) 10–12; Quinn and Rekas-Rosalbo (n 29) 17; Andrea Nicki, on the other hand, points out the limitations of a sense of self based on interdependence when the 'connectedness' in an abusive relationship leads to a diminishing sense of self: 'For people … from severely abusive families, connectedness is a great source of despair and

has historically been stigmatised both by the wider community and by disability advocates themselves, so autonomy as interdependence endeavours to normalise, render mainstream and universalise the 'dependencies' of disability.[57] Autonomy as interdependence is used to include all adults with cognitive disability as persons.

4.2 *Relational Autonomy*

Bach and Kerzner, Arstein-Kerslake, Quinn and others also invoke or refer to the notion of 'relational autonomy' to describe the autonomy envisaged by Article 12. Bach and Kerzner refer to Mackenzie and Stoljar, who describe 'relational autonomy' as 'an umbrella term, designating a range of related perspectives'.[58] Mackenzie and Stoljar describe the various theories of relational autonomy as diverse but as nevertheless 'premised on a shared conviction, the conviction that persons are socially embedded and that agents' identities are formed within the context of social relationships and shaped by a complex of intersecting social determinants, such as race, class, gender and ethnicity'.[59] Under some accounts of relational autonomy, an individual is said to be almost equivalent to the sum of their social relationships, so that 'the *identity of the self* is constituted by various social attachments'.[60]

Mackenzie and Stoljar go on to explain that some forms of feminism originally dismissed autonomy as inherently masculinist and, therefore, not a concept or condition to be given high value. Compared with men, most women lived lives of dependence (at least financial dependence), so the original feminist analysis proposed that values associated with dependency, such as trust, loyalty, friendship and caring, should be prioritised over independence and autonomy. The development of the concept of relational autonomy endorses autonomy as a normative value but rejects the 'hyperbolic abstraction' of autonomy as independent self-determination in favour of 'the possibilities for anti-individualistic conceptions'.[61]

Arstein-Kerslake explains relational autonomy as challenging traditional notions of atomistic selfhood and decision-making, and as therefore describing or allowing for a model of decision-making with support.[62] For Quinn, the concept

self-hatred': Andrea Nicki, 'The Abused Mind: Feminist Theory, Psychiatric Disability and Trauma' (2001) 16(4) *Hypatia* 80, 98.

57 Barbara Arneil, 'Disability in Political Theory versus International Practice: Redefining Equality and Freedom' in Barbara Arneil and Nancy J Hirschmann (eds), *Disability and Political Theory* (Cambridge University Press, 2016) 10, 40–2.

58 Bach and Kerzner (n 42) 39, quoting Mackenzie and Stoljar (n 15) 4.

59 Mackenzie and Stoljar (n 15) 4.

60 Ibid 61.

61 Ibid 6–8.

62 Anna Arstein-Kerslake, *Restoring Voice to People with Cognitive Disabilities: Realizing the Right to Equal Recognition before the Law* (Cambridge University Press, 2017) 63.

of relational autonomy shines a light on the interdependent nature of personhood more widely, an interdependence that is normally hidden and denied by the myth of 'the atomised rational man'.[63] Like Arstein-Kerslake, Quinn expressly applies this thinking to the paradigm of supported decision-making required by Article 12(3) CRPD, arguing that supports are not required as an exception to the norm and can therefore be provided without undermining or negating the personhood of adults with cognitive disability. For Quinn, supported decision-making should be embraced as describing and reflecting the practices of all of us.[64] Under these accounts, autonomy is reconceptualised as relational autonomy. An adult is autonomous to the extent that he or she is embedded in a network of social and personal relationships. Under this account, we are all autonomous (i.e. 'relationally' autonomous).

4.3 *Autonomy Characterised by Trust, Cooperation and the 'Cognitive Prosthesis'*

The reconceptualisation of liberal autonomy as a condition of interdependence has echoes in philosophical theories that attribute personhood through the notion of trusteeship.[65] Silvers and Francis develop a trusteeship model for adults with cognitive disability, which provides that an adult who is dependent on another (e.g. on a supporter) for decision-making should nonetheless be viewed as autonomous and attributed full moral personhood.

4.3.1 Trust and Cooperation

Francis begins by acknowledging that adults with cognitive disability do not necessarily have autonomy in the traditional Rawlsian sense but proposes a more complex conception of autonomy that includes them as persons and citizens. She lists some of the indicia typically ascribed to autonomy as follows: the capacity to value; the capacity to understand and reason; the ability to be an agent; the ability to formulate plans; the ability to act according to principles (not desires); the ability to not be subject to coercion; and the ability to act rationally.[66] Focusing on adults

[63] Quinn (n 29) 9; see also Cahill, who prefers the concept of relational autonomy to more traditional liberal accounts of autonomy, because in her view, it more readily recognises non-rational elements of decision-making, as exhibited by adults with dementia: Suzanne Cahill, *Dementia and Human Rights* (Policy Press at the University of Bristol, 2018) 14.

[64] Quinn (n 29) 10.

[65] Wasserman et al (n 8) describes theories of 'Proxy, derivative, and presumptive moral status', describing Thomas Scanlon as affirming full moral status to all human beings, including adults with cognitive disabilities who can acquire the capacity for 'judgement-sensitive' attitudes or moral personhood' 'vicariously, through trustees'; Leslie Pickering Francis also refers to Scanlon in: Leslie P Francis, 'Understanding Autonomy in Light of Intellectual Disability' in Kimberley Brownlee and Adam Cureton (eds), *Disability and Disadvantage* (Oxford University Press, 2009) 200, 210.

[66] Francis (n 65) 201.

with intellectual disability, she proposes that they may not possess all of these attributes but still may be autonomous.[67]

Silvers and Francis also propose a refashioning of Rawls's social contract by questioning his view of society as being formed by atomistic individuals, each involved in negotiations with one another. They propose instead that the social contract can more usefully be conceived of as a network of relationships developed through a process of trusting rather than bargaining.[68] Trust, according to these authors, is a quality that everyone can possess, independent of cognitive ability or rational capacity, thereby including those with cognitive disability as moral persons. While we are all individuals who, in turn, represent ourselves to others, we are also 'trustees' for others who represent others to society in a certain way, so that 'autonomy is so often a collaborative affair'.[69] Hartley likens this proposal to her own conception of the social contract as comprising relationships of 'cooperation for mutual advantage'.[70] She endorses a 'relationship model' of cooperation so that when adults cannot contribute in ways that can be readily quantified (e.g. in economic or financial terms), they nevertheless 'can contribute to society too, through the capacity for engagement'.[71] Because people with cognitive disability make a positive cooperative contribution to social relationships, they are within the social contract and personhood is attributed to them.[72] Autonomy is reconceived as a network of mutually trusting relationships that mark our personhood and in which we all participate.

4.3.2 The Supporter as Cognitive Prosthesis

Arstein-Kerslake describes how Francis and Silvers alternatively propose a 'prosthesis model' of personhood. According to this model, a support person for an adult with cognitive disability is a 'cognitive prosthesis'[73] for the adult, so as to allow that adult to convey their own conception of 'the good' and thereby exercise their autonomy. To

[67] Ibid 207.

[68] Anita Silvers and Leslie Pickering Francis, 'Justice through Trust: Disability and the "Outlier Problem" in Social Contract Theory' (2005) 116(1) *Ethics* 40, 45.

[69] Francis (n 65) 215. Arstein-Kerslake endorses the trusteeship model of Silvers and Francis, as being consistent with the concept of autonomy that underlies the CPRD and Article 12: Arstein-Kerslake, *Restoring Voice to People with Cognitive Disabilities* (n 62) 43–4; Arstein-Kerslake, 'An Empowering Dependency' (n 29) 78.

[70] Christie Hartley, 'An Inclusive Contractualism: Obligations to the Mentally Disabled' in Kimberley Brownlee and Adam Cureton (eds), *Disability and Disadvantage* (Oxford University Press, 2009) 138, 143.

[71] Ibid 148.

[72] Ibid 147ff; see also discussion of Hartley in Stacy Clifford Simplican, 'Disavowals of Disability in Rawls' Theory of Justice and His Critics' in Barbara Arneil and Nancy J Hirschmann (eds), *Disability and Political Theory* (Cambridge University Press, 2016) 79, 91–2.

[73] Arstein-Kerslake, 'An Empowering Dependency' (n 29) 78; Leslie P Francis and Anita Silvers, 'Thinking about the Good: Reconfiguring Liberal Metaphysics (or not) for People with Cognitive Disabilties' in Eva Feder Kittay and Licia Carlson (eds), *Cognitive Disability and the Challenge to Moral Philosophy* (2010) 237, 249.

ensure the adult's liberty and autonomy, trustees as 'prostheses' must represent the adult's views and preferences and not project their own onto the adult.[74] For Arstein-Kerslake, this is what marks the trusteeship/prosthesis model as underpinning and justifying a supported and not a substitute decision-making model.[75] According to the theory, the decision is the adult's own, despite the involvement of the prosthesis. If an adult is supported by a prosthesis, then he or she can have autonomy and be recognised as a person like any other, with any decision made being attributed to the adult and not to the prosthesis/supporter. Francis and Silvers describe how this process of assistive thinking, as an interaction between the 'cognitively disabled individual' and the trustee or prosthesis, enables the individual to be included in Rawls's social contract, 'revealing' their personhood.[76]

4.4 *Supports as Enabling Positive Liberty/Autonomy*

As described above, Bach and Kerzner conceptualise Article 12 autonomy as interpersonal and relational, but they also describe it as incorporating a concept of 'positive liberty'. They explain that autonomy is usually conceived of as 'negative liberty' (i.e. as the absence of restraints[77]) but suggest that Article 12 invokes a 'positive liberty' view of autonomy because it is created by the positive provision of supports.[78] They acknowledge a tension between the two concepts of positive and negative liberty but argue that a careful balancing of the two is required so that adults with cognitive disability are not left as objects of abuse and neglect. Positive liberty means that: 'the state has a positive obligation to maximise the exercise and enjoyment of autonomy by providing individuals with the goods and services they require for this purpose, and for developing their own decision-making capabilities to exercise their autonomy'.[79] A contradiction begins to emerge as autonomy is traditionally conceived of as 'negative liberty', thus requiring non-interference by the State, and yet positive actions by the State are required to ensure autonomy.

[74] Arstein-Kerslake, 'An Empowering Dependency' (n 29) 78; see also: Leslie P Francis, Barbara E Bierer and Michael Ashley Stein, 'An Externalist, Process-Based Approach to Supported Decision-Making' (2022) 22(10) *The American Journal of Bioethics* 55, 56.

[75] Ibid.

[76] Francis and Silvers (n 73) 256; see also: Leslie Francis, 'Supported Decision-Making: The CRPD, Non-Discrimination, and Strategies for Recognizing Persons' Choices about Their Good' (2021) 1 *The Journal of Philosophy of Disability* 57, 65–6.

[77] Bach and Kerzner (n 42) 7, 12, 38.

[78] Ibid 38–44. For the concepts of 'negative' and 'positive liberty', Bach and Kerzner refer to Isaiah Berlin, 'Two Concepts of Liberty' in Henry Hardy (ed), *Liberty Incorporating Four Essays on Liberty* (Oxford Scholarship Online, 2002) 166, 170, 178–81. However, Kong's view is that their use of positive liberty in this way is a misinterpretation and misapplication of Berlin's theory. See: Kong, 'The Convention on the Rights of Persons with Disabilities and Article 12' (n 21) 720.

[79] Bach and Kerzner (n 42) 40–1.

Bach and Kerzner seek to resolve this contradiction by emphasising that Article 12(3) requires just the right number of supports necessary for a person to make an autonomous decision and exercise their legal capacity – no more, no less.[80] These supports are interpreted very narrowly and insularly as only those 'goods and services' directly required for the making of a particular decision. They include life-planning supports, independent advocacy, communication and interpretive supports, relationship-building supports and administrative supports.[81] Some of these Article 12(3) supports, especially life-planning supports, are potentially extensive and would in all practicality be required continuously to be effective. But according to Bach and Kerzner's logic, it is as if Article 12(3) only engages them at the point of making a decision. There is a reluctance to acknowledge the principle of indivisibility as being the interdependence between Article 12 and those other rights in the CRPD that may demand and claim ongoing socio-economic supports. It is as if personhood remains bounded within Article 12 and individual autonomy.

4.5 *Regulation as 'Positive Liberty'?*

Article 12(4) also requires positive action by the State in terms of regulation to guard against abuse, and to 'ensure that measures relating to the exercise of legal capacity respect the rights, will and preferences of the person'.[82] As noted in Chapter 2, while Article 12(4) has been interpreted as allowing for substitute decision-making, it also requires the integrity of supported decision-making to be protected.[83] Bach and Kerzner describe some state interventions as upholding 'positive' liberty or autonomy. *General Comment No 1* provides that legal recognition of support persons must be available, as well as a 'mechanism for third parties to verify the identity of a support person' and 'a mechanism for third parties to challenge the action of a support person'.[84] In their trusteeship model, Francis and Silvers also propose procedural protections against abuse to 'respond to people's differences without disadvantaging them for being so'.[85] While such interventions

80 Ibid 95.

81 Ibid 73–6.

82 See also: 'Given the importance of safeguarding in the context of support, it is vital that supporters, particularly those who support financial decisions, are subject to appropriate levels of supervision by a public body'. Rosie Harding, 'Supporting Everyday Legal Capacity: Navigating the Complexities of Putting Rights into Practice' in Mary Donnelly, Rosie Harding and Ezgi Tascioglu (eds), *Supporting Legal Capacity in Socio-Legal Context* (Hart Publishing, 2022) 291, 312.

83 See, e.g., Bartlett who writes of Article 12(4) that it 'refers expressly to the possibility that the exercise of legal capacity may be curtailed in some circumstances'. Peter Bartlett, 'The United Nations Convention on the Rights of Persons with Disabilities and Mental Health Law' (2012) 75(5) *The Modern Law Review* 752, 765. On the other hand, see *General Comment No 1* [20]–[22].

84 *General Comment No 1* [29(d)].

85 Silvers and Francis (n 68) 66.

are necessary to protect the integrity of the decision-making process, the UN Disability Committee prescribes that such regimes should nevertheless not 'over-regulate' the lives of people with disability.[86]

There are assumptions made about what kind of positive regulatory actions would be autonomy-enhancing and those that would be autonomy-denying. State regulation (or interference) designed to protect the integrity of supported decision-making, and therefore enhance autonomy, is framed as inhering within it a concept of positive liberty or autonomy. On the other hand, decision-making by substitutes is always autonomy-denying.

4.6 *Why Refashioning Autonomy as Interdependence, Relational Autonomy or Relationships of Trust Does Not Work as Universal Personhood*

Under the above accounts, an autonomous person is ostensibly not a bounded individual, but their personhood is constituted by their interdependence and is 'shared' because the supporter contributes to their 'positive liberty'. Relational autonomy is an umbrella term used by advocates of universal legal capacity to describe many of these variations of a theory of shared personhood. The boundaries around individuals as negotiators in the social contract are ostensibly reconfigured as lines of connection, not division.[87] External interference in decision-making is reframed as positive support so that the social contract and our personhood are recognised through the trustworthy honouring of our relationships. The supporter as cognitive prosthesis is one configuration of, or metaphor for, this notion of personhood as interdependent or shared.

4.6.1 How Does Alex's Situation Reveal the Problems with Retaining Refashioned Autonomy as the Basis of Personhood?

In the case of Alex, the supporter is not separate from Alex but is part of Alex's interdependent or shared personhood. This framing means that the supporter's critical role in Alex's personal life is autonomy-enhancing and balances positive liberty against negative. Under the trusteeship model, the relationship between Alex and the supporter is one of trust and connection. Alternatively, under the prosthesis model, it is as if Alex's bounded individuality is still intact, albeit the boundary has moved to include the rational 'prosthesis'.

If the supporter is trustworthy, he or she may well respect the preference (or will) of Alex to refuse dental treatment, given the strength of Alex's objections. Alternatively,

86 *General Comment No 1* [29].

87 Note Beaudry's argument and conclusion that Francis and Silvers's attempt to redefine the social contract as being constituted by relationships of trust ultimately fails to include all adults with severe and profound cognitive disability: Jonas-Sébastien Beaudry, *The Disabled Contract: Severe Intellectual Disability, Justice and Morality* (Cambridge University Press, 2021) 50.

if the supporter is contributing the rational component of the decision-making process by way of a prosthesis, he or she may attribute a more considered decision to Alex, as reflected in his longer-term desire to be able to eat gourmet food. So, even in the case of a trusted supporter, the decision may still go either way – but in either case, it will still be attributed to Alex.

This refashioning of autonomy to underpin Alex's personhood still raises problems about the certainty, transparency and integrity of supported decision-making. The following sections consider what these problems are and ultimately reject the refashionings of autonomy described above as a way of potentially recognising universal personhood. The chapter argues that: (1) shared personhood still does not tell us who is making the decision, (2) relational autonomy is not autonomy at all, (3) 'positive' liberty may lead to less autonomy (not more), (4) rationality and bounded personhood are still privileged and (5) the residual impacts of cognitive impairment on decision-making are still not acknowledged.

4.6.2 Shared Personhood Does Not Tell Us Who Is Making the Decision, Potentially Hiding Undue Influence or Abuse

Constructing Article 12 autonomy as interdependence or shared personhood fails to address one of the central challenges in supported decision-making. Supported decision-making, in shrouding or obfuscating the locus of decision-making power, can place the adult at risk of undue influence and exploitation. This is particularly a risk in the case of informal supported decision-making undertaken in the private sphere without state scrutiny, where the nature of the relationship between adult and supporter may be unclear.[88] In many cases, the concept of shared personhood may serve to hide who is truly making the decision; and it may expose adults to abuse and exploitation by supporters who are trusted family or personal friends.[89]

The theories of supporter as trustee or prosthesis face similar challenges in determining where the adult's personhood ends and the trustee's (or prosthesis's) begins. This is especially so because, according to this account of autonomy, the prostheses would appear to have no personhood themselves but are positioned as merely instrumental to the personhood of the adult. Del Villar criticises *General Comment No 1* for potentially treating 'the family instrumentally and not relationally' so that 'support is provided to enable a person with disabilities to act as an independent individual, not as a member of a family or community'.[90] The damage in viewing a supporter in this way, as instrumental to the personhood of the adult,

[88] Malcolm Parker, 'Getting the Balance Right: Conceptual Considerations Concerning Legal Capacity and Supported Decision-Making' (2016) 13(3) *Journal of Bioethical Inquiry* 381, 388.

[89] Anita Smith, 'Are Guardianship Laws and Practices Consistent with Human Rights Instruments?' in A Kimberly Dayton (ed), *Comparative Perspectives on Adult Guardianship* (Carolina Academic Press, 2014) 247, 266.

[90] Del Villar (n 39) 194.

is best illustrated in concrete terms by the comments of a supporter in a decision-making trial who reflected that:

> 'I'm just getting so drained, physically and emotionally, that I just feel like I'm shutting down, and I'm struggling to make decisions now, because I have to switch off, emotionally, so that I don't just fall apart and I'm not going to have time to not be productive.'[91]

Beaudry further criticises the trusteeship model for its failure to sidestep the problem that the trustee is 'a kind of delegate who would occupy a more active or intrusive role than delegates for non-disabled citizens or contractees'.[92] This suggests that the trustee is no more than a substitute decision-maker who thereby signals the adult's non-membership in the social contract and associated denial of personhood.

These accounts of shared or interdependent personhood do not explain how or when a supporter or a web of influence may be coercive and lead to denial of the 'individual autonomy' of the adult. Francis and Silvers acknowledge that their trusteeship theory cannot 'offer a full account of how justice through trust conceptualises exploitation'.[93] Simplican recognises this omission when she criticises the trusteeship theory for what she describes as its unsupported assumption that the 'non-disabled possess a high level of concern for the quality of treatment shown to people with severe disabilities … in a society which we know to be infused with ableist prejudices'.[94] Further, supporters as internal cognitive prostheses risk losing their own personhood as their agency is recognised only as far as it is instrumental to the personhood of the adult.[95]

4.6.3 Relational Autonomy: Different Kinds of Relationships

Writers have criticised the way that relational autonomy has been used by some of the above commentators to justify a conception of universal autonomy and legal capacity, and I agree with these criticisms. The concept of relational autonomy is useful in the context of challenging the '…notion of autonomy [as] fundamentally individualistic and rationalistic'[96] and in bringing attention to the social determinants of autonomy and the social embeddedness of our selves. However I challenge the logic of asserting that, while adults with severe and profound cognitive disability do not have autonomy in the traditional sense, they nevertheless possess relational autonomy and can therefore be recognised as having decision-making ability and legal capacity in all cases.

[91] Carney et al (n 33) 367.
[92] Beaudry (n 87) 172.
[93] Silvers and Francis (n 68) 65.
[94] Simplican (n 72) 94.
[95] Del Villar (n 39) 194.
[96] Mackenzie and Stoljar (n 15) 3.

Nedelsky, a prominent theorist of relational autonomy, explains the concept as a theory that relationships are constitutive of the self, but also that:

> autonomy is made possible by constructive relationship (or undermined by destructive relationship) … Autonomy can thrive or wither in adults depending on the structures of relationship they are embedded in.[97]

For Nedelsky, under a relational account, autonomy is never presumed[98] and never universal. She does, however, subscribe to the idea that everyone has a capacity for autonomy, even if it cannot be achieved without the *right* supports and relationships.[99] Nedelsky uses relational autonomy as an analytic tool to show how relationships operate in society on both the interpersonal and structural levels to foster individual liberty and security.[100]

Criticisms of the way that relational autonomy has been used to explain Article 12 autonomy echo those above that criticise that 'Facilitated decision making stretches the concept of RA to its limits'. Martin et al write that relational autonomy on a 'radical interpretation' would mean that 'a person could be deemed autonomous despite lacking decision-making ability', which would be 'an abuse of language (i.e. of the language of autonomy)'.[101] Ho also raises the double-edged sword of that 'radical' conception of relational autonomy, which is that the supporter may not be benign but abusive.[102] Wilson similarly writes that the use of relational autonomy to justify or explain universal legal capacity 'misunderstands the concept' which she explains as referring to '…how a person's relations in a wider sense with other people, the state, law and the world, support or hinder an individual's autonomy and how law structures and nurtures those relationships'.[103]

I agree with these authors that using relational autonomy to explain and justify recognising universal legal capacity exhibits a narrow understanding and application of the concept. Relational autonomy ultimately retains the distinction between those adults who have autonomy and those who do not but serves as a tool to investigate which relationships and social situations enhance autonomy and which undermine it.[104]

97 Jennifer Nedelsky, *Law's Relations: A Relational Theory of Self, Autonomy, and the Law* (Oxford University Press, 2012) 39.

98 Ibid 278.

99 Ibid 46.

100 Ibid 90.

101 Wayne Martin et al, *Achieving CRPD Compliance: Is the Mental Capacity Act of England and Wales Compatible with the UN Convention on the Rights of Persons with Disabilities? If Not, What Next?* (Essex Autonomy Project, 2014) 25–6.

102 Anita Ho, 'Relational Autonomy or Undue Pressure? Family's Role in Medical Decision-Making' (2008) 22(1) *Scandinavian Journal of Caring Sciences* 128, 128–9.

103 Kay Wilson, *Mental Health Law: Abolish or Reform?* (Oxford University Press, 2021) 159.

104 Kong refers to a 'relational analysis of rights' as being required to understand and make transparent the impact of social interactions and values (including the internalisation of those values) on the individual's autonomy and decision-making processes: Kong, *Mental Capacity in Relationship* (n 46) 43; Also, Hall describes relational autonomy as providing for a more transparent and accurate

Relational autonomy as conceptualised by Mackenzie and Stoljar, Nedelsky and others[105] values autonomy but also recognises that those without autonomy need to be supported with the right kinds of supports to achieve it.

4.6.4 'Positive' Liberty Includes Regulatory Intervention by the State

Bach and Kerzner refashion the concept of autonomy from negative liberty or restraint from interference by the State to a balancing of negative and positive liberties – that is, state restraint against state action.[106] State action includes safeguards such as the registration and regulation of supporters to further preserve and support autonomy.

Existing and proposed regulatory models for supported decision-making include the same types of regulatory mechanisms as Australian guardianship regimes but with added components to deal with different complexities. They may allow for registration of supporters; establishment of a state regulatory agency and a tribunal; registration of support agreements; imposition of fees; statutory duties for supporters; access by supporters to otherwise confidential information; immunity for supporters acting in good faith; appointment of a 'monitor' to check the work of the supporter; state investigation of supporters acting contrary to law and de-registration of a support person who is acting improperly or illegally.[107] While registration of support persons would not be mandatory, the potential for a registration system to have a 'nudge' effect towards delegitimising the role of unregistered supporters would, I suggest, be strong and could undermine its voluntariness. I argue that there is a very real question as to whether such systems would undermine the autonomy of the adult any more than would a best-practice guardianship system. While other commentators have similarly admonished against overregulation, there has been no agreement on the balance to be struck.[108]

lens through which to view the way that subjectivity, personhood and decision-making actually operate for individuals. She describes how: 'Relationships per se are not sufficient for the development of autonomy in the relational account. The **right kind** of relationship context …, is required' in Margaret Isabel Hall, 'Mental Capacity in the (Civil) Law: Capacity, Autonomy, and Vulnerability' (2012) 58(1) *McGill Law Journal – Revue de Droit de McGill* 61, 87.

105 See also: Linda Barclay, 'Autonomy and the Social Self' in Catriona Mackenzie and Natalie Stoljar (eds), *Relational Autonomy: Feminist Perspectives on Autonomy, Agency and the Social Self* (Oxford University Press, 2000) 52; Marilyn Friedman, 'Autonomy, Social Disruption and Women' in Catrionia Mackenzie and Natalie Stoljar (eds), *Relational Autonomy: Feminist Perspectives on Autonomy, Agency and the Social Self* (Oxford University Press, 2000) 35.

106 Bach and Kerzner (n 42) 95.

107 For a description of the legislation in the Canadian provinces, Ireland and Victoria, see: Julia Duffy and Kelly Unsworth, *Supported Decision-making, Legal Risk and Commercial Uncertainty* (17–18 October) (Australian Guardianship and Administration Council 2016 National Conference: Reflecting Will and Preference in Decision-making) 5–9.

108 Arstein-Kerslake, 'An Empowering Dependency' (n 29) 88; of the MCA and the safeguards required under Article 12(4), Bartlett writes that it is 'difficult to say what processes would be appropriate, that would not force the system to collapse under its own administrative weight': In Bartlett (n 83) 768.

Carney has repeatedly warned against the 'net-widening' effect of formal supported decision-making systems.[109] There is a potential, if not inevitability, that if supported decision-making were widely formalised, more adults with disability would find themselves subject to state regulation than under existing guardianship regimes. And yet, if there is no formalisation, the private sphere of supported decision-making would lack transparency and accountability, and the locus of decision-making power would be obscured.[110]

4.6.5 Failure to Acknowledge the Residual Impacts of Impairment

As Plumb writes, 'Autonomy (self-determination) is fundamental to the social model of disability.' For her, the concepts are well aligned for adults with *physical* disability, whose agency can be exercised once accommodated for and recognised by people around them.[111] However, a notion of interdependent personhood or relational autonomy for adults with severe and profound cognitive disability fails to recognise the residual impacts of impairment after support is provided. The hard reality is that cognitive impairment can limit the capacity for reasoning and decision-making. Further, to universalise and normalise personhood as interdependence fails to recognise that dependencies may be different and greater for those with cognitive disability than for others and that this may make them more vulnerable to abuse and exploitation.[112] Chapter 3 has already described how impairment can be associated with a cycle of socio-economic disadvantage, and that people with disability are disproportionately poor compared with the wider population. Paradoxically, the higher levels of dependency associated with cognitive impairment are acknowledged in the consensus that support for decision-making is required. Yet that acknowledgement is paradoxically pushed aside or forgotten in the determination to retain at all

[109] Terry Carney, 'Participation and Service Access Rights for People with Intellectual Disability: A Role for Law?' (2013) 38 *Journal of Intellectual and Developmental Disability* 59, 62; Carney, 'Supported Decision-Making for People with Cognitive Impairments: An Australian Perspective?' (n 125) 41; Terry Carney, 'Supporting People with Cognitive Disability with Decision-Making: Any Australian Law Reform Contributions?' (2015) 2 *Research and Practice in Intellectual and Developmental Disabilities* 6, 10; Terry Carney and Fleur Beaupert, 'Public and Private Bricolage: Challenges Balancing Law, Services and Civil Society in Advancing the CRPD Supported Decision Making' (2013) 36(1) *University of New South Wales Law Journal* 175, 195.

[110] 'While informality advances autonomy through compliance with statutory least restrictive alternative principles … it comes at the cost of enhanced opportunities for abuse and/or misreading of wishes' in Carney and Beaupert (n 109) 195.

[111] Anne Plumb, 'UN Convention on the Rights of Persons with Disabilities: Out of the Frying Pan into the Fire? Mental Health Service Users and Survivors Aligning with the Disability Movement' in Helen Spandler et al (eds), *Madness, Distress and the Politics of Disablement* (Bristol University Press, 2015) 183, 186–7.

[112] *General Comment No 1* [22] recognises this increased vulnerability: 'All people risk being subject to "undue influence", yet this may be exacerbated for those who rely on the support of others to make decisions.'

costs liberal autonomy as the foundation of personhood. I argue that retention of autonomy as the basis for personhood is underpinned by a strict version of the social model that fails to acknowledge the residual impacts of cognitive impairment and associated disadvantages.

4.6.6 Refashioning Autonomy Retains the Privileging of Rationality (but Just Relocates It in the Supporter)

Finally, I argue that despite a disavowal of the privileging of rationality as the foundation of autonomy, autonomy as interdependence retains that privileging, merely relocating the rational element into the supporter. Series criticises Silvers and Francis's prosthetic model of decision-making because it erroneously proposes that the internal processes of decision-making can be outsourced to a third party while the decision remains the adult's own.[113] Under the prosthesis theory, 'supporters should be viewed as a prosthesis for thinking, whereby their reasoning and communication can execute part or all of a subject's own thinking processes'.[114]

Building on Series's critique, I argue that the prosthesis theory also serves to retain the Kantian privileging of rationality, but that it relocates the reasoning function into the prosthesis as supporter. Indeed, taking a broader critique, I argue that retaining autonomy as the basis of interdependent personhood risks stigmatising the adult with cognitive impairment who lacks any reasoning capability (i.e. without the help of a supporter/prosthesis). If a supporter is executing all, or even part, of a subject's thinking processes, would not transparency and accountability be better served by describing and acknowledging the outcome as a decision by a substitute?

4.7 *Returning to the Case of Alex*

In the case of Alex, we saw above that under a supported decision-making model, his decision could be interpreted as either agreeing to the dental treatment or refusing it. The outcome would depend on which view of autonomy we adopt, how we interpret Alex's life values, or how we construct his life as a coherent narrative. Autonomy reformulated as interdependence, as a relationship of trust, or as being supplied by a cognitive prosthesis takes the analysis no further. Indeed, if trust is to be wrongly assumed, Alex's autonomy may be undermined by a supporter's own reasons for refusal of dental treatment. The supporter may be a family member or worker who thought it would be easier and cheaper to care for Alex if he lost all of his teeth, didn't need high-quality food, and didn't have to be taken on so many outings. Such a decision would accord with Alex's expressed wish not to have the dental treatment, but it is not clear that it would further his autonomous personhood.

[113] Series (n 41) 86.
[114] Ibid.

If we acknowledge the impacts of impairment on Alex after all supports are provided, then we can acknowledge his personal and situational disadvantage in the decision-making situation. There are reasonable views on either side as to what is the 'right' decision in this case. But if Alex foregoes the treatment and later loses his teeth, he will ultimately feel unhappy with the resulting loss of enjoyment. This raises a legitimate ethical issue around attributing the decision to Alex. In an ableist world where many people may think that such joys could not be truly appreciated by someone with a disability, this interpretation may be perceived as placing a lesser value on Alex's life. If a substitute were to make the decision, the locus of decision-making power would be clear. If the dentist or other person felt uneasy about the decision to either forego or pursue treatment, best-practice substitute decision-making would include an independent pathway for a challenge that would take Alex's expressed views into account.

4.8 *Summary and Conclusions on Refashioning Autonomy to Underpin Universal Legal Capacity and Inclusive Personhood*

Personhood, as derived from Kant finds its foundations in autonomy as rationality and independence, thereby excluding adults with cognitive disability. To include adults with cognitive disability within conceptions of personhood, either: (1) the liberal conception of autonomy must be reformulated or (2) alternative bases for personhood must be recognised. Those commentators advocating an interpretation of Article 12 as requiring recognition of universal legal capacity and the abolition of decision-making by substitutes have followed the first strategy.

According to this first strategy, writers have refashioned autonomy as interdependence and shared personhood or relational autonomy, endeavouring to destigmatise and normalise the dependencies experienced by adults with cognitive disability, particularly under the supported decision-making model. Some theories suggest that a Rawlsian bargaining paradigm should be reconfigured as relationships of trust, or that the supporter be reconceptualised as the adult's cognitive prosthesis. To account for the role of the State and others in providing supported decision-making, Bach and Kerzner refashion Millian liberty so that it incorporates positive as well as negative liberty.

Relational autonomy has been relied on to recognise the positive impacts of a trusted supporter on an adult's autonomy. However, I argue that relational autonomy used in this way ultimately reinforces the liberal account of autonomy, as attached to and located in the personhood of the adult as an individual. More broadly, the problem with autonomy as interdependence is that the individual risks becoming lost in a web of relationships in a way that makes it impossible to determine who is actually making the decision. Shared personhood and relational autonomy as interdependence rely on a strict social model of disability that locates disability entirely in the social environment, ignoring the residual impacts of cognitive impairment.

By way of comparison, a social model that recognises the residual impacts of impairment demands recognition of the difference of impairment/disability and the impact of that difference on autonomous decision-making, even after all the supports are provided (or when they are unavailable). Acknowledging the residual impacts of impairment also allows for acknowledgement that state provision and regulation of support services, even if reframed as providing 'positive liberty', may be no more autonomy-enhancing than guardianship used as a last resort. According to Kong, the 'will and preference' paradigm and supported decision-making purport to be value-neutral in the liberal tradition but determining what counts as a restraint is value-laden.[115] Support is valued as promoting autonomy and human rights, even though it acknowledges dependency, operates in the personal sphere and attracts regulatory oversight. Decision-making by substitutes, on the other hand, is framed in all cases as perpetuating dependencies, interfering in private lives and undermining autonomy and personhood.

I argue that in all of the above refashionings of autonomy, which aim to retain its privileged position as the foundation of personhood, there are unresolved contradictions. Despite assertions to the contrary, I argue that they still privilege rationality (albeit located in the supporter/prosthesis) in a way that risks perpetuating stigmatisation and exclusion of adults with cognitive impairment. I further argue that under these refashionings, the adult's personhood is still bounded. This is because so-called interdependencies, shared personhoods, or relational autonomies (under these accounts) fail to recognise the autonomy and personhood of the supporter – who is actually described by one theory as a 'prosthesis' that is instrumental to the personhood of the adult. I would argue that the individual is still bounded in the Kantian tradition. It is just that the boundaries have moved to include as part of the individual's autonomous personhood certain carefully defined supports that the State must provide. Bach and Kerzner draw a boundary between the supports provided under Article 12(3) and those socio-economic supports that, while assisting with legal capacity and decision-making, are required separately under other articles of the CRPD. Bach and Kerzner acknowledge that provision of 'financial resources, housing and disability related supports etc. all affect the exercise of legal capacity'[116] in that, with fewer resources and supports, a person has correspondingly fewer choices. Nevertheless, they draw a boundary between the right in Article 12 to supports and the right to claim this more extensive range of financial resources and supports. According to this account, autonomy as personhood incorporates supports only to the extent that they directly assist with a particular decision. This account thereby fails to recognise the interdependency between the right in Article 12 to decision-making with supports and other rights in the convention.

[115] Kong, *Mental Capacity in Relationship* (n 46) 36.
[116] Bach and Kerzner (n 42) 73.

Universal autonomy as the basis for personhood does nothing to disrupt the liberal paradigm and risks perpetuating the marginalisation of adults with severe and profound cognitive disability who do not have autonomous decision-making capacity. Hall suggests: 'the ideological paradigm in which the capacity construct is situated and of which it is an essential part – the liberal autonomy idea – is itself, in this context, deeply problematic and even cruel'.[117] I argue that it is indeed cruel because it continues to privilege autonomy as the basis of personhood, inevitably excluding some adults with cognitive disability.

The case of Alex shows that recognising autonomy universally fails to provide certainty or transparency and does not always protect an adult's rights.[118] If Alex foregoes dental treatment, then his socio-economic rights to health and social inclusion will be compromised – and possibly his longevity. Such an outcome – whether reached by supported or substitute decision-making – could be premised on unspoken ableist assumptions that health, welfare, social inclusion and long life are not as critically important to Alex as to someone without a disability. If a substitute decision were made to have the treatment, Alex's Article 16 CRPD right to physical integrity may be compromised, but the impacts could be ameliorated by medication and the presence of a support animal. The answers in situations such as these are not easy, but the case study demonstrates that supported decision-making practices that purport to recognise autonomy in adults with compromised decision-making abilities bring their own ethical and legal problems. I further argue that, by not recognising the interdependency of Article 12 with other rights in the CRPD and the equal importance of socio-economic rights (especially in the case of disability), they fail to fully apply the principle of indivisibility of human rights.

5 DIVORCING AUTONOMY FROM PERSONHOOD: BUT STILL REFASHIONING AUTONOMY TO BE MORE INCLUSIVE

This section describes those refashionings of autonomy that align with the second strategy – that is, valuing autonomy as one among many worthy social goods but divorcing it from personhood. This strategy allows for or demands an alternative foundation for personhood inclusive of adults with cognitive disability.

I conclude that Article 12 autonomy is best aligned with those conceptions of autonomy that:

(1) conceive of autonomy as achievement or as the development of autonomy competencies; and
(2) demand a wide range of meaningful options from which to choose.

[117] Hall, 'Mental Capacity in the (Civil) Law' (n 104) 64.

[118] As Foster writes: 'it is impossible to know when a truly autonomous decision has been made, or what conditions must pertain for it to be made'. Foster, *Choosing Life, Choosing Death: The Tyranny of Autonomy in Medical Ethics and Law* (Hart Publishing, 2009) 13.

These two conceptions of autonomy require the fulfilment of a wide range of socio-economic rights.

At the end of this section, I return to the case of Alex to illustrate how autonomy as achievement, as the development of competencies and as demanding real options applies in his case. Section 6 will explain how this conception of Article 12 autonomy embodies the indivisibility of human rights.

5.1 *Autonomy as Achievement*

Donnelly reconceives autonomy as a process of achievement and also attempts to dislodge the absolute nexus between autonomy and capacity. Before the publication of *General Comment No 1*, she expressed the view that Article 12(2) CRPD was 'unlikely' to be interpreted as a prohibition on all capacity-based assessments.[119] Donnelly works from within the liberal tradition but is less determined than others to adhere to a privileging of autonomy over other rights and values, concluding that 'autonomy, capacity and incapacity are less important than under the traditional liberal view'.[120] She invokes Raz, who conceived of autonomy as 'a kind of achievement'[121] or empowerment and applies this conception of autonomy to the law and practice of health-care decision-making. She is, in particular, critical of the 'simple view of autonomy as non-interference [that] still pervades much legal discourse'.[122] Donnelly writes that:

> respect for autonomy requires more than non-interference. Instead, a legal framework for autonomy must be concerned with issues such as the adequacy of choice and the development of autonomy-building measures aimed at enhancing individual agency and a shift in decision-making power to the individual. This would seem to be the view of autonomy underlying the CRPD.... The aim is to empower individuals and to support them in making decisions for themselves regardless of capacity.[123]

Like Quinn and Arstein-Kerslake, and Bach and Kerzner, Donnelly impliedly incorporates the requirement to provide support for decision-making (i.e. 'autonomy-building measures') into her view of autonomy. However, the term 'autonomy-building measures' is much wider than the term 'support'. I suggest it envisages a more holistic and ongoing dependency on positive state measures than those that may apply to the immediate circumstances surrounding a specific decision. Donnelly is critical of the liberal account of capacity and autonomy for ignoring the impact of external social and environmental factors on decision-making capacity.[124]

119 Donnelly (n 2) 111.
120 Ibid 157.
121 Joseph Raz, *The Morality of Freedom* (Clarendon Press 1986) 204.
122 Donnelly (n 2) 23.
123 Ibid 257.
124 Ibid 7.

She proposes that an adult with cognitive disability who engages in 'participative' decision-making may have their autonomy respected while nevertheless being found to lack capacity. Ultimately, though, Donnelly unambiguously recognises that some adults will have neither autonomy nor capacity due to their cognitive disability and suggests using dignity as a value to interpret human rights would be more inclusive than autonomy.[125]

5.2 *Autonomy as the Development of Autonomy Competencies*

Similar to Donnelly's idea of autonomy as achievement are theories that propose autonomy competencies can be either developed or neglected.[126] In referring to 'autonomy competencies', these theories articulate a substantive concept of autonomy because they conceive it as more than a prescribed procedure (e.g. independence and non-interference) and value some attributes or accomplishments over others.[127] Inherent in the notion of autonomy competencies is also the idea that autonomy is something that, in many cases, can and must be achieved through positive actions; it is not simply an absence of restraints. Dodds writes that:

> it seems clear that in the provision of basic welfare services (health, education, housing, etc.) a society can promote personal autonomy by enabling access to those things needed to develop autonomy competency and to pursue an autonomous life. Health-care systems are clearly part of this provisioning, insofar as good health and decent access to health-care facilities will be a precondition for the pursuit of a very greater range of autonomous projects.[128]

Kong criticises the UN Disability Committee for its view that protection is always inconsistent with autonomy and for failing to see autonomy as one of *many* goods that need to be valued.[129] In particular, Kong points to the right to education in Article 24 CRPD as one social good that fosters autonomy competencies.[130] She endorses a scalar view of autonomy and argues that autonomy can be effected through engaging in particular types of relationships that foster the perceptual and self-reflective skills essential to achieving autonomy.[131] The idea of autonomy as a competency allows us to frame decision-making by substitutes as potentially one tool to promote or achieve autonomy.

125 Ibid 212.

126 Christman, 'Constructing the Inner Citadel' (n 6) 115; Mackenzie and Stoljar (n 15) 56, 240; Kong, *Mental Capacity in Relationship* (n 46) 147.

127 Ashley (n 18) 17. See also: 'people must have autonomy competency – the repertory of coordinated skills that makes self-discovery, self-definition and self-direction possible'. Meyers (n 32) 76.

128 Susan Dodds, 'Choice and Control in Feminist Bioethics' in Catriona Mackenzie and Natalie Stoljar (eds), *Relational Autonomy: Feminist Perspectives on Autonomy, Agency and the Social Self* (Oxford University Press, 2000) 213, 228.

129 Kong, *Mental Capacity in Relationship* (n 46) 46–7.

130 Ibid 47.

131 Ibid 98.

5.3 *Autonomy Necessitates the Provision of Real Choices and Options*

Donnelly and Dodds also consider how autonomy necessitates, or inheres within it, a demand for real options. Donnelly rejects the traditional view of autonomy as being effectively limited to the right to either consent to or, more markedly, refuse treatment.[132] Her concept of autonomy as achievement means that autonomy itself places a demand on others – health-care providers, practitioners and the State – to offer alternatives as well as to provide education and to 'create a place for a decision'.[133] Respect for autonomy as achievement and empowerment demands that the State ensure a range of alternative services. She quotes Raz as saying that 'the provision of many collective goods is constitutive of the very possibility of autonomy'.[134]

Dodds makes similar arguments about autonomy in the health-care setting.[135] She goes further to critique the dominant proceduralist view of autonomy as 'mere choice' by pointing out that how health-care choices are presented to a patient will depend on many social and environmental factors. These will include the range of available resources, institutional frameworks and the nature of health-practitioner education.[136] For example, it may be that in the mental health-care setting, it is not always the involuntariness of the treatment that is problematic but the nature of the treatment being offered and the associated lack of options.[137] As Raz writes:

> Another aspect of autonomy concerns the quality of the options open to agents. The autonomous agent is not always struggling to maintain the minimum conditions of a worthwhile life. The more one's choices are dictated by personal needs, the less autonomous one becomes.[138]

5.4 *Returning to the Case of Alex*

In the case of Alex, he is fortunate to have the option of affordable dental treatment. If affordable dental services were beyond his reach, no decision would need to be made and his legal capacity would not be compromised by the intervention of

[132] Donnelly (n 2) 39.
[133] Ibid.
[134] Ibid 42.
[135] Mackenzie and Stoljar (n 15) 25.
[136] Dodds, 'Choice and Control in Feminist Bioethics' (n 128) 223.
[137] Plumb opines that involuntary treatment is sometimes needed to keep adults safe from self-harm, but that when it comes to designing such treatment, health professionals need to be able to offer services that the adult actually feels meet their own criteria for safety: Plumb (n 111) 190.
[138] Raz (n 121) 155; see also: 'The self-governing individual must have access to an adequate assortment of options' in Oshana (n 26) 94.

either a supporter or substitute. However, if there were no dental services available, it would be hard to argue against the fact that Alex would be making the 'decision' to forego treatment from a position of relative disempowerment. Raz, Donnelly and others would argue that Alex's autonomy has been compromised not only through cognitive impairment but through a lack of alternatives, thereby recognising the reality of his disempowered position.

5.5 *Commentary and Conclusions*

Article 12, with its right to support for legal capacity, eschews a concept of autonomy as the right to be left alone and to make choices without the help of others. Donnelly conceives of Article 12 autonomy, as achievement or empowerment. She recognises that even adults who may not meet tests for decision-making capacity may still have their autonomy respected in participating in the process of decision-making. Others view autonomy in a similar vein, as a process of developing certain competencies to enable self-determination in decision-making. Dodds and Kong emphasise the provision of adequate welfare services including health, education and housing as pre-conditions for an adult to undertake autonomous pursuits.[139]

Article 12 recognises the role of other people and services in the achievement of an adult's autonomy or the development of their autonomy competencies. In doing so, Article 12 demands that the State take action in the personal realm to promote autonomy. Reformulations of autonomy as achievement or as the development of autonomy competencies, and as also demanding a range of acceptable options, are consistent with an Article 12 conception of autonomy that includes a right to support for decision-making. However, a conception of autonomy as achievement, and as incorporating a demand for a range of options, indicates not just interdependence of rights within Article 12 itself (i.e. the right to support and the right to legal capacity) but interdependence between Article 12 and other rights in the CRPD, especially socio-economic rights. Section 6 considers the implications of a conception of autonomy as achievement and as demanding a range of options for the indivisibility of human rights in the CRPD.

6 AUTONOMY AND THE INDIVISIBILITY OF HUMAN RIGHTS

Chapter 3 described how a significant element of the principle of indivisibility is the elimination of the hierarchy of rights: civil–political over socio-economic.

139 'it seems clear that in the provision of welfare services (health, education, housing, etc.) a society can promote personal autonomy by enabling access to those things needed to develop autonomy competency and to pursue an autonomous life', in: Dodds, 'Choice and Control in Feminist Bioethics' (n 128) 228; Kong refers to education: Kong, *Mental Capacity in Relationship* (n 46) 46–7.

Linked with this is the recognition that the association of certain indicia with either one category or the other is overstated or misplaced. The features typically attributed to civil–political rights are that they impose negative state obligations, can be implemented immediately, are cost-free, protect the individual from the State and are justiciable. The attributes of socio-economic rights are the converse: they impose positive state obligations, will be implemented progressively, are resource-intensive, operate in the public and private spheres and are non-justiciable. The UN Disability Committee has categorised the whole of Article 12 as a civil-political right, but I concluded in that chapter that Article 12 is better described as a 'hybrid' right.[140] As such, it disrupts the traditional dichotomies by imposing negative obligations on the State – but also positive obligations through the provision of support.

I argue in this section that the reformulations of autonomy as achievement, as the development of autonomy competencies, and as demanding a range of options reflect the principle of indivisibility of human rights. These reformulations can be interpreted as acknowledging the interdependency of the Article 12 right to legal capacity with other rights, especially socio-economic rights, thereby affirming the equal importance of the two sets of rights. At the end of the section, I return for a final time to the case of Alex to illustrate how decision-making by a substitute may be required to uphold his indivisible human rights.

6.1 *Autonomy as the Foundation of Civil-political Rights*

Autonomy is traditionally regarded as the foundation of civil–political rights, including the right to legal capacity to make decisions.[141] The European Court of Human Rights holds it as foundational to the right to privacy and family life,[142] thereby reflecting the concept of autonomy as sovereignty over one's personal sphere to be enjoyed without interference. Civil-political rights are traditionally marked as requiring restraint or negative action by the State, aligning with respect for liberal autonomy as requiring non-interference. Chapter 3 described how civil-political rights were originally framed in the ICCPR largely in terms of non-interference.[143] Behind these proscriptions are assumptions that as long as the State respects autonomy by remaining at arm's length, the default position will be

[140] See Chapter 3, Section 6.

[141] Ashley (n 18) 5.

[142] Foster (n 118) 32.

[143] For example, Article 7 *ICCPR* provides that, 'No one shall be subjected to torture or to cruel, inhuman or degrading treatment or punishment'; Article 9 that 'No one shall be deprived of his liberty except on such grounds and in accordance with such procedure as are established by law'; and Article 17 that 'No one shall be subjected to arbitrary or unlawful interference with his privacy, family, home or correspondence.'

that everyone has their rights realised. In Article 12 terms, the parallel assumption is that if the State refrains from interference in the form of guardianship, adults will have access to already available supports in the community and must not be supported against their wishes.[144]

6.2 *Autonomy Competencies and Socio-economic Rights*

The language used varies, but many of the reformulations of autonomy described above incorporate to a greater or lesser extent a concept of a right to autonomy as imposing positive obligations on the State and others. Autonomy refashioned as 'achievement' or 'empowerment', or as requiring the development of autonomy competencies, places positive obligations on the State to maximise autonomy by providing the goods and services needed to promote it. Such goods and services include immediate supports for decision-making but also the ongoing fulfilment of a wide range of socio-economic rights, including education, health, accommodation and social inclusion. In her book *Human Rights Transformed: Positive Rights and Positive Duties*, Fredman writes:

> People can only be fully autonomous if the State creates the conditions for valuable autonomy. The State's duty to promote personal autonomy requires it to create the conditions of autonomy. Crucially, this includes positively encouraging the flourishing of a plurality of incompatible and competing pursuits, projects, and relationships.[145]

DeBeco writes of the CRPD that 'the requirement to provide enabling conditions for exercise of human rights thus gives a socio-economic dimension to classical liberal rights'.[146] I argue more particularly that Article 12 demands a conception of autonomy that recognises its achievement may depend on fulfilling the range of socio-economic rights contained in the CRPD.

6.3 *A Range of Options Requires Fulfilment of a Range of Rights*

Donnelly above argues that autonomy demands a range of viable options from which an adult may choose; and, in the case of health care, not just the option

[144] Quinn refers to supports that 'occur naturally in the community' in Quinn (n 29) 10, 15; but there is 'a more muscular obligation' on the State to provide supports if an adult is in isolation. See: Quinn and Rekas-Rosalbo (n 29) 301. For the prohibition on providing supports against an adult's wishes, see *General Comment No 1* [19], [29(g)].

[145] Sandra Fredman, *Human Rights Transformed: Positive Rights and Positive Duties* (Oxford University Press, 2008) 24.

[146] Gauthier DeBeco, 'The Indivisibility of Human Rights and the Convention on the Rights of Persons with Disabilities' (2019) 68 (January) *International and Comparative Law Quarterly* 141; Michael Ashley Stein, 'Disability Human Rights' (2007) 95(1) *California Law Review* 75, 158.

of consenting to or refusing the treatment offered. Fredman similarly writes that 'autonomy is protected by placing a positive obligation on the State to provide a range of options for citizens to pursue, ensuring all have the capacity to pursue their valued options, and that all valued options are treated in the same way',[147] so that the emphasis in achieving autonomy and liberty moves 'from non-intervention to enhancing choice'.[148] She emphasises that constraints can arise as much from 'poverty, poor health, lack of education as from tyranny and intolerance' and that people need to be 'actually able to exercise their choices, rather than simply having a formal right to do so.[149]

Applying this to Article 12 decision-making, an adult with cognitive disability may be provided with the immediate supports to make a decision as to where to live. However, depending on the type of impairment and the supports required for daily living, such adults may be presented with very few suitable accommodation alternatives, if any at all. Unless the State expends resources on tailored accommodation with independent living supports, their only choice may be to live in inappropriate institutionalised accommodation that segregates them from family and the wider community and leads to diminished life skills and autonomy.[150] An abstract right to legal capacity or autonomy is impotent and meaningless without such a range of options. Fulfilment of socio-economic rights across a range of areas is a prerequisite for the exercise of an adult's legal capacity, whether decisions are made by the adult or by a substitute.

6.4 *Disrupting the Boundaries between the Individual and the State: Private and Public Spheres*

The liberal conception of autonomy traditionally draws a bright line between the personal and public realms, between the individual and the State. Fredman explains that freedom as non-interference characterises the State 'as separate from and opposed to the individual' and as 'an ever-increasing threat to individual autonomy',[151] and that recognition of the State's positive human rights obligations serves to challenge these assumptions. In the same vein, O'Cinneide writes that the interdependency recognised by the CRPD is not just between individuals but

147 Fredman (n 145) 4.

148 Ibid 10.

149 Ibid 11.

150 In Australia, this lack of funding for in-home resources has led to a large number of young adults with disability being inappropriately placed in aged-care homes. See: Australian Government, 'Younger People in Residential Aged Care – Action Plan', *Royal Commission into Violence, Abuse, Neglect and Exploitation of People with Disability* (undated), VIC.0001.0505.3677.pdf (royalcommission.gov.au).

151 Fredman (n 145) 9.

between the individual and the State.[152] The CRPD acknowledges such an interdependency because it places obligations on the State to provide the social conditions necessary for a meaningful life.[153] O'Cinneide distinguishes the CRPD from a paternalistic model because it articulates social and economic measures as the fulfilment of individual rights, not as acts by the State of discretionary benevolence.[154] Similarly, Fredman explains that with social rights the emphasis is on public goods, which anticipates a rights-bearing citizen 'rather than a passive recipient of State welfare'.[155]

The UN Disability Committee views a loss of autonomy and legal capacity as the loss of claims to any and all rights. According to this logic, recognition that a person lacks autonomy inevitably results in services being provided under a charity or welfare model. I argue that even for those who lack autonomy, the principle of the indivisibility of human rights means that services can and must be claimed – whether under a supported or substitute decision-making model – as a matter of right.

6.5 *Indivisibility and the Case of Alex*

In the case of Alex, the development of his autonomy competencies depends on fulfilling a wide range of indivisible socio-economic rights in the CRPD – such as rights to health, education and appropriate accommodation. Let us assume, however, that he is among those disproportionate numbers of people with disability who grew up in poverty and were denied access to a range of socio-economic goods and services required to fulfil their socio-economic rights. Perhaps if Alex had been provided with better, tailored education and access to a range of health services from an early age, he would either not now have dental disease or would be more accustomed to and less intimidated by health professionals so as to be in a more informed position to make a decision on treatment.

Looking forward, if Alex were left to make a decision on his own to refuse dental treatment, his Article 12 legal capacity right may ostensibly be recognised, but he would be denied other human rights. Most notably, he would be denied the right to health care (Article 25), and his rights to social inclusion (Article 19) and participation in cultural life, recreation, leisure (Article 30) would be compromised.

152 Colm O'Cinneide, 'Extracting Protection for the Rights of Persons with Disabilities from Human Rights Frameworks: Established Limits and New Possibilities' in Oddný Mjöll Arnadóttir and Gerard Quinn (eds), *The UN Convention on the Rights of Persons with Disabilities: European and Scandinavian Perspectives* (Nijhoff, 2009) 163, 172.

153 Ibid 165.

154 Ibid 165–6.

155 Fredman (n 145) 235.

I argued in the earlier sections of this chapter that autonomy is not a satisfactory foundation for personhood because it excludes adults with cognitive disability. I further argued that autonomy cannot be successfully refashioned without discarding all of its original meaning. If another basis for personhood could be recognised and a substitute were appointed to make a decision on Alex's behalf, the appointment and decision would not designate Alex as a non-person. The substitute could make a decision in which Alex's whole range of rights was considered, and the substitute could thereby claim those rights for Alex, thus recognising that his personhood would be based on other, more inclusive grounds. Chapter 5 argues that the alternative ground of personhood relevant to the case of Alex, and all of us, is dignity.

7 SUMMARY AND CONCLUSION

Article 12 CRPD has been said to mark a paradigm shift in disability rights because it situates adults with disability as the subjects, not object, of rights and recognises autonomy as the basis of personhood in all cases. However, autonomy is founded on Kantian and Rawlsian rationality; on the ability to exercise will not just desire; on the ability to make considered decisions independently; and on the premise that action by the State and others in our private, personal sphere will limit our freedom and compromise our autonomy. Adults with cognitive disability have been traditionally excluded from Kantian personhood. This means that if autonomy is retained as the basis of personhood, the traditional concept of autonomy has to shift – or an alternative, more inclusive, basis for personhood has to be recognised.

One strategy to include adults with cognitive disability in personhood has been to refashion autonomy. The Article 12 literature has attempted to refashion autonomy from being constituted by rationality, independence and lack of interference to being marked by preference and emotion, interdependence, shared personhood and positive liberty. Autonomy as interdependence, shared personhood and positive liberty acknowledges the type of autonomy envisaged by Article 12, which requires support for legal capacity. However, the language of 'interdependency' and 'shared personhood' is misplaced and misleading under a strategy that continues to privilege individual autonomy. Under these refashionings of autonomy, rationality is still privileged, the individual is still bounded, and personal space is still sovereign. It is just that the boundary has shifted to include supporters and their rational abilities – but only to the extent that they are instrumental to the adult's decision-making.

Describing all adults with cognitive disability as autonomous in their decision-making stretches the concept beyond its meaningful limits and fails to recognise the residual impacts of impairment. The case of Alex demonstrates that supported decision-making based on recognition of his legal capacity where the decision is attributed to Alex is fraught with legal and ethical challenges. It can lead to diametrically different outcomes, may lack transparency and accountability, and shroud conflicts of interest and relationships of undue influence. The retention of the privileging of autonomy over other values adheres strongly to the liberal tradition. This leads to a 'fundamental elision' in the prescription for universal legal capacity 'that a finding of mental incapacity will undermine the worth we accord to some persons'[156] who are not autonomous.

Rather than accept the premise that autonomy underpins personhood and worth, a second strategy is to privilege autonomy as one among many valuable social goods – but divorce it from personhood. This allows space for alternative values, inclusive of adults with cognitive disability, to base our recognition of personhood. This strategy refashions autonomy as demanded by Article 12 but recognises that autonomy has its limits and does not have to be privileged above all other values. Autonomy can be conceived of as an achievement or as the development of autonomy competencies, and as inhering within it a demand for choice from a broad range of goods and services.

Both strategies acknowledge the importance of socio-economic supports and services to achieving autonomy, but the first strategy is premised on internal contradictions. One such contradiction was described in Chapter 3 as the 'chicken and egg', or 'initiation', problem whereby supports cannot be claimed without first recognising legal capacity. A second contradiction is that while autonomy as non-interference is privileged, personal supports are promoted and the legal recognition and regulation of support persons are inevitably intrusive. The premises behind what is framed as 'support' and what is 'interference' are inevitably value-laden. A third contradiction is that while the privileging of rationality is disavowed, it is still valued, albeit relocated in the supporter. Under the first strategy, despite attempts to refashion autonomy as interdependence, a bounded concept of the individual is privileged, as is a bounded conception of rights, with Article 12 privileged above all others.

The reformulation of autonomy under the second strategy avoids the above contradictions by adhering less closely to the liberal tradition. It values autonomy as one very important good and Article 12 as one very important right, among others. The theories of autonomy grouped under this second strategy lend themselves to an interpretation of Article 12 that recognises the indivisibility of human rights not just within Article 12 but between Article 12 and other rights in the CRPD. They allow for recognition that the achievement of legal capacity depends on access to a range of socio-economic goods and services. Moreover, the ongoing availability of such goods and services continues to enhance autonomy as meaningful choice. The fulfilment of socio-economic rights is required for the achievement of legal capacity and autonomy. And, depending on an adult's situation in the real world, their immediate need may be the fulfilment of rights beyond Article 12.

[156] Bilchitz (n 26) 417.

In the case of Alex, the appointment of a substitute would not only allow for a decision to be made with and for Alex to have access to basic dental/health care that would ultimately foster social inclusion, but also allow clarity and certainty around who was making the decision and on what basis. In some cases, a supported decision-making model will allow for rights to health and social inclusion to be claimed with certainty and transparency. In other cases, decision-making by a substitute may be an essential tool whereby these other rights and entitlements can be claimed. In many cases, a decision by a substitute may be required to respect the adult's dignity, and it is to the concept of dignity as the basis of personhood that Chapter 5 turns.

5

Article 12 and Dignity

1 INTRODUCTION

Chapter 2 described how the progress of disability rights has frequently been charted as a journey from paternalism to autonomy, from exclusion to inclusion and from discrimination to equality. This is reflected in, and driven by, models of disability that have developed from the charity and medical models to the social model and in decision-making frameworks that have moved from institutionalisation to guardianship to supported decision-making. Chapter 3 described how the promotion of disability as a human rights issue began with acknowledging the absence of people with disability from existing human rights agendas, together with their positioning as objects of socio-economic policy at a time when socio-economic rights were not perceived as 'true' human rights.

Chapter 3 also described how civil-political rights have been underpinned by the principle of autonomy, a principle conceived of as the right to be left alone, and how a prescription that the right to legal capacity requires the abolition of guardianship assumes that guardianship in all cases constitutes rights-denying interference. Chapter 4 described how legal capacity is related to a liberal notion of autonomy as rationality, independence and self-determination, as exemplified in the abstract ideal of the bounded individual. It described how the link between rationality, autonomy and personhood has traditionally led to the relegation of adults with disability to the status of 'non-persons'. Some writers have attempted to include adults within personhood by refashioning autonomy as interdependence or shared personhood. I argue that these ultimately fail because they continue to privilege rationality and fail to recognise the residual impacts of impairment.

While the dominant narrative of disability rights development has charted a journey from paternalism to autonomy and from social policy to civil-political human rights, recognition of the residual impacts of impairment and the principle of indivisibility disrupts this trajectory. To include adults with cognitive disability as persons, an alternative basis for personhood must be found, and this chapter proposes dignity. Section 2 describes the widespread references in international and regional human rights instruments to dignity as a fundamental human rights value, and how this is reiterated in the CRPD. It considers the features of dignity in the text of the CRPD and concludes that dignity is expressly stated as inherent and as a legal principle (not a right) that influences the interpretation of the convention. It also questions what dignity means in the CRPD and proposes five dimensions of dignity, which are considered, developed and explained in Section 3, through identifying and drawing on key features of dignity, found in the philosophical and legal literature and as illustrated in jurisprudence.

Section 4 considers the literature on dignity and Article 12, which typically associates dignity with either autonomy or equality, with outlying analyses grounding dignity in vulnerability, the ethic of care or social justice. It considers and acknowledges the weight of arguments against developing dignity as a legal principle but responds to these criticisms by reiterating the proposed five-dimensional approach as a contribution, and by proposing a case-by-case approach to give determinacy and meaning to dignity. Dignity's prominent positioning in human rights law and theory, as well as in the Purpose and General Principles clauses of the CRPD, gives legitimacy and even imposes some urgency on this project. The chapter concludes by considering how the application of five-dimensional dignity would apply to the case of Sesha, a woman with a severe and profound cognitive disability, whose decisions are often made with and for her by substitutes.

2 DIGNITY IN THE TEXT OF HUMAN RIGHTS INSTRUMENTS: AN OVERVIEW

Commentators have written that the idea of twentieth-century human rights was founded on the notion of human dignity,[1] shaped significantly in response to the atrocities of Nazism.[2] Human rights are said to be 'rooted' in human dignity.[3] Dignity has been described as a 'central organising principle' for human rights[4] and as the 'anchor norm of human rights'.[5] The affirmation that dignity is foundational

[1] Klaus Dicke, 'The Founding Function of Human Dignity in the Universal Declaration of Human Rights' in Eckart Klein and David Kretzmer (eds), *The Concept of Human Dignity in Human Rights Discourse* (Kluwer Law International, 2002) 111.

[2] Brenda Hale, 'Dignity' (2009) 31(2) *Journal of Social Welfare and Family Law* 101, 104; Emily Julia Kakoullis and Yoshikazu Ikehara, 'Article 1: Purpose' in Ilias Bantekas et al (eds), *The UN Convention on the Rights of Persons with Disabilities: A Commentary* (Oxford University Press, 2018) 35, 50; Theresia Degener, 'A New Human Rights Model of Disability' in Valentina Della Fina, Rachele Cera and Giuseppe Palmisano (eds), *The United Nations Convention on the Rights of Persons with Disabilities: A Commentary* (Springer International Publishing, 2017) 4148.

[3] Jack Donnelly, *Universal Human Rights in Theory and Practice* (Cornell University Press, 3rd ed, 2013) 28.

[4] Christopher McCrudden, 'Human Dignity and Judicial Interpretation of Human Rights' (2008) 19(4) *European Journal of International Law* 655, 675.

[5] Gerard Quinn and Theresia Degener, *Human Rights and Disability: The Current Use and Future Potential of United Nations Human Rights Instruments in the Context of Disability*

to human rights is reiterated in human rights instruments both within the UN system and regionally, and the CRPD is no exception.

2.1 *United Nations and Regional Human Rights Instruments*

The Charter establishing the UN was signed on 26 June 1945 and came into force on 24 October 1945 ('the UN Charter'). Its Preamble begins with:

> We the peoples of the United Nations determined:
>
> - To save succeeding generations from the scourge of war, which twice in our lifetime has brought untold sorrow to mankind, and
> - To reaffirm faith in fundamental human rights, in the dignity and worth of the human person, in the equal rights of men and women and of nations large and small ...[6]

This foundational document gives prominence to dignity, where it is associated with human worth and equality, associations reflected consistently across the jurisprudence and commentary on dignity.[7] In 1948, the UN Declaration followed the UN Charter by foregrounding dignity both in the opening of its Preamble and in its first substantive article. The Preamble recognises 'the inherent dignity and ... the equal and inalienable rights of all members of the human family [as] the foundation of freedom, justice and peace in the world', and Article 1 states: 'All human beings are born free and equal in dignity and rights.'[8] The ICCPR and the ICESCR both include these words taken directly from the UN Declaration's Preamble and add that the rights in each covenant 'derive from the inherent dignity of the human person'.[9] The CRPD opens by reaffirming the principles of the UN Charter, including recognition of the 'inherent dignity and worth and equal ... rights of all people'.[10] None of these instruments defines

(United Nations, 2002) 14; Sarah Arduin, 'Article 3: General Principles' in Ilias Bantekas, Michael Ashley Stein and Anastasiou Dimitris (eds), *The UN Convention on the Rights of Persons with Disabilities: A Commentary* (Oxford University Press, 2018) 85, 91.

6 *UN Charter*, 1 UNTS XVI (24 October 1945) ('UN Charter').

7 See further below.

8 *Universal Declaration of Human Rights, GA Res 217A (III), UN GAOR, 3rd sess, 183rd pen mtg, UN Doc A/810 (10 December 1948)* ('*UN Declaration*').

9 *International Covenant on Civil and Political Rights, opened for signature 19 December, 1966, 999 UNTS (entered into force 23 March 1976)* ('ICCPR'); see also *International Covenant on Economic, Social and Cultural Rights, opened for signature 16 December, 1966, 993 UNTS 3 (entered into force 3 January 1976)* ('ICESCR'); and *Convention on the Elimination of All Forms of Discrimination against Women, opened for signature 1 March 1980, 1249 UNTS 8 (entered into force 3 September 1981)* Preamble para 1; *Convention on the Elimination of All Forms of Discrimination against Women, opened for signature 1 March 1980, 1249 UNTS 8 (entered into force 3 September 1981)* Preamble para 3.

10 Preamble para 1.

dignity, but all of them describe it as 'inherent' and draw links between dignity, worth, equality and the human person.

McCrudden provides a catalogue of references to human dignity in regional human rights instruments,[11] as well as in constitutional documents.[12] The *European Convention on Human Rights* ('ECHR') is one of the few human rights instruments that does not expressly recognise dignity in its text.[13] However, in *Pretty v United Kingdom* ('*Pretty*'), the European Court of Human Rights affirmed that: 'The very essence of the Convention is respect for human dignity and human freedom.'[14] The incorporation of the ECHR into UK law by the *Human Rights Act* 1998 (UK) has led to consideration and development of the concept of dignity in UK law, and this has garnered significant attention in the wider jurisprudence and literature on dignity.[15]

2.2 *Dignity in the Text of the CRPD*

The Ad Hoc Committee was originally tasked with considering: 'proposals for a comprehensive and integral international convention to promote and protect the rights *and dignity* of persons with disabilities'[16] [emphasis added]. The word 'dignity' appeared not only in the title of the Ad Hoc Committee but in the title of early working drafts of the convention. The term was ultimately dropped from the title at the seventh session of the Ad Hoc Committee because of concern that reference to 'promoting' dignity implied that dignity was not already inherent in people with disability but had to be acquired.[17]

[11] 'Increasingly, dignity language has become embedded in the texts of regional human rights instruments. Dignity is central to the Preambles to the principal Inter-American, Arab, African, and (some) European human rights instruments.' McCrudden, 'Human Dignity and Judicial Interpretation of Human Rights' (n 4) 671.

[12] 'In the 1970s, with the fall of the dictatorships in Greece, Spain, and Portugal, dignity was incorporated into the new democratic constitutions.' Also, following the fall of the Berlin Wall, dignity was incorporated in the German Constitution, which later influenced its insertion in the post-Apartheid South African Constitution and 'Israel's Basic Law on Human Dignity': ibid 672–3.

[13] *European Convention for the Protection of Human Rights and Fundamental Freedoms, as amended by Protocols Nos 11 and 14*, Council of Europe, ETS 5 (entered into force 3 September 1953) ('*ECHR*').

[14] *Pretty v United Kingdom* (2002) 35 EHRR 1, [65] ('*Pretty*'). Before this, the court had already referred to 'the fundamental objectives of the Convention, the very essence of which is respect for human dignity and human freedom' in *SW v United Kingdom* ECHR 22 Nov 1995 [44].

[15] See further below. There are also many conventions and soft law instruments regulating sensitive areas of bio-scientific research, including genomic engineering, transplantation of body parts and reproductive technology, which promote human dignity as a value in decision-making. Deryck Beyleveld and Roger Brownsword, *Human Dignity in Bioethics and Biolaw* (Oxford University Press, 2001) 9.

[16] General Assembly, *Ad Hoc Committee on a Comprehensive and Integral International Convention on the Protection and Promotion of the Rights and Dignity of Persons with Disabilities*, 56/158 (19 December 2001).

[17] Kakoullis and Ikehara (n 2) 42–3.

Nevertheless, delegates were concerned that the shorter title omitted the important principle of dignity, and on that basis agreed instead to emphasise it in a 'Purpose' clause.[18] Article 1 CRPD begins with:

> The purpose of the present Convention is to promote, protect and ensure the full and equal enjoyment of all human rights and fundamental freedoms by all persons with disabilities, and to promote *respect for their inherent dignity*. [emphasis added]

The reference to 'respect for dignity' was inserted to acknowledge that dignity was always present in people with disabilities and could never be taken away.[19]

Dignity is referred to in several other places in the CRPD, and indeed it appears more frequently than in any other UN human rights convention,[20] leading to Degener describing the CRPD as relating 'to the concept of human dignity more than any other human rights treaty'.[21] The Preamble recognises 'the inherent dignity and worth and the equal and inalienable rights of all members of the human family'[22] that 'discrimination … is a violation of the inherent dignity and worth of the human person',[23] and also that 'the rights and dignity of persons with disabilities will make a significant contribution to redressing … profound social disadvantage … and promote … participation in the civil, political, economic, social and cultural spheres, with equal opportunities'.[24] Article 3 'General Principles' also begins with 'Respect for inherent dignity'. Once again, dignity is described as inherent, is associated with worth and equality and is also associated with autonomy. It traverses the civil–political rights to non-discrimination, autonomy,[25] and the right to be free from abuse,[26] as well as the socio-economic rights to social progress, education[27] and health.[28]

[18] Resulting in the CRPD being the only core UN human rights treaty to have a separate clause expressing purpose: ibid 43.

[19] Ibid.

[20] 'The term "dignity" appears in the Convention more often than in any other United Nations human rights convention': *United Nations Committee on the Rights of Persons with Disabilities 'General Comment No. 6 (2018) on Equality and Non-discrimination CRPD/C/GC/6* [6].

[21] Theresia Degener, 'A New Human Rights Model of Disability' in Valentina Della Fina, Rachele Cera and Giuseppe Palmisano (eds), *The United Nations Convention on the Rights of Persons with Disabilities: A Commentary* (Springer International Publishing, 2017) 41, 48.

[22] Preamble para 1.

[23] Preamble para 8.

[24] Preamble para 25.

[25] Article 3 'General Principles … (1) Respect for inherent dignity, individual autonomy including the freedom to make one's own choices, and independence of persons'.

[26] Article 16 'Freedom from violence, exploitation and abuse … (4) … Such recovery and reintegration shall take place in an environment that fosters the health, welfare, self-respect, dignity and autonomy of the person and takes into account gender- and age-specific needs.'

[27] Article 24 – 'Education … (2) … With a view to realizing this right without discrimination and on the basis of equal opportunity, States Parties shall ensure an inclusive education system at all levels and lifelong learning directed to: (a) The full development of human potential and sense of dignity and self-worth, and the strengthening of respect for human rights, fundamental freedoms and human diversity.'

[28] Article 15 'Health … (d) Require health professionals to provide care of the same quality to persons with disabilities as to others, raising awareness of the human rights, dignity, autonomy and needs of persons with disabilities.'

The commentary on disability frequently emphasises that respect for dignity has particular resonance for people with disability, with one observer writing that 'disability rights advocates … have long argued that seeing persons with disabilities as equal in dignity is a necessary precondition to recognition of disability rights',[29] and another that: 'The human dignity of disabled people is often denigrated, both in popular opinion, as well as in scholarly writing.'[30] Moreover, as described below, many legal judgements that discuss the concept of dignity centre on the rights of a person with disability,[31] while philosophical writings on dignity frequently begin with a description of a person with disability whose dignity is at risk of being violated.[32]

2.2.1 Dignity Is Inherent

All of the UN instruments referred to above describe dignity as 'inherent' to human beings and yet, at least idiomatically, we often say that a person can be 'robbed' of their dignity, implying that dignity can be earned or conferred. Many commentators endeavour to resolve the apparent contradiction between affirmations of dignity as inherent and assertions that it can be earned or conferred (or taken away) by distinguishing between two different types of dignity. Gilabert describes this as the difference between status dignity and condition dignity. Status dignity is accorded to us on the basis that we are human (i.e. inherent), whereas condition-dignity is

[29] Janet E Lord, 'Preamble' in Ilias Bantekas, Michael Ashley Stein and Dēmētrēs Anastasiou (eds), *The UN Convention on the Rights of Persons with Disabilities: A Commentary* (Oxford University Press, 2018) 1, 8.

[30] Neal writes that in cases of adults with mental incapacity, including unconscious patients, protecting dignity is 'most urgent and that reminders about human dignity can be most valuable': Mary Neal, 'Respect for Human Dignity as "Substantive Basic Norm"' (2014) 10(1) *International Journal of Law in Context* 26, 28. Also, prior to the ratification of the CRPD, the only UN human rights convention that referenced disability, recognising the 'dignity' of the 'disabled child' was the *Convention on the Rights of the Child, opened for signature 20 November, 1989, 1577 UNTS 11 (entered into force 2 September 1990)* Article 23.

[31] *Price v United Kingdom* (2002) 34 EHRR 53 ('*Price*'). See also: Angela Laycock, 'Price v UK: The Importance of Human Rights Principles in Promoting the Rights of Disabled Prisoners in the United Kingdom' in Marcia H Rioux, Lee Ann Basser Marks and Melinda Jones (eds), *Critical Perspectives on Human Rights and Disability Law* (Martinus Nijhoff Publishers, 2011) 201, 209. See also cases discussed in Charles Foster, *Human Dignity in Bioethics and Law* (Hart Publishing, 2011) 104–6; also, discussed below is a case of 'dwarf-tossing': Human Rights Committee, *Views: Communication No 854/1999, Manuel Wackenheim v France*, 75 sess, UN Doc CCPR/C/75/D/854/1999 (15 July 2002) ('*Wackenheim v France*').

[32] See, e.g., Kittay's description of her daughter Sesha leaving her shower: Eva Feder Kittay, 'Equality, Dignity and Disability' in Mary Ann Lyons and Fionnuala Waldron (eds), *Perspectives on Equality: The Second Seamus Heaney Lectures* (Liffey Press, 2005) 95, 95–6; see also description of people in an asylum being hosed down: Raimond Gaita, *A Common Humanity: Thinking about Love & Truth & Justice* (Text Pub, 2nd ed, 2000) 17; see also Lady Hale who opens with a description of Mrs Price, 'a thalidomide victim without proper arms or legs': Hale (n 2) 101; and also that stealing a bicycle from a person who is disabled is an affront on their dignity: Adam Ettinson, 'What's So Special about Human Dignity?' (2020), 48(4) *Philosophy and Public Affairs* 353, 359, 394.

only accorded to us if certain rights are fulfilled to ensure we have a dignified life (i.e. earned/conferred).[33]

This chapter looks to the text of the CRPD itself, based as it is on the affirmations in the foundational human rights conventions asserting that human dignity under the CRPD is inherent. The notion of human dignity as inherent also reflects the influence of Kant, who conceived of human dignity as innate and intrinsic to all humans.[34] Since dignity is inherent, what is important is the obligation of all of us, including the State, to respect our fellow human beings in a way that recognises and respects their and our own dignity. This reflexive, interpersonal dimension of dignity is explained later in the chapter.[35] The next sections consider whether dignity in the CRPD is a legal principle or a separate human right.

2.2.2 Dignity as a Legal Principle or a Separate Human Right?

The role of dignity in law is contested, with some lawyers opposing the notion that dignity is a legal concept at all, or that it should be developed as one in the future.[36] McCrudden points out that in some human rights and constitutional instruments human dignity is expressed as a right in itself, '…whilst in other jurisdictions it is not a right but a general principle'.[37] However, most scholars who consider the role of dignity in human rights law conceptualise it as a legal principle or value that underpins or overarches human rights and, as such, that it cannot be a separate right in itself.[38] Dupre opines that dignity has been a legal concept since it was enshrined in

33 Pablo Gilabert, 'Human Rights, Human Dignity and Power' in Rowan Cruft, S Matthew Liao and Massimo Renzo (eds), *Philosophical Foundations of Human Rights* (Oxford University Press, 2015) 196, 200; other writers draw similar distinctions, for example between 'status dignity' and 'achievement dignity': Paul Formosa and Catriona Mackenzie, 'Nussbaum, Kant, and the Capabilities Approach to Dignity' (2014) 17(5) *Ethical Theory and Moral Practice* 875, 878; Miller distinguishes between 'inherent' dignity and 'performative' dignity: Sarah Clark Miller, 'Reconsidering Dignity Relationally' (2017) 11(2) *Ethics and Social Welfare* 108, 112; Carter makes a distinction between dignity as inherent and dignity as 'interdependent and dialogical', that is as requiring others to treat us wtih the respect that such inherent dignity deserves: Barbara Carter, 'The Case for Dignity as the Governing Principle in Adult Guardianship' (2010) 19(1) *Res Publica* 1, 4; Michael makes a distinction between 'full inherent dignity' and 'non-inherent dignity': Lucy Michael, 'Defining Dignity and Its Place in Human Rights' (2014) 20(1) *The New Bioethics* 12, 12.

34 'Kant played an important role historically in connecting dignity with the idea of all human beings having unconditional, intrinsic value.' Michael Rosen, *Dignity: Its History and Meaning* (Harvard University Press, 2012) 10. See further below.

35 Section 3.3.

36 Kakoullis and Ikehara (n 2) 53; Jeremy Waldron, *Is Dignity the Foundation of Human Rights?* (New York University School of Law, 2013) 7.

37 McCrudden, 'Human Dignity and Judicial Interpretation of Human Rights' (n 4) 675; Rosen suggests that unless otherwise specified in legislation, dignity may be conceived of as one particular, very important right, grounding a human being's right to be respected: Rosen (n 34).

38 Jack Donnelly (n 3) 29; Dicke argues that in the UN Declaration, dignity is 'a transcendental norm that legitimises human rights claims'; Dicke (n 1) 118; Neal categorises dignity not as a right, but as a 'substantive basic norm in a given legal system' because there is a 'necessary and

the UN Declaration in 1948 and frames it as a principle that influences the interpretation of rights, more than as a right itself.[39]

In terms of the CRPD, respect for dignity is expressed, together with autonomy and equality, as a 'General Principle' and there is no reference to dignity as a separate right. For these reasons, and because human dignity is affirmed in the UN human rights conventions as being distinct from human rights, this chapter takes as its starting point that dignity is a principle that lies behind human rights and that may be articulated through the language of rights.

Of note in the text of the CRPD is the positioning of dignity in the Preamble, the Article 1 Purpose clause, and in the General Principles. As explained in Chapter 1, the VCLT provides that a convention is to be interpreted according to its ordinary meaning in the context of its 'object and purpose'.[40] A preamble is said to 'frequently facilitate[s] the interpretation of particular provisions which are less precise than they should be, by its indication of the general idea behind them'.[41] I argue that the emphasis in these introductory provisions on dignity points to a purposive interpretation of the CRPD, and Article 12 in particular, which is informed by the principle of dignity, not just autonomy.

In terms of Article 12, I argue that dignity is the basis of our personhood, from which foundation we can claim our human rights. Both in the act of claiming our human rights and in having them fulfilled, our inherent dignity is recognised and respected. Moreover, other substantive rights in the CRPD are to be interpreted in a way that recognises and respects the dignity of the claimant.

2.2.3 What Does Dignity Mean in the CRPD?

There is no broad consensus on the meaning of dignity in philosophy or law.[42] It has indeed been described as a 'placeholder' in human rights instruments and used by drafters of the foundational instruments when there was a lack of agreement as to

foundational connection between dignity and law: Neal (n 30) 37–8; Gilabert (n 33) 200–2; Debes also considers that dignity is different from rights because rights are subsidiary to dignity: Remy Debes, 'Dignity's Gauntlet' (2009) 23(1) *Philosophical Perspectives*, 45, 57; Rosen (n 34) 10; and Foster also argues that dignity is not a right but is a legal concept that lies behind rights, and which can be 'translated into law using the language of rights': Foster, *Human Dignity in Bioethics and Law* (n 31) 17; Gearty concludes that the English courts use dignity as a 'principle', which lies behind a right, because a right can be limited or balanced, whereas recognition of dignity is non-negotiable: Conor Gearty, 'Socio-economic Rights, Basic Needs, and Human Dignity: A Perspective from the Law's Frontline' in Christopher McCrudden (ed), *Understanding Human Dignity* (Oxford University Press, 2013) 155, 160.

39 Catherine Dupre, 'Constructing the Meaning of Human Dignity: Four Questions' in Christopher McCrudden (ed), *Understanding Human Dignity* (Oxford University Press, 2013) 113, 119–20.

40 *Vienna Convention on the Law of Treaties* (opened for signature 18 December 1979), 1155 UNTS 331 (entered into force 27 January 1980) Article 31(1).

41 Lord (n 29) 3, quoting ICRC, *Commentary to the Convention (IV) relative to the Protection of Civilian Persons in Time of War*, Preamble (ICRC 1958).

42 'The variations in the use of the term "dignity" are undeniable. We can find dignity being invoked by advocates of flatly opposed moral positions.' Rosen (n 34) 5; see also Debes (n 38) 46, 61.

what rights or values should prevail.[43] However, there has started to develop a body of philosophical and legal literature and jurisprudence that considers the meaning and role of human dignity, influenced to different extents by Kantian thought.

While some theorists and practitioners equate dignity with autonomy, I argue, along with others, for a wider and more complex definition of dignity. This chapter draws on the work of philosophers, academic lawyers and judges to formulate a meaning of dignity that makes sense in the context of the CRPD, interpreted through the principle of indivisibility. It argues that the meaning of dignity in the CRPD comprises these five dimensions:

- Dignity as equal worth or value.
- Dignity as recognising the autonomy of those who are capable of autonomy.
- Dignity as recognising the interdependent, interpersonal and social nature of being human.
- Dignity as recognising the embodied nature of personhood.
- Dignity as underpinning and affirming the indivisibility of human rights.

The remainder of this chapter explores this concept of 'five-dimensional dignity'.

2.2.4 Summary and Conclusions

References to dignity are pervasive in human rights and humanitarian instruments, beginning with the UN Declaration and proliferating within the UN and regionally. The CRPD mentions dignity more times than any other UN human rights convention. It is referenced several times in its Preamble; its Purpose clause includes the promotion of respect for dignity; and respect for inherent dignity is affirmed in the first of its General Principles. In the substantive articles of the CRPD, recognition of dignity is linked with fulfilling civil-political rights (including preventing abuse) and fulfilling socio-economic rights such as the rights to education and health. This foregrounding of dignity in the CRPD reflects a broader acknowledgement in the commentary and jurisprudence that recognition of the dignity of persons with disability is often fragile and thus of particular significance. In the instruments referred to above, dignity is said to be inherent and associated with equality, worth and being human, and is also sometimes linked with autonomy.

This chapter takes as its starting point the text of the CRPD (based as it is on the wording in the foundational UN human rights instruments) to conclude that dignity is inherent in all human beings and, as such, must be recognised and respected by others through the fulfilment of their and our human rights. Further, dignity in the CRPD serves as a separate legal principle to be used to interpret and apply the human rights in the convention, including Article 12. Article 12 must be interpreted and applied in a way that recognises and respects the dignity of people with disability,

[43] McCrudden, 'Human Dignity and Judicial Interpretation of Human Rights' (n 4) 676–8; Foster, *Human Dignity in Bioethics and Law* (n 31) 93; Michael (n 33).

and the foregrounding of dignity in the text of the CRPD places a demand on us to give substantive meaning to the term. The meaning of dignity is far from agreed, but the human rights conventions themselves, including the CRPD, state that human dignity refers to the equal worth or value of all of us as humans, and many philosophers and lawyers make clear connections between dignity and autonomy.

The following sections consider the five proposed dimensions of dignity that underpin the CRPD and Article 12.

3 FIVE PROPOSED DIMENSIONS OF DIGNITY

3.1 *Dignity as Equal Worth or Value*

The first dimension of dignity proposed as underpinning the CRPD is its recognition of equal worth or value. Already noted above is the association of dignity with the concept of human worth, or equal human worth, in texts of the foundational human rights instruments, as well as in the CRPD. Dignity was originally a term of hierarchical exclusion applying only to a small portion of the privileged elite,[44] with Cicero, for instance, associating dignity with the nobility.[45] Feldman, writing in 1999, cites the Oxford English Dictionary's definition as 'The quality of being worthy or honourable; worthiness, worth, nobleness, excellence', implying retention, to an extent, of that elitist concept of dignity as an attribute of those with high status.[46] Many writers also describe how the concept of human dignity as worth was incorporated into Judeo-Christian theology to underline 'a certain exceptional position of man in God's creation',[47] signalling the universal worth or value of man as having been created in God's image.[48]

This interpretation of dignity through a Judeo-Christian lens signalled its transformation from being an attribute of the elite, to an attribute of *all* humans, so that all humans had worth or value.[49] In the eighteenth century, Kant further democratised dignity and also secularised it, with his theory that dignity is 'the idea of all human beings having unconditional, intrinsic value'.[50] However, it is important to note that in Kant's writings, attributing value or worth to a person does not serve

[44] Jack Donnelly (n 3) 2, 126–8; John F Kilner, 'Human Dignity' in Stephen G Post (ed), *Encyclopedia of Bioethics* (Macmillan Reference USA, 3rd ed, 2004) vol 2, 1193.

[45] Miller (n 33) 109; Rosen (n 34) 11.

[46] David Feldman, 'Human Dignity as a Legal Value' (Pt 1) [1999] *Public Law* 682, 686.

[47] Dicke (n 1) 113; Debes (n 38) 45; Suzy Killmister, 'Disability, Respect and Cognitive Disability' in David T Wasserman and Adam Steven Cureton (eds), *The Oxford Handbook of Philosophy and Disability* (2018) 4; Sarah Clark Miller, 'Reconsidering Dignity Relationally' (2017) 11(2) *Ethics and Social Welfare* 108.33) 109.

[48] Killmister, 'Disability, Respect and Cognitive Disability' (n 47) 4.

[49] Ibid.

[50] Rosen (n 34) 10.

to objectify or commodify them. On the contrary, for Kant 'everything has either a price or a dignity. What has a price can be replaced by something else as its equivalent; what, on the other hand, is raised above all price and therefore admits of no equivalent has a dignity'.[51] While dignity is equated with worth, the value of human dignity is immeasurable because humans and their dignity cannot be reduced to a price or commodified.

The idea of dignity as indicating human worth has been widely accepted in the philosophical and human rights literature[52] and jurisprudence.[53] In *Airedale NHS Trust v Bland* ('Bland'), the House of Lords ultimately determined that it was lawful to end life support for a young man in a persistent vegetative state ('PVS'). The judgement of Hoffman LJ in the lower Court of Appeal has been widely noted for its consideration of dignity, describing it as a value that leads to 'our belief that … it is wrong for someone to be humiliated or treated without respect for his value as a person'.[54] Quinn and Degener write:

> Recognition of the value of human dignity serves as a powerful reminder that people with disabilities have a stake in and a claim on society that must be honoured quite apart from any considerations of social or economic utility.[55]

That is, human rights are often erroneously denied to people with disability because they don't always possess capacities or functions otherwise valued by society, but their value resides in their inherent human dignity.

Consistent with the notion of dignity as signifying the incommensurable value of all humans is Kant's prescription that human beings must always be treated as ends and not merely as means – that is, valued for themselves and not used merely as instruments for the ends of others.[56] This means that a person cannot be reduced

[51] Ibid 20–1. Quoting Immanuel Kant, 'Groundwork to a Metaphysics of Morals' in Paul Menzer (ed), *Critique of Pure Reason* (Academy of Sciences, 1785) vol 4, 387, 436. See also: 'for Kant all things have a price, but man has an inestimable value' in: Paolo Becchi, 'Human Dignity in Europe: Introduction' in Paolo Becchi and Klaus Mathis (eds), *Handbook of Human Dignity in Europe* (Springer International Publishing, 2019) 1, 5.

[52] 'It is a synonym for human worth, the inherent excellence of the human person as distinguished from any other living creature.' In Dicke (n 1) 113; Charles R Beitz, 'Human Dignity in the Theory of Human Rights: Nothing but a Phrase?' (2013) 41(3) *Philosophy and Public Affairs* 259, 275; McCrudden, 'Human Dignity and Judicial Interpretation of Human Rights' (n 4) 679; 'The German word for dignity is Würde, a word that is closely related etymologically to Wert, the term for "worth" or "value"': Rosen (n 34) 19.

[53] Foster agrees that dignity in human rights means human worth and also summarises Hoffman LJ's words in *Airedale NHS Trust v Bland* [1993] AC 789, 826 ('*Bland*') as 'it is not just the sentient or self-conscious who have dignity interests protected by law' Foster, *Human Dignity in Bioethics and Law* (n 31) 94, 102.

[54] *Bland* 826 per Hoffmann LJ; cited in Foster, *Human Dignity in Bioethics and Law* (n 31) 100.

[55] Quinn and Degener (n 5) 14.

[56] See Parfit Chapter 9 – 'Merely as a Means' for a nuanced critique and analysis of this concept: Derek Parfit, *On What Matters: Volume One* (Oxford University Press, 2011) 212–32; see also Nussbaum's concept of human dignity as a foundation for personhood (see below) places this Kantian maxim at its core: Martha C Nussbaum, *Frontiers of Justice Disability, Nationality,*

to a mere object[57] and, in particular, that exploiting or abusing people with disability for the ends of others fails to recognise or respect their human dignity and their personhood. McCrudden proposes that a 'basic minimum content' of human dignity includes respect for intrinsic worth together with the recognition that the State exists for 'the sake of the individual human being, and not vice versa'.[58] He thereby implies that if the State were to treat individuals as merely instrumental to its goals, this would be a violation of human dignity. In Article 12 terms, if an adult's supporter were to unduly influence a decision merely for the supporter's own benefit, or if a substitute were to make a decision merely for the substitute's own gain, this would be treating the adult merely as a means, rather than valuing the adult in his or her own right.

3.2 *Dignity as Recognising the Autonomy of Those Who Are Capable of Autonomy*

One meaning frequently attributed to dignity in philosophy and law, and also deriving from Kant, is that dignity equates with the concept of autonomy.[59] The second dimension of dignity proposed as underpinning the CRPD is that it recognises the autonomy of those who are capable of autonomy.

3.2.1 Dignity as Meaning Only Autonomy

As one commentator summarised Kant: 'Simply put, human beings have dignity because autonomous reason rather than impulses or the pursuit of personal or social benefit governs their actions.'[60] As suggested in the quote, many writers and

Species Membership (Harvard University Press, 2009) 50. See also: 'Insofar as we exist merely in the realm of nature, we are not ends in ourselves and do not have a dignity; things in that realm simply have a price … Insofar as we enter the realm of ends, thus far, and thus far alone, we have dignity and transcend price.' Martha C Nussbaum, 'Beyond the Social Contract: Toward Global Justice', *The Tanner Lectures on Human Values* (2003) 426.

57 See, e.g., Becchi, who writes about: 'The modern idea of human dignity, which essentially prohibits us from reducing the person to a thing': Becchi (n 51) 16.

58 McCrudden, 'Human Dignity and Judicial Interpretation of Human Rights' (n 4) 679.

59 Ibid 685; also Neal (n 30) 28.

60 Kilner (n 44); see also 'Kant is generally taken to be the locus situ of the intimate connection between personhood, dignity and autonomy' in Licia Carlson and Eva Feder Kittay, 'Introduction: Rethinking Philosophical Presumptions in the Light of Cognitive Disability' (2009) 40(3–4) *Metaphilosophy* 307; 'The right to make one's own decisions about many aspects of one's fate, and to contribute to decisions made by others which affect one's life, can be seen as a major contribution to an individual's dignity, linking the notion to a Kantian perspective on morality': Feldman (Pt 1) (n 46) 685; 'In liberal theory, one's ability to act for reasons – one's "rational agency" – is regarded as valuable … It gives one a special worth or status, often called "dignity", which renders one inviolable' in Cynthia A Stark, 'Respecting Human Dignity: Contract versus Capabilities' in Eva Feder Kittay and Licia Carlson (eds), *Cognitive Disability and Its Challenge to Moral Philosophy* (2010) 111, 111; 'The Dignity Model and other dignity research also identifies autonomy and control as associated with dignity', in McCrudden, 'Human Dignity and Judicial Interpretation of Human Rights' (n 4) 685, 688.

philosophers view Kant's conception of dignity as being closely linked with the ability for rational thought, self-legislation, self-determination and personal choice, thereby excluding adults with cognitive disability.[61] McCrudden describes how in bioethics – for example, in the debate on women's right to abortion – dignity is often equated with the right to choose[62] and more widely with the right of informed consent (or refusal) of medical treatment.[63]

In arguments for limitations to, or abolition of, decision-making by substitutes, frequent reliance is placed on a prevailing right of people with cognitive disability to enjoy the 'dignity of risk'. The concept of the 'dignity of risk' was first promulgated in the 1970s by practitioners in the field of intellectual disability.[64] They recognised that institutionalisation, in denying self-determination even in daily choices, may have kept adults safe but undermined self-confidence and inhibited self-growth. Nay writes in the context of aged care: 'I would argue that risk management and "protective behaviours" are usually focused on minimising overt physical harm and often on protecting the back of the health care system'.[65] Acknowledging and promoting the dignity of risk has since become foundational to mental health treatment which promotes self-determination as a pathway to recovery.[66] The preservation

[61] Killmister, 'Disability, Respect and Cognitive Disability' (n 47) 1; Elif Celik, 'The Role of CRPD in Rethinking the Subject of Human Rights' (2017) 21(7) *The International Journal of Human Rights* 933, 940. The issue of 'individuality' or being treated as an individual also recurs frequently in dignity research; hence the concept of patient-centred care: Linda Barclay, 'In Sickness and in Dignity: A Philosophical Account of the Meaning of Dignity in Health Care' (2016) 61 *International Journal of Nursing Studies* 136, 140.

[62] McCrudden, 'Human Dignity and Judicial Interpretation of Human Rights' (n 4) 685, 688. For the US Supreme Court in relation to the right to abortion: 'The authority to make such traumatic and yet empowering decisions is an element of basic human dignity.' *Planned Parenthood of Southeastern Pa. v Casey*, 505 US 833 [916] (1992).

[63] 'Dignity has, for instance, been used to support the justification for establishing a doctrine of informed consent.' Daniel Bedford, 'Human Dignity in Great Britain and Northern Ireland' in Paolo Becchi and Klaus Mathis (eds), *Handbook of Human Dignity in Europe* (Springer Nature Switzerland, 2019) 319, 348. 'From one perspective, human dignity clearly demands protection of individual autonomy. For instance, many jurisdictions ground the autonomy of patients to make free and informed choices about their medical care in human dignity.' Paolo G Carozza, 'Human Rights, Human Dignity, and Human Experience' in Christopher McCrudden (ed), *Understanding Human Dignity* (Oxford University Press, 2013) 615, 618. 'This relevance for human dignity is associated – as is clear in particular from Article 3, in which free and informed consent becomes the fulcrum around which the "government of the body" should turn.' Becchi (n 51) 19.

[64] Robert Perske, 'The Dignity of Risk' in Wolf Wolfnsberger et al, *Principles of Normalization in Human Services* (National Institute of Mental Retardation, 1972) 194.

[65] Rhonda Nay, 'The Dignity of Risk' (2002) 9 *The Australian Nursing Journal* 33, 33.

[66] Craig Parsons, 'The Dignity of Risk: Challenges in Moving On' (2008) 15(9) *The Australian Nursing Journal* 28; 'The terms Dignity of risk (DofR) and Therapeutic Risk (TR) most commonly appear in four discourses: disability, mental health, ageing and dementia. The terms are largely interchangeable': Pauline Marsh and Lisa Kelly, 'Dignity of Risk in the Community: A Review of and Reflections on the Literature' (2018) 20 (5–6) *Health, Risk & Society* 297, 299.

of a person's 'dignity of risk' in this context equates with the preservation of their decision-making autonomy.[67]

Aligning with the view of dignity as equating with autonomy, the philosopher Ruth Macklin in 2002 concluded that dignity was a 'useless concept' because it 'means no more than respect for persons or their autonomy'.[68] However, since then a significant body of literature on the meaning of dignity, including considerations of how it functions as a wider concept than autonomy, has developed in philosophy and law.

3.2.2 Dignity as Achieving Capabilities: No More than Autonomy?

Nussbaum is one philosopher who has endeavoured to develop a concept of human dignity to expressly include adults with cognitive disability within liberal conceptions of personhood. However, it has been criticised for taking the concept of dignity no further than autonomy and ultimately failing to include the severely and profoundly cognitively impaired within moral personhood.

Nussbaum has developed a theory of justice (her capabilities approach) that proposes dignity can and should function as the marker of human personhood if divorced from the notion of Kantian rationality and autonomy. The capabilities approach defines ten central capabilities that must be achieved by citizens at threshold levels for justice to be met and human dignity recognised. She describes the ten capabilities as collectively representing a minimum threshold for human flourishing. The capabilities are as follows: 1. 'Life', 2. 'Bodily health', 3. 'Bodily integrity', 4. 'Senses, imagination and thought', 5. 'Emotions', 6. 'Practical reason', 7. 'Affiliation', 8. 'Other species' (ability to have concern for animals and plants), 9. 'Play', and 10. 'Control over one's environment'.[69] She argues intuitively that without any one of these capabilities, a life worthy of human dignity cannot be lived.[70]

Nussbaum makes a distinction between capabilities and functioning. Whilst in a just society all individuals must achieve the minimum threshold for the capabilities, the liberal emphasis on individual choice is retained in that a person can choose whether or not to exercise the functioning related to the nominated capabilities. For example, a person must live in a society that allows them the capability for health and wellbeing, but once they reach the relevant capability threshold, if they choose an unhealthy lifestyle, then the State should not intervene by imposing or mandating one.[71] Nussbaum's one exception to this tenet of free choice is that 'government … should not give people an option to be treated with respect and

[67] Suzanne Doyle and Eilionóir Flynn, 'Ireland's Ratification of the UN Convention on the Rights of Persons with Disabilities: Challenges and Opportunities' (2013) 41(3) *British Journal of Learning Disabilities* 171, 174; 'Removing the right to take risks removes autonomy and control from older people': Nay (n 65) 33.

[68] Rosen (n 34) 5; Miller (n 33) 110; Becchi (n 51) 26.

[69] Nussbaum, *Frontiers of Justice* (n 56) 76–7; Martha Nussbaum, *Creating Capabilities: The Human Development Approach* (Harvard University Press, 2011) 33–4.

[70] Nussbaum, *Frontiers of Justice* (n 56) 78.

[71] Nussbaum, *Creating Capabilities* (n 69) 26.

non-humiliation'.[72] In other words, the State should not allow us to choose to be treated by others in a way that is humiliating or degrading – that belies our human dignity.

Despite Nussbaum's express aim of correcting the ableist prejudices of Rawlsian liberalism, the capabilities approach has been widely criticised for its emphasis on reason as a capability,[73] and for espousing a concept of human dignity that is, in effect, equivalent to liberal conceptions of autonomy.[74] Nussbaum acknowledges that some adults with cognitive disability will require the assistance of a 'surrogate' decision-maker or guardian to achieve some of the capabilities.[75] The appointment of a guardian would not amount to a denial of personhood, because it would help the adult achieve the capabilities and have their dignity recognised.

More problematic, though, is Nussbaum's conclusion that some adults with a severe and profound cognitive disability will be excluded from personhood. She excludes persons in a PVS on the basis that they are 'former' human beings.[76] She also concludes that some adults with a severe and profound cognitive disability may never be capable of reaching all of the capability thresholds, even with the assistance of a surrogate or guardian.[77] The capabilities approach has been widely criticised for establishing norms that are beyond the reach of some people, thereby denying them dignity and personhood.[78] Foster reflects the view of many critics when he writes of Nussbaum that 'For her, dignity is autonomy.'[79] Nussbaum's conception of dignity as underpinning personhood ultimately fails to include the hard cases because of its privileging of autonomy, rationality and the right to make choices.[80]

72 Ibid.

73 Stark (n 60) 119–20, 12; Michael Bach and Lana Kerzner, *A New Paradigm for Protecting Autonomy and the Right to Legal Capacity: Advancing Substantive Equality for Persons with Disabilities through Law, Policy and Practice* (Law Commission of Ontario, October 2010) 69; David Bilchitz, 'Dignity, Fundamental Rights and Legal Capacity: Moving beyond the Paradigm Set by the General Comment on Article 12 of the Convention on the Rights of Persons with Disabilities' (2016) 32(3) *South African Journal on Human Rights* 410, 412; Caroline Harnacke, 'Capability and Disability: The CRPD from the Perspective of the Capabilities Approach' in Joel Andersen and Jos Philips (eds), *Disability and Human Rights: Legal, Ethical, and Conceptual Implications of the Convention on the Rights of Persons with Disabilities* (Netherlands Institute of Human Rights, 2012) 167, 177–80.

74 Leslie P Francis and Anita Silvers, 'Thinking about the Good: Reconfiguring Liberal Metaphysics (or Not) for People with Cognitive Disabilties' in Eva Feder Kittay and Licia Carlson (eds), *Cognitive Disability and the Challenge to Moral Philosophy* (2010) 237, 246; Anna Arstein-Kerslake, *Restoring Voice to People with Cognitive Disabilities: Realizing the Right to Equal Recognition before the Law* (Cambridge University Press, 2017) 45.

75 Nussbaum, *Creating Capabilities* (n 69) 24.

76 Nussbaum, *Frontiers of Justice* (n 56) 181.

77 As an example of the latter, Nussbaum refers to Kittay's daughter Sesha, ibid 192–4.

78 Eva Feder Kittay, 'At the Margins of Moral Personhood' (2005) 116(1) *Ethics* 100, 108–10.

79 Foster, *Human Dignity in Bioethics and Law* (n 31) 65.

80 See also Pinheiro and Simplican, who see Nussbaum's theory as limited at its foundations in seeking to 'correct' Rawls's theory of justice rather than embrace an understanding that the exclusion of people with cognitive disability is foundational to both Kant and Rawls: Lucas

3.2.3 Summary and Conclusions on Dignity and Autonomy

In philosophy and law, dignity is often equated with autonomy, as in bioethics, which emphasises the nexus between dignity and informed consent. The elision of dignity with autonomy is evident in the disability literature when it advocates promoting the 'dignity of risk' for people with cognitive disability, to allow them to make their own autonomous decisions in all cases. However, such a narrow concept of dignity excludes from personhood people with cognitive disability who are non-autonomous. Nussbaum attempts to reconfigure the social contract to include adults with cognitive disability but only succeeds in lowering the entry bar by retaining residual reliance on rationality in her concept of human dignity.

In the previous chapter, I argued that endeavours to extend autonomy to adults with cognitive disability ultimately fail because they continue to privilege rationality and non-interference. Nevertheless, that chapter also recognised the importance of autonomy as a human rights value, and the philosophical and legal literature demonstrates strong links between autonomy and dignity. For these reasons, five-dimensional dignity demands recognition and respect for the autonomy of those who are capable of autonomy. However, there is a growing body of literature and jurisprudence that proposes a formulation of human dignity that, while acknowledging the importance of autonomy, is broader and more inclusive.

3.3 *Dignity as Recognising the Interdependent, Interpersonal and Social Nature of Being Human*

The third proposed dimension of dignity in the CRPD is that it recognises the interdependent, interpersonal and social nature of being human. The UN Charter and human rights conventions refer not just to dignity but to *human* dignity. Dignity is an attribute that is associated with humans but also with non-human animals, so when defining *human* dignity, philosophers have been led to consider what it actually means to be human.[81]

The next section considers philosophical formulations of human dignity that reject biological definitions of the human and propose alternatives. It considers first those definitions of human dignity that identify capacities other than rationality as the foundation for personhood. However, it rejects these in favour of definitions that recognise the reflexive nature of dignity, the interdependent and interpersonal

G Pinheiro, 'The Ableist Contract: Intellectual Disability and the Limits of Justice in Kant's Political Thought' in Barbara Arneil and Nancy J Hirschmann (eds), *Disability and Political Theory* (Cambridge University Press, 2016) 43, 70–1; Stacy Clifford Simplican, 'Disavowals of Disability in Rawls' Theory of Justice and His Critics' in Barbara Arneil and Nancy J Hirschmann (eds), *Disability and Political Theory* (Cambridge University Press, 2016) 79, 91.

81 See, e.g., 'Cicero considers the dignity that human beings have solely because they are human, not animals.' And 'So, right from the outset, dignity has been transposed and extended into a way of saying something about human beings as such.' Rosen (n 34) 12.

nature of being human and the social meanings we attribute to it. Following this is a description of legal expressions of this philosophical notion of human dignity as interdependent, interpersonal and imbued with social meaning, as revealed in the jurisprudence and legal commentary on dignity.

3.3.1 Philosophical Approaches to Dignity as Human

If human dignity and moral personhood were said to attach to humans merely because of their different biological makeup from animals, then there is a widely held view that this would amount to 'speciesism'. Speciesism describes a conception of moral personhood that is linked entirely to biology and therefore opens a space for implying more broadly that certain biological characteristics – for example, race, sex, ability or disability – are either superior or inferior to others.[82]

3.3.2 Human Dignity Based on Sentience or Other Psychological Capacities

To avoid speciesism, some philosophers such as Singer have endeavoured to formulate conceptions of personhood based on the capacity for sentience – that is, the capacity for sensation or feeling or other psychological capacities.[83] Such arguments, however, inevitably lead to conclusions that some animals may have equal or greater sentience or psychological capacity than some people with a severe and profound cognitive disability.[84] Disability advocates criticise these arguments both because they are insensitive to the history of marginalisation and 'dehumanisation' of people with disability[85] and because comparisons between the psychology of humans and animals are to a large extent inapt or unintelligible.[86] A definition of personhood based on the capacity for sentience is, therefore, both over-inclusive and under-inclusive.[87] It is over-inclusive because it encompasses some animals, and it is under-inclusive by excluding some people with a severe and profound cognitive

[82] See, e.g., Cora Diamond, 'Eating Meat and Eating People' in Cass R Sunstein and Martha C Nussbaum (eds), *Animal Rights: Current Debates and New Directions* (Oxford Scholarship Online 2012) DOI: 10.1093/acprof:oso/9780195305104.001.0001 93–4; Becchi (n 51) 21.

[83] McMahan proposes similarly that claims to moral personhood may be based on whether an animal – human or non-human – has the requisite higher levels of psychological capacity: Jeff McMahan, 'Radical Cognitive Limitation' in Kimberley Brownlee and Adam Steven Cureton (eds), *Disability and Disadvantage* (Oxford University Press, 2018) 240; Elizabeth Anderson, 'Animal Rights and the Values of Nonhuman Life' in Cass R Sunstein and Martha C Nussbaum (eds), *Animal Rights: Current Debates and New Directions* (Oxford University Press, 2004) 277, 277; Alice Crary, 'Cognitive Disability and Moral Status' in David T Wasserman and Adam Steven Cureton (eds), *The Oxford Handbook of Philosophy and Disability* (Oxford University Press, 2018) 6.

[84] McMahan (n 83).

[85] Crary (n 83) 7.

[86] Kittay, 'At the Margins of Moral Personhood' (n 78) 117.

[87] David T Wasserman et al, 'Cognitive Disability and Moral Status' in Edward N Zalta (ed), *The Stanford Encyclopedia of Philosophy* (Fall 2017 Edition), <https://plato.stanford.edu/archives/fall2017/entries/cognitive-disability/> [4.1].

disability. This leads to the conclusion that any concept of human dignity or personhood based on the possession of identified capacities – whether the capacity for rationality, autonomy or sentience – must always fail. Instead, it has been argued that human dignity is imbued with meaning through the relational, interpersonal and social nature of being human.

3.3.3 Human Dignity as Reflexive, Interpersonal or Interrelational

Debes describes how several philosophers have argued for a concept of human dignity that is constituted by an interpersonal or inter-human component.[88] This does *not* mean that dignity is conferred on us by others. It does mean, however, that dignity as an essentially human attribute is constituted by our interpersonal relationships, communications and affinities with other humans, including our emotional and affective gestures or responses (or, in the case of the patient in a PVS, non-responses). Felder proposes a similar, inclusive concept of the human as specifically underpinning the CRPD when she writes that 'human beings alone' have a '"we" capability', and that 'our normative expectations are met by beings "we count on", and whom we consider in a fundamental sense to "belong to us"'.[89]

Neal draws out this interpersonal component of dignity when she proposes that, when we violate another's dignity, we reflexively may compromise our own. Conversely, we may impinge on the autonomy of someone else without compromising our own.[90] Unlike autonomy, dignity's core is not found in rationality, nor in the ideal of the bounded, atomistic individual of Rawls's thinking. Nor is dignity based on a concept of contractual reciprocity between individuals. Dignity implies the existence of a moral community between humans,[91] and it is because of this that dignity underpins all human rights and demands that people be treated as subjects, not objects, as ends and not merely as means.[92] Mosissa argues similarly that dignity is a 'relational normative principle underlying our complex social relations'; and that '…as opposed to autonomy and equality, the principle of respect for human dignity does not in any way imply the idea of atomised individualism…'.[93] However, it could be argued that this type of reasoning still leaves it open to argue that our interactions

[88] Debes (n 42) 48; see also: 'It is also helpful in this context to conceive of human dignity as a relational value. According to this notion we are interconnected beings.' Sandra Liebenberg, 'The Value of Human Dignity in Interpreting Socio-Economic Rights' (2005) 21(1) *South African Journal on Human Rights* 1, 11.

[89] Franziska Felder, 'What Does the CRPD Tell Us about Being Human?' in Franziska Felder, Laura Davy and Rosemary Kayess (eds), *Disability Law and Human Rights: Theory and Policy* (Palgrave, 2022) 47, 58–9, citing Hans Bernhard Schmid, '"Person" – Nostrologische Notizen' in Frank Kannetzky and Henning Tegtmeyer (eds) *Personalität* (Universitätsverlag, 2007).

[90] Neal (n 30) 29.

[91] Debes (n 42) 58.

[92] Ibid 54.

[93] Getahun A Mosissa, *A Re-examination of Economic, Social and Cultural Rights in a Political Society in the Light of the Principle of Human Dignity* (Intersentia, 2020) 89, 121.

with animals are also based on a type of inter-relationality, without identifying what marks us as human.

Anderson avoids accusations of speciesism by proposing that personhood is grounded in dignity as constituted and generated by the social meanings we attribute to being human. Central to her theory of personhood is the fact that adults with a severe and profound cognitive disability will not have the capacity for autonomy but are still recognised as persons and have moral considerability. Human dignity inheres in them and in all of us, through our bodies, through the material experiences of our everyday lives, and, importantly, through the social meanings attributed to and generated by our existence and actions.[94] By way of illustration, Anderson describes how our interests in respecting a woman with advanced Alzheimer's disease who can no longer care for herself cannot be attributed merely to an instrumental concern for her health and hygiene. Respect for her as a person 'make[s] sense only within a complex system of social relations and meanings' around the notion of being human.[95]

Killmister argues in similar terms as Anderson when she conceives of humans not just as a biological category of the 'natural kind' but as a category of the 'social kind'. Like Anderson, she places great weight on 'social meanings' generated by us all around the concept of being human, writing that 'dignity refers to the worth of being human, where that worth is an upshot of the meaning we've given to the social kind human'.[96]

A potential critique of a conception of human dignity as being generated or constituted by social meaning, may be based on observaions of how easy it has been for society to position certain individuals as 'sub-human' or 'non-human'. Indeed, we would all agree with the analysis that placing people with disabilities and Jewish people on cattle trucks to be industrially exterminated, 'dehumanises' them. But such a statement only makes sense within a framework of meaning that acknowledges implicitly that people with disabilities and Jews *are* human. To treat someone 'like a dog' means that we have 'de-humanised' them but saying that we treat a cat 'like a dog' or a cow 'like a dog', would mean something very different. In short, we operate within systems of social meaning that implicitly define and acknowledge what is human.

Some proponents of an ethic of care as the basis for personhood also connect care theory with dignity. Unfortunately, there is not space here for a description of the

[94] Anderson (n 83) 282–4.

[95] Ibid.

[96] Killmister, 'Disability, Respect and Cognitive Disability' (n,47) 8. Note that elsewhere Killmister writes that human dignity is 'conferred', but I argue that her concept of the human as 'social kind' is not inconsistent with the concept of human dignity as inherent. Suzy Killmister, Dignity: Personal, Social, Human' (2017) 174(8) *Philosophical Studies* 2063. For a social or relational concept of human, see also Diamond who writes that the difference between humans and animals is that: 'The moral expectations of other human beings demand something of me as other than an animal': Diamond (n 82) 106.

nuances and complexities of care theory.[97] However, of significance is that an ethic of care has developed as an alternative basis for personhood to Kantian and Rawlsian autonomy, focusing on context and relationships as constitutive of personhood.[98] Kittay searches for a concept of human dignity grounded in an ethic of care that will include her daughter Sesha who has a profound and severe cognitive disability. She concludes, not dissimilarly to Anderson and Killmister, that 'Philosophers have been on the right path when they have located human dignity in the possibility of a moral life lived out amongst fellow human beings.'[99] Human dignity is to be found in our capacity to care and in being cared for by others. In care ethics, relationships are not instrumental but constitutive of personhood and the inherent dignity of the carer and the cared for.[100]

3.3.4 Jurisprudence and Legal Commentary: The Dignity Interests of the Many; Article 8 ECHR and the Right to Respect for Private and Family Life; 'Public Order' in *Wackenheim v France*

The subsections above have described a philosophical conception of dignity as respecting autonomy but as nevertheless grounded in the interdependent and interpersonal nature of being human and the social meanings attached to it. I argue that this conception is also suggested in some of the key jurisprudence and legal commentary relating to dignity.

Lady Hale writes that 'Although respect for individual autonomy is an essential part of respect for human dignity, we are also required to respect the human dignity of those who are unable to make an autonomous choice.'[101] Much of the UK jurisprudence on autonomy and dignity arises from an examination of Articles 3 and 8 ECHR. Article 3 contains the prohibition against torture and inhuman or degrading treatment, and the Article 3 formulation of dignity is discussed later in this chapter.[102] The jurisprudence around Article 8, the 'Right to respect for private and family life', is of interest in its consideration of the role of dignity and its interface with autonomy. Article 8 ECHR provides that:

(1) Everyone has the right to respect for his private and family life, his home and his correspondence.
(2) There shall be no interference by a public authority with the exercise of this right except such as is in accordance with the law and is necessary in

97 See Carol Gilligan, *In a Different Voice: Psychological Theory and Women's Development* (Harvard University Press, 1993); Jonathan Herring, *Caring and the Law* (Hart Publishing, 2013); Virgina Held, *The Ethics of Care: Personal, Political, Global* (Oxford University Press, 2006).

98 Jennifer Nedelsky, *Law's Relations: A Relational Theory of Self, Autonomy, and the Law* (Oxford University Press, 2012) 87.

99 Kittay, 'Equality, Dignity and Disability' (n 32) 111.

100 Miller similarly proposes an ethic of care can be founded in a concept of dignity as relationality: Miller (n 33) 113–14.

101 Hale (n 2) 106; Neal (n 30) 28–9.

102 See Section 3.5.

> a democratic society in the interests of national security, public safety or the economic well-being of the country, for the prevention of disorder or crime, for the protection of health or morals, or for the protection of the rights and freedoms of others.

Article 8(1) establishes a right to respect for private and family life, while Article 8(2) sets out circumstances where paragraph (1) rights may be limited.

In *Pretty*, Ms Pretty had argued for the legality of assisted suicide, submitting that, as part of her Article 8 right to protection of her private life, she had the right to choose when and how her life was to end in accordance with her own autonomous wishes. The European Court of Human Rights confirmed that Article 8 equates with a right to autonomy,[103] and this interpretation of Article 8 has since been widely acknowledged and accepted in both the jurisprudence and commentary.[104] Nevertheless, the Court acknowledged that, while Ms Pretty's Article 8(1) autonomy rights had been engaged,[105] she failed in her argument because the Court held that Article 8(2) allowed for limitations on her autonomous wishes. The Court explained that Article 8(2) allows for restrictions on autonomy in cases of 'pressing social need', when 'necessary in a democratic society', and for the protection of the rights of others. In this case, these social factors meant that state restrictions on the active facilitation of suicide were not unjustifiable.[106]

Foster summarises how the relevant principles derived from *Pretty* are that both autonomy and dignity are aspects of the 'private life' guaranteed respect by Article 8.[107] He further concludes from the reasoning in this and other Article 8 cases that:

> whatever dignity is, it is a deeper concept than autonomy, and so has a right to priority. That autonomy rights, crucially important though they are, are rights that are rooted in and find their only conceivable justification in dignity: autonomy is a manifestation of dignity.[108]

According to Foster, autonomy is an important value and upholding autonomy may be necessary to respect dignity in many cases. However, in complex and difficult cases, such as *Pretty*, autonomy may conflict with other important values including

[103] 'Although no previous case has established as such any right to self-determination as being contained in Article 8 of the Convention, the Court considers that the notion of personal autonomy is an important principle underlying the interpretation of its guarantees.' *Pretty* 33.

[104] 'It is important to note that personal autonomy and dignity are both aspects of the "private life", respect for which is guaranteed by article 8 of the Convention.' *R (Burke) v General Medical Council (Official Solicitor intervening)* [2005] QB 424, 445 ('*Burke*'); Dupre (n 39) 114; Jonathan Herring, 'Elder Abuse: A Human Rights Agenda for the Future' in Israel Doron and Ann M Soden (eds), *Beyond Elder Law* (Springer-Verlag, 2012) 175, 182.

[105] *Pretty* [67].

[106] Ibid [78].

[107] Foster, *Human Dignity in Bioethics and Law* (n 31) 110.

[108] Ibid 101.

'justice', and in these instances, the ethically justifiable decision is the one that upholds dignity in the wider sense.[109]

Foster endorses the reasoning of Munby J in a long line of Article 8 cases,[110] culminating in His Honour's judgement at first instance in *R (Burke) v General Medical Council* ('*Burke*'). One of the cases discussed by Munby J is *R (A, B, X and Y) v East Sussex County Council (No 2)* ('*East Sussex*'), in which the applicants alleged the unlawfulness of council policies mandating mechanical lifting by disability workers of adults under their care. The applicants claimed that mechanical lifting amounted to violations of Articles 3 and 8 ECHR and sought instead that lifting be provided manually. Munby J found that Article 8 was engaged: first, through Article 8(1) by asserting the dignity interests of the applicants, including their rights to autonomy and to participate in the community, and second, through Article 8(2) by asserting and protecting the dignity rights of the carers.[111] Munby J ultimately decided that the policies should be rewritten to acknowledge the dignity interests of all parties, not just of the applicant, more adequately.

It is notable that, according to Munby J's judgement, Article 8(2) ECHR brings the interdependent, interpersonal and social dimensions of lives into focus, eschewing the liberal conception of the individual as an independent isolate. Foster further describes Article 8(2) as protecting 'the dignity rights of the many', but also as affirming the dignity interests of the claimant by placing an objective lens over Article 8(1) autonomy rights and placing them in a community setting.[112] In other words, considering the dignity interests of the claimant as an isolate does not make sense, given that dignity is constituted by a human, interpersonal component. Recognition of our human dignity is linked to, or generated by, our recognition of ourselves and others as fellow human beings.

The UN Human Rights Committee has not dissimilarly recognised the social and relational nature of dignity as compared with autonomy. In *Wackenheim v France* ('*Wackenheim*'), Monsieur Wackenheim applied to the Committee for a determination that an ordinance banning 'dwarf-tossing' competitions was discriminatory on the basis of disability. Monsieur Wackenheim was a man with dwarfism who wished to continue to earn his living by being 'tossed' and argued his case on the basis that his human dignity rested on his right to the work of his choice.

[109] Ibid 104.

[110] Foster considers a number of cases considered in *Burke*: Foster, *Human Dignity in Bioethics and Law* (n 31) 97–107. These include *Bland*; *D v United Kingdom* (1997) 24 EHRR 423 ('*D v UK*'); *Keenan v United Kingdom* 2001) 33 EHRR 913 ('*Keenan*'); *R (A, B, X and Y) v East Sussex County Council (No 2)* [2003] EWHC 167 (Admin) ('*East Sussex*'); *Price*; this and other jurisprudence on dignity is also discussed in: Mary Donnelly, *Healthcare Decision-Making and the Law: Autonomy, Capacity and the Limits of Liberalism* (Cambridge University Press, 2010) 213–23.

[111] Ultimately, orders were made that an appropriate lifting protocol be drafted according to the principles that he laid down in the judgement: *East Sussex*.

[112] Foster, *Human Dignity in Bioethics and Law* (n 31) 124–5.

However, the Human Rights Committee ultimately endorsed the argument of the State, which had submitted that 'dwarf-tossing' offended human dignity in the sense of 'public order' and the ban was upheld on that basis.[113]

Commentators alike agree that the Human Rights Committee came to a just decision in upholding a ban on 'dwarf-tossing' on the basis that it was a violation of human dignity.[114] This case is widely interpreted as one where the applicant relied on a concept of dignity as autonomy while the State and the Human Rights Committee relied on a different type of dignity that applied to society as a whole. It has been interpreted as not just respecting the applicant's dignity, but also the dignity of other people with dwarfism who, because of their disability, are typically subject to discrimination or unequal status.[115]

3.3.5 Summary and Conclusions on Dignity Recognising the Human as Interdependent

Dignity in the CRPD refers to the equal worth of all human beings, and dignity incorporates respect for autonomy but is also broader and more inclusive than autonomy. The section above addressed the challenging philosophical question of what it means to be human when we talk about human dignity. It rejected the concept of human in this context as a biological category on the grounds that it would amount to speciesism. It went on to consider, as an alternative, theories of personhood that depend on capacities other than autonomy as determinants, notably the capacity for sentience. However, it rejected such formulations of human dignity on the basis that any capacity-based theory – whether the capacity for autonomy or sentience – will be either over-inclusive (by including animals) or under-inclusive (by excluding adults with a severe and profound cognitive disability).

The concept of human dignity underpinning the CRPD must instead rest on a recognition of the interpersonal and interdependent components of personhood as informed by social meanings of the human. Dignity reflects this interpersonal component in particular because when we violate another's dignity, we also compromise our own. This conception of dignity draws on the work of philosophers including Anderson, who describes the human as imbued with social meaning, and Killmister, who recognises the difference between humans as 'natural kind' and humans as 'social kind'. Another way of explaining this is that we have different moral expectations of people whom we recognise as fellow humans.[116]

113 United Nations Human Rights Committee, UN Doc CCPR/C/75/D/854/1999 (n 31).

114 See, e.g., Foster, *Human Dignity in Bioethics and Law* (n 31) 96; Bedford (n 63) 320.

115 Christopher McCrudden, 'In Pursuit of Human Dignity: An Introduction to the Current Debates' in Christopher McCrudden (ed), *Understanding Human Dignity* (Oxford University Press, 2013) 1, 40; Becchi (n 51) 24. See also Barclay, who describes 'dwarf throwing' as an affront to dignity because it is a violation of the equal status of people with dwarfism: Barclay, 'In Sickness and in Dignity: A Philosophical Account of the Meaning of Dignity in Health Care' (n 61) 138.

116 Diamond (n 82) 106.

There are similarities between philosophical conceptions of the human and of human dignity as interpersonal, on the one hand, and legal formulations of dignity as revealed in the jurisprudence and commentary, on the other. The European Court of Human Rights has interpreted Article 8(2) ECHR as acknowledging the interdependence of the individual autonomous claimant, with the dignity interests of others. In *Wackenheim*, the Human Rights Committee found that the dignity of the claimant, the dignity of people with disability and the dignity of the community as a whole were violated by the practice of 'dwarf-tossing'. Mr Wackenheim's dignity was violated for the following reasons: his humanity was devalued; he was treated unequally due to his disability; he was tossed like a 'thing', not a person; and the 'dwarf-tossing' violated our moral expectations of his and our human personhood. In conclusion, human dignity as underpinning the CRPD includes but is broader than respect for autonomy.

3.4 *Dignity as Recognising the Embodied Nature of Personhood*

The fourth dimension of dignity is that it inheres in the person as embodied and as existing and living in a concrete, material world. Discussions on the meaning of dignity invariably focus on a person's body and the impact of the person's physical state on their mind and feelings, and on the feelings of the onlooker. In doing so, these discussions also emphasise the particular, and often begin with an examination of the marginalised, hard cases.

Foster describes how the autonomous man never really existed except in the abstract as an ideal, but that dignity, on the other hand, recognises that 'We exist in our bodies, and we exist in a social, political and physical environment.'[117] Foster's concept of human dignity looks at what makes humans 'thrive', suggesting' a link between nourishing the body and mind in a way that disrupts mind–body dualism.[118] Carozza similarly writes of dignity that: 'It … inher[es] always in an embodied 'I' rather than in a disembodied discourse … it is a hard fact.'[119] Autonomy, on the other hand, relates more readily to abstract legal and philosophical concepts including legal recognition, legal capacity, liberty and equality, and the associated civil–political rights. I argue, with others, that dignity puts flesh on these abstract concepts and rights by looking at what flows from them both in the adherence and the breach.

When writers try to explain dignity, they invariably begin with the image of a person whose dignity is being violated or compromised because of an infliction affecting both body and mind. Kittay begins her discussion of human dignity with the image of her daughter Sesha, naked except for her bath towel, an example both Killmister

[117] Foster, *Human Dignity in Bioethics and Law* (n 31) 12; Nedelsky criticises Kantian autonomy and independence as an 'illusion': Nedelsky (n 98) 45.

[118] Foster, *Human Dignity in Bioethics and Law* (n 31) 17.

[119] Carozza (n 63) 628.

and Crary draw on in their own considerations of dignity.[120] Anderson also opens with the depiction of an Alzheimer's patient suffering personal and physical neglect and explains how human dignity demands that her body be made 'fit for human society'.[121] Lady Hale opens her essay on dignity with a description of *Price v UK*, which concerned the physical ill-treatment and neglect of a woman with only partially formed limbs, a case referred to frequently in the dignity jurisprudence and literature.[122]

Dignity considers the particularities of human existence, with Foster describing his formulation of dignity as 'anthropological' because he derives it through examining a series of hard cases.[123] For him, dignity is a concept that, unlike autonomy, is grounded in the real, material world, applying to embodied people who have complex material lives intertwined with the lives of others.[124] Philosophers and lawyers alike tend to begin with the hard cases, with the case of the PVS patient or the conscious person with a severe and profound cognitive disability, to understand how human dignity works. These hard cases are not always easily or logically resolved by reference to autonomy but may be explained by respect for human dignity.[125]

In summary, the fourth dimension of human dignity proposed in this chapter is that human dignity inheres in the embodied person, and its meaning is derived from the particularities of peoples' lives. Considerations of dignity in the philosophical and legal literature and jurisprudence typically begin with depictions of a person who is fragile in body and mind. For this reason, understanding dignity requires examination of the hard cases, which are often put to one side and marginalised in interpretations of Article 12 that privilege autonomy. Recognition of universal legal capacity requiring a 'best interpretation' of autonomous wishes begins with assumptions of what is typical, extending general rules to marginal cases without always acknowledging the actualities of a person's existence. Autonomy underpins a conception of personhood premised on the ideal of the abstract, independent, isolated man, who has never really existed in the real world.

Chapter 2 described how a strict social model of disability risks denying the reality of impairment. A strict social model would focus solely on the changes in society required to accommodate impairment, and in so doing would take no account of the specificity and particularity of impairment. Human dignity as attaching to the embodied person, interdependent and interrelated with others, recognises that

120 Kittay, 'Equality, Dignity and Disability' (n 32) 96; Killmister, 'Disability, Respect and Cognitive Disability' (n 47) 3; Crary (n 83) 2.

121 Anderson (n 83) 282.

122 Hale (n 2) 101–2. See also Foster, who opens with a depiction of a naked girl with an intellectual disability, lying exposed on a hospital trolley: Foster, *Human Dignity in Bioethics and Law* (n 31) 2.

123 Foster, *Human Dignity in Bioethics and Law* (n 31) 1.

124 For his argument that autonomy does not account for people's lives in the real world, see: Foster, Charles, *Choosing Life, Choosing Death: The Tyranny of Autonomy in Medical Ethics and Law* (Hart Publishing, 2009) 4.

125 Foster, *Human Dignity in Bioethics and Law* (n 31) 3.

impairment has an impact on a person's body and mind, as well as on the lives of others. It positions disability within a social model that recognises the residual impacts of impairment.

3.5 *Dignity as Underpinning and Affirming the Indivisibility of Human Rights*

The fifth and final dimension of dignity proposed as underpinning the CRPD is that it embodies and affirms the indivisibility of human rights. While autonomy has traditionally been viewed as underpinning civil–political rights, I argue that dignity underpins both civil–political and socio-economic rights, and in so doing demonstrates and drives the principle of indivisibility.

As established in Chapter 3, this book has adopted a concept of the principle of indivisibility of human rights with two broad components. First, indivisibility recognises interdependencies between rights, so that some rights cannot be realised without the realisation of other rights; and second, it demands that the two categories of rights – civil–political and socio-economic – be considered as of equal importance. The bifurcation of rights into the two categories has historically framed civil–political rights as requiring restraint by the State, abstention from intervening in the private sphere, as cost-free, and as requiring immediate implementation. The corollary is that socio-economic rights are framed as requiring positive state action and intervention in the private realm, considerable resources, and progressive implementation. Indivisibility is further evidenced and driven by disruption of these indicators between and across the two categories.

This section begins with a review of those provisions in human rights instruments, including the CRPD, that emphasise the link between dignity and socio-economic rights. Following this is an examination of some of the jurisprudence on dignity that illustrates how the fulfilment of civil–political rights can depend on the fulfilment of socio-economic rights, demonstrating the principle of indivisibility.

3.5.1 In Human Rights Instruments – Dignity and Socio-economic Rights

Section 2 set out those provisions in the foundational human rights instruments and the CRPD where the inherent dignity of all human beings is affirmed as an overarching principle. Dignity is usually listed as a pre-eminent value or quality preceding, or alongside, affirmations of the rights to liberty, justice and equality,[126] all of which traditionally fall within the category of civil–political rights. As explained above, dignity is closely associated with the civil–political rights to be free from

[126] For example, 'To reaffirm faith in fundamental human rights, in the dignity and worth of the human person, in the equal rights of men and women and of nations large and small' UN Charter (n 6) Preamble para 1. See also 'the inherent dignity and … the equal and inalienable rights of all members of the human family [as] the foundation of freedom, justice and peace in the world': *UN Declaration* Preamble.

torture and inhuman or degrading treatment, as well as the right to privacy and family life. But that dignity's impact extends beyond the category of civil–political rights, is evident through its express referencing in the ICESCR, as well as in other human rights instruments where it is linked with socio-economic rights.

In this respect, the UN Declaration's Preamble reads:

> Whereas the peoples of the United Nations have in the Charter reaffirmed their faith in fundamental human rights, in the dignity and worth of the human person and in the equal rights of men and women and have determined to promote social progress and better standards of life in larger freedom. [emphasis added][127]

In the above paragraph, dignity is linked with rights to 'social progress' and improved standards of living; and the fulfilment of the traditionally civil–political right to freedom is also linked with achievement of these socio-economic rights. Article 22 of the UN Declaration provides that every person has 'the right to social security and … realisation … of the economic, social and cultural rights indispensable for his dignity and the free development of his personality'. It thus expressly provides that fulfilment of socio-economic rights is 'indispensable' for human dignity – and our development as human persons. Article 23(3) provides:

> Everyone has the right to just and favourable remuneration ensuring for himself and his family an existence worthy of human dignity, and supplemented, if necessary, by other means of social protection. [emphasis added]

Articles 22 and 23 are the only two substantive articles of the UN Declaration that refer to dignity, and they unequivocally ground the recognition of dignity in the realisation of socio-economic rights that require positive action from the State, impacting the family and private sphere (i.e. the provision of 'social protection' or welfare).

The socio-economic right to education has been linked with human dignity, both in the ICESCR and the CRPD,[128] and Article 25 CRPD also links the right to health care with respect for human dignity.[129] That dignity is linked with living conditions, and the right to shelter and accommodation is also expressly recognised by the UN Disability Committee, which, in relation to Article 19 'Living independently and being included in the community', explains that 'The foundation of the Article is the

[127] *UN Declaration* Preamble para 5.

[128] 'Dignity is also implicated in certain particular claims about socio-economic rights. Article 13(1) *ICESCR*, recognizes a right to education and lays it down that "education shall be directed to the full development of the human personality and the sense of its dignity"': Waldron (n 36) 3; see also how education allows for the 'development of human potential and sense of dignity and self-worth': *CRPD* Article 24 para 1(a).

[129] See also: 'States Parties shall take measures … to ensure that working and living conditions of migrant workers and members of their families in a regular situation are in keeping with the standards of fitness, safety, health and principles of human dignity.' *International Convention on the Protection of the Rights of All Migrant Workers and Members of Their Families*, signed 18 December 1990, 2220 UNTS 3, Article 70 (entered into force 1 July 2003).

core human rights principle that all human beings are born equal in dignity and rights and all life is of equal worth.'[130] The UN Disability Committee further acknowledges that Article 19 CRPD includes a mix of civil–political and socio-economic rights,[131] incorporating a specific instance of the right to legal capacity in choice of residence.[132]

The Vienna World Conference on Human Rights in 1993 had also adopted dignity as an organising principle, boosting its status as a human rights norm. As described in Chapter 3, a significant outcome from this conference was an affirmation of the indivisibility of human rights, such affirmation proving pivotal in the growing recognition of the principle of indivisibility in UN doctrine.[133] The Vienna Declaration's affirmation of dignity as a fundamental human rights principle was closely linked with the achievement of socio-economic rights and the alleviation of poverty.[134] In this way, the Vienna Declaration reflects the nexus in the UN human rights conventions of dignity and socio-economic rights and the principle of indivisibility.

3.5.2 The Jurisprudence on Socio-economic Rights and Dignity

These links between dignity, socio-economic rights and the principle of indivisibility are beginning to emerge in the growing jurisprudence on dignity. The following cases show that rights to liberty, equality and asylum may depend on fulfilment of rights to shelter, subsistence or social assistance; and that the right to be free from inhuman treatment may depend on fulfilment of the right to access adequate health care.

The South African constitution is noteworthy for its inclusion of socio-economic rights to housing, health care, food, water, social security, and education,[135] as well

130 Committee on Economic Social and Cultural Rights, *General Comment 5: Persons with Disabilities*, 11th sess (9 December 1994) [2].

131 Ibid [7].

132 Ibid [20]. McCrudden also catalogues how dignity has been linked with the socio-economic right to work: McCrudden, 'Human Dignity and Judicial Interpretation of Human Rights' (n 4) 661, 669.

133 World Conference on Human Rights, *Vienna Declaration and Programme of Action*, UN Doc A/CONF.157/24 (25 June 1993) part 1 [5].

134 '...further major fillip to the use of dignity in the international sphere was given by the adoption of dignity as the central organizing principle of the Vienna World Conference on Human Rights in 1993. The Declaration and Programme of Action adopted dignity as foundational not just to human rights in general but also adopted the concept of dignity in their provisions dealing with particular areas of human rights, such as the treatment of indigenous peoples, the prohibition of torture, the prohibition of gender-based violence and harassment, the abolition of extreme poverty, and the issue of biomedical ethics.' McCrudden, 'Human Dignity and Judicial Interpretation of Human Rights' (n 4) 670. See also 'It is now undisputed that all human rights are indivisible, interdependent, interrelated and of equal importance for human dignity. Therefore, states are as responsible for violations of economic, social and cultural rights as they are for violations of civil and political rights.' Stephen P Marks, 'The Past and Future of the Separation of Human Rights into Categories' (2009) 24 *Maryland Journal of International Law* 209, 233, quoting International Commission of Jurists, *Maastricht Guidelines on Violations of Economic, Social and Cultural Rights* (26 January 1997) [4].

135 *Constitution of the Republic of South Africa* (Act 108 of 1996) s 26 'Everyone has the right to have access to adequate housing'; s 27(1) 'Everyone has the right to have access to: (a) health

as the inclusion of a 'right [for persons] to have their dignity respected and protected', and a provision that applies dignity as an 'interpretive principle'.[136] *Government of the Republic of South Africa and Others v Grootboom and Others* ('*Grootboom*') is a case from the Constitutional Court of South Africa that has attracted wide interest, both because it involves the adjudication of socio-economic rights,[137] and it grounds the value of these rights in respect for human dignity.[138]

Grootboom concerned squatters who had been evicted off private land and found themselves homeless and living in deplorable conditions. Article 26 of the South African Constitution provides for a right to adequate housing and Article 28(1)(c) provides for a child's right to shelter. Yacoob J, in delivering the Court's unanimous decision, wrote that: 'A society must seek to ensure that the basic necessities of life are provided to all if it is to be a society based on human dignity, freedom and equality'[139] and 'In short, I emphasise that human beings are required to be treated as human beings.'[140] These affirmations suggest that human dignity is perceived as founding our civil, economic, social, political and cultural personhood. They also

care services, including reproductive health care; (b) sufficient food and water; and (c) social security, including, if they are unable to support themselves and their dependants, appropriate social assistance'; s 29 'Everyone has the right to a basic education, including adult basic education; and to further education.'

136 Ibid s 1 'The republic of South Africa is … founded on the following values: (a) Human dignity, the achievement of equality and the advancement of human rights and freedoms …' s 19 'Everyone has inherent dignity and the right to have their dignity respected and protected.'

137 Marks (n 134) 230–1 quoting from *Draft International Covenant on Human Rights and Measures of Implementation: Future Work of the Commission on Human Rights*, GA Res 421E (V), UN Doc A/1775 (4 December 1950); Dorothea Anthony, 'The Human Rights Principle of Indivisibility and Its Ideological Significance in the Contemporary Age' (Dissertation, University of New South Wales, 2018) 173 http://unsworks.unsw.edu.au/fapi/datastream/unsworks:51572/SOURCE02?view=true>; Jennifer Sellin, 'The Justiciability of the Right to Health – Access to Medicines – The South African and Indian Experience' (2009) 2(4) *Erasmus Law Journal* 445, 456; Venitia Govender, 'Economic, Social and Cultural Rights in South Africa: Entitlements, Not Mere Policy Options' in Berma Klein Goldewijk, Adalid Contreras Baspineiro, Paulo Câesar Carbonari (eds) *Dignity and Human Rights: The Implementation of Economic, Social and Cultural Rights* (Intersentia 2002) 75, 79; Ida Elizabeth Koch, 'Economic, Social and Cultural Rights as Components in Civil and Political Rights: A Hermeneutic Perspective' (2006) 10(4) *International Journal of Human Rights* 405, 427; Li-Ann Thio, 'The Universal Declaration of Human Rights at 60: Universality, Indivisibility and the Three Generations of Human Rights' (2009) 21(1) *Singapore Academy of Law Journal* 293, 316.

138 Andrea Broderick, *The Long and Winding Road to Equality and Inclusion for Persons with Disabilities: The United Nations Convention on the Rights of People with Disabilities* (Intersentia, 2015) 197; Liebenberg (n 88) 3; McCrudden, 'Human Dignity and Judicial Interpretation of Human Rights' (n 4) 694; Evadné Grant, 'Human Dignity and Socio-economic Rights' (2012) 33(3) *Liverpool Law Review* 235, 236–7; Christian Courtis, 'Standards to Make ESC Rights Justiciable: A Summary of Exploration' (2009) 2 *Erasmus Law Review* 379, 391; Carozza (n 63) 618.

139 *Government of the Republic of South Africa and Others v Grootboom and Others* (2000) (1) SA 46 ('*Grootboom*').

140 Ibid [83].

echo the words of the UN General Assembly in 1950 that '[W]hen deprived of economic, social and cultural rights … the man does not represent the human person whom the Universal Declaration regards as the ideal of the free man.'[141]

Noteworthy in drawing the relationship between dignity and the indivisibility of human rights is the statement of Yacoob J in *Grootboom* that:

> All the rights in our Bill of Rights are inter-related and mutually supporting. There can be no doubt that human dignity, freedom and equality, the foundational values of our society, are denied those who have no food, clothing or shelter.[142]

Govender writes of the South African Constitution that 'the very core of economic, social and cultural rights is human dignity and equality', and Liebenberg observes that the South African Constitutional Court has 'invoked dignity as the central value informing its approach to the interpretation of socio-economic rights.[143]

According to Feldman, in some cases dignity is used to limit autonomy, as if socio-economic rights are invoked by dignity to limit civil–political rights. He describes *R v Secretary of State for Social Security, ex parte Joint Council for the Welfare of Immigrants* ('*Council for the Welfare of Immigrants*')[144] in which regulations that withdrew government benefits from asylum seekers were found to be unlawful. The Court held that the regulations made the right to asylum 'nugatory' by making it impossible for asylum seekers to remain in the UK unless they lived in a state of intolerable destitution. The outcome implicitly acknowledges that the civil–political right to asylum depended on the fulfilment of the basic socio-economic rights to food and subsistence. Feldman explains this decision in terms of the Court upholding dignity, concluding that:

> dignity is an important value which may generate duties on public authorities to provide assistance to those who would otherwise be left destitute. This gives rise to something in the nature of a socio-economic right, which extends at least as far as is necessary to maintain life and a minimum level of dignity.[145]

In *Council for the Welfare of Immigrants*, the rights to civil–political liberty and asylum depended on fulfilling the socio-economic right to social assistance. Fulfilment of this latter right required positive action from the State, expenditure of resources and intervention in the private lives of the claimants.

Grootboom and the *Council of Welfare of Immigrants* also illustrate, I argue, the proposition that dignity recognises embodied personhood, underpinning the indivisibility of human rights. In post-Apartheid South Africa, many people have access to new-found civil–political personhood; but, without material subsistence to

141 Marks (n 134) 240.
142 *Grootboom* [23].
143 Govender (n 137) 89; Liebenberg (n 88) 3; *Khosa and Others v Minister for Social Development and Others* 2004 (6) SA 505 (Constitutional Court).
144 [1996] 4 All ER 385.
145 David Feldman, 'Human Dignity as a Legal Value' (Pt 2) [2000] *Public Law* 61, 61.

nourish both mind and the body, those rights are hollow. Similarly, in *Council for the Welfare of Immigrants*, while the asylum seekers had their civil–political personhood recognised in acknowledgement of their right to asylum, the right was nugatory without recognition of the needs generated by the embodied nature of their personhood. These same connections between the indivisibility of human rights, dignity and embodied personhood are also evident in the following cases on the right to be free from torture and inhuman or degrading treatment.[146]

In *D v United Kingdom* (1997) 24 EHRR 423 ('*D v UK*'), the applicant was in the terminal stages of an HIV-related illness and obtained relief from deportation on the basis that deportation would amount to a breach of Article 3 ECHR. The European Court of Human Rights concluded that the lack of adequate medical facilities and social support in Mr D's home country of St Kitts would have resulted in him suffering inhuman and degrading treatment if deported. The judgement can be interpreted as asserting that the Article 3 right to be free from inhuman treatment depended on fulfilling the socio-economic rights to health and social support services. Koch describes this judgement as illustrating 'the organic interdependence between Article 3 and the social right to health care of a dying AIDS patient';[147] that is, it illustrates the principle of the indivisibility of human rights.

The European Court of Human Rights in *Pretty* described the judgement in *D v UK* as being founded on the recognition of human dignity, a finding affirmed by Munby J in *Burke*.[SS] Commenting on *D v UK* but also extrapolating more widely, Munby J opines that the dignity interest of the dying may ground either the right to be protected from unwanted medical treatment or the right to be 'protected from lack of treatment'.[148] That is, respect for the dignity of the dying requires the fulfilment of the socio-economic right to adequate health care. In emphasising that adequate health care may require either restraint or positive action by the state, Munby J's comment also suggests a disruption of the dichotomy of the traditional indicia associated with civil–political and socio-economic rights. The fulfilment of the right to adequate health care may even require the withdrawal of services for the dying.[149]

146 In another case, the House of Lords held that it was unlawful for the Secretary of State to deny all means of subsistence to an asylum seeker so that he was reduced to living and begging on the streets: see *R (Adam and Limbuela) v Secretary of State for the Home Department* [2005] UKHL 66 ('*Limbuela*'). Lady Hale writes of *Limbuela* that 'Human dignity was the fundamental value which underlay that decision even if we did not say so.' Hale (n 2) 107.

147 Ida Elisabeth Koch, 'Social Rights as Components in the Civil Right to Personal Liberty: Another Step Forward in the Integrated Human Rights Approach?' (2002) 20(1) *Netherlands Quarterly of Human Rights* 29, 35.

148 *Burke* [80].

149 See also *Keenan* in which the European Court of Human Rights found a violation of Article 3 when a mentally ill prisoner was held in solitary confinement without proper medical monitoring, and where he ultimately committed suicide. The Court in this case found that 'The lack of appropriate medical treatment may amount to treatment contrary to Article 3.' *Keenan* [110] cited in *Burke* [67]. Donnelly explains the Court's reasoning as imposing positive obligations

Human rights theorists more broadly have expressed the view that dignity underpins all human rights, both civil–political and socio-economic. Carbonari argues for human dignity as a coherent ethical underpinning for human rights as moral, legal, political and social subjects.[150] Dignity is the basis of our personhood in the civil, social, economic, political and cultural spheres because 'ESCR [economic, social and cultural rights] are as fundamental to human agency and dignity and as definitional of human existence and fulfillment as CPR [civil and political rights].'[151]

3.5.3 Summary and Conclusions on Dignity and the Principle of Indivisibility

It is proposed that dignity recognises the inherent and equal worth of all human persons, and includes respect for autonomy, but is also wider than being merely equivalent to autonomy. Historically, autonomy has been privileged in rights discourse because it underpins civil–political rights, which have, in turn, been privileged over socio-economic rights. Dignity in the CRPD encompasses autonomy but is broader and underpins both civil–political and socio-economic rights, recognising their indivisibility.

The link between respect for dignity and the fulfilment of civil–political rights is widely accepted and manifest in associations between dignity and the right to be free from torture, the right to legal capacity, the right to liberty, and the right to equality. However, links are also frequently drawn between dignity and the fulfilment of socio-economic rights, as expressed in the UN Declaration, the ICESCR and the CRPD. Rights to shelter and accommodation, education and social progress are all closely associated with respect for fundamental human dignity.

The jurisprudence on dignity is only emerging, but the South African Constitutional Court is taking the lead in developing dignity as a legal principle and grounding it in the indivisibility of socio-economic and civil–political rights. In *Grootboom*, fulfilment of the civil rights to liberty and equality depended on fulfilling the socio-economic rights to shelter and subsistence. In the UK case of *Council for the Welfare of Immigrants*, the fulfilment of the civil–political right to asylum was meaningless without the provision of basic subsistence. In *D v UK*, violation of the prohibition against inhuman treatment resulted from failure to fulfil rights of access to adequate health care and support services.

Of note in these cases is that, while the applicants may have had legal personhood and legal capacity, such personhood was impotent and those rights were hollow,

on the state to provide mental health care, in order to protect a person from inhumane treatment and respect their dignity: Mary Donnelly, 'From Autonomy to Dignity: Treatment for Mental Disorders and the Focus for Patient Rights' (2008) 26(2) *Law in Context* 37, 55.

150 Paulo Câesar Carbonari, 'Human Dignity as a Basic Concept of Ethics and Human Rights' in Berma Klein Goldewijk, Adalid Contreras Baspiniero and Paulo Câesar Carbonari (eds), *Dignity and Human Rights: The Implementation of Economic, Social and Cultural Rights* (Insentia, 2002) 35, 39–40.

151 That is, civil-political rights: Marks (n 134) 240; see also Mosissa (n 93) 128.

given their actual circumstances. To recognise their dignity, acknowledgement of their interdependent and embodied personhood was required, together with fulfilment of their socio-economic rights.

4 DIGNITY AND THE ARTICLE 12 LITERATURE

The sections above have argued that dignity as a legal principle is underpinned by the indivisibility of human rights, recognising the interdependence of rights and the equal importance of socio-economic and civil–political rights. This section goes on to explain how dignity, while underpinning the indivisibility of human rights, can also fill the breach left by autonomy to recognise the personhood of all adults and to provide a legal principle for decision-making under Article 12.

It begins by identifying that there has been scant attention paid to the complexities of dignity in interpreting Article 12. In this context, dignity has often been invoked in the limited sense of autonomy and has also been linked with equality and non-discrimination.[152] However, as described below, a few commentators have promoted dignity as a value to underpin personhood and Article 12 decision-making.[153]

4.1 *Article 12 and Autonomy*

Much of the commentary relating to Article 12 that mentions dignity contends or assumes that dignity is linked with autonomy[154] or is limited in meaning to the

[152] See further discussion in Chapter 7.

[153] For the most part, except for the connections made with autonomy and equality, the Article 12 literature tends to refer to dignity incidentally or rhetorically. For example: 'The Convention draws on the principles of the UN Charter – namely, the inherent dignity and the equal and inalienable rights of all members of the human family as the foundation of freedom, justice and peace in the world'; Rosemary Kayess and Ben Fogarty, 'The Rights and Dignity of Persons with Disabilities' (2007) 32(1) *Alternative Law Journal* 22, 23. Or sometimes dignity is merely incorporated in a list of other important values and human rights, for example 'a long list of CRPD rights, including those of inherent dignity, non-discrimination, liberty and security, freedom from torture or cruel, inhuman or degrading treatment': Terry Carney et al, 'Realising "Will, Preferences and Rights": Reconciling Differences on Best Practice Support for Decision-Making?' (2019) *Griffith Law Review* 357, 370–1; see also: 'Equality and non-discrimination along with respect for dignity, individual autonomy and freedom to make one's choices have been recognized as general principles of the CRPD': International Disability Alliance, *Legal Opinion on Article 12 of the CRPD* (www.internationaldisability alliance.org/representation/legal-capacity-working-group, 2008).

[154] See Gerard Quinn and Abigail Rekas-Rosalbo, 'Civil Death: Rethinking the Foundations of Legal Personhood for Persons with a Disability' (2016) 56 *Irish Jurist* 286, 299; de Bhailís, Clíona and Eilionóir Flynn, 'Recognising Legal Capacity: Commentary and Analysis of Article 12 CRPD' (2017) 13(01) *International Journal of Law in Context* 6, 17; 'A statutory measure that limits a person's legal capacitiy affects that person's rights to equality, dignity and psychological integrity.' Holness (n 25) 330; Bach and Kerzner (n 73) 86, 89, 134, 153, 163, 178, 184.

dignity of risk.[155] The concept of the dignity of risk has already been described in Section 3.2.1 above. It is often used to ground the right of adults with cognitive disability to make unwise or risky decisions in the same way that others are free without paternalistic intervention to make decisions that may risk harm to themselves or others.[156] In this way, the dignity of risk, while an important component of dignity, reflects the limited meaning of dignity as autonomy.

For example, the ALRC defines dignity as one of the guiding principles of the CRPD and then goes on to write that 'dignity as a human being is linked to self-determination, decision making and choice'; and it makes frequent references to the importance of respecting the dignity of risk.[157] As explained in Chapter 2, the outcome-based test for legal capacity – whereby the unreasonableness of a decision is the starting point to work backwards to a determination of incapacity – has been heavily criticised as violating an individual's autonomy and their 'dignity of risk'.[158] This limited formulation of dignity as the dignity of risk is used widely to justify interpreting Article 12 as requiring universal legal capacity and the abolition of guardianship.

Düwell is one writer who endeavours to formulate a wider conception of dignity in the CRPD by proposing that it include the '*possibility* of living an autonomous life'[159] [emphasis added]. Düwell views dignity as an attribute of all human humans; as having an empirical, not just abstract, dimension; as underpinning claims to both positive and negative human rights; and as requiring both state restraint and state action, depending on an individual's contingent circumstances.[160] His theory of dignity aligns, to an extent, with the concept of five-dimensional dignity, with

155 Gerard Quinn, 'Concept Paper "Personhood and Legal Capacity": Perspectives on the Paradigm Shift of Article 12 of the CRPD' (Conference Paper, HPOD Conference, 20 February, 2010) 19 www.inclusiveirelandie/document/HarvardLegalcapacitygqdraft2.doc; Eilionóir Flynn and Anna Arstein-Kerslake, 'State Intervention in the Lives of People with Disabilities: The Case for a Disability-Neutral Framework' (2017) 13(1) *International Journal of Law in Context* 39, 48; Bruce Alston (n 134) 24.

156 Doyle and Flynn (n 67) 174.

157 Australian Law Reform Commission, *Equality, Capacity and Disability in Commonwealth Laws: A Final Report* (2014) 43, 53, 75, 85, 102, 154, 170, 174, 213.

158 'It is to recognise the "dignity of risk" so that individuals with impairments are allowed to make unwise choices without paternalistic incursions into their lives': Camillia Kong, 'The Convention on the Rights of Persons with Disabilities and Article 12: Prospective Feminist Lessons against the "Will and Preferences" Paradigm' (2015) 4(4) *Laws* 709725; 'The General Comment states that there must be safeguards to protect against undue influence, yet these must respect the rights, will and preferences of the person, including the right to take risks and make mistakes.' Lucy Series and Anna Nilsson, 'Article 12 CRPD: Equal Recognition before the Law' in Ilias Bantekas, Michael Ashley Stein and Anastasiou Dimitris (eds), *The UN Convention on the Rights of Persons with Disabilities: A Commentary* (Oxford University Press, 2018) 339, 371.

159 Marcus Düwell, 'Setting the Agenda for Ethical Debates about the Rights of Persons with Disabilities' in Joel Andersen and Jos Philips (eds), *Disability and Universal Human Rights: Legal, Ethical, and Conceptual Implications of the Convention on the Rights of Persons with Disabilities* (Netherlands Institute of Human Rights, 2012) 185, 187.

160 Ibid 186–91.

its embrace of positive and negative rights and recognition of the materiality of our existence. However, dignity as 'the possibility of living an autonomous life' excludes someone like Sesha and does not explain how, when we fail to recognise Sesha's dignity, we ultimately fail to respect our own humanity and self-worth. Düwell's concept of dignity elides with or equates to a very thin version of autonomy.

4.2 *Article 12 and Equality*

While dignity conceptualised as no more than autonomy is a persistent theme in some of the Article 12 literature, there is also a recurring theme linking discrimination with a violation of inherent dignity. *General Comment No 1* suggests that dignity is equivalent to autonomy, but that it is also closely linked with the right to non-discrimination and equality in that 'Freedom from discrimination in the recognition of legal capacity restores autonomy and respects the human dignity of the person.'[161] According to the UN Disability Committee, denial of autonomy together with discrimination in the recognition of legal capacity combine to violate the dignity of people with disability.[162]

Chapter 6 argues that the notion of substantive, inclusive equality underpinning the CRPD and Article 12 allows for or demands the differential treatment of decision-making by substitutes in some cases, in order to achieve inclusive equality. It also describes how *General Comment No 6* proposes a four-dimensional approach to inclusive equality, with two of those dimensions expressly recognising the close relationship between inclusive equality and the recognition of dignity. Suffice to say here that to promote social inclusion and recognise dignity, substantive, inclusive equality does not always demand identical treatment for persons with disability but may require a differential response that recognises the difference of impairment.

4.3 *Article 12: Beyond Autonomy and Equality*

As already mentioned, there is scant consideration in the literature of how dignity formulated as a wider concept than autonomy may underpin an interpretation of Article 12. And yet at least one submission to the ALRC from the Australian Research Network on Law and Ageing ('Law and Ageing') does advocate this broader role – in

161 *United Nations Committee on the Rights of Persons with Disabilities 'General Comment No. 1 (2014) Article 12: Equal Recognition Before the Law CRPD/C/GC/1' (2014)* [33]. See also [4] which provides more generally: 'The present general comment reflects an interpretation of Article 12 which is premised on the general principles of the Convention, as outlined in Article 3, namely respect for the inherent dignity, individual autonomy – including the freedom to make one's own choices – and independence of persons'.

162 The *CRPD*'s Preamble para 8 also draws a link between discrimination and dignity in 'Recognising … that discrimination against any person on the basis of disability is a violation of the inherent dignity and worth of the human person.'

particular, to uphold the human rights of people with cognitive disability whose capacity for autonomy may be limited. Law and Ageing noted:

> the importance of looking beyond the concept of promoting the personal autonomy of persons, to include the wider right of respect for the person's dignity. It has been recognised that dignity is a wider concept than autonomy, and a universal value to which all persons are entitled. It therefore has special relevance for those whose capacity is compromised, either because of conditions producing fluctuating capacity, or for more chronic situations.[163]

A handful of commentators have considered what this wider conception of dignity may be in the specific context of Article 12.

Bilchitz considers how dignity can be used to interpret Article 12 as allowing for decision-making by substitutes for adults with mental illness, acknowledging that some people at some times will not have the autonomy to make decisions. For Bilchitz, autonomy is to be valued if present; but if not present, then it is essential to find other qualities in people's lives that found their inherent dignity. However, Bilchitz's account of dignity is based on capacities: either the capacity for an individual to consciously experience the world or 'the ability of individuals to develop purposes and to seek to achieve them'.[164] As explained above,[165] any concept of dignity that is based on capacities or abilities is ultimately either over-inclusive or under-inclusive.[166] Bilchitz's criteria are both: the capacity to have a conscious experience of the world is over-inclusive as it would include non-human animals, and it is under-inclusive in terms of excluding people in a PVS.

Celik draws on an extensive body of philosophical and political literature on the 'vulnerable subject' to argue that the personhood envisaged by Article 12 CRPD is founded on a concept of dignity grounded in relational autonomy and vulnerability. Fineman proposed that the 'vulnerable subject' should replace the autonomous, independent, rational subject of liberal theory, as a starting point to understanding the relationship between individuals and the State, and the extent and nature of the State's obligations towards us.[167] The vulnerable subject recognises that we are all vulnerable to greater or lesser extents at different times in our lives and that the nature of our relationship with each other and with the State varies accordingly.

[163] ALRC Report 76.

[164] Bilchitz (n 73) 431.

[165] See Section 3.3.2.

[166] 'These accounts are attractive in identifying attributes that may offer a more intuitively appealing basis for moral status than practical rationality or self-awareness, and in reducing, to varying extents, the proportion of humanity excluded from full moral status. But because they exclude some humans, and may include some non-human animals, they do not fully capture common sense views about moral status and will be unacceptable to some philosophers': Wasserman et al (n 87).

[167] Martha Fineman, 'Beyond Identities: The Limits of an Anti-discrimination Approach to Equality' (2012) 92(6) *Boston University Law Review* 1713.

Celik argues that the very concept of supported decision-making recognises the vulnerable, dependent subject, whose autonomy is not found through enjoying 'negative liberties' but achieved through the guarantee of rights.[168] She rejects both a 'negative liberty' view of autonomy as fulfilled only through State restraint and a Kantian view of dignity as limited to rationality. Vulnerability for Celik acknowledges the embodied nature of personhood and our dependencies on others and becomes a tool for defining the obligations of the State towards us.

Celik's concept of dignity, in referencing the vulnerable subject, has much in common with other concepts of dignity that reject pure Kantianism. It implies recognition of the equal worth of all humans but recognises the embodied subject and the relational and social nature of personhood. Celik proposes that Article 12 anticipates the universal, vulnerable subject because personhood is defined by the State's obligations to us to provide supports, and relational autonomy is the analytic tool used to determine which supports are lacking and which are needed. However, I argue that dignity as a basis for recognising personhood and respect for dignity as a basis for intervention have more resonance in a human rights context, given their reiterative affirmation in human rights and humanitarian instruments. Human dignity acknowledges our vulnerability as humans (not just as one species of animal) and also that personhood cannot be achieved or measured in degrees.

Donnelly considers how dignity can be used as a way of valuing people who are not autonomous. She writes that 'a consequence of the legal and ethical fixation on autonomy has been a lack of conceptual engagement with the position of people who cannot make autonomous decisions'.[169] She argues that for adults with impaired capacity, autonomy should be respected by promoting participative decision-making, but that dignity should serve as a 'right' or value to ensure that the human rights of the non-autonomous are upheld. She does not expressly propose dignity as an inclusive basis for personhood to replace autonomy but does rely on the ECHR jurisprudence to argue for ongoing development of the concept of dignity to protect the rights of adults with impaired capacity in the provision of mental health services.

Donnelly's description of dignity as a legal right or principle that underpins human rights aligns in some respects with the formulation of five-dimensional dignity. It preserves recognition and respect for autonomy for those adults who are capable of autonomy, and, in relying on Article 3 and Article 8 ECHR jurisprudence, it emphasises the importance of positive rights to protection.[170] By way of comparison however, the formulation of five-dimensional dignity is more expressly grounded in philosophical as well as legal formulations of dignity. I also propose five-dimensional dignity to serve not just as an interpretive legal principle but as a foundation for recognition of personhood in specifically interpreting the CRPD and Article 12.

168 Celik (n 61) 941.

169 Donnelly, *Healthcare Decision-Making and the Law* (n 110) 176.

170 Ibid 218, 221.

Carter is critical of interpretations of Article 12 that require the abolition of guardianship and argues that guardianship and the decisions made by guardians can recognise human dignity. She is sceptical of the benefits of a human rights approach to decision-making for adults with cognitive disability because it has resulted in a disproportionate focus on civil–political rights at the expense of socio-economic rights.[171] She defends best practice guardianship as ensuring human flourishing and as achieving social justice for adults with cognitive disability.[172] Carter criticises the dominance of the 'least restrictive means' principle found in mental health and guardianship legislation because it allows state intervention only as a last resort, leading to an over-emphasis on proceduralism at the expense of ensuring positive substantive outcomes for adults. Carter describes the 'least restrictive means' as emphasising concepts of 'negative liberty' and criticises it as becoming a justification for the 'lazy state' whereby governments disavow responsibilities towards their citizens on the basis that they are upholding their human rights.[173] She concludes that:

> the governing philosophical principle for guardianship legislation should be the promotion of the human dignity of the person with a disability. The operational principle that flows from this is the promotion of the personal and social well-being of the person with a disability.[174]

For Carter, dignity allows for positive state actions, intervention in the private sphere, recognition of relationships including relationships of care, and a focus on substantive outcomes to be achieved in the real world. Carter's concept of dignity is consistent with the concept of dignity developed in this chapter to underpin an interpretation of Article 12. However, she is reluctant or ambivalent to apply it within a human rights framework because of the dominance traditionally accorded to civil–political rights.

In conclusion, there has been scant consideration of how Article 12 can be interpreted and applied to recognise human dignity, not just autonomy. Bilchitz's

[171] Barbara Carter, 'Adult Guardianship: Human Rights or Social Justice?' (2010) 18(1) *Journal of Law and Medicine* 122, 145–6.

[172] 'Guardianship is about working in the way that will best enable the represented person to grow and flourish. In order to grow and flourish, the environment must be stable and healthy.… Much of a guardian's work is about trying to clear away the impediments to a person's growth and flourishing and help them reach a stage where they do not need the intensive support of a guardian any longer.' Barbara Carter, 'Seeking the Essence of Guardianship: Beyond the United Nations Convention on the Rights of Persons with Disabilities' (Conference Paper, World Guardianship Congress, 15–16 October 2012) 3 <https://agac.org.au/conference-papers/72-2012-oct-2nd-world-congress-melbourne>; see also: 'Supported and substituted decision makers do this best when they act as agents for the promotion of human dignity and human flourishing.' Anita Smith, 'Are Guardianship Laws and Practices Consistent with Human Rights Instruments?' in A Kimberly Dayton (ed), *Comparative Perspectives on Adult Guardianship* (Carolina Academic Press, 2014) 247, 271.

[173] Carter, 'The Case for Dignity as the Governing Principle in Adult Guardianship' (n 33) 3.

[174] Ibid 4.

concept of dignity as the capacity to experience the world, or as the ability to develop purposes and seek to achieve them, ultimately takes the value of dignity no further than a thin conception of autonomy. Celik links dignity with the idea of the vulnerable person, but vulnerability has the disadvantage of being novel terminology in the human rights lexicon. Donnelly identifies that the legal focus on autonomy has resulted in failure to consider adequately the rights of the non-autonomous. She proposes that dignity as a legal principle developed in the ECHR jurisprudence should be relied on and developed to fill that gap. Carter directly and expressly provides that dignity in an Article 12 context has the potential to dislodge the privileging of autonomy. She views the privileging of autonomy as having a damaging influence on States that justify abnegation of responsibility in the name of upholding human rights. Her critique of the 'lazy state' could readily describe the actions (or inaction) of the state in *Grootboom, Council for the Welfare of Immigrants* and *D v UK*.

5 SUPPORTED DECISION-MAKING, DECISION-MAKING BY SUBSTITUTES AND DIGNITY

This section considers how the five proposed dimensions of dignity can be used to interpret and apply Article 12, including explaining how decision-making by substitutes can uphold human rights. Five-dimensional dignity is a novel formulation of human dignity, which has drawn from and built on the work of philosophers and lawyers who have endeavoured to develop a definition of human dignity that extends beyond Kantian rationalism.

The literature has ventilated many criticisms of the idea that dignity is or should be a legal principle, and there is indeed some merit in elements of these critiques. One major criticism is that, as both a philosophical and legal principle, dignity is inevitably indeterminate and vague[175] and that it has not infrequently been used to justify opposing arguments in a debate.[176] Related to this is the criticism that dignity does not lend itself to adjudication, especially because its indeterminacy may allow for political considerations to impinge.[177] There have been several defences of these criticisms, and the five-dimensional formulation of dignity proposed in this chapter is intended as a step towards meeting some of them. However, ultimately, because inherent dignity is a recognition of the particularity of people's lives and their embodied selfhood, an 'anthropological' or case-by-case approach to developing dignity is urged.

[175] Liebenberg (n 88) 9–10; Evadné Grant, 'Dignity and Equality' (2007) 7(2) *Human Rights Law Review* 299, 299; Kakoullis and Ikehara (n 2) 53.

[176] McCrudden, 'Human Dignity and Judicial Interpretation of Human Rights' (n 4) 698; Michael (n 33) 24; Hale (n 2) 106; Rosen (n 34) 5.

[177] Gearty (n 38) 255.

The criticisms that dignity is indeterminate and could be shaped by political considerations are similar to arguments made against the recognition of socio-economic rights as 'true' human rights (the criticisms briefly canvassed in Chapter 3).[178] Socio-economic rights have historically been dismissed either as policy or mere political aspirations. However, since the introduction of the Optional Protocol to the ICESCR in 2013,[179] and given the emerging jurisprudence on socio-economic rights and dignity in South Africa, the strength of the criticism that they are not justiciable has been undermined. Furthermore, given the mingling of civil, social, political, economic and cultural rights in the CRPD, the challenge of adjudicating and giving shape to these rights is already pressing. Feldman is ambivalent about the role of dignity as a legal principle because it can lead to socio-economic rights limiting the reach of civil–political rights, including those rights linked with autonomy.[180] However, such uneasiness is, I argue, borne out of a reluctance to embrace the principle of indivisibility.

Grant combats the charge of indeterminism by arguing that in the case of South Africa, the 'malleability of the concept' is ultimately its strength.[181] In examining the particular facts of each case and through a case-by-case approach, the Constitutional Court is gradually developing a line of jurisprudence that will ultimately provide greater determinacy.[182] Because of its central place in human rights, in the text of the CRPD, and disability studies and commentary more widely, an understanding of what is meant by human dignity is imperative to interpret and apply the CRPD, including Article 12. The following discussion of the case of Sesha is offered as a contribution to this developing project.

SESHA

Philosopher Eva Feder Kittay describes her daughter Sesha as a girl and now woman, who 'was diagnosed as having severe to profound retardation'.[183] Kittay describes Sesha as 'enormously responsive, forming deep personal relationships with her family and long-standing caregivers and friendly relations

[178] Ibid 165.

[179] *Optional Protocol to the International Covenant on Economic, Social and Cultural Rights*, opened for signature 24 September 2009, UN Doc A/RES/63/117 (entered into force 5 May 2013).

[180] Feldman (Pt 1) (n 46) 684–6.

[181] See also Carozza, who views the pluralism in the concept of dignity as a strength: 'where there is not a strong practical agreement, grounded in concrete experience, we should tolerate, and indeed embrace, a generous pluralism of understandings across cultures and legal systems. The risk of a hegemonic imposition of one idea of dignity is great' in Carozza (n 63) 629.

[182] Grant, 'Dignity and Equality' (n 175) 319; Carozza argues that dignity's strength is its ability is able to embrace and respond to different cultural practices: Carozza (n 63) 629.

[183] Eva Feder Kittay, 'The Personal Is Philosophical Is Political: A Philosopher and Mother of a Cognitively Disabled Person Sends Notes from the Battlefield' (2009) 40(3–4) *Metaphilosophy* 606, 616.

with her therapists and teachers'. Kittay has written quite a bit about her daughter's love of music, especially but not exclusively classical symphonic music, Beethoven being on the top of her list. Sesha cannot read, and Kittay says that she cannot 'engage in moral reasoning' or 'participate in political life' but that her life is full. It is hard to know what cognitive capacities Sesha possesses because she cannot speak. She also has physical functional limitations, with unsteady legs and no dexterity with a spoon or knife. Kittay is fortunate enough to have the material resources to provide her daughter with carers, therapists and teachers. As an adult, Sesha lives in supported accommodation – a group home with five other young people who are also described as having cognitive and multiple disabilities.[184]

I was presenting a paper at a conference where an audience member asked me a question using Sesha as an exemplum. The question was to the effect of:

> One of Sesha's great joys in life is her love of classical music. Suppose Sesha's family were to be given medical advice that she had a life-threatening condition that could only be remedied by an operation that would cause her total hearing loss. The choice was between saving her life or losing her hearing.

(1) How could I justify imposing a substitute decision under a 'best interests' principle that saved Sesha's life but caused her deafness? And
(2) Wouldn't it be better to make a 'best interpretation' determination to allow Sesha to die?

The clear assumption behind the questions is that the second option of foregoing the operation would be the autonomous one under Article 12 because it would respect Sesha's will and preferences, respect her life story, and recognise her authentic personhood.

There are multiple other assumptions behind the question – including that a substitute decision-maker, using a 'best interests' approach, would always or necessarily have to decide to save Sesha's life. I don't see why this would be the case, but there are further issues of autonomy and dignity at stake here.

If Sesha were able to decide that life without music was not worth living, then respect for her dignity would require respect for her autonomy to make the grave decision to refuse treatment. However, the ethical lines are much less clear when a supporter assumes that Sesha herself would find her life not worth living with the additional impairment of hearing loss. Certainly, if any of us were confronted

[184] Kittay, 'Equality, Dignity and Disability' (n 32); Kittay, 'At the Margins of Moral Personhood' (n 78); Kittay, 'The Personal Is Philosophical Is Political' (n 183) 624.

with that choice at Sesha's age of forty-something,[185] we would invariably choose the hearing loss. The problem with the 'best interpretation' approach in this case is twofold. First, it feeds into widely held, ableist assumptions that people would rather die than be disabled and that the lives of people with disability are not worth living.[186] Second, it is problematic for such a decision to be made by a supporter (via 'best interpretation') but attributed to Sesha herself. It effectively risks absolving the supporter from accountability and responsibility for the life-and-death decision that they are in reality making for Sesha. So, what is the answer in this vexed scenario?

Dignity is most useful in the 'hard cases' such as this, where autonomy cannot give a certain and transparent answer. My answer would be that the 'supporter', whether a family member, guardian or court, should acknowledge the decision as their own and not Sesha's. The appointment of a substitute decision-maker in itself would recognise Sesha's dignity. It would recognise the embodied nature of her personhood – that she does, in fact, have significant impairments, meaning that she cannot make the decision herself in any material way; she lacks decision-making autonomy. Recognition that a decision is being made by a substitute would, I argue, more clearly respect Sesha's incommensurable worth; the vulnerability of her dependency; the value of her humanity (no matter what the extent of her impairments), and the dignity of her personhood. I argue that this would also acknowledge the dignity and personhood of the substitute decision-maker – that is, the gravity of their role in making this decision on behalf of someone else, not just as their interpreter. The substitute's role (and the supporter's) is more than as an instrumental interpreter.

Much harder is to decide which outcome could be justified as respecting Sesha's dignity. I don't profess to have the answer, but any decision would with great transparency and accountability have to:

1. acknowledge Sesha's equal worth as a human being with or without her sense of hearing;
2. acknowledge that even with total hearing loss, Sesha may have other joys in life – in particular, joys in family relationships – and that she could still bring joy to others;
3. consider how the loss of hearing may dilute her joys and could not be replaced by others;
4. treat Sesha as an end in herself, to ensure that a decision to allow her to die was not merely justified by the convenience of the decision-maker and society, or to save money in the health or service system; and

[185] In 2005 Sesha was thirty-two years old: Kittay, 'Equality, Dignity and Disability' (n 32) 95.

[186] 'There has long been serious concern amongst disabled people and their families that DNR decisions may be made on the basis of false assumptions that the quality of their life would be unacceptable to them.' Anna Lawson, 'The Human Rights Act 1998 and Disabled People: A Right To Be Human?' in Colin Harvey (ed), *Human Rights in the Community: Rights as Agents for Change* (Hart Publishing, 2005) 135, 139.

5. recognise that the strict social model of disability would not justify a decision to allow Sesha's life to end, and that such a decision would flow from recognition of the residual impacts of her severe impairments on her embodied personhood, after all accommodations had been made.

It may seem evasive to leave the question unanswered, but perhaps to provide an answer on an imaginary, abstract scenario would not respect Sesha's dignity. In hard cases, the facts are complex, and the few facts given here are unlikely to be all there are.

One consideration worth mentioning, though, is that, despite Sesha's disadvantages and dependencies, she is indeed fortunate to have joys in her life, especially a loving family who also has personal resources to fund a team of carers and access medical treatment. Without this wide range of intensive health and social supports, Sesha's life – with or without the capacity to hear – would be one of even greater disadvantage, marginalisation and social exclusion. Fulfilment of both her socio-economic and civil–political rights allows Sesha to have the choice of medical treatment, have her dignity respected, and her personhood recognised.

6 OVERVIEW AND CONCLUSION

This chapter has argued for recognising, as a foundation for personhood, a concept of human dignity that includes adults with severe and profound cognitive impairments. Dignity is chosen because it is a value claimed in UN human rights instruments, including the CRPD, to be foundational to all human rights and to be inherent in all human beings. As inherent, it cannot be earned or conferred, but it places demands on us to recognise the dignity in others and ourselves by acting in ways that respect our personhood. Dignity has been said to underpin the CRPD and is referred to in the CRPD more than in any other human rights convention, and yet it is a concept that has been under-explored in both the CRPD and Article 12 literature.

To formulate a concept of dignity that can be used to interpret the CRPD and Article 12, this chapter has considered and adopted key features of dignity as explained and developed by philosophers, lawyers and disability advocates, organising them into 'five dimensions'. The first dimension acknowledges that, as described in human rights instruments, dignity is associated with the equal worth of all humans, and also demands that we treat people as ends, not merely as means. The second dimension recognises the autonomy of those who are capable of autonomy. Dignity is viewed by many as equivalent to autonomy, and as thereby promoting the 'dignity of risk'. However, a growing body of literature is developing dignity as a philosophical value and legal principle, imbuing it with a wider role and meaning than just respect for autonomy. Nussbaum's capabilities approach attempts to develop such a concept by emphasising the material and embodied aspects of human dignity as a basis for personhood. However, it ultimately fails to include adults with a severe and profound cognitive disability because of its over-reliance on rationality in its conception of human dignity. Other capability or capacity-based conceptions of personhood, including the capacity for sentience, are rejected as either over-inclusive (because they include animals) or under-inclusive by excluding persons with severe cognitive impairments.

The third dimension of human dignity is found in philosophical writings that conceive of the human not as biological but as social personhood, with the essence of being human evident in our interpersonal relations and the meanings we ascribe to being human. These conceptions of human dignity as reflecting the interdependency of personhood also align with the proposals of some care theorists who found an ethic of care on the value of human dignity. This dimension of dignity is reflected in the jurisprudence. For example, in *East Sussex*, the Court considered not just the dignity interests of the claimants but also of the carers. The European Court of Human Rights affirmed in *Pretty* that the ECHR has as its 'very essence … respect for human dignity and human freedom'. The jurisprudence on Article 8 ECHR, Respect for private and family life, finds that while 8(1) recognises dignity as autonomy, respect for autonomy may be subject to Article 8(2) dignity interests, which demand recognition of the rights and freedoms of others. In *Wackenheim*, the Human Rights Committee decided that the dignity constituted by the interests of the wider public (i.e. the dignity of the audience, the community and other people with disability) was violated in the practice of 'dwarf-tossing', which therefore also failed to recognise the dignity of the claimant.

The fourth dimension of dignity is found in its recognition of embodied personhood. Writings about dignity nearly always open with the image of a person's body as tortured, neglected or objectified, and with the material particulars of their situation carefully drawn. These depictions impliedly situate disability within a social model that recognises the residual impacts of the impaired body and mind. These are the hard cases and it is from these hard cases, which are typically marginalised in assertions of universal legal capacity, that the essential features of dignity and of what it means to be a person can be ascertained.

The fifth dimension of dignity is that it reflects and drives the interdependence and indivisibility of human rights. While dignity is widely recognised as being associated with autonomy and the civil–political rights to legal capacity and freedom from torture, the human rights instruments and jurisprudence recognise that dignity also underpins socio-economic rights. The jurisprudence of the South African Constitutional Court reveals that in the particularities of hard cases, rights to liberty and equality depend on rights to shelter and subsistence. In the UK, the cases reveal that the right to be free from inhuman and degrading treatment is conditional on the fulfilment of the right to access health care.

For the most part, the literature on dignity and Article 12 links dignity with autonomy and equality, with a handful of commentators proposing wider definitions. These include the following: dignity as the ability for conscious experience of the world or to develop purposes, dignity as underpinning the vulnerable subject or person, dignity as a legal principle interpreting the rights of the non-autonomous and dignity as social justice. The idea of dignity as the ability to have conscious experience or to develop purposes is both too wide (includes animals) and too narrow (excludes some adults with a severe and profound cognitive disability). Dignity as underpinning the vulnerable subject has synergies with five-dimensional dignity in recognising the equal worth of human beings and the interdependent and embodied nature of personhood. Dignity as social justice recognises that a human rights framework privileging civil–political rights has failed to promote justice for all adults with cognitive disability. The inclusion of the principle of the indivisibility of human rights as the fifth dimension of human dignity seeks to redress this failure.

This chapter concluded by applying the concept of five-dimensional dignity to situations where Article 12 is engaged, and the ethics and justice of privileging autonomy are clearly challenged. There will never be an easy resolution to the dilemmas posed by all of the hard cases, but it is nevertheless proposed that dignity can start to provide answers. It can recognise the personhood of the non-autonomous and offer transparency and accountability for how we make decisions with and for them. On an equal basis with others, adults with a severe and profound cognitive disability require recognition of equal dignity, equal personhood, and legal capacity. The principle of equality – what it means in the CRPD and how it applies in interpreting Article 12 – is the subject of the next chapter.

6

Article 12 and Equality

1 INTRODUCTION

Chapter 2 described the dominant narrative of disability rights development as reflecting a journey from protection to autonomy, from exclusion to inclusive personhood and from discrimination to equality. The chapter tracked policy and rights progression from reflecting the dominance of a charity model of disability to a social model. It also began a critique of that dominant narrative by discarding a strict social model of disability in favour of one that recognises the residual impacts of impairment. I have also explained how disability rights developed from being framed as a mere socio-economic policy issue to its eventual inclusion on the agenda of civil-political human rights, the latter being widely considered the only 'true' human rights. I further argued that the framing of Article 12 as fundamental to all other rights is an over-correction to the historical exclusion of disability from civil-rights agendas. The over-correction fails to acknowledge the principle of indivisibility as recognising interdependencies between rights, together with the equal importance of socio-economic with civil–political rights.

In Chapter 4, I argued that the narrative of rights development – from protection to autonomy, and from exclusion to personhood – has led to endeavours to include adults with cognitive disability in liberal conceptions of autonomy and personhood. However, these endeavours fail because they continue to privilege rationality as the basis of personhood, emphasise civil-political rights over socio-economic rights and fail to acknowledge the residual dependencies and disadvantages experienced by adults with cognitive impairment. In Chapter 5, I argued that because autonomy excludes some adults with cognitive disability from personhood, it should be replaced by the concept of five-dimensional dignity. Dignity can be formulated to be more inclusive than autonomy – in particular, by acknowledging the residual impacts of impairment, the social dimensions of being human, and by valuing embodied (not just abstract) personhood. Acknowledgement of impairment and associated disadvantages serves to disrupt the notion that recognition of autonomy is the goal of rights recognition by emphasising the equal importance of socio-economic rights with civil–political rights (the latter more traditionally associated with the value of autonomy).

This chapter considers how the condition of equality in Article 12, which demands recognition of legal capacity 'on an equal basis with others', does not simply equate with the right to be free from discriminatory action, nor the right to be treated the same as others. Section 2 begins with an introduction to the UN Disability Committee's '*General Comment No 6 (2018) on equality and non-discrimination*' ('*General Comment No 6*'),[1] and how it reiterates that the fulfilment of Article 12 is a pre-condition to the fulfilment of all other rights, including the right to equality. This is followed by a description of how *General Comment No 6* interprets key concepts in equality law, by reference to existing human rights law. It explains how *General Comment No 6* prescribes a model of substantive, not just formal, equality, which requires recognition of difference and demands positive actions by the State to achieve equality. Section 3 describes the complexities of deciding what equality means when we are all situated differently and argues that *General Comment No 6* reflects proposals in the literature that equality for people with disability is an approximation for inclusion. It goes on to consider commentaries that describe substantive equality as embodying the principle of indivisibility by bridging civil-political and socio-economic rights, applying these commentaries to the concept of inclusive equality in *General Comment No 6*.

In considering the four dimensions of inclusive equality prescribed by *General Comment No 6*, Section 4 focuses on what equality means in Article 12 – that is, redressing socio-economic disadvantage, addressing stigma and reducing violence, encouraging participation and inclusion and accommodating difference, while respecting dignity. It first reviews the literature on Article 12 that endeavours to formulate 'disability-neutral' tests for legal capacity, concluding that neutrality is elusive under a test of indirect discrimination. Second, it reviews the literature that justifies the differential response of decision-making by substitutes as non-discriminatory (and promoting equality), according to various tests of substantive equality later built on in *General Comment No 6*.

In Section 5, I argue that while *General Comment No 6* reiterates that Article 12 requires the abolition of decision-making by substitutes, this conclusion is premised on an outmoded concept of formal equality that demands the same treatment for all. Section 5 concludes by arguing that applying the four dimensions of inclusive equality, as driven by the principle of indivisibility, leads to an interpretation of Article 12 that allows for both supported decision-making and decision-making by

[1] *United Nations Committee on the Rights of Persons with Disabilities 'General Comment No. 6 (2018) on equality and non-discrimination* CRPD/C/GC/6 ('*General Comment No 6*').

substitutes as a last resort. The chapter begins and concludes with the case of Jess to consider what inclusive equality may mean for her.

Jess, aged 76, has advanced dementia and lives on a rural property with her adult son. The property has been in the family for generations and Jess has always wanted it to stay in the family. She has also been very house-proud in the past.

To 'manage' her dementia, her son has placed Jess in the laundry under the house and locked the door to prevent her from wandering. Jess does not object to her living situation and appears acquiescent or compliant, always favouring her son over her other children.

Neighbours report the situation to the police, who find Jess under the house, malnourished and soiled.

2 EQUALITY AND NON-DISCRIMINATION IN HUMAN RIGHTS LAW

'Equality' has been described as a 'moral and analytical mechanism for ensuring that all people effectively enjoy human rights guarantees'.[2] According to Wouter Vandenhole, it is 'without doubt one of the central principles of human rights law and of the UN core human rights treaties in particular'.[3] Equality thus affirms the universality of human rights. It also implies that, when it comes to their fulfilment, no one person or group of persons should be privileged or disadvantaged over another. Beyond that, however, the meaning and application of equality are widely contested.

In the case of Jess, we know that she is being treated unfairly, and most of us would agree she is being discriminated against or treated unequally because of her dementia. If we were to respect Jess's expressed will and preferences to be 'supported' by her son and to live under the house, then we could be said to be respecting her will and preferences or her legal capacity (or, on some accounts, her autonomy)[4] 'on an equal basis with others'. This raises these questions: When responding to inequality, to what extent do we consider differences in starting positions? Is it the treatment or the result that must be 'equal'? And what does 'equal' mean anyway? Different

[2] Jarlath Clifford, 'Equality' in Dinah Shelton (ed), *The Oxford Handbook of International Human Rights Law* (Oxford University Press, 2013) 420, 421.

[3] Wouter Vandenhole, *Non-Discrimination and Equality in the View of the UN Human Rights Treaty Bodies* (Intersentia, 2005) 1.

[4] See Chapter 4 for discussion of various concepts and applications of autonomy.

answers to these questions have led to contested concepts of equality in human rights law, as well as different mechanisms for its realisation.[5]

This section introduces *General Comment No 6*, sets out the provisions in the CRPD that affirm the right to equality and non-discrimination, and describes the key concepts of formal and substantive equality and direct and indirect discrimination. Following this is a description of those mechanisms expressly prescribed by the CRPD and explained in *General Comment No 6* as tools for achieving substantive equality – that is, the provision of reasonable accommodation and 'specific measures'. It explains how these mechanisms demand, as their starting point, a recognition of the difference of disability.

2.1 *Introduction to* General Comment No 6

In 2018, the UN Disability Committee published *General Comment No 6*, which describes both equality and non-discrimination as being 'at the heart of the Convention',[6] as being 'interconnected with human dignity',[7] and as not just principles but as separate human rights.[8] It goes on to describe and interpret those provisions in the CRPD that relate to the right to equality and describes how the CRPD has developed a 'new model of equality', which it calls 'inclusive equality'. This model:

> embraces a substantive model of equality and extends and elaborates on the content of equality in: (a) a fair redistributive dimension to address socioeconomic disadvantages; (b) a recognition dimension to combat stigma, stereotyping, prejudice and violence and to recognize the dignity of human beings and their intersectionality; (c) a participative dimension to reaffirm the social nature of people as members of social groups and the full recognition of humanity through inclusion in society; and (d) an accommodating dimension to make space for difference as a matter of human dignity.
>
> The Convention is based on inclusive equality.[9]

[5] Clifford (n 2) 422.

[6] *General Comment No 6* [7].

[7] Ibid [4].

[8] Ibid. 'The effective enjoyment of the rights to equality and non-discrimination calls for the adoption of enforcement measures, such as: … (f) Effective, proportionate and dissuasive sanctions for breach of the right to equality and adequate remedies; …': [31]; 'the right to equality and non-discrimination …': [47]; 'the right to equality and non-discrimination …': [73(h)]; 'the rights to non-discrimination and equality …' [73(k)]; equality is universally recognised as a 'principle' of human rights law, and it has been said that the right to non-discrimination has become the dominant legal gateway to enforcing equality: Clifford (n 2) 426; there is no broad consensus on whether there exists in human rights law an independent *right* to equality, but some discussions in the literature suggest that either this is, or at least should be, the case: ibid 442; Broderick refers to the CRPD as including the 'right to equality': Andrea Broderick, *The Long and Winding Road to Equality and Inclusion for Persons with Disabilities: The United Nations Convention on the Rights of People with Disabilities* (Intersentia, 2015) 120, 221.

[9] *General Comment No 6* [11].

General Comment No 6 describes how inclusive equality operates in interpreting and applying a range of articles in the CRPD,[10] including Article 12,[11] and further explains the importance of enforcement and remedies for violation.[12] The focus of this chapter is on how *General Comment No 6* formulates substantive, inclusive equality and how it helps interpret Article 12.

General Comment No 6 reiterates the UN Disability Committee's existing interpretation of Article 12 as providing that 'The right to legal capacity is a threshold right, that is, it is required for the enjoyment of almost all other rights in the Convention', prescribing that the fulfilment of the right to legal capacity is required for the fulfilment of the right to equality and non-discrimination.[13] It further reiterates that: 'Discrimination through denial of legal capacity may be present in different ways, including status-based, functional and outcome-based systems. Denial of decision-making on the basis of disability through any of these systems is discriminatory;'[14] and 'guardianship laws and other rules infringing upon the right to legal capacity' must be repealed.

2.2 *Key Equality Provisions in the CRPD*

The concept of equality pervades the text of the CRPD. The Preamble refers to the 'equal and inalienable rights of all members of the human family',[15] to the rights of people with disability to participate 'as equal members of society'[16] and 'on an equal basis with others',[17] and endorses the UN Standard Rules on the Equalisation of Opportunities for Persons with Disabilities.[18] The convention's purpose is stated in Article 1 as 'to promote, protect and ensure the full and *equal* enjoyment of all human rights and fundamental freedoms by all persons with disabilities' [emphasis

10 Article 6 (Awareness raising), Article 7 (Children with disabilities), Article 9 (Accessibility), Article 11 (On situations of risk and humanitarian emergencies), Article 13 (On access to justice), Article 14 (On liberty and security of the person), Article 15 (On freedom from torture, cruel, inhuman or degrading treatment or punishment), Article 16 (On freedom from exploitation, violence and abuse), Article 17 (On protecting the integrity of the person), Article 19 (On living independently and being included in the community), Article 23 (On respect for home and the family), Article 24 (On education), Article 25 (On health), Article 27 (On work and employment), Article 28 (On adequate standard of living and social protection), Article 29 (On participation in political and social life), and Article 32 (On international cooperation).

11 *General Comment No 6* [47]–[51].

12 Ibid [30]–[34].

13 Ibid [47].

14 Ibid.

15 Preamble para 1.

16 Preamble para 10.

17 Ibid Preamble para 5.

18 Ibid Preamble para 6. See also: 'children with disabilities' should enjoy human rights 'on an equal basis with other children': [18]; providing that persons with disabilities and their families should receive assistance 'to contribute towards the full and equal enjoyment of the rights of persons with disabilities': [24].

added].[19] The General Principles include 'Non-Discrimination' (principle 2) and 'Equality of Opportunity' (principle 5).

Article 5 also establishes a stand-alone right to equality and non-discrimination, which can be engaged independently of a violation of any other provision.[20] The inclusion of this stand-alone right to equality and non-discrimination contributes to the broad-based rights framework of the CRPD, as being more than just an anti-discrimination convention.[21] Article 5 CRPD 'Equality and non-discrimination' provides that:

1. States Parties recognize that all persons are equal before and under the law and are entitled without any discrimination to the equal protection and equal benefit of the law.
2. States Parties shall prohibit all discrimination on the basis of disability and guarantee to persons with disabilities equal and effective legal protection against discrimination on all grounds.
3. In order to promote equality and eliminate discrimination, States Parties shall take all appropriate steps to ensure that reasonable accommodation is provided which are necessary to accelerate or achieve de facto equality of persons with disabilities shall not be considered discrimination under the terms of the present Convention.

In addition to this overarching right to equality and non-discrimination in Article 5 (the meaning of which is considered at some length below), other specific rights, including Article 12, are to be enjoyed 'on an equal basis with others'. These include the right to accessibility (Article 9), the right to life (Article 10), access to justice (Article 13), and the right to liberty and security of the person (Article 14). The words 'on an equal basis with others' appear a total of thirty-one times in the convention.[22]

[19] Ibid Article 1.

[20] Jessica Lynn Corsi, 'Article 5: Equality and Non-Discrimination' in Ilias Bantekas et al (eds), *The UN Convention on the Rights of Persons with Disabilities: A Commentary* (Oxford University Press, 2018) 140, 157; Rachele Cera, 'Article 5: Equality and Non-Discrimination' in Valentina Della Fina, Rachele Cera and Giuseppe Palmisano (eds), *The United Nations Convention on the Rights of Persons with Disabilities: A Commentary* (Springer International Publishing, 2017) 157, 160. In this respect, it follows the discrimination prohibition in Article 26 *International Covenant on Civil and Political Rights, opened for signature 19 December, 1966, 999 UNTS, (entered into force 23 March 1976)* ('ICCPR') which is broader than its counterpart in *International Covenant on Economic, Social and Cultural Rights, opened for signature 16 December, 1966, 993 UNTS 3 (entered into force 3 January 1976)* ('ICESCR') Article 2(2), the latter being limited to prohibiting discrimination only in respect of upholding rights listed in that covenant.

[21] See Chapter 3, Section 5.1.

[22] As noted by Broderick, *The Long and Winding Road to Equality and Inclusion for Persons with Disabilities* (n 8) 92. In addition to the articles referenced above, see Article 15 'Freedom from torture or cruel, inhuman or degrading treatment or punishment', Article 17 'Protecting the integrity of the person', Article 18 'Liberty of movement and nationality', Article 21 'Freedom of expression and opinion, and access to information', Article 22 'Respect for privacy', Article 23 'Respect for home and the family', Article 24 'Education', Article 27 'Work and employment', Article 29 'Participation in political and public life', Article 30 'Participation in cultural life, recreation leisure and sport'.

The UN Disability Committee has described the concept of equality as a 'golden thread' weaving throughout the CRPD.[23]

'Discrimination on the basis of disability' (referred to in Article 5 above) is defined in Article 2 as:

> any distinction, exclusion or restriction on the basis of disability which has the purpose or effect of impairing or nullifying the recognition, enjoyment or exercise, on an equal basis with others, of all human rights and fundamental freedoms in the political, economic, social, cultural, civil or any other field. It includes all forms of discrimination, including denial of reasonable accommodation.

The definition has two elements. The first element is an act that makes a 'distinction, exclusion or restriction on the basis of disability', and the second is that the act has to affect the person's 'human rights and fundamental freedoms' unequally and adversely. This means that different treatment for people with disability in the form of a 'distinction, exclusion or restriction' is not in itself sufficient to constitute discrimination. To be discriminatory, the different treatment must have a detrimental effect on, be disadvantageous to or have an unfavourable result for the person subject to the treatment, in relation to the recognition of their human rights.

The inclusion of the catch-all that discrimination on the basis of disability 'includes all forms of discrimination' is a result of a consensus reached during drafting that the prohibition be as wide as possible. There was agreement that the definition should include both direct and indirect discrimination and failure to provide reasonable accommodation. It would also clarify that affirmative action or special measures were not discriminatory if designed to achieve equality of opportunity and treatment.[24]

The meanings of direct and indirect discrimination, reasonable accommodation and positive or specific measures are complex and frequently contested. To understand them, it is first necessary to consider the different understandings of formal and substantive equality that have developed in international human rights law and that are also explained in *General Comment No 6*.

2.3 *Formal Equality*

Formal equality is rooted in the much-quoted Aristotelian axiom that things that are alike should be treated alike.[25] This axiom forms the basis of formal equality, where

[23] Corsi (n 20) 156.

[24] Anna Nilsson, 'Article 2: Definitions' in Ilias Bantekas, Michael Ashley Stein and Dēmētrēs Anastasiou (eds), *The UN Convention on the Rights of Persons with Disabilities: A Commentary* (Oxford University Press, 2018) 63, 65–6.

[25] Clifford (n 2) 421; Sandra Fredman, *Discrimination Law* (Oxford University Press, 2nd ed, 2011) 8; Rosie Harding, 'Equality, Social Justice and Older People' in Israel Doron and Nena Georgantzi (eds), *Ageing, Ageism and the Law: European Perspectives on the Rights of Older Persons* (2019) 15, 19.

the legal system on its face treats people the same as others. *General Comment No 6* describes how 'Formal equality seeks to combat direct discrimination by treating persons in a similar situation similarly'.[26] It requires that preferential treatment never be given to any one group over another but that everyone be treated on their merits.[27] Paragraph 1 of Article 5 CRPD is said to embody formal equality in recognising that all persons 'are equal before and under the law'.[28] Equality before the law is generally understood to require equal treatment by legal institutions (including the courts and police)[29] so that all people are treated alike.[30] Formal equality focuses on commonalities and the universal to require and justify equal treatment.[31]

Arnadóttir describes how formal equality was the predominant model in rights law and discourse from the 1950s to the 1970s, but since then has come under sustained critique and been replaced by other concepts of equality including substantive equality.[32] In requiring 'universal sameness' of treatment, formal equality has had the effect of ignoring significant inequalities where people were placed differently.[33] It assumes a 'benign social norm' and ignores differences, including the difference of disability.[34] Arnadóttir describes formal equality as a type of procedural equality, 'void of normative content', demanding equal treatment even when it leads to unequal results.[35] Formal equality also focuses on negative state obligations,[36] privileges the idea of the laissez-faire liberal state and emphasises individual merit or fault. In failing to distinguish between discrimination against privileged groups and those experiencing disadvantage,[37] formal equality excludes from protection members of marginalised groups, including people with disability.[38]

In the case of Jess, if we apply a model of formal equality, then in allowing Jess to make her own decision, she is being treated under the law the same 'as others'. If a guardianship order were imposed on Jess, however, then this amounts to different, and some would say 'unequal', treatment. This analysis assumes, however, a 'benign

26 *General Comment No 6* [10].
27 Corsi (n 20) 157.
28 Cera, 'Article 5' (n 20) 161; Corsi (n 20) 161.
29 Corsi (n 20) 161.
30 Cera, 'Article 5' (n 20) 161.
31 Camillia Kong, *Mental Capacity in Relationship: Decision-Making, Dialogue and Autonomy* (Cambridge University Press, 2017) 24.
32 Oddný Mjöll Arnadóttir, 'A Future of Multidimensional Disadvantage Equality' in Oddný Mjöll Arnadóttir and Gerard Quinn (eds), *The UN Convention on the Rights of Persons with Disabilities: European and Scandinavian Perspectives* (Nijhoff, 2009) 41, 47.
33 Jonas-Sebastien Beaudry, 'Welcoming Monsters: Disability as a Liminal Legal Concept' (2017) 29(2) *Yale Journal of Law & the Humanities* 291, 321.
34 Rosemary Kayess and Philip French, 'Out of Darkness into Light? Introducing the Convention on the Rights of Persons with Disabilities' (2008) 8(1) *Human Rights Law Review* 1, 8.
35 Arnadóttir (n 32) 48; Beaudry, 'Welcoming Monsters' (n 33) 321.
36 Arnadóttir (n 32) 49.
37 Ibid.
38 Ibid; Kayess and French (n 34) 8.

social norm' and ignores difference.[39] It ignores the fact that Jess is situated in a disadvantageous position because of her dementia and associated dependence on her son. We are all allowed to pursue our personal lives according to our wishes – but, in the case of Jess, most would agree that life is more complex.

There are limits to the fairness of a simple formal model of equality, and these limitations have led to the development of the concept of substantive equality.

2.4 *Substantive Equality*

The drafters of the CRPD focused, from the start, on a substantive equality approach, which demands positive actions by the State to accommodate the difference of impairment.[40] For example, Article 21 provides for freedom of expression, which is typically construed as a negative obligation on the State to refrain from silencing its citizens. However, Article 21 recognises that people with disability will only be able to exercise this right equally with others in a substantive sense if they are provided with access to information in appropriate formats. Substantive equality, or versions of it, has also been referred to as 'material equality'[41] or sometimes 'equality of opportunity',[42] the latter recognising a person's specific socio-economic context[43] and requiring equality of results.[44] *General Comment No 6* states that 'Equalization of opportunities, as a general principle of the Convention under Article 3, marks a significant development from a formal model of equality to a substantive model of equality'.[45]

[39] 'In other words, formal equality assumes a benign social norm, and focuses on the elimination of perverse personal behaviour. It does not seek to change the fundamental structure of the norm. The central premise of formal equality – the disregard of difference – is particularly problematic in a disability context for another reason. Perhaps more so than for any other disadvantaged group, treatment of persons with disability "equally" will often require specific recognition and accommodation of their difference; that is, "different" treatment': Kayess and French (n 34) 8.

[40] Sarah Arduin, 'Article 3: General Principles' in Ilias Bantekas, Michael Ashley Stein and Anastasiou Dimitris (eds), *The UN Convention on the Rights of Persons with Disabilities: A Commentary* (Oxford University Press, 2018) 85, 85, 101.

[41] María Soledad Cisternas Reyes, 'Foreword' in Valentina Della Fina (ed), *The United Nations Convention on the Rights of Persons with Disabilities: A Commentary* (Springer, 2017) v, v.

[42] Cera, 'Article 5' (n 20) 158.

[43] Sergiu Bălan, 'Formal and Substantive Equality of Opportunity' (2012) IV(4) *Cogito* 85, 86.

[44] Corsi (20) 157; note in the literature more widely there is some lack of clarity as to whether equality of opportunity means formal or substantive equality; see ibid 100–11; 'Professor Terry Carney stated that equality, in the sense used in Article 12, "can be variously formulated": It can be expressed as a purely *formal* concept (i.e. an 'opportunity') or in more substantive terms, as an achievement of distributive equity': Australian Law Reform Commission, *Equality, Capacity and Disability in Commonwealth Laws: A Final Report* (2014) 43; Bălan writes that there can be either formal or substantive equality of opportunity: Bălan (n 43) 100; Arduin (n 40) 100.

[45] *General Comment No 6* [10]; see also 'Equalization of opportunities means the process through which the general system of society, such as the physical and cultural

Substantive equality recognises difference[46] but challenges 'the equation of difference with inferiority'.[47] It recognises the effects of indirect discrimination – that identical treatment, including being subject to the same merit criteria, may nevertheless constitute discrimination. Prohibitions solely against direct discrimination – that is, rules that, on their face, select a person with disability for unfavourable treatment on the basis of their disability – may lead to formal equality but can ignore the needs of members of already marginalised groups.[48]

In the case of Jess, attempts at formal equality that applied the same rule to her 'as others' – in terms of non-interference in her decision-making – failed to result in what most of us would consider to be substantive equality. The abolition of guardianship on its own may lead to formal equality, but I argue that unless there is another type of remedy or intervention, the needs and rights of Jess as an already marginalised member of the community have been ignored.

2.5 *Direct and Indirect Discrimination*

Direct discrimination is said to be 'the most obvious form of discrimination',[49] occurring when 'in a similar situation, persons with disabilities are treated less favourably than other persons … for a reason related to a prohibited ground'.[50] According to *General Comment No 6*, indirect discrimination occurs when 'laws, policies or practices appear neutral at face value but have a disproportionate negative impact on a person with a disability'.[51] A claim of indirect discrimination was considered by the UN Disability Committee in *HM v Sweden*, where discrimination on the basis of disability was found even though a planning Act was 'applied in the same way to all,

environment, housing and transportation, social and health services, educational and work opportunities, cultural and social life, including sports and recreational facilities, are made accessible to all': Gerard Quinn and Theresia Degener, *Human Rights and Disability: The Current Use and Future Potential of United Nations Human Rights Instruments in the Context of Disability* (United Nations, 2002) 18 quoting from the *Vienna Declaration* [12].

46 Arnadóttir (n 32) 50.

47 Kayess and French (n 34) 8.

48 Arnadóttir (n 32) 47–50.

49 Nilsson (n 24).

50 *General Comment No 6* [18(a)].

51 Ibid [18(b)]. *General Comment No 6* expressly adopts the definitions of direct and indirect discrimination first promulgated in Committee on Economic, Social and Cultural Rights *General Comment No 20: Non-Discrimination in Economic, Social and Cultural Rights (Art 2, [2], of the International Covenant on Economic, Social and Cultural Rights)*, 42nd sess, Agenda Item 3, UN Doc E/C.12/GC/20 (2 July 2009) [10(b)]). See also Fredman, who defines indirect discrimination as having three elements: 'equal treatment, a disproportionately exclusionary impact on those sharing a protected characteristic, and the absence of acceptable justification' in Fredman, *Discrimination Law* (n 25) 154.

whether they have disabilities or not'.[52] The applicant was a person with disability who claimed indirect discrimination when the State refused her permission to build a hydrotherapy pool at her home.

While the UN Disability Committee in its findings in *HM v Sweden* did not use the terms 'direct' or 'indirect', it is reasonable to describe these circumstances as an example of indirect discrimination, because identical treatment led to discrimination when 'the particular circumstances of the individual(s) … [were] disregarded'.[53] The difference experienced by the adult as a result of her impairment had not been recognised by the State in its refusal for building permission. Applying the same response to the applicant as to adults without disability had resulted in a detriment to the applicant not suffered by others. Several human rights were breached, including the rights to live independently and receive supports in the community (Article 19) and the rights to health (Article 25) and habilitation (Article 26). The UN Disability Committee found that the State had breached its obligation under the general anti-discrimination provision in Article 5(1) and its more specific obligation to provide 'reasonable accommodation' under Article 5(3).[54]

In the case of Jess, she has 'chosen' to live under the house. The rule that applies to all of us is that we can choose where and with whom we live, and Jess has a choice of selling the house to live in supported accommodation. In *HM v Sweden*, where the disability related to physical needs, the State had to consider an exception to identical treatment by way of allowing for a physical accommodation in terms of a hydrotherapy pool.[55] When accommodating cognitive impairment, the type of assistance or exception required may be more complex,[56] but this chapter argues that not only support for decision-making but, in some cases, decision-making by a substitute can provide this type of assistance.

[52] Committee on the Rights of Persons with Disabilities, *Views: Communication No 3/2011*, 7th sess, UN Doc CRPD/C/7/D/3/2011 (19 April 2012) [4.12] ('*HM v Sweden*').

[53] 'Although indirect discrimination does not appear in the CRPD, it is not disputable that this form of discrimination is covered by Article 2 as well. A statement in support of this view can be found in *HM v Sweden*, where the CRPD Committee owed for the possibility that a national law, though applied in a neutral way, may lead to discriminatory consequences if the particular circumstances of the individuals to whom it is applied are disregarded'. Rachele Cera, 'Article 2: Definitions' in Valentina Della Fina, Rachele Cera and Giuseppe Palmisano (eds), *The United Nations Convention on the Rights of Persons with Disabilities: A Commentary* (2017) 107, 112.

[54] *HM v Sweden* (n 52) [9].

[55] Ibid [8.8].

[56] See, for example, the comments of Plumb, a 'survivor of psychiatry' who writes that: '…it is much harder to express my immediate needs and not everyone is able to respond as easily to another's emotional needs or apparent "madness" as to a request for physical assistance. And even if I do express my wishes, say for "sanctuary", chances are such support is not available anyway': Anne Plumb, 'UN Convention on the Rights of Persons with Disabilities: Out of the Frying Pan into the Fire? Mental Health Service Users and Survivors Aligning with the Disability Movement' in Helen Spandler et al (eds), *Madness, Distress and the Politics of Disablement* (Bristol University Press, 2015) 183, 194.

The case of Jess will be returned to when considering the particular application of substantive, inclusive equality to Article 12. The next section describes and considers what is meant by the terms 'reasonable accommodation' and 'appropriate' or 'specific measures', how they can be used to achieve equality, and how they are incorporated into the text of the CRPD.

2.6 *Differential Treatment for Substantive Equality*

General Comment No 6 reflects explanations previously published by the ESCR Committee in describing two types of different treatment that will not be discriminatory in the case of disability.[57] The first is reasonable accommodation as provided for in Article 5(3) CRPD, and the second type is constituted by the 'specific measures' (called 'appropriate measures' by the ESCR Committee)[58] necessary to achieve equality as provided for in Article 5(4) CRPD. Human rights law more broadly recognises that these two categories of differential treatment may be necessary to prevent indirect discrimination and achieve substantive equality.[59]

2.6.1 Denial of Reasonable Accommodation

The concept of reasonable accommodation is prevalent in anti-discrimination law[60] but was first expressly recognised in UN instruments by the ESCR Committee in its *General Comment No 5 on Person with Disabilities*.[61] It is defined in Article 2 CRPD as:

> necessary and appropriate modification and adjustments not imposing a disproportionate or undue burden, where needed in a particular case, to ensure to persons with disabilities the enjoyment or exercise on an equal basis with others of all human rights and fundamental freedoms …

General Comment No 6 further explains that reasonable accommodation is an action that is taken in a particular case either by way of removing barriers or providing assistance, the cost of which is not borne by the person with disability but by the State or the provider of the service or facility.[62] Further, 'An accommodation is

57 Committee on Economic Social and Cultural Rights, *General Comment 5: Persons with Disabilities*, 11th sess (9 December 1994) ('*ESCR General Comment No 5*') [5], [18]; note that *General Comment No 6* does not acknowledge that it has replicated the wording in the earlier instrument.

58 Ibid.

59 Broderick, *The Long and Winding Road to Equality and Inclusion for Persons with Disabilities* (n 8) 115–35, 152–3.

60 Sometimes referred to as 'reasonable adjustment' or 'reasonable measures', for example *Disability Discrimination Act 1992* (Cth) ss 5–6.

61 *ESCR General Comment No 5* [15].

62 *General Comment No 6* [18(c)].

reasonable … if it achieves the purpose (or purposes) for which it is being made, and is tailored to meet the requirements of the person with a disability'.[63] In *Beasley v Australia*, the UN Disability Committee decided that there was a failure to provide reasonable accommodation in the form of an Auslan interpreter to allow a deaf person to participate on a jury.[64] An example of reasonable accommodation for an adult with cognitive disability may be to provide relevant information from a retailer or health provider in Easy Read format. It has been argued that this express inclusion of reasonable accommodation as part of the right to non-discrimination is transformative of the right to equality. This is because reasonable accommodation is no longer just an exception to the equal treatment principle but has the effect of placing the burden on the State or third party to show that accommodations were not possible.[65]

Reasonable accommodation purportedly is to be negotiated on a case-by-case basis in each situation, rather than constituting a systemic response;[66] however, boundaries and definitions do blur. This is because even though initiated on a case-by-case basis, the availability of reasonable accommodations may become a public good,[67] and its provision on a case-by-case basis can lead eventually to system-wide change.[68] While the duty to provide reasonable accommodation is mandatory under the CRPD, it is limited so that it does not impose a 'disproportionate or undue burden' in terms of cost and convenience on the provider of goods or services. In the CRPD, reasonable accommodation ensures that indirect discrimination is remedied or prevented so as to uphold a wide range of human rights. It can be distinguished from situations where discrimination is prevented through state restraint – that is, restraint from making a 'distinction, exclusion or restriction' on the basis of disability.

2.6.2 Specific or Appropriate Measures

Like reasonable accommodation, specific measures include positive action and provision of socio-economic resources and could be rearticulated in some cases as responses to socio-economic rights claims. However, *General Comment No 6* explains how they categorically differ from reasonable accommodation in that (as

[63] Ibid [25(a)].

[64] Committee on the Rights of Persons with Disabilities, *Views: Communication No 11/2013*, 15th sess, UN Doc CRPD/C/15/D/11/2013 (1 April 2016) ('*Beasley v Australia*').

[65] 'For the first time in a UN human rights treaty, denial of reasonable accommodation is included as a distinct form of discrimination … This strengthens considerably the protection provided to persons with disabilities under international human rights law'. Broderick, *The Long and Winding Road to Equality and Inclusion for Persons with Disabilities* (n 8) 155.

[66] *General Comment No 6* [26(e)].

[67] Ibid 24(b).

[68] '…reasonable accommodation has the potential to result in fundamental structural transformations of the norm': Kayess and French (n 34) 9.

described above) reasonable accommodation is ostensibly an 'individualised, reactive duty' that arises when an accommodation request is received.[69] By way of contrast, specific measures imply that 'preferential treatment' is required to address historic or systemic abuse. *General Comment No 6* explains how a second difference is that specific measures are usually temporary, the clear implication being that once specific temporary measures (e.g. preferential recruitment strategies for people with disability) achieve their purpose of remedying structural or systemic inequalities, they will no longer be needed.[70] I note, however, that the temporary nature of specific measures is not expressed in the text of the CRPD itself[71] and that *General Comment No 6* does acknowledge that permanent specific measures may sometimes be required, 'depending on context and circumstances, including by virtue of a particular impairment or the structural barriers of society'.[72]

What reasonable accommodation and specific measures have in common is that, in order to identify a need for either of them, material and relevant difference relating to a disability must be recognised. Recognition of these differences is fundamental to achieving substantive equality. The next section reviews those parts of the CRPD and *General Comment No 6* that demand recognition of the difference of disability, as well as recognition of the differences within disability.

2.6.3 Recognising Difference

The Preamble to the CRPD recognises 'the diversity of persons with disabilities'[73] and their communities[74] and acknowledges the socio-economic differences experienced by people with disability.[75] *General Principle No 4* affirms 'Respect for difference and acceptance of persons with disabilities as part of human diversity and humanity'.[76] Article 21 (Freedom of expression and opinion, and access to information) refers to 'different kinds of disabilities'[77] and Article 24 (Education) refers to recognition of 'human diversity'.[78] *General Comment No 6* also recognises that people with disabilities can be 'disproportionately affected by violence, abuse and

69 Ibid [24(b)].
70 Ibid [25(c)].
71 For more information on the permanent versus temporary special measures and her observation that: 'Article 5(4) *CRPD* does not contain this temporal limitation and it is therefore akin to Article 4 *Convention on the Elimination of All Forms of Discrimination against Women*, opened for signature 1 March 1980, 1249 UNTS 8 (entered into force 3 September 1981), under which both temporary special measures and permanent protective measures are permissible': Broderick, *The Long and Winding Road to Equality and Inclusion for Persons with Disabilities* (n 8) 125.
72 *General Comment No 6* [25(c)]–[29].
73 *CRPD* Preamble para 9.
74 Ibid para 13.
75 Ibid para 19.
76 Ibid Article 3.
77 Ibid Article 21(a).
78 Ibid Article 24(a).

other cruel and degrading treatment', indicating that they may be situated differently when it comes to potential exposure to violence. It has already been pointed out above that older people may be recognised as a different sub-group and that permanent (not just temporary) specific measures may be required for different types of impairment.

General Comment No 6 also acknowledges that substantive equality entails acknowledgement of difference, describing how:

> Formal equality seeks to combat direct discrimination by treating persons in a similar situation similarly. It may help to combat negative stereotyping and prejudices, but it cannot offer solutions for the 'dilemma of difference', as it does not consider and embrace differences among human beings. Substantive equality, by contrast, also seeks to address structural and indirect discrimination and takes into account power relations. It acknowledges that the 'dilemma of difference' entails both ignoring and acknowledging differences among human beings in order to achieve equality.[79]

This 'dilemma of difference' is illustrated further below in relation to supported decision-making, which I argue relies on recognising the difference of disability in the obligation to provide support. Wolff recognises this dilemma of difference when he points out that 'Disability advocates sometimes seem to want to argue both that there is no hard and fast line between able-bodied people and disabled people, yet, at the same time, that disabled people should receive special legal protection'.[80] Wolff is correct in that some differences matter because they are material and relevant when it comes to providing differential treatment to ensure equality, but others are not, and should be ignored. In short, 'we can conclude that a society of equals is one that accepts people in their differences'.[81] Difficult questions arise as to what differences matter and what does it mean to achieve equality when we are situated differently.

2.7 *Analysis and Conclusions*

In summary, the CRPD was drafted not as a narrow, non-discrimination convention along the lines of *CEDAW* and *CERD* but as a convention that includes the full range of substantive human rights, civil-political and socio-economic, as they apply to disability. The emphasis on equality and non-discrimination in both the Preamble and the General Principles, together with the reiteration of the phrase 'on an equal basis with others' in many of the substantive articles, demonstrates

[79] *General Comment No 6* [10].

[80] Jonathan Wolff, 'Disability among Equals' in Kimberley Brownlee and Adam Cureton (eds), *Disability and Disadvantage* (Oxford University Press, 2009) 112, 134.

[81] Ibid 123.

the central role of equality as a right and a principle, as also affirmed by the UN Disability Committee in *General Comment No 6*. The CRPD also includes a stand-alone right to equality and non-discrimination in Article 5 so that any discriminatory treatment on the basis of disability, whether or not it relates to one of the other substantive articles in the convention, constitutes a violation.

General Comment No 6 confirms that the CRPD demands not just formal but substantive equality,[82] explaining how formal equality, in requiring everyone to be treated alike, ignores differences between people, including differences in their impairments and socio-economic starting positions. Principles of formal equality will recognise direct discrimination (i.e. when different treatment is evident on the face of a particular law) but will not look behind the law to recognise indirect discrimination to determine if the application of the law leads to substantive inequality in effect. Non-discrimination and substantive equality in the CRPD may demand positive, differential actions by the State or third parties to recognise and respond to difference. These differential responses have been identified in international human rights law – including the CRPD (and as confirmed by *General Comment No 6*) – as including reasonable accommodation or specific or appropriate measures. The text of the CRPD acknowledges the difference of disability, including the associated disproportionate levels of socio-economic disadvantage, and recognises the differences within disability.

Equality and non-discrimination are traditionally considered civil-political rights,[83] and formal equality, in typically requiring restraint by the State and being immediately realisable, bears the markers of a civil-political right. However, equality and non-discrimination apply across both categories of rights, and both reasonable accommodation and specific measures can amount to the provision of socio-economic resources. How the right to equality drives the indivisibility of human rights in the CRPD and Article 12 is considered further in Section 4. But first, Section 3 considers the four dimensions of inclusive equality as outlined in *General Comment No 6*.

3 INCLUSIVE EQUALITY: AN ADAPTATION OF TRANSFORMATIVE EQUALITY

This section describes how the concept of inclusive equality in *General Comment No 6* is a specific application or adaptation of substantive, transformative equality to disability rights.[84] In applying the concept of transformative equality to disability,

[82] *General Comment No 6* [14].

[83] Rachele Cera, 'Preamble' in Valentina Della Fina, Rachele Cera and Giuseppe Palmisano (eds), *The United Nations Convention on the Rights of Persons with Disabilities: A Commentary* (Springer International Publishing, 2017) 80, 167.

[84] See Broderick, *The Long and Winding Road to Equality and Inclusion for Persons with Disabilities* (n 8) 36–8.

General Comment No 6 has added the requirement that inclusive equality in the CRPD demands the recognition of universal legal capacity and the abolition of guardianship.[85] This chapter ultimately argues that a coherent application of the concept of transformative equality to disability – to recognise legal capacity (not universally but 'on an equal basis with others') – may in some cases require the actions of a substitute decision-maker.

3.1 *Foundations in 'Transformative' Equality: A Four-Dimensional Approach*

General Comment No 6 describes inclusive equality as having four dimensions:

> (a) a fair redistributive dimension to address socioeconomic disadvantages; (b) a recognition dimension to combat stigma, stereotyping, prejudice and violence and to recognise the dignity of human beings and their intersectionality; (c) a participative dimension to reaffirm the social nature of people as members of social groups and the full recognition of humanity through inclusion in society; and (d) an accommodating dimension to make space for difference as a matter of human dignity.[86]

The formulation of inclusive equality as incorporating four dimensions has been adapted from a submission to the UN Disability Committee on a draft of *General Comment No 6* made by Fredman et al,[87] which, in turn, has its origin in Fredman's *Human Rights Transformed: Positive Rights and Positive Duties*.[88] In their submission on *General Comment No 6*, Fredman et al propose a 'four-dimensional evaluative framework' of 'transformative' equality, prescribing four dimensions that approximate those incorporated in the final version (above).[89] Before the publication of *General*

[85] *General Comment No 6* [47]–[50].
[86] *General Comment No 6* [11].
[87] Sandra Fredman et al, 'Achieving Transformative Equality for Persons with Disabilities', Submission to the Committee on the Rights of Persons with Disabilities, for General Comment No 6 on Article 5 of the UN Convention on the Rights of Persons with Disabilities' (Oxford Human Rights Hub, undated) <www.ohchr.org/EN/HRBodies/CRPD/Pages/WSPersonsDisabilitiesEqualityResponsability.aspx>.
[88] That more broadly applicable concept was described as: 'First, it should promote respect for the equal dignity and worth of all, thereby redressing stigma, stereotyping, humiliation, and violence because of membership of an out-group … Secondly, it should entail an accommodation and positive affirmation and celebration of identity within community. Thirdly, it should break the cycle of disadvantage associated with out-groups. Finally, it should facilitate full participation in society. The content of positive duties can more easily be specified in relation to these four aims or dimensions': Sandra Fredman, *Human Rights Transformed: Positive Rights and Positive Duties* (Oxford University Press, 2008) 179.
[89] 'We recommend that a four-dimensional evaluative framework be incorporated. This would give clarity and strength to the conception of transformative equality … This conception requires that, to achieve transformative equality, measures must (i) redress the social and economic disadvantage associated with disability; (ii) address stigma, stereotyping, prejudice and violence on the basis of disability; (iii) enhance participation and voice of people with disabilities and (iv) accommodate difference by achieving structural change': Fredman et al (n 87) 3.

Comment No 6, several writers had already described the CRPD as embracing transformative equality.[90] This is because the CRPD demands a redistribution of resources, equal access to and participation in society,[91] elimination of stereotypes and prejudices (especially through Article 8 'Awareness-raising'),[92] and structural transformation.[93]

3.2 *Equal to What or with Whom? Equality as an Approximation for Inclusion*

The terminology of 'inclusive equality' is apt because it reflects views in the literature that the goal of equality for people with disability is an approximation for socio-economic and civil-political inclusion. Kayess and French describe discrimination against people with disability as having the effect of segregating or excluding them from 'participating fully in society',[94] and in cataloguing the types of rights in the CRPD, Quinn and Rekas-Rosalbo group 'equality and participation rights' together.[95] Goldschmidt opines that the CRPD demands the recognition of difference to achieve substantive equality, but once recognised, the focus is not on difference but on 'how a maximum inclusion of all can be realised in our society'.[96] Arnadóttir links equality with the CRPD's emphasis on 'inclusion and accessibility',[97] and Broderick, in her endorsement of transformative equality, writes of the CRPD that 'Equality and non-discrimination norms are linked intrinsically to the notions of participation and inclusion in society'.[98] Beaudry, more explicitly than others, opines that the concept of 'equality' for people with disability has effectively been substituted as 'political idiom' for 'social integration'[99] and that social inclusion is in reality the crucial issue.[100]

90 Broderick, *The Long and Winding Road to Equality and Inclusion for Persons with Disabilities* (n 8) 36–7; Andrea Broderick, 'Article 4: General Obligations' in Ilias Bantekas et al (eds), *The UN Convention on the Rights of Persons with Disability: A Commentary* (Oxford University Press, 2018) 116, 117; Corsi (20) 140ff; Cera, 'Article 5' (n 20) 153.

91 Broderick, *The Long and Winding Road to Equality and Inclusion for Persons with Disabilities* (n 8) 39.

92 '1. States Parties undertake to adopt immediate, effective and appropriate measures: … b) To combat stereotypes, prejudices and harmful practices relating to persons with disabilities, including those based on sex and age, in all areas of life' *CRPD* Article 8(1)(b).

93 Clifford describes transformative equality in human rights law more broadly as requiring equality of results for disadvantaged groups through changing both social structures and 'the way organisations and institutions function': Clifford (n 2) 429–30.

94 Kayess and French (n 34) 5.

95 Gerard Quinn and Abigail Rekas-Rosalbo, 'Civil Death: Rethinking the Foundations of Legal Personhood for Persons with a Disability' (2016) 56 *Irish Jurist* 286, 299.

96 Jenny E Goldschmidt, 'New Perspectives on Equality: Towards Transformative Justice through the Disability Convention?' (2017) 35 *Nordic Journal of Human Rights* 1, 12.

97 Arnadóttir (n 32) 44–5.

98 Broderick, *The Long and Winding Road to Equality and Inclusion for Persons with Disabilities* (n 8) 69.

99 Beaudry, 'Welcoming Monsters' (n 33) 291.

100 Jonas-Sébastien Beaudry, 'Beyond (Models of) Disability?' (2016) 41(2) *Journal of Medicine and Philosophy* 210, 211; Rioux proposes a concept of equality for people with disability as

The goal of participation and inclusion for people with disability is, like the principle of equality, threaded throughout the CRPD. Article 9 asserts the right of accessibility to enable persons to 'participate fully in all aspects of life'; Article 19, the right to 'full inclusion and participation in the community'; Article 24, the right to 'equal participation in education and as members of the community'; Article 26, the right to habilitation and rehabilitation so as to enable 'full inclusion and participation in all aspects of life', and Articles 29 and 30 refer to participation in 'political and public life' and 'cultural, life, recreation, leisure and sport', respectively. Notably, 'full and effective participation and inclusion in society' is one of the eight General Principles in Article 3 CRPD; and it is the first time that the principle of 'inclusion' has been incorporated in an international human rights treaty.[101] The goal of equality as inclusion has particular resonance for people with disability, given their historical and lingering exile in institutional settings; and the text of the CRPD, *General Comment No 6*, and the commentary above all point to a concept of equality as social inclusion. Fredman et al are explicit that it is the simultaneous achievement of all four dimensions that is required for inclusion,[102] and I would add, therefore, that it requires the fulfilment of a range of interdependent human rights according to the principle of indivisibility.[103]

3.3 *Equality and Indivisibility*

While Fredman et al explicitly provide that the four dimensions of transformative equality must be applied simultaneously, this is also implicit in *General Comment No 6* which states that 'human rights are interdependent, interrelated and indivisible'.[104] I argue that the four-dimensional approach is underpinned by the principle of indivisibility.

amounting to achievement of 'well being', which requires recognising difference while ensuring socio-economic as well as civil and political inclusion: Martha Rioux, 'On Second Thoughts: Constructing Knowledge, Law, Disability and Inequality' in Stanley S Herr and Lawrence O Gostin (eds), *The Human Rights of Persons with Intellectual Disabilities: Different but Equal* (Oxford University Press, 2003) 287, 300–2; see also Melinda Jones, 'Inclusion, Social Inclusion and Participation' in Marcia H Rioux, Lee Ann Basser Marks and Melinda Jones (eds), *Critical Perspectives on Human Rights and Disability Law* (Martinus Nijhoff, 2011) 57; see also 'The CRPD builds on the knowledge that to realize human rights, persons must be included in society': Kjersti Skarstad, 'Disability and the Dilemma of Difference' in Franziska Felder et al (eds), *Disability Law and Human Rights: Theory and Policy* 87, 103.

101 Arduin (n 40) 96.

102 'These measures need to be considered simultaneously in evaluating whether a measure advances equality': Fredman et al (n 87) 3.

103 See also: 'Instead, social inclusion is better facilitated under a human rights paradigm that applies civil and political rights (that equalize treatment) in combination with economic, social and cultural rights (that equalize opportunity': Michael Ashley Stein, 'Disability Human Rights' (2007) 95(1) *California Law Review* 75, 92.

104 *General Comment No 6* [9].

3.3.1 Equality as Disrupting the Hierarchy of Civil-Political over Socio-economic Rights

Non-discrimination and equality are traditionally categorised as civil-political rights. They bear the indicia of civil-political rights to the extent that they require restraint by the State from taking discriminatory action. It is also widely agreed that because a denial of reasonable accommodation is part of the right to non-discrimination, it is considered a civil-political right, subject to immediate realisation.[105] This is despite the fact that reasonable accommodation may constitute the provision of socio-economic goods or services. As Lawson suggests, the definition of 'discrimination' in Article 2 CRPD, by expressly including a 'denial of reasonable accommodation', requires States to spend money (in the tradition of socio-economic rights) to achieve equality;[106] and that this emphasis is specific to disability. Lawson argues that the emphasis in the CRPD on requiring reasonable accommodation[107] serves to form a 'bridge' between civil-political rights and socio-economic rights, because both sets of rights are subject to the non-discrimination requirement, concluding that in this respect 'The CRPD is an extraordinarily far-reaching convention'.[108] Similarly, Broderick writes that the duty to reasonably accommodate, as part of the non-discrimination requirement, is an important facilitator of economic rights in the disability field.[109] Lord and Brown also recognise the relationship between non-discrimination, equality and indivisibility when they write:

> The CRPD serves to re-conceptualize and unite civil and political rights and economic, social and cultural rights in the realization of equality for persons with disabilities by requiring reasonable accommodation through positive measures in all areas of life.[110]

105 Ibid [12]. Quinn and Rekas-Rosalbo (n 95) 315; Anna Lawson, 'The UN Convention on the Rights of Persons with Disabilities and European Disability Law: A Catalyst for Cohesion?' in Oddný Mjöll Arnadóttir and Gerard Quinn (eds), *The UN Convention on the Rights of Persons with Disabilities: European and Scandinavian Perspectives* (Nijhoff, 2009) 81, 103.

106 Albeit 'reasonable accommodation' is defined in Article 2 CRPD to be those adjustments 'not imposing a disproportionate or undue burden'.

107 Article 5(3): 'In order to promote equality and eliminate discrimination, States Parties shall take all appropriate steps to ensure that reasonable accommodation is provided'. Lawson points out at that 'reasonable accommodation' is also explicitly mentioned in CRPD in Article 14(2) (Liberty and security of the person), Articles 24(2)(c) and 24(5) (Education); Article 27(1)(i) (Employment): Lawson, 'The UN Convention on the Rights of Persons with Disabilities and European Disability Law' (n 105) 103.

108 Lawson, 'The UN Convention on the Rights of Persons with Disabilities and European Disability Law' (n 105) 104–7.

109 Andrea Broderick, 'Harmonisation and Cross-fertilisation of Socio-Economic Rights in the Human Rights Treaty Bodies: Disability and the Reasonableness Review Case Study' (2016) 5 *Laws* 38.

110 Rebecca Brown and Janet Lord, 'The Role of Reasonable Accommodation in Securing Substantive Equality for Persons with Disabilities' in Marcia H Rioux, Lee Ann Basser Marks and Melinda Jones (eds), *Critical Perspectives on Human Rights and Disability Law* (Martinus Nijhoff, 2011) 273, 281.

The emphasis on substantive equality challenges the traditional dichotomy between the two sets of rights. This is because it demands that all human rights, in requiring realisation on an equal basis, impose positive obligations on states to expend resources and that, depending on the nature of the obligations, this may only be achieved progressively. Returning to the case of *HM v. Sweden*, the applicant's civil–political right to be treated without discrimination depended on the fulfilment of her socio-economic right to habilitation in the form of access to an in-home hydrotherapy pool.[111] *General Comment No 6* provides further examples of reasonable accommodation that clearly involve claims to the fulfilment of socio-economic rights (e.g. transport services that may be required to take children with disability to school).[112]

The right to equality not only disrupts the traditional negative versus positive action bifurcation but also impacts the immediate versus progressive implementation obligations for civil-political and socio-economic rights, respectively. *General Comment No 6* makes it clear that reasonable accommodation is part of the right to non-discrimination and, as such, is a civil-political right and immediately realisable.[113] Ostensibly a civil–political right, the right to non-discrimination and equality disrupts the stereotypical markers of the traditional categories of rights by demanding urgent, if not immediate, realisation of human rights across both categories.[114] The emphasis in the CRPD on non-discrimination and substantive, inclusive equality develops the principle of indivisibility in its disruption of differences between the two sets of rights and associated denial of traditional hierarchies.

3.3.2 Equality as Demonstrating the Interdependencies between Rights

The second component of the indivisibility principle is the interdependence of rights: they depend on one another. Explained above is how the civil-political right to non-discrimination and equality may depend on the fulfilment of socio-economic rights related to the provision of reasonable accommodation and specific measures. The ESCR Committee has emphasised that failure to fulfil the socio-economic right to education for people with disability has led to the denial of equal opportunities more widely, as demanded by other rights.[115]

General Comment No 6 does make clear this interdependence, with one whole section describing and analysing the relationship of the rights to non-discrimination

[111] *HM v Sweden* (n 52).
[112] *General Comment No 6* [64].
[113] Ibid [12].
[114] Clifford (n 2) 434; Gauthier DeBeco, 'The Indivisibility of Human Rights and the Convention on the Rights of Persons with Disabilities' (2019) 68 (January) *International and Comparative Law Quarterly* 141; Stein (n 103) 149.
[115] Broderick, 'Harmonisation and Cross-fertilisation of Socio-Economic Rights in the Human Rights Treaty Bodies' (n 109) 9.

and equality to other rights in specific articles of the CRPD. Included in this section is a discussion of Article 6 on women with disabilities; Article 8 on 'awareness-raising'; Article 9 on 'Accessibility'; Article 12 on 'Equal recognition before the law'; Article 14 on 'Liberty and security of person'; Article 15 on 'Freedom from torture or cruel, inhuman or degrading treatment or punishment'; Article 16 on 'Freedom from exploitation, violence and abuse'; and Article 17 on 'Protecting the integrity of the person'.[116] Inclusive equality, as formulated in *General Comment No 6*, impliedly requires fulfilment of both civil–political and socio-economic rights interdependently, expressly requiring socio-economic redistribution, social and political inclusion, and the end of violence and abuse. The notion of inclusive equality is far more wide-reaching than other conceptions of substantive equality and is specifically focused on the human rights of people with disability.

Notably, inclusive equality also includes respect for dignity in two of its dimensions: '(b) a recognition dimension to combat stigma, stereotyping, prejudice and violence and to recognize the dignity of human beings and their intersectionality;' and '(d) an accommodating dimension to make space for difference as a matter of human dignity'.[117] The concept of dignity – its interrelationship with indivisibility and its role in interpreting the CRPD and Article 12 – was the subject of the previous chapter. However, it serves here to reiterate that dignity is closely related to equality in its demand that all humans be respected as having equal worth because of their humanity and that it is a value that underpins all human rights, emphasising their interdependence and indivisibility. In particular, like inclusive equality (or as an intrinsic part of it), dignity demands recognition of the embodied reality of peoples' lives and the interrelationship of socio-economic needs and rights with access to civil–political rights.

3.4 *Inclusive Equality, Difference and Models of Disability*

The starting point for achieving substantive equality, including the inclusive equality proposed by *General Comment No 6*, is to acknowledge difference and diversity because inclusive equality demands 'an accommodating dimension to make space for difference as a matter of human dignity'.[118] *General Comment No 6* provides that inclusive equality can only be achieved by addressing a range of civil–political and socio-economic rights claims (i.e. by addressing socio-economic disadvantage, combating prejudice and violence, and encouraging social participation). It thereby acknowledges conversely that this requires recognition of how individuals are differently situated at the centre of a web of distinct civil, economic, social, political and cultural structures, and influences.

[116] *General Comment No 6* [36]–[70].
[117] Ibid [11].
[118] Ibid.

The strict social model would recognise social and environmental differences between people with disability and others but would fail to acknowledge the particularity of an individual's impairment and associated inequalities and disadvantage. Under a medical model, disability had been associated with a deficit, with 'less' and with personal fault; so services tailored and targeted to people with disability reflected this patronising attitude both in substance and in the mode of delivery, encouraging social and political exclusion.[119] In this context, the terminology of 'special needs' or 'special education' became rapidly stigmatised and, for this reason, the terminology of 'special measures' used in relation to other UN human rights conventions was replaced by the 'specific' or 'appropriate' measures terminology in the CRPD.[120] I propose that the concept of inclusive equality for people with disability is underpinned by a social model of disability that recognises the residual impacts of impairment (i.e. recognises the difference and diversity of impairment and any associated socio-economic disadvantage).

There is some agreement in the literature that formal equality is underpinned by a strict social model of disability, while substantive equality demands recognition of the residual difference of impairment or disability.[121] Stein writes that a *strict* social model is limited to formal notions of equality by implying that all individuals are the same and that identical treatment leads to equality.[122] He goes on to argue that formal equality and the strict social model of disability fail to account for 'some individual variations … even when using broad and inclusive principles' and that while civil–political rights ensure procedural equality of opportunity, socio-economic rights are needed to 'effectuate first-generation rights' to ensure substantive equality of opportunity in terms of actual social participation and inclusion.[123] The emphasis in a strict social model on achieving the same level of functioning for all, so that disability is ultimately erased as a minority category, risks denying the humanity and dignity of those whose functional limitations remain, despite the efforts to achieve structural change.[124] In its comprehensive, multi-dimensional formulation, inclusive equality recognises that difference must be recognised but need to be

[119] See, for example, explanation of the 'medical model' in Broderick, *The Long and Winding Road to Equality and Inclusion for Persons with Disabilities* (n 8) 22–3.

[120] Ibid 122–3.

[121] Broderick appears to describe what I call a 'social model that recognises the residual impacts of impairment', when she writes that 'a model of disability has evolved which focuses both on the individualised impairment, as well as factors external to the disabled person – I will call this a social-contextual model of disability'. She argues that this socio-contextual model explains the CRPD's approach to transformative, substantive equality: ibid 24, 139.

[122] Stein (n 103) 91; see also: '…the [social] model has so far been expressed as requiring only formal equality – treating all persons the same – or as requiring only that people should have equal opportunities …': Skarstad, 'Disability and the Dilemma of Difference' (n 100) 94.

[123] Ibid 92–3.

[124] Stein applies a 'human-rights-based model' of disability, as a corrective to the strict social model, concluding that 'because advocates have limited the social model to formal equality theory, its application is limited within the human rights arena': ibid 83.

responded to in a way that defies stigmatisation, respects dignity, and results in civil, social, political, economic and cultural inclusion.

3.5 *Analysis and Conclusions*

This section has described the four-dimensional approach to inclusive equality prescribed by *General Comment No 6*, and how it is based on earlier formulations of substantive, transformative equality. The previous section already explained how substantive equality demands recognition of difference so that a differential response can be made to achieve equality, but this leaves open the question of what equality really means if we are all different and are responded to in different ways. This section has explained how in disability advocacy and literature, 'inequality' has been associated with civil, economic, political, social and cultural segregation and exclusion, and that the goal of equality has thus become synonymous with the goal of inclusion. This is evidenced in the literature and also reflected in the renaming of transformative equality as 'inclusive equality' when applied to the particular case of disability.

Several writers have described how the rights to non-discrimination and equality, although ostensibly civil-political rights, disrupt the traditional distinctions between categories of rights, and also demonstrate the interdependency between rights. The CRPD requires that all rights be fulfilled on a non-discriminatory basis so that the abolition of discrimination in the fulfilment of socio-economic rights is required to be realised immediately,[125] even though the socio-economic character of those rights would normally demand only progressive realisation.[126] The right to non-discrimination can require the provision of socio-economic measures both on an individual basis in the form of reasonable accommodation and on a system-wide basis in the form of specific or appropriate measures.

The trigger for differential treatment is the recognition of difference – both the differences attached to the individual and associated with their impairment and accompanying differences in the civil, economic, social, political and cultural environment. These differences are responded to, and inclusive equality realised, through a four-dimensional response that demands the simultaneous fulfilment of a wide range of civil–political and socio-economic rights to (a) address socio-economic disadvantage; (b) combat stigma, stereotyping and violence to recognise dignity; (c) ensure participation and inclusion; and (d) accommodate difference as a matter of human dignity.[127] This simultaneous achievement means that resources must be redistributed and difference recognised in a way that ensures participation and avoids stigma and ultimately leads to equality as inclusion.

[125] *General Comment No 6* [12].
[126] ICESCR Article 2(1); *CRPD* Article 4(2).
[127] *General Comment No 6* [11].

The next section considers how this concept of four-dimensional, transformative, inclusive equality, infused by the principle of indivisibility, can be applied to interpret Article 12 of the CRPD: the right to recognition of legal capacity 'on an equal basis with others'.

4 DISCRIMINATION, EQUALITY AND ARTICLE 12

General Comment No 6 reiterates that inclusive equality demands recognition of legal capacity under Article 12.[128] I argue in this section and the next, however, that if the four dimensions of transformative/inclusive quality are applied to interpret Article 12, then equality does allow for or demand decision-making by substitutes as a last resort because it can lead to inclusion.[129]

General Comment No 1 is clear in its prescription that the status and outcome tests of capacity constitute direct discrimination, and (as described in Chapter 2) there is wide agreement with this view.[130] It goes on to conclude that functional tests of capacity also constitute indirect discrimination because they disproportionately affect people with cognitive disability,[131] a conclusion that is contested by some of the commentary described below. In an endeavour to imbue meaning into the phrase 'on an equal basis with others', *General Comment No 1* does, however, go on to explain that Article 12 allows for denials of legal capacity that are not triggered by disability. It provides that:

> the right to equal recognition before the law and freedom from discrimination requires that when the State denies legal capacity, it must be on the same basis for all persons. Denial of legal capacity must not be based on a personal trait such as gender, race, or disability, or have the purpose or effect of treating the person differently.[132]

This section first discusses and analyses proposals for disability-neutral triggers for interfering in decision-making and concludes that these will inevitably

[128] Ibid [47]–[51].

[129] A footnote in the draft provided that the reference to 'on an equal basis with others' is to allow for some difference as to legal capacity between children and adults. This difference had already been acknowledged in the *Convention on the Rights of the Child, opened for signature 20 November, 1989, 1577 UNTS 11 (entered into force 2 September 1990)* by the limiting of some children's rights as compared to those of adults by reference to the 'evolving capacity of the child' in Articles 5 and 14: see comments of the Coordinator in: Ad Hoc Committee, *Daily Summary of the Fifth Session* (25 January 2005) www.un.org/esa/socdev/enable/rights/ahc5sum25jan.htm ('*Daily Summary 25 January 2005*').

[130] Chapter 2, Sections 3.2.1 and 3.2.2; see also Cera, 'Article 2' (n 53) 112.

[131] *General Comment No 1* [15]; Eilionóir Flynn and Anna Arstein-Kerslake, 'The Support Model of Legal Capacity: Fact, Fiction, or Fantasy?' (2014) 32(1) *Berkeley Journal of International Law* 124, 127–8; Piers Gooding and Eilionóir Flynn, 'Querying the Call to Introduce Mental Capacity Testing to Mental Health Law: Does the Doctrine of Necessity Provide an Alternative?' (2015) 4(2) *Laws* 245, 256.

[132] *General Comment No 1* [32].

disproportionately affect adults with cognitive disability. Second, it describes and analyses commentary that concludes a trigger of cognitive disability is not discriminatory in itself and can indeed be justified under theories of substantive equality. These conclusions are consistent with the argument in this chapter, albeit they apply tests of substantive equality that pre-date *General Comment No 6*.

4.1 *The Search for 'Disability-Neutral' Criteria*

General Comment No 1 suggests that legal capacity may be lawfully denied on the basis of bankruptcy or criminal conviction, given that neither of these conditions falls within prohibited bases of discrimination in human rights law.[133] However, these examples have been criticised by at least one commentator as ignoring the human rights of prisoners.[134] I propose further that these remarks reveal a lack of recognition that people with cognitive disability are widely over-represented in the prison system[135] and that a denial of legal capacity for prisoners would most likely constitute indirect discrimination against adults with cognitive disability.[136] This illustrates just how challenging it is to find truly 'disability-neutral' ' criteria for determining when a State should intervene in the area of decision-making.[137]

4.1.1 Extending the Doctrine of Necessity: Or Risk of Harm

Gooding and Flynn propose as a 'disability-neutral' basis for intervention, an expansion of the doctrine of necessity in the law of medical consent, such doctrine already

[133] Ibid.

[134] Quinn and Rekas-Rosalbo (n 95) 314.

[135] In relation to acquired brain injury, see Kristin Booth Glen, 'Introducing a New Human Right: Learning from Others, Bringing Legal Capacity Home' (2018) 49(3) *Columbia Human Rights Law Review* 1, 48; in relation to mental illness, see: Michael Perlin, 'Understanding the Intersection between International Human Rights and Mental Disability law: The Role of Dignity' in Bruce Arrigo and Heather Bersot (eds), *Routledge Handbook of International Crime and Justice Studies* (Routledge, 2013) 191, 191, 201; 'Aboriginal and Torres Strait Islander peoples with mental and cognitive disbilities are significantly over-represented in Australian criminal justice systems': in Eileen Baldry et al, *A Predictable and Preventable Path: Aboriginal People with Mental and Cognitive Disabilities in the Criminal Justice System* (University of New South Wales, 2015) 9.

[136] Caycho makes a similar analysis of legislation passed in Peru, which, although ostensibly forbidding denials of legal capacity based on disability, nevertheless allows for such declarations for 'habitual drunkards, drug addicts, persons with criminal convictions, bad administrators and spendthrifts'. He points out that adults with cognitive disability would be disproportionately represented in those cohorts: Caycho (n 99) 162–3.

[137] As indicated in Chapter 1 (Section 4.2), the interpretation and application of Article 12 in the criminal law environment is outside scope. Of interest though is an article by Wondemaghen, who in interpreting Article 12 in the criminal context concludes that: 'It soon becomes apparent then that 'on an equal basis with others' does not translate to 'on an identical basis with others': Wondemaghen (n 108) 182.

allowing for medical intervention without consent in emergencies.[138] They suggest that the test of 'serious adverse effects' proposed by Bach and Kerzner[139] could be used, provided that 'serious adverse effects' are explained as occurring 'when a person's life, health or safety is at imminent and grave risk, and failure to intervene would constitute criminal or civil negligence'.[140] Elsewhere, Flynn and Arstein-Kerslake propose a 'risk of imminent and grave harm to life, health or safety'.[141] However, in both cases, the authors acknowledge that the tests require further formulation so as not to impact disproportionately in practice on adults with disability.[142]

4.1.2 A Test of 'Special or Heightened Vulnerabilities'

Chapter 5 has already described some of the literature that proposes the vulnerable subject should be recognised as the foundation for personhood, in place of Kant's rational, autonomous person.[143] Hall proposes vulnerability as a universal human condition, but that when an individual is exposed to 'special or heightened vulnerabilities',[144] this could justify state intervention, whether or not a person had a cognitive disability. She explains that determining the degree or kind of vulnerability may include considerations of mental capacity; but, if so, it would consider a person's thinking processes in the context of their 'material, social and relationship' context, and may propose guardianship as one response among many to address the situation of heightened vulnerability.[145] Similarly, Herring has suggested heightened vulnerability may be a determinant for when state intervention, including guardianship,

[138] On consent and emergency situations, see: Bernadette Richards, 'Chapter 5: General Principles of Consent to Medical Treatment' in Ben White, Fiona McDonald and Lindy Willmott (eds), *Health Law in Australia* (Lawbook Co, 2018) 133, 154–6.

[139] For Bach and Kerzner's proposed test of 'serious adverse effects' in 'facilitated decision making', see Michael Bach and Lana Kerzner, *A New Paradigm for Protecting Autonomy and the Right to Legal Capacity: Advancing Substantive Equality for Persons with Disabilities through Law, Policy and Practice* (Law Commission of Ontario, October 2010).

[140] Gooding and Flynn (n 131) 261.

[141] Eilionóir Flynn and Anna Arstein-Kerslake, 'State Intervention in the Lives of People with Disabilities: The Case for a Disability-Neutral Framework' (2017) 13(1) *International Journal of Law in Context* 39, 49–50.

[142] Flynn and Arstein-Kerslake's caveats include that: 'we want to emphasise that this approach is based specifically on the legal, political, social and cultural context within which we as authors are located', and that 'Finally, there is a need to codify the criteria for intervention in legislation in order to constrain judicial discretion to authorise a broad range of interventions in the perception that these would be in the "best interests" of vulnerable adults': ibid 50; 'We also consider the need for deliberative law reform processes to identify such measures': Gooding and Flynn (n 131) 246.

[143] See Chapter 5, Section 4.3.

[144] Margaret Hall, 'Relational Autonomy, Vulnerability Theory, Older Adults and the Law: Making it Real' (2019) 12(1) *Elder Law Review* [i] [i], [ix].

[145] Margaret Hall, 'Rethinking Adult Guardianship: Mental Capacity and Vulnerability in the Context of Dementia in Old Age' (PhD Thesis, University of British Columbia, 2018) 13, 14.

may be justified[146] and that such a test should apply to adults both with and without impairments.[147] Herring expressly argues that such a test would be more compliant with the CRPD because intervention is not determined by disability but by broader criteria.[148] Like Hall, he sees guardianship as only one intervention among others to address heightened vulnerability, depending on the circumstances and the needs of the individual.[149]

A test of intervention based on vulnerability has attracted wide interest. Of note, however, is commentary pointing out that a vulnerability test would still disproportionately affect people with disability.[150] It has also been described as potentially throwing an even wider net than a capacity test, and allowing more readily for the dismissal of a person's avowed views and preferences.[151] In short, a test of vulnerability would, in all likelihood, affect people with disability (especially cognitive disability) more than others and, like the other tests proposed above, would not, therefore, be 'disability-neutral'.

4.1.3 Analysis and Conclusions on 'Disability-Neutrality'

General Comment No 1 recognises direct discrimination as unlawful but also prescribes that functional tests of capacity constitute unlawful discrimination on the basis that they disproportionately affect adults with cognitive disability, implying that they constitute indirect discrimination (see further below).[152] However, *General Comment No 1* interprets Article 12 as allowing for denials of, or limitations to, recognition of legal capacity, provided that they are not based on disability (i.e. they must be 'disability-neutral'). Several commentators have endeavoured to meet the challenge of finding a 'disability-neutral' basis for making distinctions as to legal capacity, including extending the doctrine of necessity; using a test of serious, imminent risk of harm; or replacing a capacity test with a test of heightened vulnerability.

146 Jonathan Herring and Jesse Wall, 'Autonomy, Capacity and Vulnerable Adults: Filling the Gaps in the Mental Capacity Act' (2015) 35(4) *Legal Studies* 698, 719.

147 He argues in the United Kingdom context that because the reach of the *Mental Capacity Act 2005* (England and Wales) is limited to people with 'impairments of the mind or brain', the inherent jurisdiction of the Supreme Court of England and Wales should be preserved to address the heightened vulnerability of others. For adults without impairments, functional capacity may not be at issue, but he argues that genuine autonomy may be impaired due to social and personal vulnerabilities. Despite the existing split jurisdiction in England and Wales (i.e. under the MCA for those with impairments and the inherent jurisdiction for others), Herring's overarching theoretical model is that the one test of vulnerability should apply to all adults, whether or not they have a cognitive disability.

148 Herring and Wall (n 146) 717.

149 Hall, Relational Autonomy, Vulnerability Theory, Older Adults and the Law' (n 144).

150 Flynn and Arstein-Kerslake, 'State Intervention in the Lives of People with Disabilities' (n 141) 45.

151 Mary Donnelly, *Healthcare Decision-Making and the Law: Autonomy, Capacity and the Limits of Liberalism* (Cambridge University Press, 2010) 125–7.

152 See Section 4.2.1.

However, it is likely all of these proposed tests would nevertheless disproportionately affect adults with cognitive disability.

I conclude that under a conception of substantive, transformative or inclusive equality, privileging 'disability-neutral' responses is misplaced and counterproductive. Wilson goes so far as to say in this context that she is '…generally sceptical of claims of disability neutrality or the general claim that neutrality of any kind is ever possible'.[153] Inclusive equality makes clear that differential responses – including in the form of reasonable accommodation or specific measures – are not only allowed but may be required to redress the inequalities experienced by people with disability. The critical test for whether an action is discriminatory is not whether it is based on the distinguishing feature of impairment or disability, but whether it leads to disadvantage, unfavourable outcomes or exclusion.

4.2 *'Disability-Neutrality' Is Not Essential for Equality*

As referred to above, *General Comment No 1* considers a functional test of capacity to be unlawful under Article 12 because although it avoids a diagnostic or status distinction, it nevertheless impacts disproportionately on adults with cognitive disability, and is said to therefore constitute indirect discrimination. However, several critics point out that differential treatment – including through applying a functional test of capacity – is not in itself discriminatory and may be lawful if it upholds human rights. One commentator has suggested that guardianship could constitute reasonable accommodation.[154] This proposal is technically challenging, given the case-by-case nature of reasonable accommodation and the programmatic nature of guardianship. However, others have asserted its lawfulness by applying a test of discrimination promulgated in 1989 by the Human Rights Committee in its *General Comment No 18: Non-Discrimination*.[155]

4.2.1 Pursuing a Legitimate Aim with Objective and Reasonable Means

Martin et al argue that a functional test of capacity, although disproportionately affecting adults with cognitive disability, is justified under the Human Rights

[153] Kay Wilson, *Mental Health Law: Abolish or Reform?* (Oxford University Press, 2021) 184.

[154] 'Some decision-making impairments may be accommodated or rectified but at the end of the spectrum there will be a very small proportion of persons whose impairments mean that they lack decision-making ability, even with infinite resources available for support. For those persons, the appointment of a substitute decision maker becomes a reasonable accommodation to ensure that they are afforded basic human rights including the right to exercise legal capacity': Anita Smith, 'Are Guardianship Laws and Practices Consistent with Human Rights Instruments?' in A Kimberly Dayton (ed), *Comparative Perspectives on Adult Guardianship* (Carolina Academic Press, 2014) 247, 264.

[155] Human Rights Committee, *General Comment No 18 Non-Discrimination*, 37th sess, UN Doc CCPR/C21/1/Rev.1/Add.1 (21 November 1989).

Committee's test set out in *General Comment No 18: Non-Discrimination* because this test provides that:

> not every differentiation of treatment will constitute discrimination, if the criteria for such differentiation are reasonable and objective and if the aim is to achieve a purpose which is legitimate under the Covenant.[156]

Martin et al review the functional element of the capacity test under the MCA and conclude that it sets 'reasonable and objective' criteria because it is based on the 'presence or absence of decision-making ability', which is a 'plain objective, empirical fact' one way or the other.[157] It also pursues legitimate aims: the promotion of the independence of adults with disability, ensuring access to services, allowing for autonomous decision-making where possible and protecting adults when this is not possible.[158] They conclude that a functional capacity test is a 'reasonable means' to achieve the MCA's aims because it can result in protecting an adult's right to life, physical and mental integrity and access to health services in a situation where the adult cannot understand the information provided to them.[159] In short, at least in situations where an adult's health is at stake, it is reasonable to treat people differently when they can't understand that lack of treatment would lead to longer-term illness and disadvantage. Such differential treatment, although disproportionately applying to adults with cognitive disability, is not discriminatory because it upholds human rights.[160]

Dawson and Szmukler arrive at a similar conclusion when endorsing a functional test of capacity for involuntary mental health treatment. Although such a test may disproportionately affect people with mental illness, they conclude that it would *not* constitute unlawful discrimination. Szmukler argues, as do Martin et al above, that the test would be supported by reasonable and objective criteria in pursuit of a legitimate aim.[161] The legitimate aim would align with the principles of the CRPD to respect the 'inherent dignity of the person, and individual autonomy'. Support would be provided to enable autonomous decision-making, and treatment would

[156] Ibid [13].

[157] Wayne Martin et al, *Achieving CRPD Compliance: Is the Mental Capacity Act of England and Wales Compatible with the UN Convention on the Rights of Persons with Disabilities? If Not, What Next?* (Essex Autonomy Project, 2014) 17.

[158] Ibid 16.

[159] Ibid 18.

[160] See also 'It needs to be recognised that autonomy in decision-making, although a central component of the legal capacity protected by Article 12 of the CPRD, is not the only value the CRPD seeks to protect. Other central rights include the right to life (Article 10) and the right to the "highest attainable standard of [mental] health"' (Article 25); Katrine Del Villar, 'Should Supported Decision-Making Replace Substituted Decision-Making? The Convention on the Rights of Persons with Disabilities and Coercive Treatment under Queensland's Mental Health Act 2000' (2015) 4(2) *Laws* 173, 183.

[161] George Szmukler, '"Capacity", "Best Interests", "Will and Preferences" and the UN Convention on the Rights of Persons with Disabilities' (2019) 18(1) *World Psychiatry: Official Journal of the World Psychiatric Association (WPA)* 34, 37.

be provided to restore autonomy for those who previously had impaired capacity. Szmukler argues that the test is reasonable because decision-making ability and autonomy are intimately linked.[162] Dawson points out that such a test would only be discriminatory if it resulted in disadvantage for the adult, but if the adult received appropriate health treatment, this would be advantageous and, therefore, would not constitute unlawful discrimination.[163] Dawson's analysis in this respect aligns with the argument in this book, contesting the underlying premise of *General Comment No 1* that decision-making by a substitute is always and inevitably rights-denying.

4.2.2 Commentary and Conclusions

The writers above, who argue that Article 12 allows for the retention of decision-making by substitutes, do so on the basis that not all differential treatment constitutes discrimination. Before the publication of *General Comment No 6* with its formulation of inclusive equality, writers have relied upon the Human Rights Committee's *General Comment No 18: Non-Discrimination* to argue that decision-making by substitutes can lead to equality by pursuing a legitimate aim in accordance with reasonable and objective criteria. Several writers conclude that despite its disproportional effect on adults with cognitive disability, a functional test of capacity is justified on this basis, often to uphold the rights to life and access to health care.

The UN Disability Committee has not referred to the Human Rights Committee's *General Comment No 18* in its *General Comment No 6*, making it unclear whether it considers it applicable to the CRPD.[164] However, I argue that the 'objective and reasonable' test in *General Comment No 18* is consistent with the concept of inclusive equality, the latter serving to flesh out the earlier test. Inclusive equality could be interpreted as implying that to be reasonable and pursue a legitimate aim, any action taken must be implemented in a way that: (a) ensures a 'fair' redistribution of resources 'to address socio-economic disadvantages'; (b) combats 'stigma, stereotyping, prejudice and violence' to recognise dignity; (c) ensures participation and social inclusion; and (d) has 'an accommodating dimension to make space for difference as a matter of human dignity'.[165] Martin et al and Dawson make clear in their analyses (although it is sometimes lost in the larger debate) that for decision-making by substitutes to constitute discrimination, it has to lead

[162] Ibid.

[163] John Dawson, 'A Realistic Approach to Assessing Mental Health Laws' Compliance with the UNCRPD' (2015) 40 *International Journal of Law and Psychiatry* 70, 71.

[164] Gurbai's view is that: 'In sum, particularly when read in light of its drafting history, the CRPD Committee's general comment on equality and non-discrimination sends mixed messages in relation to the validity of the pragmatic definition in the context of the CRPD'. By 'pragmatic definition', Gurbai means that: 'differential treatment does not constitute discrimination if the purpose or effect of the differential treatment is to achieve a legitimate aim and if the differential treatment can be objectively and reasonably justified': Sándor Gurbai, 'Beyond the Pragmatic Definition? The Right to Non-Discrimination of Persons with Disabilities in the Context of Coercive Interventions' (2020) *Health and Ruman Rights Journal* 279, 279, 285.

[165] *General Comment No 6* [11].

to a disadvantageous or an unfavourable outcome. Guardianship and involuntary mental health treatment can result in subsequent denials of human rights depending on what decisions are made and how they are made. In many cases, however, guardians and other substitutes may be required to make decisions to uphold the adult's human rights, without which the adult would become subject to neglect if not ill-treatment or abuse.[166]

5 'INCLUSIVE EQUALITY' AND THE RIGHT TO LEGAL CAPACITY

In interpreting the words 'on an equal basis with others', I argue that an interpretation of Article 12 as a threshold right, which must be realised for the rights to equality and non-discrimination to be realised,[167] overlooks that Article 12 is itself subject to an understanding of what equality means. I further argue that both supported decision-making and decision-making by substitutes respond to the difference of cognitive disability and the differences within cognitive disability, to provide differential treatment that ensures inclusive equality.

5.1 *Supported Decision-Making and Inclusive Equality*

To ensure non-discrimination and inclusive equality, *General Comment No 6* reiterates that support must be provided for persons with disability to exercise their legal capacity.[168] Supported decision-making has, as its starting point, the recognition of difference (i.e. the difference of cognitive disability) and the differential 'appropriate measure' of support allows recognition of legal capacity 'on an equal basis with others'.[169]

As described and discussed in Chapter 4, many commentators argue that everyone requires support for decision-making – those with cognitive disability and those without – and that we all make decisions supported or influenced to greater or lesser extents by those around us.[170] However, as also pointed out in that chapter,

[166] Dawson recognises that involuntary treatment may in some cases uphold human rights, but in other cases violate them when he asks the question: 'Involuntary psychiatric treatment, for instance, could both limit a person's autonomy and promote their social inclusion, health, and standard of living. Would it therefore violate or promote the person's rights under the Convention as a whole?' Dawson (n 140) 71.

[167] 'The right to legal capacity is a threshold right, that is, it is required for the enjoyment of almost all other rights in the Convention, including the right to equality and non-discrimination'. *General Comment No 6* [47].

[168] Ibid [48].

[169] Note that Article 12(3) provides that 'States Parties shall take *appropriate measures* to provide access by persons with disabilities to the support they may require in exercising their legal capacity' (emphasis added).

[170] Gerard Quinn and Anna Arstein-Kerslake, 'Restoring the "Human" in "Human Rights": Personhood and Doctrinal Innovation in the UN Disability Convention' in Costas Douzinas

registration of supporters and accompanying administrative systems and safeguards are required to ensure the protection of adults with cognitive disability from abusive and exploitative supporters.[171] Some commentators contend that formal safeguards are not required for supported decision-making.[172] However, Carney et al point out that such a position 'downplays difference as between abled and disabled to leave safeguarding entirely to natural social processes'.[173] Moreover, it is highly unlikely that adults not identifying as having a cognitive disability would submit their relationships to oversight by a formal support system.

Informal supported decision-making trials also acknowledge the difference between adults with cognitive disability and those without, by requiring, for example, written agreements with supporters, or the establishment of triadic relationships between the adult, the supporter and a monitor.[174] Supported decision-making systems will be disproportionately used by adults with cognitive disability because the difference of cognitive disability requires a differential response to recognise legal capacity on an equal basis with others. Consistently with this analysis, Kanter writes that support for decision-making in Article 12 is one example of how 'the CRPD recognises the ways in which formal equality is not adequate to protect the rights of persons with disabilities'.[175] Other writers note the similarities and even

and C A Gearty (eds), *Cambridge Companion to Human Rights Law* (Cambridge University Press, 2012) 36, 46.

171 *General Comment No 1* [17].

172 Terry Carney et al, 'Realising "Will, Preferences and Rights": Reconciling Differences on Best Practice Support for Decision-Making?' (2019) *Griffith Law Review* 357, 374, citing Eilionóir Flynn, 'The Rejection of Capacity Assessments in Favor of Respect for Will and Preferences: The Radical Promise of the UN Convention on the Rights of Persons with Disabilities' (2019) 18(1) *World Psychiatry* 50.

173 Carney et al (n 172) 374.

174 Office of the Public Advocate (Qld), *Decision-Making Support and Queensland's Guardianship System: A Systemic Advocacy Report* (A Systemic Advocacy Report, April 2016) 171; Jacinta Douglas et al, 'Factors That Underpin the Delivery of Effective Decision-Making Support for People with Cognitive Disability' (2015) 2(1) *Research and Practice in Intellectual and Developmental Disabilities* 37, 40.

175 Arlene S Kanter, *The Development of Disability Rights under International Law from Charity to Human Rights* (Routledge, 2015) 3; Dawson similarly implies that supported decision-making may be differential treatment which is not discriminatory because it is highly advantageous for the adult when he writes that: 'Evidence of impairment in such functioning can be highly relevant, and permitting such evidence to be used may be highly advantageous to the person, preventing inappropriate punishment, for example, or triggering entitlements to additional support:. Dawson (n 163) 73. Keys also arguably acknowledges this when she writes that: 'The Council of Europe Commissioner for Human Rights commented on the functional approach as having "given too little attention to the importance of support. It may have a future not as a measure of legal capacity but as a means of determining what kinds of supports should be available"': Mary Keys, 'Article 12' in Valentina Della Fina, Rachele Cera and Giuseppe Palmisano (eds), *The United Nations Convention on the Rights of Persons wtih Disabilities: A Commentary* (Springer International Publishing, 2017) 263, 276.

the overlap between the functions of support for decision-making and reasonable accommodation.[176]

General Comment No 6 provides that inclusive equality demands, 'an accommodating dimension to make space for difference as a matter of human dignity' to offer a solution for the 'dilemma of difference'.[177] To ensure equality of results and social inclusion, substantive, inclusive equality demands recognition of difference to provide support for decision-making for adults with cognitive disability. The right to supported decision-making acknowledges the residual impacts of impairment, even after legal capacity is recognised at a formal, legal level. According to the precepts of inclusive equality, supported decision-making will be used to redress economic disadvantage, combat stigma and violence and enable social inclusion, all based on a recognition of difference and dignity. It is a specific or appropriate measure in the form of the provision of socio-economic resources, which recognises difference and allows for (or demands) the State to be involved in personal relationships to ensure the right to equality. While the right to non-discrimination and equality is ostensibly a civil–political right, the achievement of inclusive equality depends on fulfilling a range of other civil–political and socio-economic rights.

Returning to the case of Jess, a best-case scenario would be for Jess to choose a different person as a supporter – not her son. Chapter 3 has already investigated what it calls the 'chicken and egg' or 'initiation problem' in this scenario – that is, that the first decision that she needed assistance with was indeed her choice of supporter.[178] If she refuses to change supporter because she has absolute trust in her son, then it is inevitable that a substitute decision would have to be made to appoint a new supporter.

Alternatively, we will assume that her son has died but that Jess still seems to want to live in the house and still does not care about her hygiene, health or appearance. All would agree that Article 12(3) CRPD requires recognition that the impairment associated with Jess's dementia means that she has a right to supported decision-making. Her daughter steps into the role without objection from Jess. A good scenario for Jess would be that her daughter could live with her and provide the necessary services and supports, with Jess's agreement or compliance.

Or if the daughter can't live with Jess because she has a young family in town, perhaps with a more trustworthy supporter for decision-making, Jess would be aided to understand the real choices open to her, and would express a preference to sell the farm and use the money to live somewhere more appropriate. Perhaps the daughter may interpret Jess's true will and preference to be that she wants to live elsewhere,

[176] Quinn and Rekas-Rosalbo note that: 'The concept of "reasonable accommodation" can perform some of the tasks of supported decision-making.... But it has its limits. It is not a replacement for a programme of supported decision-making': Quinn and Rekas-Rosalbo (n 95) 315; Bach and Kerzner (n 139) 112.

[177] *General Comment No 6* [11].

[178] See Chapter 3, Section 6.3.

where she can be houseproud as she always has been. (As illustrated through the case of Alex in Chapter 4, depending on what concept of autonomy we adopt, and how we interpret Jess's will and preferences, different decisions could be attributed to Jess.)[179] This would also be a good scenario for Jess – through utilising a supported decision-making framework.

But what if, even with her daughter as a trustworthy supporter, Jess continues to express a preference to live in the house, and there is overwhelming agreement that this accords with her lifelong wish not to sell the farm?

This is a hard case where, despite ostensibly recognising Jess's right to legal capacity, she remains subject to ongoing human rights abuses – including potentially violations of Article 16 ('Freedom from exploitation, violence and abuse'), Article 17 ('Protecting the integrity of the person'), Article 19 ('Living independently and being included in the community'), Article 25 ('Health'), Article 26 ('Habilitation and rehabilitation'), Article 28 ('Adequate standard of living and social protection') and Article 30 ('Participation in cultural life, recreation, leisure and sport'). Supported decision-making, while ostensibly upholding a right to legal capacity on an equal basis with others, may in hard or troubling cases shroud undue influence and allow for ongoing violations of a range of other indivisible human rights.

The position that supported decision making *always* upholds human rights ignores the reality that not all family relationships are benign and that limits to resources – both family and government – mean that decision-making 'choices' are likewise limited. Fulfilment of socio-economic rights may be a fundamental prerequisite for achieving decision-making autonomy and recognising legal capacity 'on an equal basis with others'.

5.2 *Equality, Substitute Decision-Making and Indivisibility*

I suggested above that the UN Disability Committee's view of guardianship as inherently discriminatory assumes a concept of formal equality premised on the argument that equality requires the same treatment for all. In limiting its analysis of Article 12 to one of formal equality, *General Comment No 6* fails to acknowledge the difference of impairment and disability as experienced in these cases of adults with severe and profound cognitive disability, such as the case of Jess. The difference inherent in such hard cases – both impairment and the disadvantages associated with cognitive impairment – is obscured by the assertion that *all* adults can be supported to make their own decisions.

The questions of who is 'different' and who is 'the same' is indeed complex, as acknowledged by *General Comment No 6* in its reference to the 'dilemma of

[179] See Chapter 4, Section 3.

difference'.[180] Some commentators have concluded that basing arguments for and against substitute decision-making on equality theory will never arrive at a satisfactory consensus because of the subjectivity involved in determining difference.[181] I suggest, however, that there is some consensus on difference when it comes to cognitive disability and decision-making. First, as explained above, there is an implicit agreement that the difference of cognitive impairment is a material one, evidenced in the consensus that supported decision-making may be required in some cases.

Second, there is wide acknowledgement that there are 'hard cases' that cannot be satisfactorily responded to with supported decision-making. As explained in Chapter 1, it is beyond the scope of this book to investigate or recommend a specific test or criteria for when decision-making by substitutes may be required (e.g. different capacity tests or heightened vulnerability).[182] But, as also explained in Chapter 1, there is wide agreement that, in some circumstances, supported decision-making has its limitations, either because of the nature or severity of the cognitive impairment, or the circumstances surrounding and associated with the impairment.[183] In this sense, there is broad agreement that some cases, because of their 'difference', are not adequately addressed by supported decision-making.

Despite general recognition of the differences between adults with cognitive impairment, *General Comment No 1* extends the will and preference test to all cases. Such an identical legal response for all adults with cognitive disability shrouds the reality of hard cases, obscuring their difference together with adults' associated different legal, economic and social needs. I argue that recognition of difference demands acknowledgement of the residual impacts of impairment, even after all possible social and environmental supports are provided. Once difference is recognised, differential treatment to achieve non-discrimination and substantive, inclusive equality is warranted and necessary to uphold a range of interdependent human rights beyond the right to legal capacity. There is express resistance to basing a legal regime on the 'hard cases' because acknowledgement of such difference may invert the paradigm for all.[184] However, in many cases, decision-making by substitutes may

180 Ibid [10].

181 Lucy Series and Anna Nilsson, 'Article 12 CRPD: Equal Recognition before the Law' in Ilias Bantekas, Michael Ashley Stein and Anastasiou Dimitris (eds), *The UN Convention on the Rights of Persons with Disabilities: A Commentary* (Oxford University Press, 2018) 339, 354.

182 See Chapter 1, Section 4.2.

183 Anna Arstein-Kerslake and Eilionóir Flynn, 'The General Comment on Article 12 of the Convention on the Rights of Persons with Disabilities: A Roadmap for Equality before the Law' (2016) 20(4) *The International Journal of Human Rights* 471, 482; Ron McCallum, *The United Nations Convention on the Rights of Persons with Disabilities: An Assessment of Australia's Level of Compliance* (Royal Commission into Violence, Abuse, Neglect and Exploitation of People with Disability, 2020) 49–50; Glen (n 135) 7; Peter Bartlett, 'Will and Preferences in the Overall CRPD Project' (2019) 18(1) *World Psychiatry: Official Journal of the WPA* 48, 49.

184 Jillian Craigie et al, 'Legal Capacity, Mental Capacity and Supported Decision-Making: Report from a Panel Event' (2019) 62 *International Journal of Law and Psychiatry* 160, 162;

be the only way (or be one necessary tool among others) to achieve inclusive equality for an adult and respect their dignity and personhood.

5.3 Case Study: Jess, Decision-Making and Inclusive Equality

For Jess, transformational, inclusive equality requires that she:

(a) not be subject to socio-economic disadvantage;
(b) not be the object of stigma, stereotype or violence and that her dignity be respected;
(c) participate in society and be included; and
(d) have accommodations 'to make space for [her] difference as a matter of human dignity'.[185]

Depending on which view of autonomy we hold and how we apply the 'best interpretation' principle, supported decision-making could lead to different outcomes for Jess with very little transparency or accountability for the decision. If a substitute were appointed, then it would be clear who was making the decision, and if a decision were made that Jess remain in squalor, then the substitute's decision could be challenged.

In describing guardianship as 'reasonable accommodation' to ensure substantive equality, Smith writes that:

> the right to a secure environment, nutrition and necessary health care (tangible rights) should not be sacrificed in order to prevent a limited (in time and content) loss of legal capacity where that limited denial of legal capacity is properly adjudicated and subject to regular review and monitoring.[186]

In the above quote, Smith refers to the appointment of a guardian as a '*loss* of legal capacity' [emphasis added], which is required for an adult's socio-economic rights to food and health care to be realised. Later in the same article, she surmises that an adult's legal capacity may actually be '*enhanced* by the appointment of a substitute decision maker. In its essence substitute decision and supported decision making is a form of agency' [emphasis added].[187] Whether substitute decision-making amounts to a loss of capacity or an enhancement to capacity may depend on the particular way that future legislation is drafted. It is the actual, practical and material effects and implications of any finding of incapacity that determines whether a finding, one way or the other, leads to substantive inequality and social exclusion.

Gerard Quinn, 'Concept Paper "Personhood and Legal Capacity": Perspectives on the Paradigm Shift of Article 12 of the CRPD' (Conference Paper, HPOD Conference, 20 February, 2010) 17 www.inclusiveirelandie/document/HarvardLegalcapacitygqdraft2.doc; McCallum (n 183) 51.

185 *General Comment No 6* [11].

186 Smith (n 154) 268.

187 Ibid 271.

In Jess's case, if a substitute decided to sell the farm and move Jess to more suitable accommodation, this would recognise that Jess is in a 'different' situation from others because of her impairment. It would address her socio-economic disadvantage, end her neglect and abuse, and enable her to participate in society with the goal of achieving inclusive equality. A substitute could make a decision that acknowledges Jess's personhood by respecting her dignity. Dignity (as we have seen in the previous chapter) acknowledges Jess's equal worth and the social dimensions of her humanity, respects her autonomy in those areas of life where she can exercise autonomy, takes account of her embodied selfhood and material situation, and recognises the indivisibility of human rights.

6 CONCLUSION

Article 12 requires recognition of legal capacity 'on an equal basis with others', and this chapter has argued that Article 12 may require decision-making by substitutes as a last resort to achieve substantive equality. In 2018, the UN Disability Committee published its *General Comment No 6*, which explains how the rights to equality and non-discrimination apply to the particular case of disability. It describes how the right to equality is referred to in the Preamble, recognised in two of the General Principles, established as a stand-alone right in Article 5 and reiterated in the refrain of 'on an equal basis with others' in sixteen of the substantive articles of the CRPD including Article 12.

The chapter has described and explained different concepts of discrimination and equality as they have evolved in human rights law and theory and as explained in *General Comment No 6*. It described how the concept of formal equality, which focuses on commonalities and demands identical treatment to achieve non-discrimination, has been largely abandoned as the prevailing concept of equality in human rights theory, especially in addressing the rights of marginalised people, including adults with disability. The novel inclusion of an express right to reasonable accommodation in the CRPD recognises the importance of substantive equality for people with disability. The obligation to provide reasonable accommodation recognises that different treatment may be required to achieve substantive equality for people with disability – albeit ostensibly applying only on a case-by-case basis. The CRPD recognises that reasonable accommodation alone will not achieve structural, systemic and substantive equality for people with disability, because it is limited to a case-by-case approach and qualified by the proviso that it does not impose a disproportionate or undue burden on a third party. For this reason, the CRPD requires specific measures appropriate to disability to be pursued and provided by the State and others, to ensure substantive equality.

The provision of both reasonable accommodation and specific measures depends on recognising the differences associated with disability, in order to respond with appropriate differential responses. *General Comment No 6* acknowledges the dilemma that difference raises for assessing and measuring substantive equality and proposes the concept of inclusive equality as a solution. The term 'inclusive equality' reflects views in the literature that suggest or propose that equality in the area of disability advocacy and policy has been used as an approximation for inclusion. Inclusive equality adapts a four-dimensional account of transformative equality to the particular case of disability. It provides that equality is achieved or marked by redressing socio-economic disadvantage; eliminating stigma, prejudice and abuse; enabling participation and inclusion and accommodating difference to respect dignity.

I argue that inclusive equality, in requiring all four dimensions to be achieved simultaneously, recognises the indivisibility of human rights as the interdependency of rights and affirming the equal importance of socio-economic with civil–political rights. The literature on equality more widely argues that substantive equality is driven by the principle of indivisibility. It explains how reasonable accommodation displays indicia of a socio-economic right but is part of the civil-political right to non-discrimination, and also that the civil-political right to non-discrimination applies across both categories of rights. Rights to specific measures, while needed to ensure the fulfilment of a range of rights, including civil–political rights, can resemble socio-economic rights. They frequently demand positive state action, involvement in the personal sphere, and the provision of socio-economic resources. For this reason, the notion of substantive equality in the CRPD has been said to function as a bridge between socio-economic and civil-political rights, emphasising and driving the indivisibility of human rights as espoused in the CRPD. I further argued that the notion of substantive and inclusive equality for people with disability is premised on a social model of disability that recognises the residual impacts of impairment and the differences and disadvantages associated with such impairments. A strict social model elides these differences in its aspiration that ultimately, with appropriate social and environmental changes, disability will no longer exist or be recognised.

I argue that both *General Comment No 1* and *General Comment No 6*, by asserting that realisation of all other rights depends on recognising legal capacity, fail to recognise interdependencies between Article 12 and other rights and instead privilege the civil-political right to legal capacity above all others. *General Comment No 1* interrogates, to an extremely limited extent, the concept of equality as it applies to legal capacity. There are two key gaps in its equality analysis. First, it provides that legal capacity may be denied if done according to disability-neutral criteria, without solving the dilemma of what disability neutrality may mean in practical terms. Commentators have considered extending the doctrine of necessity, relying on tests of harm or introducing the test of heightened vulnerability. Ultimately, however, these formulations still impact disproportionately on adults with cognitive disability, responding to them with differential treatment and revealing that disability neutrality is not the key to substantive equality. Second, *General Comment*

No 1 incorrectly assumes that decision-making by a substitute will always result in unfavourable treatment. Scholars have to date used the test in the Human Rights Committee's *General Comment No 18 Non-Discrimination* to argue that such differential treatments do not amount to inequality for people with disability if they pursue a legitimate aim in accordance with reasonable and objective criteria.

I argued that, in interpreting and applying Article 12, *General Comment No 6* fails to apply the four dimensions of inclusive equality to adults with severe and profound cognitive disability. The requirement that adults with cognitive disability may need support to exercise legal capacity does implicitly acknowledge the residual impact of cognitive impairment and the need for an appropriate measure or differential response to achieve substantive, inclusive equality. I argued that there is also wide acknowledgement of the difference posed by hard cases, although it is beyond the scope of this book to determine precisely where that boundary may lie. Extending supported decision-making to hard cases may result in formal equality, but differential treatment in the form of decision-making by substitutes may be required to achieve inclusive equality and to recognise personhood in respecting human dignity. For Jess, the privileging of her autonomy could lead to opposing results, depending on our view of autonomy. But respecting her, and *our* dignity, demands that any decisions enable her civil, economic, political, social and cultural inclusion by respecting her indivisible human rights. In hard cases, decision-making by substitutes can be one appropriate measure or tool through which an adult with cognitive disability can be situated as a claimant of a broad range of human rights.

7

Conclusion

1 INTRODUCTION

This final chapter summarises the main findings and outcomes of the book. Section 2 summarises the interpretive problem surrounding Article 12. Section 3 summarises the argument made in this book: that Article 12 should be interpreted through the principle of indivisibility and the values of autonomy, dignity and equality to require both supported decision-making and decision-making by substitutes as a last resort. Section 4 reflects on its implications for advocacy and law reform, and Section 5 contains concluding remarks, acknowledging the historical and ongoing neglect and abuse of people with disability.

2 ARTICLE 12: A SITE OF CONTENTION

There is significant contention over the interpretation of the right to 'legal capacity on an equal basis with others' in Article 12 of the CRPD. On the one hand, there is the authoritative but non-binding view espoused by the UN Disability Committee and others that the paradigm shift in disability rights required by Article 12 demands the abolition of decision-making by substitutes in all cases. This interpretation is based on understandings of legal capacity as the capacity both to hold rights and act on them, and assertions that the fulfilment of the right to legal capacity is a precondition for claiming other rights. It assumes that autonomy in decision-making can always exist and that equal recognition of legal capacity demands 'disability neutrality' in applying identical treatment.[1] I argue that what unites these arguments is that they are premised on the privileging of autonomy as a human rights value above all others and on a strict social model of disability that fails to acknowledge the residual difference of impairment.

[1] See Chapter 2, Section 4.1.

On the other hand, there are arguments for an interpretation of Article 12 as allowing for or requiring decision-making by substitutes as a last resort. The dominant arguments supporting this interpretation are that:

(1) legal capacity means only the capacity to hold rights;
(2) decision-making by substitutes is equivalent to 100% support;
(3) decision-making by substitutes is an Article 12(4) safeguard; and
(4) the difference of cognitive disability demands differential treatment to achieve substantive equality.[2]

I argued that what unites these arguments is the assumption that the residual impacts of cognitive impairment (after all available supports have been provided) mean that some adults (as a matter of hard reality) will not have autonomy in decision-making. Once this is recognised, the 'best interpretation principle' as underpinning supported decision-making in hard cases lacks transparency and accountability and is both ethically and legally problematic.

3 A SUMMARY OF THE ARGUMENT

Interpreting Article 12 through the principle of indivisibility and the fundamental human rights values of autonomy, dignity and equality, this book situated the interpretive debate over Article 12 against the development in the twentieth and twenty-first centuries of different concepts in disability policy, law and human rights. It described how these developments – from the charity to the social model, from mass institutionalisation through to supported decision-making – have been predominantly framed as a progression from protection to autonomy, from exclusion to inclusion, and from discrimination to equality.[3] It further explained that, in terms of UN institutional arrangements, disability had been sidelined as the province of socio-economic rights only, at a time when socio-economic rights were being framed as social policy and subordinated as not 'true' human rights. This led in the 1990s to the urgency to promote disability as a civil-political rights issue so that people with disability would have visibility as subjects of 'true' human rights,[4] representing a paradigm shift in disability law and policy that culminated in the development of the CRPD and Article 12.

The book identified the limitations of this dominant narrative in its failure to acknowledge how the recognition of the residual impacts of cognitive impairment, and the importance of the principle of indivisibility of human rights, disrupt its apparent simplicity. Interpreting Article 12 as the endpoint on a trajectory from paternalism to autonomy fails to account for what are agreed to be the hard cases. These hard cases

[2] See Chapter 2, Section 4.2.
[3] See Chapter 2, Sections 2 and 3.
[4] See Chapter 3, Section 4.1.

arise where decisions relate to adults with a severe and profound cognitive disability; there is a fine line between whether the adult or the supporter made the decision, and a supported decision may result in unacceptable harm to the adult or others.

This book has interpreted Article 12 not as a standalone provision but in the context of the whole of the CRPD. It has done this by demonstrating its critical interdependencies with other articles in the convention, and also by considering how the values of autonomy, dignity and equality, which are fundamental to the whole of the CRPD, affect Article 12's interpretation. The interpretation of Article 12 argued for in this book is grounded in the principle of indivisibility of human rights and a social model of disability that recognises the residual impacts of impairment. The interpretive framework is applied consistently because it explains how Article 12 allows for or requires both supported decision-making and decision-making by substitutes. It demonstrates how decision-making practices are justified as differential treatment, accounting for the difference of disability to maximise autonomy, recognise personhood through dignity and achieve inclusive equality. Both supported decision-making and decision-making by substitutes, together with the values of autonomy, dignity and equality that underpin them, are, in turn, all reinterpreted through the principle of indivisibility.

3.1 *Privileging Autonomy, Civil-political Rights and Article 12*

The concept of autonomy has its roots in the liberal philosophical tradition, with Kant emphasising rationality as the basis of autonomy and autonomy as the foundation for personhood. Mill's concept of liberty has heavily influenced contemporary notions of autonomy, which see it as the right to be free from interference by the State and others, and as therefore demanding state exclusion from the personal sphere.[5] However, autonomy as rationality or the ability to reason excludes adults with cognitive disability from personhood. Autonomy as non-interference fails to acknowledge the residual impacts of impairment and socio-economic disadvantage associated with disability, which may demand state support as an ethical imperative. Chapter 3 identified that autonomy as the right to be left alone underpins civil-political rights in the liberal tradition and serves to perpetuate the subordination of socio-economic rights, the latter framed as demanding positive actions from the State that interfere in the personal sphere.[6]

3.2 *The CRPD and the Principle of Indivisibility*

The principle of indivisibility of human rights demands recognition of the interdependence of rights and the equal importance of socio-economic with civil–political

[5] See Chapter 4, Section 2.
[6] See Chapter 3.

rights. The right to legal capacity is categorised as a civil-political right and interpretations of Article 12 that require recognition of universal legal capacity frame it as a right fundamental to all others. I argued that the framing of Article 12 as fundamental to all other rights over-corrects the historical exclusion of people with disability from the human rights agenda and promotes civil-political rights at the expense of socio-economic rights, contrary to the principle of indivisibility. As liberal autonomy is a value that traditionally underpins civil-political rights, I further argued that the principle of indivisibility disrupts the privileging of autonomy as a human rights value above all others. This disruption is evident within Article 12 itself, which can more convincingly be categorised as a mixed civil-political and socio-economic right where the fulfilment of the civil-political right to legal capacity may depend on the fulfilment of the socio-economic right to support. I described how the principle of indivisibility can resolve the 'chicken and egg' or 'initiation problem', otherwise posed by the dependence in practice of the right to legal capacity on the initial provision of trustworthy support.[7]

Some of the literature has described the CRPD as evincing a new type of indivisibility of human rights, whereby the two categories of rights collapse into one another. I agreed with suggestions that the CRPD – through its declaration of indivisibility in the Preamble and its mingling of traditionally civil-political rights and socio-economic rights in the same articles – evinces the principle of indivisibility more than any other human rights convention. I argued, however, that it is premature to describe the CRPD as developing a principle of indivisibility according to which the significance of the two separate categories is obliterated. This is because people with disability disproportionately experience socio-economic disadvantage associated with their impairment, and thus their immediate need may be to fulfil a socio-economic right to claim a range of other rights, including potentially the right to legal capacity. The distinction between the two categories is embedded in UN human rights institutions, and there is residual ongoing privileging of civil-political human rights, contrary to the principle of indivisibility. I argue that in this context, an ostensible collapsing of the two categories risks a situation where socio-economic rights are subsumed and subordinated to civil–political rights under a rhetorical cloak of indivisibility.[8]

3.3 *Article 12 and Autonomy*

Chapter 4 explained how the interpretation of Article 12 as requiring the abolition of decision-making by substitutes has been driven by the urgent demand to include adults with cognitive disability as persons, coupled with a desire to retain autonomy as the basis of personhood. I used the case of Alex to illustrate

[7] See Chapter 3, Section 6.3.
[8] See Chapter 3, Section 5.4.

how attributing autonomy to an adult who has impaired capacity to make decisions can result in a lack of transparency and accountability for decision-making. Depending on what concept of autonomy is relied upon and how Alex's will and preferences are interpreted, opposing decisions may be attributed to Alex regarding 'his decision' to consent to or refuse dental treatment. Alex does not have a severe and profound disability, but he may nevertheless be considered a hard case because, under a supported decision-making regime that eliminated guardianship, the line between supporting Alex to decide and deciding for him could be too fine to discern, and a decision to refuse treatment will result in long-term personal harm to Alex.

To include Alex and others (especially adults with a severe and profound cognitive disability) within personhood, commentators have endeavoured to refashion liberal autonomy from being marked by rationality, independence, and freedom from interference to autonomy marked by emotion, interdependence or positive liberty. I argued that the limitations of these arguments are found in their internal inconsistencies. While ostensibly rejecting traditional liberal models of autonomy and personhood, the refashionings nevertheless retain a privileging of rationality, and bounded personhood, in a way that risks perpetuating the exclusion and stigmatisation of adults with cognitive impairment. Under these refashionings, the autonomous person is still rational, independent and bounded; it is just that the boundary has shifted to include the supporter, but only to the extent that the supporter is instrumental to the adult's personhood. Not only does this leave adults with cognitive disabilities (especially those without support) vulnerable to ongoing stigmatisation as non-rational and dependent, but it also risks denying the autonomy and personhood of the supporter. It also reveals an inconsistent logic in framing state intervention in the form of 'support' as always rights-affirming, but intervention in the form of decision-making by substitutes as always rights-denying.

I concluded that because of the above limitations, the notion of the autonomous person cannot be stretched or refashioned to include all adults with cognitive disability and that another basis for personhood must be found. Autonomy is nevertheless an important value that underpins human rights and the CRPD in particular, and I thus affirmed the value of autonomy as one very important good, among others. However, I argue that the traditional view of autonomy as rationality, independence and non-interference does not align well with the concept of autonomy anticipated by Article 12, with its demand for supported decision-making. I concluded that a concept of autonomy as achievement or as the development of autonomy competencies, and as inhering within it a demand for real options, best aligns with the Article 12 right to legal capacity with support. I further argued that this concept of autonomy can be interpreted as recognising the indivisibility of human rights. In particular, for adults who experience socio-economic disadvantage associated with their impairment, the fulfilment of socio-economic rights may be a pre-condition to achieving autonomy and legal capacity.

3.4 Article 12 and Dignity

The case of cognitive disability reveals the inadequacy of autonomy as an inclusive basis for personhood, so Chapter 5 proposed that dignity take its place. I argued that the emphasis on dignity in the text of the CRPD and the disability rights literature and jurisprudence means that there is not only legitimacy but a degree of urgency to formulate dignity as a coherent legal principle. I described how some of the philosophical literature and much of the Article 12 literature attributes a limited meaning to dignity as being equivalent to autonomy as the 'dignity of risk'. Drawing on the philosophical and legal literature, I argued for a wider concept of five-dimensional dignity, which recognises dignity as inherent and as an important legal principle but not as a separate human right. I proposed the five dimensions of dignity as:

(1) meaning equal worth or value and thereby treating persons as ends and not merely means;
(2) placing a high value on autonomy, especially for those who are capable of autonomy;
(3) reflexive and as acknowledging the interdependent, interpersonal and social nature of being human;
(4) recognising personhood as embodied and particular; and
(5) recognising and incorporating the indivisibility of human rights.

I argued that dignity can serve to recognise personhood where adults, as a matter of hard reality, are not autonomous in their decision-making.

I drew upon the jurisprudence in South Africa and the United Kingdom to demonstrate how dignity is more readily associated with upholding socio-economic as well as civil–political rights than is autonomy, according to the principle of indivisibility. In *Grootboom*, the South African Constitutional Court described how dignity, freedom and equality could depend on fulfilling the right to adequate shelter.[9] In *D v UK*,[10] the European Court of Human Rights decided that D's civil right to be free from inhumane or degrading treatment depended on fulfilling his right to health care, a decision that Munby J subsequently explained as respecting D's dignity.[11]

Endeavours to emphasise dignity as a concept wider than autonomy, in interpreting Article 12 specifically, have to date been limited. Chapter 5 described a proposal by Donnelly for dignity as a principle to guide decision-making for adults with impaired capacity[12] and also a proposal by Carter that dignity should be accorded

9 *Government of the Republic of South Africa and Others v Grootboom and Others* (2000) (1) SA 46.

10 *D v United Kingdom* (1997) 24 EHRR 423.

11 *R (Burke) v General Medical Council (Official Solicitor intervening)* [2005] QB 424.

12 Mary Donnelly, *Healthcare Decision-Making and the Law: Autonomy, Capacity and the Limits of Liberalism* (Cambridge University Press, 2010) 176, 218, 221; Mary Donnelly, 'From Autonomy to Dignity: Treatment for Mental Disorders and the Focus for Patient Rights' (2008) 26(2) *Law in Context* 37.

more weight than autonomy in decision-making for people with impaired capacity.[13] However, Donnelly situates her argument in a broader context than the CRPD and Article 12, and Carter favours a social justice framework in preference to a human rights one, because of the ongoing privileging of civil–political rights and autonomy in human rights.[14]

Chapter 5 concluded by applying the concept of five-dimensional dignity to analyse and interpret Article 12, focusing on the case study of Sesha. It shows that the same decision may result, whether undertaken through a support model or by a substitute. However, Sesha's situation illustrates how the privileging of autonomy and legal capacity in a case of severe and profound cognitive disability leads to uncertainty and undermines transparency in decision-making. It argued that in Sesha's circumstances, a process of supported decision-making, which makes a 'best interpretation' of Sesha's will and preferences, is ethically unacceptable, as illustrated by the example of life-or-death decision-making. I argued that if a decision were made by a substitute, there would be more accountability and transparency and that a substitute could respect Sesha's dignity and personhood by claiming her civil, economic, political, social and cultural rights.

3.5 *Article 12 and Equality*

Chapter 6 argued that the phrase 'on an equal basis as others' in Article 12 invokes a concept of substantive, inclusive equality. This means that decision-making by substitutes is not necessarily discriminatory because it may be necessary to achieve equality in hard cases. Relying on human rights law and theory, as also described in *General Comment No 6*, I affirmed equality as a fundamental value in the CRPD. I further traced the development of the human rights norm of equality through its origins as being limited to formal equality, to the current understanding of it as embodying substantive equality. Formal equality assumes that equality will be realised by treating everyone the same. I argued that an interpretation of Article 12 that demands the abolition of decision-making by substitutes is premised on accepting an outdated concept of formal equality.

Achieving substantive equality has as its starting point the recognition of difference. The CRPD itself, as explained in *General Comment No 6*, affirms the importance of recognising the difference of disability as well as the differences within disability. Once difference is recognised, then differential treatment will

[13] Barbara Carter, 'The Case for Dignity as the Governing Principle in Adult Guardianship' (2010) 19(1) *Res Publica* 1, 1.

[14] Barbara Carter, 'Adult Guardianship: Human Rights or Social Justice?' (2010) 18(1) *Journal of Law and Medicine* 122, 147–53; Carter, 'The Case for Dignity as the Governing Principle in Adult Guardianship' (n 13).

be required to achieve equality. The challenge with substantive equality models is to determine what constitutes equality when we are all situated differently, and also to determine which differences matter. I described the UN Disability Committee as answering the first question by developing its concept of inclusive equality, thereby reflecting suggestions in the literature that for people with disability, equality is measured by their degree of civil, economic, political, social and cultural inclusion. *General Commen No 6* provides that inclusive equality demands:

(1) a fair redistributive dimension to address socioeconomic disadvantages;
(2) a recognition dimension to combat stigma, stereotyping, prejudice and violence and to recognise the dignity of human beings and their intersectionality;
(3) a participative dimension to reaffirm the social nature of people as members of social groups and the full recognition of humanity through inclusion in society; and
(4) an accommodating dimension to make space for difference as a matter of human dignity.[15]

The literature on equality and human rights more broadly recognises that the right to equality and non-discrimination cuts across the two categories of rights in a way that drives the principle of indivisibility. The prescription of these four dimensions further illustrates that inclusive equality depends on the fulfilment of interdependent rights that cut across the traditional categories.

I answered the second question of what differences matter by arguing that the difference of cognitive disability is widely recognised as being a material difference in achieving rights related to decision-making. I further argued that the importance of recognising difference is premised on a social model of disability that recognises the residual impacts of impairment. Article 12 requires a recognition of the difference of cognitive disability so that the differential response of supported decision-making can help adults achieve legal capacity and social inclusion. I argued further that the wide acceptance that there are hard cases of cognitive disability, where supported decision-making cannot offer a satisfactory response, signals consensus that the difference constituted by hard cases is a difference that matters. To extend the same treatment of supported decision-making to hard cases will not achieve inclusive equality, so differential treatment in the form of decision-making by substitutes will be required to uphold a wide range of indivisible human rights. I used the case of Jess, a woman with advanced dementia who is being neglected by her son/supporter, to demonstrate how decision-making by a substitute may be needed to ensure her civil, economic, social, political and cultural inclusion and fulfilment of her indivisible human rights.

[15] [11].

4 IMPLICATIONS FOR ADVOCACY AND LAW REFORM

This book makes a significant contribution to the debate around Article 12, by interpreting it in the context of the whole of the CRPD. However the arguments it develops around cognitive disability, personhood, human dignity, inclusive equality and the principle of indivisibility are of much wider application. I understand why disability advocates assert the value of autonomy over all other values, given the history and lingering practice of institutionalisation of people with disability. However while autonomy is indeed important, there needs to be acknowledgement by advocates and governments of the dependencies associated with impairment so that the value of autonomy – acknowledged by many to be a liberal abstraction or ideal – is not privileged over all others. Insistence that decision-making autonomy be the basis of our personhood, risks ongoing stigmatisation of adults who as a matter of empirical reality require appropriate supports or substitutes in making decisions and being held accountable for them.[16]

Instead, I have argued that the conception of autonomy that underpins Article 12 and the CRPD is autonomy as achievement or the development of autonomy competencies, together with a demand for the provision of options. This can be interpreted not as the right to be left alone from state intervention but as a demand for the fulfilment of civil–political and socio-economic rights, according to the principle of indivisibility.[17] There is a wide consensus that supported decision-making upholds the human rights of adults with cognitive disability and positions them as subjects and claimants of human rights. Arguments against the retention of decision-making by substitutes have as their premise that to have a decision made for an adult by a substitute, and for the substitute to be accountable for that decision rather than the adult, automatically situates the adult as an object of charity and an object of rights.

Arguments that advocate for an interpretation of Article 12 that allows for decision-making by substitutes, together with the accountability of the substitute for that decision, are frequently articulated in terms of protecting the adult from harm. In being framed in terms of protection, they invoke historical paternalisms and associated abuses. Sometimes these interpretations may describe how decision-making by substitutes is necessary to uphold human rights beyond Article 12.[18] However, this book has as its central argument that it is the indivisibility of human rights that allows for or demands that adults with cognitive disability are positioned as subjects and claimants of human rights. This analysis allows us to discard the language and practice of paternalism and protection in order to reposition adults with cognitive disability as claimants of rights across the civil, economic, social, political and cultural domains.

[16] See Chapter 4, Section 4.6.

[17] See Chapter 4, Section 6.

[18] Wayne Martin et al, *Achieving CRPD Compliance: Is the Mental Capacity Act of England and Wales Compatible with the UN Convention on the Rights of Persons with Disabilities? If Not, What Next?* (Essex Autonomy Project, 2014) 27.

4.1 'Choice and Control' in the Real World

This book began in Chapter 1 by referring to the Disability Royal Commission[19] and how it has used the CRPD as a framework for its investigations and research.[20] Chapter 1 also referred to the impressive commitment made by the Australian Government through the introduction and ongoing implementation of the NDIS and referred to similar programmes in other Western nations where disability services are provided through programmes based on individual budgeting. The structure of these programmes and the rhetoric and legal framing of 'choice and control' embedded in them clearly align with a human rights framework for disability service provision that is centred on the right to legal capacity.

I argued that the positioning of the civil-political right to legal capacity, as a foundational human right, risks privileging 'choice and control' under the NDIS (and other self-directed support systems) in a way that severely disadvantages adults with cognitive disability. The NDIS assumes as a starting point that all people with disability have the ability to make their own decisions and yet the literature is beginning to reveal the limitations of framing service delivery in this way. First, many adults with cognitive disability may not have immediate decision-making capability and also may not have readily available supports. Second, adults with disability are not always presented with an adequate array of options to exercise a meaningful choice.

In relation to the first issue, the disability community has advised the National Disability Insurance Agency of the critical need for support for decision-making. But, to date, decision-making support is not funded under the NDIS,[21] and practitioners and researchers have started to criticise it more broadly for its practice of 'dedifferentiation' of people with cognitive disability, thus failing to recognise or meet needs

[19] https://disability.royalcommission.gov.au/

[20] See, for example, Ron McCallum, *The United Nations Convention on the Rights of Persons with Disabilities: An Assessment of Australia's Level of Compliance* (Royal Commission into Violence, Abuse, Neglect and Exploitation of People with Disability, 2020).

[21] Christine Bigby et al, 'Delivering Decision Making Support to People with Cognitive Disability – What Has Been Learned from Pilot Programs in Australia from 2010 to 2015' (2017) 52(3) *Australian Journal of Social Issues* 222, 224; see also 'the majority of participants' in the NDIS will have some kind of cognitive impairment and therefore 'good support for decision-making is crucial': Jacinta Douglas et al, 'Factors That Underpin the Delivery of Effective Decision-Making Support for People with Cognitive Disability' (2015) 2(1) *Research and Practice in Intellectual and Developmental Disabilities* 37, 41; also, there are gaps in NDIS service provision relating to decision-making support, i.e., shortfalls in advocacy funding and conflicts of interest between support coordinators and service providers: Office of the Public Advocate (Vic), *'I'm Too Scared to Come out of My Room': Preventing and Responding to Violence and Abuse between Co-Residents in Group Homes* (Research Report, 2019); see also recent consultation on supported decision-making: National Disability Insurance Agency, *National Disability Insurance Scheme Consultation Paper: Supporting you to make your own decisions* (2021).

for differentiated, tailored and targeted treatment to promote inclusion.[22] Without support, many adults with cognitive disability are being placed in a central decision-making role without requisite capability. This means that planners are often imposing their own decisions on participants and making their own judgements about what are 'reasonable and necessary disability-related needs'.[23] Moreover, without the funding and provision of supports, there is a risk that guardianship appointments will actually increase as service providers wish to reduce their commercial risks in a system based on choice, control and contracts.[24]

In relation to the second issue, there is frequently a lack of adequate service and accommodation options. In the area of housing, for example, this means that participants may still be subject to ongoing neglect and abuse in situations that amount to institutionalisation.[25] Further, the market-driven nature of service provision means that support workers are poorly paid and provide correspondingly inadequate services.[26] Concern has been expressed that 'the NDIS may fail to produce a meaningful change for people with intellectual disability and further marginalise them if there is no workforce capable of supporting their decision-making needs'.[27] Without meaningful choice, autonomy, legal capacity and equality with others are very abstract concepts.

4.2 *The Right to Legal Capacity as a Right above All Others: Legitimising the Role of the 'Lazy State'*

Carter has written that:

> adoption of the 'least restrictive means' principle … is an expression of the view that the state should keep out of the lives of its citizens, except as a last resort.

[22] Michelle King, 'Dedifferentiation and Difference: People with Profound Intellectual and Multiple Disabilities and the National Disability Insurance Scheme (NDIS)' (2020) 45(4) *Journal of Intellectual & Developmental Disability* 320; Christine Bigby and Jacinta Douglas, 'Supported Decision Making' in Roger J. Stancliffe et al (eds), *Choice, Preference, and Disability: Promoting Self-Determination Across the Lifespan* (Springer International Publishing, 2020) 45.

[23] Erin Wilson et al, 'Exploring the Personal, Programmatic and Market Barriers to Choice in the NDIS for People with Psychosocial Disability' (2021) *Australian Journal of Sociology* 1, 10–12.

[24] 'OPA has seen the incidence of guardianship rise since the introduction of the NDIS'. OPA guardians are asked to make decisions about participants' access to services and the agreements that govern these service arrangements. Office of the Public Advocate (Vic), Submission No 57 to Joint Standing Committee on the National Disability Insurance Scheme, Parliament of Australia, *Inquiry into Independent Assessments* (29 March 2021) 2.

[25] Office of the Public Advocate (Vic), *'I'm Too Scared To Come out of My Room'* (n 20) 6; Erin Wilson et al (n 22) 14.

[26] Tom Edwards, 'A Disabling Ideology: Challenging the Neoliberal Co-Optation of Independent Living under the NDIS' (2019) 83 *Journal of Australian Political Economy* 32, 38, 48.

[27] Elyse Perry, Rebecca Waters and Angus Buchanan, 'Experiences of National Disability Insurance Scheme Planning from the Perspective of Adults with Intellectual Disability' (2019) 54(3) *The Australian Journal of Social Issues* 210, 212.

> Unfortunately, it can become a justification for 'the lazy state', where government neglects its positive responsibility towards its citizens.[28]

Like Carter, I caution against the privileging of the right to legal capacity, and autonomy as non-interference, over other rights and values. The risks of doing so have revealed themselves in the NDIS, but other examples can be found in the rhetoric of the UK government, in US law reform endeavours, and even in Sweden's social service provision.[29] In 2015, the UN Disability Committee criticised the UK government for violating its treaty obligations in severely cutting back services and benefits to people with disability under the banner of 'welfare reform'.[30] The government responded by 'strongly refuting' the findings, and also criticising the UN Disability Committee for holding an 'outdated view of disability which was patronising and offensive'.[31] This response disingenuously suggests that the provision of much-needed welfare is somehow inherently human-rights-denying and that welfare cut-backs are somehow rights-affirming. The UK government impliedly aligns this argument with the framing of civil-political rights as the only true human rights, and as always requiring restraint and non-interference by the State. And yet inclusive equality as a fundamental human right for people with disability demands that socio-economic disadvantage be addressed to combat prejudice, eliminate stigma and enable participation, by accommodating difference as a matter of human dignity.

Along the same lines are arguments made in several jurisdictions in the US for the introduction of supported decision-making as a measure that will decrease government costs by reducing reliance on guardianship systems.[32] Theodorou '...cautions against overstating the salience of international human rights law in accounting for interest in supported decision-making in the United States', describing how conservatives in Texas hailed its introduction as a move away from big-government and towards cost-savings.[33] These claims are in direct contradiction to the widespread acknowledgement in the disability and human rights literature that effective supported decision-making will require extensive resourcing by the State. They also align with an understanding of human rights as privileging civil–political rights,

28 Carter, 'The Case for Dignity as the Governing Principle in Adult Guardianship' (n 13) 3.

29 See Chapter 2, Section 3.4.1, for description of the Swedish 'god man'.

30 Committee on the Rights of Persons with Disabilities, *Concluding Observations on the Intial Report of the United Kingdom of Great Britain and Northern Ireland*, UN Doc CRPD/C/GBR/CO/1; see also discussion by Theresia Degener and María Gómez-Carrillo de Castro, 'Toward Inclusive Equality: Ten Years of the Human Rights Model of Disability in the Work of the UN Committee on the Rights of Persons with Disabilities' in Franziska Felder, Laura Davy and Rosemary Kayess (eds), *Disability Law and Human Rights* (Palgrave, 2022) 33.

31 Tom Shakespeare, *Disability: The Basics* (Routledge, 2018) 146–7.

32 Kristin Booth Glen, 'Supported Decision-Making from Theory to Practice: Further Reflections on an Intentional Pilot Project' (2020) 13 *Albany Government Law Review* 94, 160–6; Eliana J Theodorou, 'Supported Decision-Making in the Lone-Star State' (2018) 93(4) *New York University Law Review* 973, 981–5.

33 Theodorou (n 32).

especially the right to legal capacity and autonomy as the right to be left alone, and thereby purportedly justify inaction and abnegation of responsibility for some of the most disadvantaged members of our community.

Even in Sweden, known both for its highly developed social safety net and its early moves towards recognition of universal legal capacity, challenges have arisen in service provision.[34] For older adults with dementia, when they refuse much-needed services, neither families nor social workers in local authorities have the authority to make decisions for them. Mattsson and Giertz explain that one consequence of this is that many people do not get the supports to which they are entitled and therefore can live in situations of neglect.[35]

For self-directed support systems to be positioned to uphold the human rights of people with cognitive disability, the right to autonomy as choice and control needs to be reconceived, and the right to equality needs to be reconceived as promoting not identical treatment, but inclusion. Autonomy should not be primarily about the right to be left alone, nor the right to make 'decisions' on zero-sum options. This book argued that autonomy depends on developing competencies through providing socio-economic supports, and on the availability of an adequate range of choices. It argued that personhood can still be acknowledged for those who lack decision-making capability by claiming rights on their behalf in a way that respects their human dignity. It argued that social inclusion will only be achieved if the different and specific needs of adults with disability are recognised, so that differential responses can be made that ensure civil, economic, social, political and cultural inclusion. Article 12 requires supported decision-making but also decision-making by substitutes as a last resort, so as to recognise and claim the interdependent and indivisible human rights of all adults with cognitive disability.

5 CONCLUDING REMARKS

I would like to conclude by acknowledging the abuse and neglect of people with disability that has occurred and that unfortunately continues to occur under guardianship and involuntary treatment regimes, but also outside of these regimes. The aim of this book is not to pit guardianship against supported decision-making or paternalism against autonomy, but to position adults with cognitive disability as subjects of human rights, not just in legislation but in daily practice. Given that the lexicon of human rights has such great purchase in our community and is widely viewed as placing demands of great moral and political urgency, I believe it is important that claims for social justice for people with disability are understood and advocated for in human rights terms.

[34] See Chapter 2, Section 3.4.1.

[35] Titti Mattsson and Lottie Giertz, 'Vulnerability, Law and Dementia: An Interdisciplinary Discussion of Legislation and Practice' (2020) 21(1) *Theoretical Inquiries in Law* 139.

References

Alston, Bruce, 'Towards Supported Decision-Making: Article 12 of the Convention on the Rights of Persons with Disabilities and Guardianship Law Reform' (2017) 35(2) *Law in Context* 21

Alston, Philip, 'Disability and the Covenant on Economic, Social and Cultural Rights' in Theresia Degener and Yolan Koster-Dreese (eds), *Human Rights and Disabled Persons: Essays and Relevant Human Rights Instruments* (Martinus Nijhoff, 1995) 94

Alston, Philip and Gerard Quinn, 'The Nature and Scope of States Parties' Obligations under the International Covenant on Economic, Social and Cultural Rights' (1987) 9(2) *Human Rights Quarterly* 156

Amundson, Ron, 'Against Normal Function' (2000) 31(1) *Studies in the History and Philosophy of Biology and Biomedical Science* 33

Anderson, Elizabeth, 'Animal Rights and the Values of Nonhuman Life' in Cass R Sunstein and Martha C Nussbaum (eds), *Animal Rights: Current Debates and New Directions* (Oxford University Press, 2004) 277

Anthony, Dorothea, 'The Human Rights Principle of Indivisibility and Its Ideological Significance in the Contemporary Age' (PhD Dissertation, University of New South Wales, 2018)

Arduin, Sarah, 'Article 3: General Principles' in Ilias Bantekas, Michael Ashley Stein and Anastasiou Dimitris (eds), *The UN Convention on the Rights of Persons with Disabilities: A Commentary* (Oxford University Press, 2018) 85

Arnadóttir, Oddný Mjöll, 'A Future of Multidimensional Disadvantage Equality' in Oddný Mjöll Arnadóttir and Gerard Quinn (eds), *The UN Convention on the Rights of Persons with Disabilities: European and Scandinavian Perspectives* (Nijhoff, 2009) 41

Arneil, Barbara, 'Disability in Political Theory versus International Practice: Redefining Equality and Freedom' in Barbara Arneil and Nancy J Hirschmann (eds), *Disability and Political Theory* (Cambridge University Press, 2016) 10

Arstein-Kerslake, Anna, 'An Empowering Dependency: Exploring Support for the Exercise of Legal Capacity' (2016) 18 *Scandinavian Journal of Disability Research* 77

Arstein-Kerslake, Anna, *Restoring Voice to People with Cognitive Disabilities: Realizing the Right to Equal Recognition before the Law* (Cambridge University Press, 2017)

Arstein-Kerslake, Anna and Eilionóir Flynn, 'The General Comment on Article 12 of the Convention on the Rights of Persons with Disabilities: A Roadmap for Equality before the Law' (2016) 20(4) *The International Journal of Human Rights* 471

Arstein-Kerslake, Anna et al, 'Future Directions in Supported Decision-Making' (2017) 37(1) *Disability Studies Quarterly*

Ashley, Viv, *Green Paper Technical Report: Philosophical Models of Autonomy* (Essex Autonomy Project 2012) https://autonomy.essex.ac.uk/wp-content/uploads/2016/11/Essex-Autonomy-Project-Philosophical-Models-of-Autonomy-October-2012.pdf

Australian Council of Social Service and University of New South Wales, *Poverty in Australia 2018* (Australian Council of Social Service, in partnership with the University of New South Wales, 2018)

Australian Law Reform Commission, Equality, Capacity and Disability in Commonwealth Laws: A Final Report (Report No 124, August 2014)

Bach, Michael, 'Inclusive Citizenship: Refusing the Construction of "Cognitive Foreigners" in Neo-liberal Times' (2017) 4(1) *Research and Practice in Intellectual and Developmental Disabilities* 4

Bach, Michael and Lana Kerzner, A New Paradigm for Protecting Autonomy and the Right to Legal Capacity: Advancing Substantive Equality for Persons with Disabilities through Law, Policy and Practice (Law Commission of Ontario, October 2010)

Balakrishnan, Rhadhika, James Heintz and Diane Elson, *Rethinking Economic Policy for Social Justice: The Radical Potential of Human Rights* (Routledge, 2016)

Bălan, Sergiu, 'Formal and Substantive Equality of Opportunity' (2012) IV(4) *Cogito* 85

Baldry, Eileen et al, *A Predictable and Preventable Path: Aboriginal People with Mental and Cognitive Disabilities in the Criminal Justice System* (University of New South Wales, 2015)

Barclay, Linda, 'In Sickness and in Dignity: A Philosophical Account of the Meaning of Dignity in Health Care' (2016) 61 *International Journal of Nursing Studies* 136

Barclay, Linda, 'Autonomy and the Social Self' in Catriona Mackenzie and Natalie Stoljar (eds), *Relational Autonomy: Feminist Perspectives on Autonomy, Agency and the Social Self* (Oxford University Press, 2000) 52

Bartlett, Peter, 'The United Nations Convention on the Rights of Persons with Disabilities and Mental Health Law' (2012) 75(5) *The Modern Law Review* 752

Bartlett, Peter, 'Will and Preferences in the Overall CRPD Project' (2019) 18(1) *World Psychiatry: Official Journal of the World Psychiatric Association (WPA)* 48

Beauchamp, Tom L and James F Childress, *Principles of Biomedical Ethics* (Oxford University Press, 6th ed, 2009)

Beaudry, Jonas-Sébastien, 'Beyond (Models of) Disability?' (2016) 41(2) *Journal of Medicine and Philosophy* 210

Beaudry, Jonas-Sébastien, *The Disabled Contract: Severe Intellectual Disability, Justice and Morality* (Cambridge University Press, 2021)

Beaudry, Jonas-Sébastien, 'Theoretical Strategies to Define Disability' in David T Wasserman and Adam Cureton (eds), *The Oxford Handbook of Philosophy and Disability* (Oxford University Press, 2019) DOI: 10.1093/oxfordhb/9780190622879.013.3 2019

Beaudry, Jonas-Sebastien, 'Welcoming Monsters: Disability as a Liminal Legal Concept' (2017) 29(2) *Yale Journal of Law & the Humanities* 291

Becchi, Paolo, 'Human Dignity in Europe: Introduction' in Paolo Becchi and Klaus Mathis (eds), *Handbook of Human Dignity in Europe* (Springer International Publishing, 2019) 1

Bedford, Daniel, 'Human Dignity in Great Britain and Northern Ireland' in Paolo Becchi and Klaus Mathis (eds), *Handbook of Human Dignity in Europe* (Springer Nature Switzerland, 2019) 319

Beitz, Charles R, 'Human Dignity in the Theory of Human Rights: Nothing but a Phrase?' (2013) 41(3) *Philosophy and Public Affairs* 259

Bell, Justice Virginia 'Equality, Proportionality and Dignity: The Guiding Principles for a Just Legal System' (2017) 42(1) *Alternative Law Journal* 4

Berlin, Isaiah, 'Two Concepts of Liberty' in Henry Hardy (ed), *Liberty Incorporating Four Essays on Liberty* (Oxford Scholarship Online, 2002) 166

Beyleveld, Deryck and Roger Brownsword, *Human Dignity in Bioethics and Biolaw* (Oxford University Press, 2001)

Bigby, Christine and Jacinta Douglas, 'Supported Decision Making' in Roger J Stancliffe et al (eds), *Choice, Preference, and Disability: Promoting Self-Determination across the Lifespan* (Springer International Publishing, 2020) 45

Bigby, Christine et al, 'Delivering Decision Making Support to People with Cognitive Disability – What Has Been Learned from Pilot Programs in Australia from 2010 to 2015' (2017) 52(3) *Australian Journal of Social Issues* 222

Bigby, Chris et al, *Diversity, Dignity, Equity and Best practice: A Framework for Supported Decision-making. Royal Commission into Violence, Abuse, Neglect and Exploitation of People with Disability* (2023) https://disability.royalcommission.gov.au/policy-and-research/research-program

Bilchitz, David, 'Dignity, Fundamental Rights and Legal Capacity: Moving beyond the Paradigm Set by the General Comment on Article 12 of the Convention on the Rights of Persons with Disabilities' (2016) 32(3) *South African Journal on Human Rights* 410

Björgvinsson, Davíð Þór, 'The Protection of the Rights of Persons with Disabilities in the Case Law of the European Court of Human Rights' in Oddný Mjöll Arnadóttir and Gerard Quinn (eds), *The UN Convention on the Rights of Persons with Disabilities: European and Scandinavian Perspectives* (Nijhoff, 2009) 141

Boorse, Christopher, 'On the Distinction between Disease and Illness' (1975) 5(1) *Philosophy & Public Affairs* 49

Boorse, Christopher, 'Disability and Medical Theory' in D Christopher Ralston and Justin Ho (eds), *Philosophical Reflections on Disability* (Springer, 2010) 55

Boorse, Christopher, 'Health as a Theoretical Concept' (1977) 44(4) *Philosophy of Science* 542

Boyle, Sam, 'Is the Wisdom of a Person's Decision Relevant to their Capacity to Make That Decision?' (2020) 46(1) *Monash University Law Review* 39

Boyle, Sam, 'Medical Evidence of Capacity in a Legal Setting: To What Extent Do Courts and Tribunals Make Their Own Decisions?' (2018) 25(2) *Journal of Law and Medicine* 572

Broderick, Andrea, 'Article 4: General Obligations' in Ilias Bantekas et al (eds), *The UN Convention on the Rights of Persons with Disability: A Commentary* (Oxford University Press, 2018) 116

Broderick, Andrea, 'Harmonisation and Cross-Fertilisation of Socio-Economic Rights in the Human Rights Treaty Bodies: Disability and the Reasonableness Review Case Study' (2016) 5 *Laws* 38

Broderick, Andrea, *The Long and Winding Road to Equality and Inclusion for Persons with Disabilities: The United Nations Convention on the Rights of Persons with Disabilities* (Intersentia, 2015)

Brolan, Claire E et al, 'The Right to Health of Australians with Intellectual Disability' (2011) 17(2) *Australian Journal of Human Rights* 1

Brown, Rebecca and Janet Lord, 'The Role of Reasonable Accommodation in Securing Substantive Equality for Persons with Disabilities' in Marcia H Rioux, Lee Ann Basser Marks and Melinda Jones (eds), *Critical Perspectives on Human Rights and Disability Law* (Martinus Nijhoff, 2011) 273

Buchanan, Allen E and Dan W Brock, *Deciding for Others: The Ethics of Surrogate Decision Making* (Cambridge University Press, 1989)

Burch, Matthew, 'Autonomy, Respect, and the Rights of Persons with Disabilities in Crisis' (2017) 34(3) *Journal of Applied Philosophy* 389

Byrne, Iain, 'The Importance of Economic, Social and Cultural Rights in Guaranteeing Civil and Political Rights within the Euro-Mediterranean Partnership' (2004) 9(3) *Mediterranean Politics* 344

Cahill, Suzanne, *Dementia and Human Rights* (Policy Press at the University of Bristol, 2018)

Caivano, Nicholas, 'Conceptualizing Capacity: Interpreting Canada's Qualified Ratification of Article 12 of the UN Disability Rights Convention' (2014) 4(1) *Western Journal of Legal Studies* 1

Carbonari, Paulo Câesar, 'Human Dignity as a Basic Concept of Ethics and Human Rights' in Berma Klein Goldewijk, Adalid Contreras Baspiniero and Paulo Câesar Carbonari (eds), *Dignity and Human Rights: The Implementation of Economic, Social and Cultural Rights* (Insentia, 2002) 35

Carlson, Licia, 'Cognitive Ableism and Disability Studies: Feminist Reflections on the History of Mental Retardation' (2001) 16(4) *Hypatia* 124

Carlson, Licia and Eva Feder Kittay, 'Introduction: Rethinking Philosophical Presumptions in the Light of Cognitive Disability' (2009) 40(3–4) *Metaphilosophy* 307

Carney, Terry, 'Participation and Service Access Rights for People with Intellectual Disability: A Role for Law?' (2013) 38 *Journal of Intellectual and Developmental Disability* 59

Carney, Terry, 'Prioritising Supported Decision-Making: Running on Empty or a Basis for Glacial-to-Steady Progress?' (2017) 6(4) *Laws* 18

Carney, Terry, 'Searching for Workable Alternatives to Guardianship for Vulnerable Populations?' (2015) 1(1) *Ethics, Medicine and Public Health* 113

Carney, Terry, 'Supported Decision-Making for People with Cognitive Impairments: An Australian Perspective?' (2015) 4 *Laws* 37

Carney, Terry, 'Supporting People with Cognitive Disability with Decision-Making: Any Australian Law Reform Contributions?' (2015) 2 *Research and Practice in Intellectual and Developmental Disabilities* 6

Carney, Terry and Fleur Beaupert, 'Public and Private Bricolage: Challenges Balancing Law, Services and Civil Society in Advancing the CRPD Supported Decision Making' (2013) 36(1) *University of New South Wales Law Journal* 175

Carney, Terry et al, 'Realising "Will, Preferences and Rights": Reconciling Differences on Best Practice Support for Decision-Making?' (2019) 28(4) *Griffith Law Review* 357

Carozza, Paolo G, 'Human Rights, Human Dignity, and Human Experience' in Christopher McCrudden (ed), *Understanding Human Dignity* (Oxford University Press, 2013) 615

Carter, Barbara, 'Adult Guardianship: Human Rights or Social Justice?' (2010) 18(1) *Journal of Law and Medicine* 122

Carter, Barbara, 'The Case for Dignity as the Governing Principle in Adult Guardianship' (2010) 19(1) *Res Publica* 1

Carter, Barbara, 'Seeking the Essence of Guardianship: Beyond the United Nations Convention on the Rights of Persons with Disabilities' (Conference Paper, World Guardianship Congress, 15–16 October 2012)

Caycho, Renato Antonio Constantino, 'The Flag of Imagination: Peru's New Reform on Legal Capacity for Persons with Intellectual and Psychosocial Disabilities and the Need for New Understandings in Private Law' (2020) 14(June) *The Age of Human Rights Journal* 155

Celik, Elif, 'The Role of CRPD in Rethinking the Subject of Human Rights' (2017) 21(7) *The International Journal of Human Rights* 933

Cera, Rachele, 'Article 2: Definitions' in Valentina Della Fina, Rachele Cera and Giuseppe Palmisano (eds), *The United Nations Convention on the Rights of Persons with Disabilities: A Commentary* (2017) 107

Cera, Rachele, 'Article 5: Equality and Non-Discrimination' in Valentina Della Fina, Rachele Cera and Giuseppe Palmisano (eds), *The United Nations Convention on the Rights of Persons with Disabilities: A Commentary* (Springer International Publishing, 2017) 157

Cera, Rachele, 'Preamble' in Valentina Della Fina, Rachele Cera and Giuseppe Palmisano (eds), *The United Nations Convention on the Rights of Persons with Disabilities: A Commentary* (Springer International Publishing, 2017) 80

Clifford, Jarlath, 'Equality' in Dinah Shelton (ed), *The Oxford Handbook of International Human Rights Law* (Oxford University Press, 2013) 420

Chesterman, John, 'The Future of Adult Guardianship in Australia' (2013) 66(1) *Australian Social Work* 26

Chesterman, John, 'The Review of Victoria's Guardianship Legislation: State Policy Development in an Age of Human Rights' (2010) 69(1) *Australian Journal of Public Administration* 61

Christman, John, 'Autonomy in Moral and Political Philosophy', *The Stanford Encyclopedia of Philosophy* (Fall 2020 Edition), in Edward N Zalta (ed) https://plato.stanford.edu/archives/fall2020/entries/autonomy-moral/

Christman, John, 'Constructing the Inner Citadel: Recent Work on the Concept of Autonomy' (1988) 99(1) *Ethics* 109

Clifton, Shane, *Hierarchies of Power: Disability Theories and Models and Their Implications for Violence against, and Abuse, Neglect, and Exploitation of, People with Disability* (Royal Commission into Violence, Abuse, Neglect and Exploitation of People with Disability, 2020)

Copelon, Rhonda, 'The Indivisible Framework of International Human Rights: A Source of Social Justice in the U.S.' (1998) 3(1) *New York City Law Review* 59

Corsi, Jessica Lynn, 'Article 5: Equality and Non-Discrimination' in Ilias Bantekas et al (eds), *The UN Convention on the Rights of Persons with Disabilities: A Commentary* (Oxford University Press, 2018) 140

Courtis, Christian, 'Standards to Make ESC Rights Justiciable: A Summary of Exploration' (2009) 2 *Erasmus Law Review* 379

Craigie, Jillian et al, 'Legal Capacity, Mental Capacity and Supported Decision-Making: Report from a Panel Event' (2019) 62 *International Journal of Law and Psychiatry* 160

Crary, Alice, 'Cognitive Disability and Moral Status' in David T Wasserman and Adam Cureton (eds), *The Oxford Handbook of Philosophy and Disability* (Oxford University Press, 2018) DOI: 10.1093/oxfordhb/9780190622879.013.40

Crooms, Lisa A, 'Indivisible Rights and Intersectional Identities or, "What Do Women's Human Rights Have to Do with the Race Convention?"' (1997) 40(3) *Howard Law Journal* 619

Daniels, Norman, Susannah Rose and Ellen Daniels Zide, 'Disability, Adaptation and Inclusion' in Kimberley Brownlee and Adam Cureton (eds), *Disability and Disadvantage* (Oxford University Press, 2009) 54

Davy, Laura, 'Philosophical Inclusive Design: Intellectual Disability and the Limits of Individual Autonomy in Moral and Political Theory' (2015) 30(1) *Hypatia* 132

Davy, Laura and Celia Green, 'The Right to Autonomy and the Conditions That Secure It: The Relationship between the UNCRPD and Market-Based Policy Reform' in Franziska Felder, Laura Davy and Rosemary Kayess (eds), *Disability Law and Human Rights* (Palgrave, 2022) 127

Dawson, John, 'A Realistic Approach to Assessing Mental Health Laws' Compliance with the UNCRPD' (2015) 40 *International Journal of Law and Psychiatry* 70

DeBeco, Gauthier, 'The Indivisibility of Human Rights and the Convention on the Rights of Persons with Disabilities' (2019) 68(January) *International and Comparative Law Quarterly* 141

Debes, Remy, 'Dignity's Gauntlet' (2009) 23(1) *Philosophical Perspectives* 45
de Bhailís, Clíona and Eilionóir Flynn, 'Recognising Legal Capacity: Commentary and Analysis of Article 12 CRPD' (2017) 13(1) *International Journal of Law in Context* 6
Degener, Theresia, 'Editor's Foreword' (2017) 13(1) *International Journal of Law in Context* 1
Degener, Theresia, 'A New Human Rights Model of Disability' in Valentina Della Fina, Rachele Cera and Giuseppe Palmisano (eds), *The United Nations Convention on the Rights of Persons with Disabilities: A Commentary* (Springer International Publishing, 2017) 41
Degener, Theresia and Andrew Begg, 'From Invisible Citizens to Agents of Change: A Short History of the Struggle for the Recognition of the Rights of Persons with Disabilities at the United Nations' in Valentina Della Fina, Rachele Cera and Giuseppe Palmisano (eds), *The United Nations Convention on the Rights of Persons with Disabilities: A Commentary* (Springer International Publishing, 2017) 1
Degener, Theresia and María Gómez-Carrillo de Castro, 'Toward Inclusive Equality: Ten Years of the Human Rights Model of Disability in the Work of the UN Committee on the Rights of Persons with Disabilities' in Franziska Felder, Laura Davy and Rosemary Kayess (eds), *Disability Law and Human Rights* (Palgrave, 2022) 33
Della Fina, Valentina, 'Article 4 General Obligations' in Valentina Della Fina, Rachele Cera and Giuseppe Palmisano (eds), *The United Nations Convention on the Rights of Persons with Disabilities: A commentary* (Springer International Publishing, 2017) 149
Del Villar, Katrine, 'Should Supported Decision-Making Replace Substituted Decision-Making? The Convention on the Rights of Persons with Disabilities and Coercive Treatment under Queensland's Mental Health Act 2000' (2015) 4(2) *Laws* 173
Devi, Nandini, 'Supported Decision-Making and Personal Autonomy for Persons with Intellectual Disabilities: Article 12 of the UN Convention on the Rights of Persons with Disabilities' (2013) 41(4) *The Journal of Law, Medicine & Ethics* 792
Dhanda, Amita, 'Constructing a New Human Rights Lexicon: Convention on the Rights of Persons with Disabilities' (2008) 8 *Sur – Revista Internacional de Direitos Humanos* 43
Dhanda, Amita, 'Conversations between the Proponents of the New Paradigm of Legal Capacity' (2017) 13(1) *International Journal of Law in Context* 87
Dhanda, Amita, 'From Duality to Indivisibility: Mental Health Care and Human Rights' (2016) 32(3) *South African Journal on Human Rights* 438
Dhanda, Amita, 'Legal Capacity in the Disability Rights Convention: Stranglehold of the Past or Lodestar of the Future' (2007) 34 *Syracuse Journal of International Law and Commerce* 429
Dhanda, Amita and Gabor Gombos, 'Questions of Criminal Culpability and Persons with Disabilities' in Eilionoir Flynn, Anna Arstein-Kerslake, Clíona De BhailíS and Maria Laura Serra (eds), *Global Perspectives on Legal Capacity Reform: Our Voices, our Stories* (Routledge, 2018) 32
Diamond, Cora, 'Eating Meat and Eating People' in Cass R Sunstein and Martha C Nussbaum (eds), *Animal Rights: Current Debates and New Directions* (Oxford Scholarship Online, 2012) DOI: 10.1093/acprof:oso/9780195305104.001.0001
Dicke, Klaus, 'The Founding Function of Human Dignity in the Universal Declaration of Human Rights' in Eckart Klein and David Kretzmer (eds), *The Concept of Human Dignity in Human Rights Discourse* (Kluwer Law International, 2002) 111
Dinerstein, Robert D, 'Implementing Legal Capacity under Article 12 of the UN Convention on the Rights of Persons with Disabilities: The Difficult Road from Guardianship to Supported Decision-Making' (2012) 19(2) *Human Rights Brief* 8

Dodds, Susan, 'Choice and Control in Feminist Bioethics' in Catriona Mackenzie and Natalie Stoljar (eds), *Relational Autonomy: Feminist Perspectives on Autonomy, Agency and the Social Self* (Oxford University Press, 2000) 213

Dodds, Susan, 'Depending on Care: Recognition of Vulnerability and the Social Contribution of Care Provision' (2017) 21(9) *Bioethics* 500

Donnelly, Jack, *Universal Human Rights in Theory and Practice* (Cornell University Press, 3rd ed, 2013)

Donnelly, Mary, 'Best Interests in the Mental Capacity Act: Time to Say Goodbye?' (2016) 24 *Medical Law Review* 318

Donnelly, Mary, 'Deciding in Dementia: The Possibilities and Limits of Supported Decision-Making' (2019) 66 *International Journal of Law and Psychiatry* 101466

Donnelly, Mary, 'From Autonomy to Dignity: Treatment for Mental Disorders and the Focus for Patient Rights' (2008) 26(2) *Law in Context* 37

Donnelly, Mary, *Healthcare Decision-Making and the Law: Autonomy, Capacity and the Limits of Liberalism* (Cambridge University Press, 2010)

Douglas, Jacinta et al, 'Factors That Underpin the Delivery of Effective Decision-Making Support for People with Cognitive Disability' (2015) 2(1) *Research and Practice in Intellectual and Developmental Disabilities* 37

Douzinas, Costas, *The End of Human Rights: Critical Legal Thought at the Turn of the Century* (Hart, 2000)

Doyle, Suzanne and Eilionóir Flynn, 'Ireland's Ratification of the UN Convention on the Rights of Persons with Disabilities: Challenges and Opportunities' (2013) 41(3) *British Journal of Learning Disabilities* 171

Duffy, Julia, 'What If Britney Spears Lived in Australia? Disrupting the Binary Framing of Guardianship versus Supported Decision-Making' (forthcoming 2023) 30 *Transnational Law and Contemporary Problems*

Duffy, Julia, Sam Boyle and Katrine Del Villar, 'What Does 'Least Restrictive or 'Less Restrictive' Mean in Mental Health Law? Contradictions and Confusion in the Case of Queensland, Australia' (forthcoming 2023, symposium issue) *American Journal of Law and Medicine*

Duffy, Julia and Kelly Unsworth, 'Supported Decision-Making, Legal Risk and Commercial Uncertainty' (Conference Paper, Australian Guardianship and Administration Council National Conference: Reflecting Will and Preference in Decision-Making, 17–18 October 2016)

Dupre, Catherine, 'Constructing the Meaning of Human Dignity: Four Questions' in Christopher McCrudden (ed), *Understanding Human Dignity* (Oxford University Press, 2013) 113

Düwell, Marcus, 'Setting the Agenda for Ethical Debates about the Rights of Persons with Disabilities' in Joel Andersen and Jos Philips (eds), *Disability and Universal Human Rights: Legal, Ethical, and Conceptual Implications of the Convention on the Rights of Persons with Disabilities* (Netherlands Institute of Human Rights, 2012) 185

Dworkin, Gerald, *The Theory and Practice of Autonomy* (Cambridge University Press, 1998)

Edwards, Tom, 'A Disabling Ideology: Challenging the Neoliberal Co-Optation of Independent Living under the NDIS' (2019) 83 *Journal of Australian Political Economy* 32

Erevelles, Nirmala, *Disability and Difference in Global Contexts: Enabling a Transformative Body Politic* (Macmillan, 2011)

Ettinson, Adam, 'What's so Special about Human Dignity?' (2020) 48(4) *Philosophy and Public Affairs* 353

Felder, Franziska, 'What Does the CRPD Tell Us about being Human?' in Franziska Felder, Laura Davy and Rosemary Kayess (eds), *Disability Law and Human Rights: Theory and Policy* (Palgrave, 2022) 47

Feldman, David, 'Human Dignity as a Legal Value' (Pt 1) [1999] *Public Law* 682

Feldman, David, 'Human Dignity as a Legal Value' (Pt 2) [2000] *Public Law* 61

Fineman, Martha, 'Beyond Identities: The Limits of an Anti-Discrimination Approach to Equality' (2012) 92(6) *Boston University Law Review* 1713

Flóvenz, Brynhildur G, 'The Implementation of the UN Convention and the Development of Economical and Social Rights as Human Rights' in Oddný Mjöll Arnadóttir and Gerard Quinn (eds), *The UN Convention on the Rights of Persons with Disabilities: European and Scandinavian Perspectives* (Martinus Nijhoff, 2009) 257

Flynn, Eilionóir, 'The Rejection of Capacity Assessments in Favor of Respect for Will and Preferences: The Radical Promise of the UN Convention on the Rights of Persons with Disabilities' (2019) 18(1) *World Psychiatry* 50

Flynn, Eilionoir and Anna Arstein-Kerslake, 'Legislating Personhood: Realising the Right to Support in Exercising Legal Capacity' (2014) 10(1) *International Journal of Law in Context* 81

Flynn, Eilionóir and Anna Arstein-Kerslake, 'State Intervention in the Lives of People with Disabilities: The Case for a Disability-Neutral Framework' (2017) 13(1) *International Journal of Law in Context* 39

Flynn, Eilionóir and Anna Arstein-Kerslake, 'The Support Model of Legal Capacity: Fact, Fiction, or Fantasy?' (2014) 32(1) *Berkeley Journal of International Law* 124

Formosa, Paul and Catriona Mackenzie, 'Nussbaum, Kant, and the Capabilities Approach to Dignity' (2014) 17(5) *Ethical Theory and Moral Practice* 875

Foster, Charles, *Choosing Life, Choosing Death: The Tyranny of Autonomy in Medical Ethics and Law* (Hart Publishing, 2009)

Foster, Charles, *Human Dignity in Bioethics and Law* (Hart Publishing, 2011)

Francis, Leslie Pickering, 'Supported Decision-Making: The CRPD, Non-Discrimination, and Strategies for Recognizing Persons' Choices about their Good' (2021) 1 *The Journal of Philosophy of Disability* 57

Francis, Leslie Pickering, 'Understanding Autonomy in Light of Intellectual Disability' in Kimberley Brownlee and Adam Cureton (eds), *Disability and Disadvantage* (Oxford University Press, 2009) 200

Francis, Leslie Pickering, Barbara E Bierer and Michael Ashley Stein, 'An Externalist, Process-Based Approach to Supported Decision-Making' (2022) 22(10) *The American Journal of Bioethics* 55

Francis, Leslie Pickering and Anita Silvers, 'Thinking about the Good: Reconfiguring Liberal Metaphysics (or Not) for People with Cognitive Disabilities' in Eva Feder Kittay and Licia Carlson (eds), *Cognitive Disability and the Challenge to Moral Philosophy* (2010) 237

Frankfurt, Harry, 'Freedom of the Will and the Concept of a Person' (1971) 68 (1) *Journal of Philosophy* 5

Fredman, Sandra, *Discrimination Law* (Oxford University Press, 2nd ed, 2011)

Fredman, Sandra, *Human Rights Transformed: Positive Rights and Positive Duties* (Oxford University Press, 2008)

Freeman, Melvyn Colin et al, 'Reversing Hard Won Victories in the Name of Human Rights: A Critique of the General Comment on Article 12 of the UN Convention on the Rights of Persons with Disabilities' (2015) 2(9) *The Lancet Psychiatry* 844

Friedman, Marilyn, 'Autonomy, Social Disruption and Women' in Catriona Mackenzie and Natalie Stoljar (eds), *Relational Autonomy: Feminist Perspectives on Autonomy, Agency and the Social Self* (Oxford University Press, 2000) 35

Gaita, Raimond, *A Common Humanity: Thinking about Love & Truth & Justice* (Text Pub, 2nd ed, 2000)

Galderisi, Silvana, 'The UN Convention on the Rights of Persons with Disabilities: Great Opportunities and Dangerous Interpretations' (2019) 18(1) *World Psychiatry* 47

Gavison, Ruth, 'On the Relationships between Civil and Political Rights, and Social and Economic Rights' in Jean-Marc Coicaud, Michael W Doyle and Anne-Marie Gardner (eds), *The Globalization of Human Rights* (United Nations University Press, 2003) 23

Gearty, Conor, 'Socio-Economic Rights, Basic Needs, and Human Dignity: A Perspective from the Law's Frontline' in Christopher McCrudden (ed), *Understanding Human Dignity* (Oxford University Press, 2013) 155

Gilabert, Pablo, 'Human Rights, Human Dignity and Power' in Rowan Cruft, S Mattthew Liao and Massimo Renzo (eds), *Philosophical Foundations of Human Rights* (Oxford University Press, 2015) 196

Gilabert, Pablo, 'The Importance of Linkage Arguments for the Theory and Practice of Human Rights: A Response to James Nickel' (2010) 32(2) *Human Rights Quarterly* 425

Gilligan, Carol, *In a Different Voice: Psychological Theory and Women's Development* (Harvard University Press, 1993)

Glen, Kristin Booth, 'Changing Paradigms: Mental Capacity, Legal Capacity, Guardianship and Beyond' (2012) 44 *Columbia Human Rights Law Review* 93

Glen, Kristin Booth, 'Introducing a New Human Right: Learning from Others, Bringing Legal Capacity Home' (2018) 49(3) *Columbia Human Rights Law Review* 1

Glen, Kristin Booth, 'Piloting Personhood: Reflections from the First Year of a Supported Decision-Making Project' (2017) 39(2) *Cardozo Law Review* 495

Glen, Kristin Booth, 'Supported Decision-Making from Theory to Practice: Further Reflections on an Intentional Pilot Project' (2020) 13 *Albany Government Law Review* 94

Goldschmidt, Jenny E, 'New Perspectives on Equality: Towards Transformative Justice through the Disability Convention?' (2017) 35 *Nordic Journal of Human Rights* 1

Gooding, Piers, 'Supported Decision-Making: A Rights-Based Disability Concept and Its Implications for Mental Health Law' (2013) 20(3) *Psychiatry, Psychology and Law* 431

Gooding, Piers et al, 'Unfitness to Stand Trial and the Indefinite Detention of Persons with Cognitive Disabilities in Australia: Human Rights Challenges and Proposals for Change' (2017) 40 *Melbourne University Law Review* 816

Gooding, Piers and Eilionóir Flynn, 'Querying the Call to Introduce Mental Capacity Testing to Mental Health Law: Does the Doctrine of Necessity Provide an Alternative?' (2015) 4(2) *Laws* 245

Govender, Venitia, 'Economic, Social and Cultural Rights in South Africa: Entitlements, Not Mere Policy Options' in Berma Klein Goldewijk, Adalid Contreras Baspineiro and Paulo Câesar Carbonari (eds) *Dignity and Human Rights: The Implementation of Economic, Social and Cultural Rights* (Intersentia 2002) 75

Grant, Evadné, 'Dignity and Equality' (2007) 7(2) *Human Rights Law Review* 299

Grant, Evadné, 'Human Dignity and Socio-Economic Rights' (2012) 33(3) *Liverpool Law Review* 235

Gurbai, Sándor, 'Beyond the Pragmatic Definition? The Right to Non-Discrimination of Persons with Disabilities in the Context of Coercive Interventions' (2020) 22(1) *Health and Human Rights Journal* 279

Hale, Brenda, 'Dignity' (2009) 31(2) *Journal of Social Welfare and Family Law* 101

Hall, Margaret, 'Rethinking Adult Guardianship: Mental Capacity and Vulnerability in the Context of Dementia in Old Age' (PhD Thesis, University of British Columbia, 2018).

Hall, Margaret Isabel, 'Mental Capacity in the (Civil) Law: Capacity, Autonomy, and Vulnerability' (2012) 58(1) *McGill Law Journal — Revue de Droit de McGill* 61

Hall, Margaret Isabel 'Putting the Pieces Together: Article 12, 'Safeguarding' and the Right to Legal Capacity' in Mary Donelly, Rosie Harding and Ezgi Tascioglu (eds), *Supporting Legal Capacity in Socio-Legal Context* (Hart Publishing 2022) 273

Hall, Margaret Isabel, 'Relational Autonomy, Vulnerability Theory, Older Adults and the Law: Making It Real' (2019) 12(1) *Elder Law Review* [i]

Hamlyn, Victoria, 'The Indivisibility of Human Rights: Economic, Social and Cultural Rights and the European Convention on Human Rights' (2008) 40 *Bracton Law Journal* 13

Harding, Rosie, 'Equality, Social Justice and Older People' in Israel Doron and Nena Georgantzi (eds), *Ageing, Ageism and the Law: European Perspectives on the Rights of Older Persons* (Edward Elgar Publishing, 2019) 15

Harding, Rosie, 'Supporting Everyday Legal Capacity: Navigating the Complexities of Putting Rights into Practice' in Mary Donnelly, Rosie Harding and Ezgi Tascioglu (eds), *Supporting Legal Capacity in Socio-Legal Context* (Hart Publishing, 2022) 291.

Harnacke, Caroline, 'Capability and Disability: The CRPD from the Perspective of the Capabilities Approach' in Joel Andersen and Jos Philips (eds), *Disability and Human Rights: Legal, Ethical, and Conceptual Implications of the Convention on the Rights of Persons with Disabilities* (Netherlands Institute of Human Rights, 2012) 167

Harpur, Paul, 'The Evolving Nature of the Right to Life: The Impact of Positive Human Rights Obligations' (2007) 9 *University of Notre Dame Australia Law Review* 95

Harpur, Paul and Heather Douglas, 'Disability and Domestic Violence: Protecting Survivors' Human Rights' (2014) 23(3) *Griffith Law Review* 405

Hartley, Christie, 'An Inclusive Contractualism: Obligations to the Mentally Disabled' in Kimberley Brownlee and Adam Cureton (eds), *Disability and Disadvantage* (Oxford University Press, 2009) 138

Held, Virginia, *The Ethics of Care: Personal, Political, Global* (Oxford University Press, 2006)

Henrard, Kristin, 'Introduction: The Justiciability of ESC Rights and the Interdependence of All Fundamental Rights' (2009) 2(4) *Erasmus Law Review* 373

Herring, Jonathan, *Caring and the Law* (Hart Publishing, 2013)

Herring, Jonathan, 'Elder Abuse: A Human Rights Agenda for the Future' in Israel Doron and Ann M Soden (eds), *Beyond Elder Law* (Springer-Verlag, 2012) 175

Herring, Jonathan and Jesse Wall, 'Autonomy, Capacity and Vulnerable Adults: Filling the Gaps in the Mental Capacity Act' (2015) 35(4) *Legal Studies* 698

Hirschmann, Nancy J, 'Disability Rights, Social Rights, and Freedom' (2016) 12(1) *Journal of International Political Theory* 42

Ho, Anita, 'Relational Autonomy or Undue Pressure? Family's Role in Medical Decision-Making' (2008) 22(1) *Scandinavian Journal of Caring Sciences* 128

Holness, Willene, 'Equal Recognition and Legal Capacity for Persons with Disabilities: Incorporating the Principle of Proportionality' (2014) 30(2) *South African Journal on Human Rights* 313

Inclusion Europe, *Key Elements of a System of Supported Decision-Making* (Position Paper, 2018) http://inclusion-Europe.org/images/stories/documents/PositionPapers/Position_Supported_Decision_Making_EN.pdf

International Disability Alliance, *Legal Opinion on Article 12 of the CRPD* disability-studies.leeds.ac.uk/wp-content/uploads/sites/40/library/legal-opinion-LegalOpinion-Art12-FINAL.pdf, 2008

Jackman, Martha and Bruce Porter, 'Social and Economic Rights' in Peter Oliver, Patrick Macklem and Nathalie Des Rosiers (eds), *The Oxford Handbook of the Canadian Constitution* (Oxford University Press, 2017) 843

Jones, Melinda, 'Inclusion, Social Inclusion and Participation' in Marcia H Rioux, Lee Ann Basser Marks and Melinda Jones (eds), *Critical Perspectives on Human Rights and Disability Law* (Martinus Nijhoff, 2011) 57

Kahneman, Daniel, *Thinking, Fast and Slow* (Farrar, Strauss and Giroux, 2011)

Kakoullis, Emily Julia and Yoshikazu Ikehara, 'Article 1: Purpose' in Ilias Bantekas et al (eds), *The UN Convention on the Rights of Persons with Disabilities: A Commentary* (Oxford University Press, 2018) 35

Kallehauge, Holger, 'General Themes Relevant to the Implementation of the UN Disability Convention into Domestic Law: Who Is Responsible for the Implementation and How Should It Be Performed?' in Oddný Mjöll Arnadóttir and Gerard Quinn (eds), *The UN Convention on the Rights of Persons with Disabilities: European and Scandinavian perspectives* (Nijhoff, 2009) 201

Kant, Immanuel, 'Groundwork to a Metaphysics of Morals' in Pauyl Menzer (ed), *Critique of Pure Reason* (Academy of Sciences, 1785) vol 4, 387

Kanter, Arlene S, *The Development of Disability Rights under International Law from Charity to Human Rights* (Routledge, 2015)

Kayess, Rosemary and Ben Fogarty, 'The Rights and Dignity of Persons with Disabilities' (2007) 32(1) *Alternative Law Journal* 22

Kayess, Rosemary and Philip French, 'Out of Darkness into Light? Introducing the Convention on the Rights of Persons with Disabilities' (2008) 8(1) *Human Rights Law Review* 1

Kayess, Rosemary and Therese Sands, *Convention on the Rights of Persons with Disabilities: Shining a Light on Social Transformation* (UNSW Social Policy Research Centre, 2020)

Keys, Mary, 'Article 12' in Valentina Della Fina, Rachele Cera and Giuseppe Palmisano (eds), *The United Nations Convention on the Rights of Persons with Disabilities: A Commentary* (Springer International Publishing, 2017) 263

Killmister, Suzy, 'Dignity: Personal, Social, Human' (2017) 174(8) *Philosophical Studies* 2063

Killmister, Suzy, 'Disability, Respect and Cognitive Disability' in David T Wasserman and Adam Steven Cureton (eds), *The Oxford Handbook of Philosophy and Disability* (2018)

Kilner, John F, 'Human Dignity' in Stephen G Post (ed), *Encyclopedia of Bioethics* (Macmillan Reference USA, 3rd ed, 2004) vol 2, 1193

King, Michelle, 'Dedifferentiation and Difference: People with Profound Intellectual and Multiple Disabilities and the National Disability Insurance Scheme (NDIS)' (2020) 45(4) *Journal of Intellectual & Developmental Disability* 320

Kingma, Elselijn, 'What Is It to Be Healthy? (Boorse's Biostatistical Theory)' (2007) 67(2) *Analysis* 128

Kittay, Eva Feder, 'At the Margins of Moral Personhood' (2005) 116(1) *Ethics* 100

Kittay, Eva Feder, 'Equality, Dignity and Disability' in Mary Ann Lyons and Fionnuala Waldron (eds), *Perspectives on Equality: The Second Seamus Heaney Lectures* (Liffey Press, 2005) 93

Kittay, Eva Feder, 'The Personal Is Philosophical Is Political: A Philosopher and Mother of a Cognitively Disabled Person Sends Notes from the Battlefield' (2009) 40(3–4) *Metaphilosophy* 606

Knight, Amber, 'Democratizing Disability: Achieving Inclusion (without assimilation) through "Participatory Parity"' (2015) 30(1) *Hypatia* 97

Koch, Ida Elisabeth, 'Economic, Social and Cultural Rights as Components in Civil and Political Rights: A Hermeneutic Perspective' (2006) 10(4) *International Journal of Human Rights* 405

Koch, Ida Elisabeth, 'From Invisibility to Indivisibility: The International Convention on the Rights of Persons with Disabilities' in Oddný Mjöll Arnadóttir and Gerard Quinn (eds), *The UN Convention on the Rights of Persons with Disabilities: European and Scandinavian Perspectives* (Nijhoff, 2009) 67

Koch, Ida Elisabeth, 'Social Rights as Components in the Civil Right to Personal Liberty: Another Step Forward in the Integrated Human Rights Approach?' (2002) 20(1) *Netherlands Quarterly of Human Rights* 29

Kong, Camillia, 'The Convention on the Rights of Persons with Disabilities and Article 12: Prospective Feminist Lessons against the "Will and Preferences" Paradigm' (2015) 4(4) *Laws* 709

Kong, Camillia, *Mental Capacity in Relationship: Decision-Making, Dialogue and Autonomy* (Cambridge University Press, 2017)

Law Commission, *Mental Capacity and Deprivation of Liberty* (Report No 372, 2017)

Law Commission, *Mental Incapacity* (Report No 231, 1995)

Lawson, Anna, 'The Human Rights Act 1998 and Disabled People: A Right to be Human?' in Colin Harvey (ed), *Human Rights in the Community: Rights as Agents for Change* (Hart Publishing, 2005) 135

Lawson, Anna, 'The UN Convention on the Rights of Persons with Disabilities and European Disability Law: A Catalyst for Cohesion?' in Oddný Mjöll Arnadóttir and Gerard Quinn (eds), *The UN Convention on the Rights of Persons with Disabilities: European and Scandinavian Perspectives* (Nijhoff, 2009) 81

Lawson, Anna, 'The United Nations Convention on the Rights of Persons with Disabilities: New Era or False Dawn?' (2007) 34(2) *Syracuse International Journal of Law and Commerce* 563

Lawson, Anna and Mark Priestley, 'The Social Model of Disability: Questions for Law and Legal Scholarship?' in Peter Blanck and Eilionoir Flynn (eds), *Routledge Handbook of Disability Law and Human Rights* (Routledge, 2016) 3

Laycock, Angela, 'Price v UK: The Importance of Human Rights Principles in Promoting the Rights of Disabled Prisoners in the United Kingdom' in Marcia H Rioux, Lee Ann Basser Marks and Melinda Jones (eds), *Critical Perspectives on Human Rights and Disability Law* (Martinus Nijhoff Publishers, 2011) 201

Liebenberg, Sandra, 'The Value of Human Dignity in Interpreting Socio-Economic Rights' (2005) 21(1) *South African Journal on Human Rights* 1

Lipp, Volker and Julian O Winn, 'Guardianship and Autonomy: Foes or Friends?' (2011) 5 *Journal of International Aging, Law & Policy* 41

Lord, Janet E, 'Preamble' in Ilias Bantekas, MA Stein and Dēmētrēs Anastasiou (eds), *The UN Convention on the Rights of Persons with Disabilities: A Commentary* (Oxford University Press, 2018) 1

Marks, Stephen P, 'The Past and Future of the Separation of Human Rights into Categories' (2009) 24 *Maryland Journal of International Law* 209

Marsh, Pauline and Lisa Kelly, 'Dignity of Risk in the Community: A Review of and Reflections on the Literature' (2018) 20 (5–6) *Health, Risk & Society* 297

Martin, Wayne et al, Achieving CRPD Compliance: Is the Mental Capacity Act of England and Wales Compatible with the UN Convention on the Rights of Persons with Disabilities? If Not, What Next? (An Essex Autonomy Project Position Paper, 22 September, 2014) EAP Position Paper FINAL copy (essex.ac.uk)

Martin, Wayne et al, *Three Jurisdictions Report: Towards Compliance with CRPD Article 12 in Capacity/Incapacity Legislation across the UK* (An Essex Autonomy Project Position Paper, 6 June 2016) EAP 3J Final Report revised (essex.ac.uk)

Martiniez-Pujalte, Antonio, 'Legal Capacity and Supported Decision-Making: Lessons from Some Recent Legal Reforms' (2019) 8(1) *Laws* 4

Mackenzie, Catriona and Natalie Stoljar, 'Introduction: Autonomy Reconfigured' in Catriona Mackenzie and Natalie Stoljar (eds), *Relational Autonomy: Feminist Perspectives on Autonomy, Agency and the Social Self* (Oxford University Press, 2000) 3

Mattsson, Titti and Lottie Giertz, 'Vulnerability, Law and Dementia: An Interdisciplinary Discussion of Legislation and Practice' (2020) 21(1) *Theoretical Inquiries in Law* 139

Mayessa, Amsalu Darge, 'Overview of the Notion of Integration of Human Rights: Giving Pragmatic Value to Socio-Economic Rights Rather Than Rim Service' (2014) 83 *Nordic Journal of International Law* 168

McCallum, Ron, *The United Nations Convention on the Rights of Persons with Disabilities: An Assessment of Australia's Level of Compliance* (Royal Commission into Violence, Abuse, Neglect and Exploitation of People with Disability, 2020)

McCrary, Lorraine Krall, 'Hannah Arendt and Disability: Natality and the Right to Inhabit the World' in Barbara Arneil and Nancy J Hirschmann (eds), *Disability and Political Theory* (Cambridge University Press, 2016) 198

McCrudden, Christopher, 'Human Dignity and Judicial Interpretation of Human Rights' (2008) 19(4) *European Journal of International Law* 655

McCrudden, Christopher, 'In Pursuit of Human Dignity: An Introduction to the Current Debates' in Christopher McCrudden (ed), *Understanding Human Dignity* (Oxford University Press, 2013) 1

McMahan, Jeff, 'Radical Cognitive Limitation' in Kimberley Brownlee and Adam Cureton (eds), *Disability and Disadvantage* (Oxford University Press, 2018) 240

McSherry, Bernadette, 'Legal Capacity under the Convention on the Rights of Persons with Disabilities' (2012) 20 *Journal of Law and Medicine* 22

McSherry, Bernadette and Penelope Weller, 'Rethinking Rights-Based Mental Health Laws' in Bernadette McSherry and Penelope Weller (eds), *Rethinking Rights-Based Mental Health Laws* (Bloomsbury Publishing, 2010) 6

Mégret, Frédéric, 'The Disabilities Convention: Towards a Holistic Concept of Rights' (2008) 12(2) *International Journal of Human Rights* 261

Meyers, Diana, *Self, Society and Personal Choice* (Columbia University Press, 1989)

Michael, Lucy, 'Defining Dignity and Its Place in Human Rights' (2014) 20(1) *The New Bioethics* 12

Mill, John Stuart, *On Liberty* (Routledge, 1991)

Miller, Sarah Clark, 'Reconsidering Dignity Relationally' (2017) 11(2) *Ethics and Social Welfare* 108

Minkowitz, Tina, 'Legal Capacity: Fundamental to the Rights of Persons with Disabilities' (2007) 56(1) *International Rehabilitation Review* 25

Minkowitz, Tina et al, 'Advancing the Rights of Users and Survivors of Psychiatry Using the UN Convention on the Rights of Persons with Disabilities: An Interview with Tina Minkowitz' in Helen Spandler, Jill Anderson and Bob Sapey (eds), *Madness, Distress and the Politics of Disablement* (Bristol University Press; Policy Press, 2015) 171

Mitra, Sophie, 'The Capability Approach to Disability' (2006) 16(4) *Journal of Disability Policy Studies* 236

Morris, Jenny, 'Impairment and Disability: Constructing an Ethics of Care That Promotes Human Rights' (2001) 16(4) *Hypatia* 1

Morrissey, Fiona, 'The United Nations Convention on the Rights of Persons with Disabilities: A New Approach to Decision-Making in Mental Health Law' (2012) 19 *European Journal of Health Law* 423

Mosissa, Getahun A, *A Re-examination of Economic, Social and Cultural Rights in a Political Society in the Light of the Principle of Human Dignity* (Intersentia, 2020)

National Disability Insurance Agency, National Disability Insurance Scheme Consultation Paper: Supporting You to Make Your Own Decisions (2021)

Nay, Rhonda, 'The Dignity of Risk' (2002) 9 *The Australian Nursing Journal* 33

Neal, Mary, 'Respect for Human Dignity as "Substantive Basic Norm"' (2014) 10(1) *International Journal of Law in Context* 26

Nedelsky, Jennifer, *Law's Relations: A Relational Theory of Self, Autonomy, and the Law* (Oxford University Press, 2012)

New South Wales Law Reform Commission, *Review of the Guardianship Act 1987* (Report No 145, May 2018)

Nickel, James W, 'Rethinking Indivisibility: Towards a Theory of Supporting Relations between Human Rights' (2008) 30(4) *Human Rights Quarterly* 984

Nicki, Andrea, 'The Abused Mind: Feminist Theory, Psychiatric Disability and Trauma' (2001) 16(4) *Hypatia* 80

Nilsson, Anna, 'Article 2: Definitions' in Ilias Bantekas, Michael Ashley Stein and Dēmētrēs Anastasiou (eds), *The UN Convention on the Rights of Persons with Disabilities: A Commentary* (Oxford University Press, 2018) 63

Nussbaum, Martha C, 'Beyond the Social Contract: Toward Global Justice', *The Tanner Lectures on Human Values* (2003)

Nussbaum, Martha, *Creating Capabilities: The Human Development Approach* (Harvard University Press, 2011)

Nussbaum, Martha C, *Frontiers of Justice Disability, Nationality, Species Membership* (Harvard University Press, 2009)

O'Cinneide, Colm, 'Extracting Protection for the Rights of Persons with Disabilities from Human Rights Frameworks: Established Limits and New Possibilities' in Oddný Mjöll Arnadóttir and Gerard Quinn (eds), *The UN Convention on the Rights of Persons with Disabilities: European and Scandinavian Perspectives* (Nijhoff, 2009) 163

Office of the Public Advocate (Qld), Decision-Making Support and Queensland's Guardianship System: A Systemic Advocacy Report (A Systemic Advocacy Report, April 2016)

Office of the Public Advocate (Qld), Submission No 73 to Senate Standing Committee on Community Affairs, Parliament of Australia, *Inquiry into Violence, Abuse and Neglect against People with Disability in Institutional and Residential Settings, Including the Gender and Age Related Dimensions, and the Particular Situation of Aboriginal and Torres Strait Islander People with Disability, and Culturally and Linguistically Diverse People with Disability* (June 2015)

Office of the Public Advocate (Qld), Upholding the Right to Life and Health: A Review of the Deaths in Care of People with Disability in Queensland (A Systemic Advocacy Report, February 2016)

Office of the Public Advocate (Vic), 'I'm Too Scared to Come out of My Room': Preventing and Responding to Violence and Abuse between Co-Residents in Group Homes (Research Report, 2019)

Office of the Public Advocate (Vic), Submission No 57 to Joint Standing Committee on the National Disability Insurance Scheme, Parliament of Australia *Inquiry into Independent Assessments* (29 March 2021)

O'Neill, Nick, 'From Parens Patriae to Advance Personal Planning – Guardianship in Australia 1824–2016' (Conference Paper, Australian Guardianship and Administration

Council National Conference: Reflecting Will and Preference in Decision-Making, 17–18 October, 2016)

O'Neill, Nick and Carmel Peisah, 'Beware the New Paternalisms: Capacity as a Means of Achieving the Goals of the Convention on the Rights of Persons with Disabilities' (Conference Paper, World Guardianship Congress, 15–16 October 2012)

Oshana, Marina, 'Personal Autonomy and Society' (1998) 29(1) *Journal of Social Philosophy* 81

Owen, Frances and Gillian MacKinnon, 'The Right to Community Living' in Dorothy Griffiths, Frances Owen and Shelley L Watson (eds), *The Human Rights Agenda for Persons with Intellectual Disabilities* (NADD, 2012) 39

Parfit, Derek, *On What Matters: Volume One* (Oxford University Press, 2011)

Parker, Malcolm, 'Getting the Balance Right: Conceptual Considerations Concerning Legal Capacity and Supported Decision-Making' (2016) 13(3) *Journal of Bioethical Inquiry* 381

Parsons, Craig, 'The Dignity of Risk: Challenges in Moving On' (2008) 15(9) *The Australian Nursing Journal* 28

Penson, William J, 'Unsettling Impairment: Mental Health and the Social Model of Disability' in Helen Spandler, Jill Anderson and Bob Sapey (eds), *Madness, Distress and the Politics of Disablement* (Bristol University Press, 2015) 57

Perlin, Michael, 'Understanding the Intersection between International Human Rights and Mental Disability Law: The Role of Dignity' in Bruce Arrigo and Heather Bersot (eds), *Routledge Handbook of International Crime and Justice Studies* (Routledge, 2013) 191

Perry, Elyse, Rebecca Waters and Angus Buchanan, 'Experiences of National Disability Insurance Scheme Planning from the Perspective of Adults with Intellectual Disability' (2019) 54(3) *The Australian Journal of Social Issues* 210

Perske, Robert, 'The Dignity of Risk' in Wolf Wolfensberger et al, *Principles of Normalization in Human Services* (National Institute of Mental Retardation, 1972) 194

Pinheiro, Lucas G, 'The Ableist Contract: Intellectual Disability and the Limits of Justice in Kant's Political Thought' in Barbara Arneil and Nancy J Hirschmann (eds), *Disability and Political Theory* (Cambridge University Press, 2016) 43

Plumb, Anne, 'UN Convention on the Rights of Persons with Disabilities: Out of the Frying Pan into the Fire? Mental Health Service Users and Survivors Aligning with the Disability Movement' in Helen Spandler, Jill Anderson and Bob Sapey (eds), *Madness, Distress and the Politics of Disablement* (Bristol University Press, 2015) 183

Price, Margaret, 'The Bodymind Problem and the Possibilities of Pain' (2015) 30(1) *Hypatia* 268

Puta-Chekwe, Chisanga and Nora Flood, 'From Division to Integration: Economic, Social and Cultural Rights as Basic Human Rights' in Isfahan Merali and Valerie Oosterveld (eds), *Giving Meaning to Economic, Social, and Cultural Rights* (University of Pennsylvania Press, 2001) 39

Queensland Law Reform Commission, *A Review of Queensland's Guardianship Laws* (Report No67, September 2010)

Quinn, Gerard, 'Concept Paper "Personhood and Legal Capacity": Perspectives on the Paradigm Shift of Article 12 of the CRPD"' (Conference Paper, HPOD Conference, 20 February, 2010)

Quinn, Gerard, 'From Civil Death to Civil Life: The Decay and Re-Birth of Legal Capacity Law around the World' (Conference Paper, Australian Guardianship and Administration Council National Conference: Reflecting Will and Preference in Decision-Making, 17–18 October, 2016)

Quinn, Gerard, 'The International Covenant on Civil and Political Rights and Disability: A Conceptual Framework' in Theresia Degener and Yolan Koster-Dreese (eds), *Human Rights and Disabled Persons* (Martinus Nijhoff, 1995) 69

Quinn, Gerard, 'Resisting the "Temptation of Elegance": Can the Convention on the Rights of Persons with Disabilities Socialise States to Right Behaviour?' in Oddný Mjöll Arnadóttir and Gerard Quinn (eds), *The UN Convention on the Rights of Persons with Disabilities: European and Scandinavian Perspectives* (Nijhoff, 2009) 215

Quinn, Gerard and Abigail Rekas-Rosalbo, 'Civil Death: Rethinking the Foundations of Legal Personhood for Persons with a Disability' (2016) 56 *Irish Jurist* 286

Quinn, Gerard and Anna Arstein-Kerslake, 'Restoring the "Human" in "Human Rights": Personhood and Doctrinal Innovation in the UN Disability Convention' in Costas Douzinas and C A Gearty (eds), *Cambridge Companion to Human Rights Law* (Cambridge University Press, 2012) 36

Quinn, Gerard and Theresia Degener, *Human Rights and Disability: The Current Use and Future Potential of United Nations Human Rights Instruments in the Context of Disability* (United Nations, 2002)

Ralston, D Christopher and Justin Ho, 'Introduction: Philosophical Reflections on Disability' in D Christopher Ralston and Justin Ho (eds), *Philosophical Reflections on Disability* (Springer, 2010) 1

Rawls, John, *A Theory of Justice* (Harvard University Press, 1971)

Raz, Joseph, *The Morality of Freedom* (Clarendon Press 1986)

Reyes, María Soledad Cisternas, 'Foreword' in Valentina Della Fina (ed), *The United Nations Convention on the Rights of Persons with Disabilities: A Commentary* (Springer, 2017)

Richards, Bernadette, 'Chapter 5: General Principles of Consent to Medical Treatment' in Ben White, Fiona McDonald and Lindy Willmott (eds), *Health Law in Australia* (Lawbook Co., 2018) 133

Rioux, Martha, 'On Second Thoughts: Constructing Knowledge, Law, Disability and Inequality' in Stanley S Herr and Lawrence O Gostin (eds), *The Human Rights of Persons with Intellectual Disabilities: Different but Equal* (Oxford University Press, 2003) 287

Rosen, Michael, *Dignity: Its History and Meaning* (Harvard University Press, 2012)

Royal Commission into Violence Abuse Neglect and Exploitation of People with Disability, *Health Care for People with Cognitive Disability* (Issues Paper, 16 December 2019)

Royal Commission into Violence, Abuse, Neglect and Exploitation of People with Disability, *Group Homes* (Issues Paper, 28 November 2019)

Royal Commission into Violence Abuse Neglect and Exploitation of People with Disability, *Overview of Responses to Group Homes* (Issues Paper, September 2020)

Royal Commission into Violence Abuse Neglect and Exploitation of People with Disability, *Overview of Responses to Health Issues Paper* (Issues Paper, October 2020) 4

Ruck Keene, Alex, Nuala B Kane, Scott Y H Kim and Gareth S Owen, 'Mental Capacity _ Why Look for a Paradigm Shift?' Medical Law Review, 10.1093/m3elaw/fwac052

Salzman, Leslie, 'Guardianship for Persons with Mental Illness: A Legal and Appropriate Alternative' (2011) 4 *St Louis University Journal of Health Law and Policy* 279

Schabas, William A, 'Freedom from Want: How Can We Make Indivisibility More Than a Mere Slogan?' (1999/2000) 11 *National Journal of Constitutional Law* 189

Schneewind, Jerome Borges, 'Kant on the Will' in Thomas Pink and Martin William Francis Stone (eds), *The Will and Human Action: From Antiquity to the Present Day* (Routledge, 2004) 154

Schulze, Marianne, 'Chapter 16: The Human Rights of Persons with Disabilities' in Anja Mihir and Mark Gibney (eds), *The SAGE Handbook of Human Rights* (SAGE Publications, 2014) 267

Scott, Craig, 'The Interdependence and Permeability of Human Rights Norms: Towards a Partial Fusion of the International Covenants on Human Rights' (1989) 27(4) *Osgoode Hall Law Journal* 769

Scully, Jackie Leach, 'Disability and the Thinking Body' in Simo Vehmas, Kristjana Kristiansen and Tom Shakespeare (eds), *Arguing about Disability: Philosophical Perspectives* (Taylor and Francis, 2008) 57

Sellin, Jennifer, 'The Justiciability of the Right to Health – Access to Medicines – The South African and Indian Experience' (2009) 2(4) *Erasmus Law Journal* 445

Series, Lucy, 'Relationships, Autonomy and Legal Capacity: Mental Capacity and Support Paradigms' (2015) 40 *International Journal of Law and Psychiatry* 80

Series, Lucy and Anna Nilsson, 'Article 12 CRPD: Equal Recognition before the Law' in Ilias Bantekas, Michael Ashley Stein and Anastasiou Dimitris (eds), *The UN Convention on the Rights of Persons with Disabilities: A Commentary* (Oxford University Press, 2018) 339

Shakespeare, Tom, *Disability Rights and Wrongs* (Routledge, 2006)

Shakespeare, Tom, *Disability: The Basics* (Routledge, 2018)

Shue, Henry, *Basic Rights: Subsistence, Affluence, and U.S. Foreign Policy* (Princeton University Press, 40th anniversary ed, 2020)

Silvers, Anita and Leslie Pickering Francis, 'Justice through Trust: Disability and the "Outlier Problem" in Social Contract Theory' (2005) 116(1) *Ethics* 40

Simplican, Stacy Clifford, 'Disavowals of Disability in Rawls' Theory of Justice and His Critics' in Barbara Arneil and Nancy J Hirschmann (eds), *Disability and Political Theory* (Cambridge University Press, 2016) 79

Skarstad, Kjersti, 'Disability and the Dilemma of Difference' in Franziska Felder et al (eds), *Disability Law and Human Rights: Theory and Policy* (Springer, 2022) 87

Skarstad, Kjersti, 'Ensuring Human Rights for Persons with Intellectual Disabilities?' (2018) 22(6) *International Journal of Human Rights* 774

Skarstad, Kjersti, 'Human Rights through the Lens of Disability' (2018) 36(1) *Netherlands Quarterly of Human Rights* 24

Skowron, Paul, 'Giving Substance to "the Best Interpretation of Will and Preferences"' (2019) 62 *International Journal of Law and Psychiatry* 125

Smith, Anita, 'Are Guardianship Laws and Practices Consistent with Human Rights Instruments?' in A Kimberly Dayton (ed), *Comparative Perspectives on Adult Guardianship* (Carolina Academic Press, 2014) 247

Smith, Stephen R, 'Social Justice and Disability: Competing Interpretations of the Medical and Social Models' in Kristjana Kristiansen, Simo Vehmas and Tom Shakespeare (eds), *Arguing about Disability: Philosophical Perspectives* (Routledge, 2008) 15

Snelling, Jeanne and Alison Douglass, 'Legal Capacity and Supported Decision-Making' in Iris Reuvecamp and John Dawson (eds), *Mental Capacity Law in New Zealand* (Thomson Reuters, 2019) 163

Stark, Cynthia A, 'Respecting Human Dignity: Contract versus Capabilities' in Eva Feder Kittay and Licia Carlson (eds), *Cognitive Disability and its Challenge to Moral Philosophy* (Wiley-Blackwell 2010) 111

Stavert, Jill, 'Supported Decision-Making and Paradigm Shifts: Word Play or Real Change?' (2020) 11 *Frontiers in Psychiatry* 571005

Stein, Michael Ashley, 'Disability Human Rights' (2007) 95(1) *California Law Review* 75

Stein, Michael Ashley and Janet E Lord, 'Future Prospects for the United Nations Convention on the Rights of Persons with Disabilities' in Oddný Mjöll Arnadóttir and Gerard Quinn (eds), *The UN Convention on the Rights of Persons with Disabilities: European and Scandinavian Perspectives* (Nijhoff, 2009) 17

Stein, Michael Ashley and Penelope J S Stein, 'Beyond Disability Civil Rights' (2006) 58 *Hastings Law Journal* 1203

Szmukler, George, '"Capacity", "Best Interests", "Will and Preferences" and the UN Convention on the Rights of Persons with Disabilities' (2019) 18(1) *World Psychiatry: Official Journal of the World Psychiatric Association (WPA)* 34

Szmukler, George, 'The UN Convention on the Rights of Persons with Disabilities: "Rights, Will and Preferences" in Relation to Mental Health Disabilities' (2017) 54 *International Journal of Law and Psychiatry* 90

Szmukler, George, Rowena Daw and Felicity Callard, 'Mental Health Law and the UN Convention on the Rights of Persons with Disabilities' (2014) 37(3) *International Journal of Law and Psychiatry* 245

Terzi, Lorella, 'Vagaries of the Natural Lottery? Human Diversity, Disability, and Justice: A Capability Perspective' in Kimberley Brownlee and Adam Cureton (eds), *Disability and Disadvantage* (Oxford University Press, 2009) 86

Then, Shih-Ning, 'Evolution and Innovation in Guardianship Laws: Assisted Decision-Making' (2013) 35(1) *Sydney Law Review* 133

Then, Shih-Ning et al, 'Supporting Decision-Making of Adults with Cognitive Disabilities: The Role of Law Reform Agencies — Recommendations, Rationales and Influence' (2018) 61 *International Journal of Law and Psychiatry* 64

Theodorou, Eliana J, 'Supported Decision-Making in the Lone-Star State' (2018) 93(4) *New York University Law Review* 973

Thio, Li-Ann, 'The Universal Declaration of Human Rights at 60: Universality, Indivisibility and the Three Generations of Human Rights' (2009) 21(1) *Singapore Academy of Law Journal* 293

Traustadóttir, Rannveig, 'Disability Studies, the Social Model and Legal Development' in Oddný Mjöll Arnadóttir and Gerard Quinn (eds), *The UN Convention on the Rights of Persons with Disabilities: European and Scandinavian Perspectives* (Nijhoff, 2009) 3

Turner, Bryan S, *Vulnerability and Human Rights* (Pennsylvania State University Press, 2006)

Vehmas, Simo and Pekka Mäkelä, 'The Ontology of Disability and Impairment: A Discussion of the Natural and Social Features' in Simo Vehmas, Kristjana Kristiansen and Tom Shakespeare (eds), *Arguing about Disability: Philosophical Perspectives* (Taylor and Francis, 2008) 42

Waddington, Lisa, 'Evolving Disability Policies from Social Welfare to Human Rights: An International Trend from a European Perspective' (2001) 19 *Netherlands Quarterly of Human Rights* 141

Waldron, Jeremy, *Is Dignity the Foundation of Human Rights?* (Public Law Research Paper No 12–73, New York University School of Law, 3 January 2013)

Wallcraft, Jan and Kim Hopper, 'The Capabilities Approach and the Social Model of Mental Health' in Helen Spandler, Jill Anderson and Bob Sapey (eds), *Madness, Distress and the Politics of Disablement* (Policy Press at the University of Bristol, 2015) 83

Ward, Adrian, 'Abolition of Guardianship? "Best Interests" versus "Best Interpretation"' (2015) 32 *Scots Law Times* 150

Wasserman, David, Adrienne Asch, Jeffrey Blustein, and Daniel Putnam, 'Cognitive Disability and Moral Status', *The Stanford Encyclopedia of Philosophy* (Fall 2017 Edition), in Edward N Zalta (ed) https://plato.stanford.edu/archives/fall2017/entries/cognitive-disability/

Watson, Joanne, 'The Right to Supported Decision-Making for Those Rarely Heard' (PhD Thesis, Deakin University, 2016)

Watson, Shelley L and Stephanie Hayes, 'The Right to Accessible Health Care for Persons with Intellectual Disabilities' in Dorothy Griffiths, Frances Owen and Shelley L Watson (eds), *The Human Rights Agenda for Persons with Intellectual Disabilities* (NADD, 2012) 59

Weller, Penelope, 'The Right to Health: The Convention on the Rights of Persons with Disabilities' (2010) 35(2) *Alternative Law Journal* 66

Whelan, Daniel J, *Indivisible Human Rights: A History* (University of Pennsylvania Press, 2010)

Whelan, Daniel J and Jack Donnelly, 'The West, Economic and Social Rights, and the Global Human Rights Regime: Setting the Record Straight' (2007) 29(4) *Human Rights Quarterly* 908

White, Ben, Fiona McDonald and Lindy Willmott, *Health Law in Australia* (Lawbook Co, 3rd ed, 2018)

White, Ben, Lindy Willmott and Shih-Ning Then, 'Chapter 7: Adults Who Lack Capacity: Substitute Decision Making' in Ben White, Fiona McDonald and Lindy Willmott (eds), *Health Law in Australia* (Lawbook Co, 3rd ed, 2018) 207

Willmott, Lindy, Ben White and Ben Matthews, 'Law, Autonomy and Advance Directives' (2010) 18 *Journal of Law and Medicine* 366

Wilson, Erin et al, 'Exploring the Personal, Programmatic and Market Barriers to Choice in the NDIS for People with Psychosocial Disability' (2021) *Australian Journal of Sociology* 1

Wilson, Kay, *Mental Health Law: Abolish or Reform?* (Oxford University Press, 2021)

Winick, Bruce, 'The Side Effects of Incompetency Labelling and the Implications for Mental Health Law' (1995) 1(1) *Public Policy and the Law* 6

Winston, Morton Emmanuel, 'Indivisibility and Interdependence of Human Rights' (Public Lecture, Nebraska Union, 3 September 1999)

Wolff, Jonathan, 'Disability among Equals' in Kimberley Brownlee and Adam Cureton (eds), *Disability and Disadvantage* (Oxford University Press, 2009) 112

Wondemaghen, Meron, 'Testing Equality: Insanity, Treatment Refusal and the CRPD' (2018) 25(2) *Psychiatry, Psychology and the Law* 174

World Health Organization and The World Bank, World Report on Disability 2011 (World Health Organization, 2011)

World Network of Users and Survivors of Psychiatry, 'Implementation Manual for the United Nations Convention on the Rights of Persons with Disabilities' (February 2008) www.wnusp.net/documents/WNUSP_CRPD_Manual.pdf

Zylbermas, Ariel, 'The Indivisibility of Human Rights' (2017) 36(4) *Law and Philosophy* 389

Index

CAMBRIDGE BIOETHICS AND LAW

Books in the Series

Marcus Radetzki, Marian Radetzki and Niklas Juth *Genes and Insurance: Ethical, Legal and Economic Issues*

Ruth Macklin *Double Standards in Medical Research in Developing Countries*

Donna Dickenson *Property in the Body: Feminist Perspectives*

Matti Häyry, Ruth Chadwick, Vilhjálmur Árnason and Gardar Árnason *The Ethics and Governance of Human Genetic Databases: European Perspectives*

J. K. Mason *The Troubled Pregnancy: Legal Wrongs and Rights in Reproduction*

Daniel Sperling *Posthumous Interests: Legal and Ethical Perspectives*

Keith Syrett *Law, Legitimacy and the Rationing of Health Care: A Contextual and Comparative Perspective*

Alasdair Maclean *Autonomy, Informed Consent and Medical Law: A Relational Change*

Heather Widdows and Caroline Mullen *The Governance of Genetic Information: Who Decides?*

David Price *Human Tissue in Transplantation and Research: A Model Legal and Ethical Donation Framework*

Matti Häyry *Rationality and the Genetic Challenge: Making People Better?*

Mary Donnelly *Healthcare Decision-Making and the Law: Autonomy, Capacity and the Limits of Liberalism*

Anne-Maree Farrell, David Price and Muireann Quigley *Organ Shortage: Ethics, Law and Pragmatism*

Sara Fovargue *Xenotransplantation and Risk: Regulating a Developing Biotechnology*

John Coggon *What Makes Health Public?: A Critical Evaluation of Moral, Legal, and Political Claims in Public Health*

Mark Taylor *Genetic Data and the Law: A Critical Perspective on Privacy Protection*

Anne-Maree Farrell *The Politics of Blood: Ethics, Innovation and the Regulation of Risk*

Stephen W. Smith *End-of-Life Decisions in Medical Care: Principles and Policies for Regulating the Dying Process*

Michael Parker *Ethical Problems and Genetics Practice*

William W. Lowrance *Privacy, Confidentiality, and Health Research*

Kerry Lynn Macintosh *Human Cloning: Four Fallacies and Their Legal Consequence*

Heather Widdows *The Connected Self: The Ethics and Governance of the Genetic Individual*

Amel Alghrani, Rebecca Bennett and Suzanne Ost *Bioethics, Medicine and the Criminal Law Volume I: The Criminal Law and Bioethical Conflict: Walking the Tightrope*

Danielle Griffiths and Andrew Sanders *Bioethics, Medicine and the Criminal Law Volume II: Medicine, Crime and Society*

Margaret Brazier and Suzanne Ost *Bioethics, Medicine and the Criminal Law Volume III: Medicine and Bioethics in the Theatre of the Criminal Process*

Sigrid Sterckx, Kasper Raus and Freddy Mortier *Continuous Sedation at the End of Life: Ethical, Clinical and Legal Perspectives*

A. M. Viens, John Coggon and Anthony S. Kessel *Criminal Law, Philosophy and Public Health Practice*

Ruth Chadwick, Mairi Levitt and Darren Shickle *The Right to Know and the Right Not to Know: Genetic Privacy and Responsibility*

Eleanor D. Kinney *The Affordable Care Act and Medicare in Comparative Context*

Katri Lõhmus *Caring Autonomy: European Human Rights Law and the Challenge of Individualism*

Catherine Stanton and Hannah Quirk *Criminalising Contagion: Legal and Ethical Challenges of Disease Transmission and the Criminal Law*

Sharona Hoffman *Electronic Health Records and Medical Big Data: Law and Policy*

Barbara Prainsack and Alena Buyx *Solidarity in Biomedicine and Beyond*

Camillia Kong *Mental Capacity in Relationship: Decision-Making, Dialogue, and Autonomy*

Oliver Quick *Regulating Patient Safety: The End of Professional Dominance?*

Thana Cristina de Campos *The Global Health Crisis: Ethical Responsibilities*

Jonathan Ives, Michael Dunn and Alan Cribb *Empirical Bioethics: Theoretical and Practical Perspectives*

Alan Merry and Warren Brookbanks *Merry and McCall Smith's Errors, Medicine and the Law* (second edition)

Donna Dickenson *Property in the Body: Feminist Perspectives* (second edition)

Rosie Harding *Duties to Care: Dementia, Relationality and Law*

Ruud ter Meulen *Solidarity and Justice in Health and Social Care*

David Albert Jones, Chris Gastmans and Calum MacKellar *Euthanasia and Assisted Suicide: Lessons from Belgium*

Muireann Quigley *Self-Ownership, Property Rights, and the Human Body: A Legal Perspective*

Françoise Baylis and Alice Dreger *Bioethics in Action*

John Keown *Euthanasia, Ethics and Public Policy: An Argument against Legislation* (second edition)

Amel Alghrani *Regulating Assisted Reproductive Technologies: New Horizons*

Britta van Beers, Sigrid Sterckx and Donna Dickenson *Personalised Medicine, Individual Choice and the Common Good*

David G. Kirchhoffer and Bernadette J. Richards *Beyond Autonomy: Limits and Alternatives to Informed Consent in Research Ethics and Law*

Markus Wolfensberger and Anthony Wrigley *Trust in Medicine: Its Nature, Justification, Significance, and Decline*

Catriona A. W. McMillan *The Human Embryo in vitro: Breaking the Legal Stalemate*

Benjamin Peter White and Lindy Willmott (editors) *International Perspectives on End-of-Life Law Reform: Politics, Persuasion and Persistence*

Carolyn Adams, Judy Allen and Felicity Flack *Sharing Linked Data for Health Research: Toward Better Decision Making*

Emily Postan *Embodied Narratives: Protecting Identity Interests through Ethical Governance of Bioinformation*

Jaime Lindsey *Reimagining the Court of Protection: Access to Justice in Mental Capacity Law*

Marcelo Corrales Compagnucci, Michael Lowery Wilson, Mark Fenwick, Nikolaus Forgó, Till Bärnighausen *AI in eHealth: Human Autonomy, Data Governance and Privacy in Healthcare*

Steph Jowett *Consent for Medical Treatment of Trans and Gender Diverse Youth*

Julia Duffy *Mental Capacity, Dignity and the Power of International Human Rights*

For EU product safety concerns, contact us at Calle de José Abascal, 56–1°,
28003 Madrid, Spain or eugpsr@cambridge.org.

www.ingramcontent.com/pod-product-compliance
Ingram Content Group UK Ltd.
Pitfield, Milton Keynes, MK11 3LW, UK
UKHW022141020426
469639UK00019B/432
9781009304498